Jeannie Robertson

Jeannie Robertson

Emergent Singer,

Transformative Voice

James Porter

Herschel Gower

TUCKWELL PRESS

First published in the United States of America
by The University of Tennessee Press / Knoxville.

First published in Great Britain by Tuckwell Press Ltd,
Mill House, Phantassie, East Linton EH40 3DG.

Frontispiece. Jeannie Robertson, c. 1953.
Courtesy of School of Scottish Studies.

Musical transcriptions by Richard Keeling.

British Library Cataloguing in Publication Data
A catalogue record is available on request

Printed and bound in Great Britain by
Redwood Books, Trowbridge, Wilts.

This volume is dedicated to

Hamish Henderson

who introduced Jeannie Robertson to the world

and who, with Jeannie, sparked the

revival of Scottish song

Contents

Illustrations

Jeannie Robertson, c. 1953 *Frontispiece*

Figures

Preface

The collaboration for this volume followed a good deal of individual work. Studying as a Fulbright Scholar in Scotland from 1954 to 1956, Herschel Gower (HG) first listened to tapes of Jeannie Robertson's singing at the School of Scottish Studies, University of Edinburgh. These had been made by Hamish Henderson, a Research Fellow at the school and the scholar who, convinced of the worth of traveller expressive culture, "found" Jeannie in 1953. She had sprung from the nomadic people known also as tinkers. Henderson urged Gower to transcribe the texts of Jeannie's ballads for comparative purposes, but this led to more basic questions about the nature of her repertoire. So, in 1955, HG visited Jeannie, her husband Donald, and her brother-in-law Isaac Higgins, all of whom were living in the small house at 21 Causewayend in the city of Aberdeen. Over successive years, HG returned for summer visits, continuing to supplement Henderson's recordings of Jeannie's life and repertoire by interviews that tried to clarify the tangled web of social structures binding Jeannie's and other traveller families. In 1967, HG and James Porter (JP) agreed to collaborate on an extended work devoted to Jeannie.

James Porter first encountered Jeannie in 1958, at the height of the British Folksong Revival, while studying musicology at the University of Edinburgh. After postgraduate work abroad, he began a detailed investigation of Jeannie's singing style. Seeing that distinctive changes had taken place in her later singing style, he recognized that explaining these posed something of a challenge and thus was drawn further into the study. Shortly thereafter, in 1968, when he had spent several years transcribing and analyzing Jeannie's repertoire at the School of Scottish Studies, he continued research at the University of California, Los Angeles, until her recorded repertoire was prepared for publication.

❧

What could we, two male scholars, say about Jeannie Robertson that was new and had not been said before? As collaborators with Jeannie herself, we frequently returned to Scotland to explore issues central to the study and continued to rely on Henderson's indispensable recordings of Jeannie. Despite the difficulties imposed by time and distance, we worked with this remarkable woman even after she had ceased singing in public. The collaboration, then, though it began at a stage when most of Jeannie's life story had been recorded, gained in depth and perspective from the sustained analysis of over two hundred hours of tape-recorded material and from personal interviews and correspondence with Jeannie, her family, and many figures involved in the Folksong Revival. The time lag allowed us not only to check the process of change in the songs, but also to assess the relatively long-term effects of Jeannie's influence.

Studies such as this one on the travellers, or any other group regarded by a "mainstream society" as different, have their limits. For one thing, as Johannes Fabian has cautioned, distancing makes us place the referents (of anthropology) in a time other than the present or the time of the producer of anthropological discourse.[1] The danger of objectifying, or distancing, was compounded by another hazard. The sociologist Georg Simmel noted as far back as 1911 how the psychological superiority assigned to male behavior in Western society is given normative significance—a transsexual validity as the yardstick of truth and justice for both men and women. Women thus come to occupy a position in the world that is full of "otherness."[2] In recent work, sociologists have intensified awareness of male hegemony in musical (and musicological) processes.[3] The literature on music and gender also has burgeoned.[4] As researchers, then, we are conscious of being "others" from the traveller point of view, and of being males assessing a woman singer. We have therefore tried to account not only for differentials of class and group identity but of gender as well.

In our research with Jeannie's family we experienced warmth, courtesy, and ready cooperation over several years of study. But we were far from being the first to appreciate traveller life and culture. After the sturdy example of Hamish Henderson, who lived in traveller tents during those pioneer years of the early 1950s, a drive to understand the ethnographic reality behind traveller expressive forms led to Stephanie Smith's study of Lizzie Higgins, Jeannie Robertson's daughter.[5] Identifying with that culture by becoming a traveller's wife, as the American Linda Headlee (Williamson) did, is to experience a unity with the subject denied to other researchers. Headlee's marriage to Duncan Williamson in 1976 yielded, in her dissertation, an intimate ethnography of traveller life and a detailed study of stanzaic variation in traveller singing.[6] Additional studies have added substance and depth: those of MacColl and Seeger,[7] and Betsy Whyte's[8] and Stanley Robertson's[9] published autobiographies. Work on Irish travellers has resulted in useful comparative material.[10]

We found some benefit in approaching the traveller world (or worlds) from outside, in that we could interpret the web of traveller social structure and cultural relationships from several angles. Still, we have tried to focus centrally on the emergent process of Jeannie as a singer and the transformative nature of her singing. Despite the ambiguities and ethical pitfalls of fieldwork and its analysis, we describe and analyze one person's transformation in a period of cultural change. In a sense, as James Clifford has noted, all ethnographic interpretation is allegorical, as well as artisanal, bound to the worldly work of writing.[11] Whatever its merits, our analysis represents a reflective, long-term study rather than a synchronic ethnography. At the same time, it aims at uncovering cognitive patterns, sometimes conflicting, within a socially constructed reality.

The introduction and commentary provide an explanatory frame for the biography. Their function is to clarify the major issues that arise from a reading of the narrative, both broad questions of definition and approach and more precise matters of genre, mode, text, texture, and context, to use the terms suggested by Dundes and Toelken.[12] In the initial division of labor, HG contributed the biographical narrative, stitching together the diachronic sequence of events from accounts recorded at different times; JP drafted the introductory and concluding essays and transcribed the song texts and tunes. All of these parts were subjected to comment by readers as well as by each of us.

All citations made in the songs and notes to Child and to Laws are to designations in Francis J. Child's *The English and Scottish Popular Ballads* (1882-98) and G. Malcolm Laws, Jr., *American Balladry from British Broadsides* (1957).

Various individuals lent indispensable aid to this project; to them we shall always be grateful. The late Lizzie Higgins Youlden permitted us to use her mother's and her own material. John MacQueen, former director of the School of Scottish Studies, gave permission to use the archives and facilities of the school. Hamish Henderson, "discoverer" of Jeannie, has been more than generous in sharing her life and artistry with us and with a worldwide audience. Members of the staff of the School of Scottish Studies, in particular Dr. Emily Lyle, Mary Macdonald, Ailie Munro, and the late Pat Shaw, helped greatly. Fred Kent and the late Tom Atkinson provided invaluable technical assistance.

We want especially to pay tribute to the work of the late Robert Garioch, poet and champion of Scots as a literary medium, in his painstaking transcription of Jeannie's autobiography; and we thank Richard Keeling for his elegant copying of the tune transcriptions. Further acknowledgment is due George Bruce, Russell Hart, and David Murison for reading and commenting on the manuscript at various stages, and for numerous helpful suggestions. Others who should be mentioned in this regard are Peter Ladefoged and Alan Lomax. Crucial information was cheerfully and willingly provided by Joyce Colley, Ray

Fisher, Andy Hunter, Stephanie Smith, Jean Redpath, and Stanley Robertson. Our late friends, Arthur Argo, Norman Buchan, Bertrand Bronson, and D. K. Wilgus, are warmly remembered for their interest in this project. For general assistance in preparing this work for the press, we would like to mention Erica Meltzer, Susan Kelly, and Seeme Ali.

We are further indebted to the Department of English, Vanderbilt University; the Department of Ethnomusicology, UCLA; and the Center for the Study of Comparative Folklore and Mythology, UCLA, for generously providing time and facilities; and to the Academic Senates of both these universities for grants-in-aid, without which the completion of the project would have been impossible. Charles Speroni, late dean of the College of Fine Arts, UCLA, helped with a grant for copying the tunes. We owe, above all, a huge debt to our families, whose patience and understanding over the years contributed in a thousand ways to this work's realization. For much help and patience at UT Press we cite Stan Ivester, Mavis Bryant, and Meredith Morris-Babb.

Finally, though we see ourselves as "outsiders" in relation to the traveller community and experience, we also were Jeannie's friends, a fact that bestows on us a more important identity. We have been privileged to know her family over years of fellowship, joy, and hardship. Our "fieldwork" with her and with them has been more like a dialogue with neighbors and acquaintances. In a very real sense, it was through Jeannie that we came to know ourselves, with a greater understanding, as both Self and Other. This study, then, is meant not only for students of "folksong" or social history, or even for admirers of Jeannie and her art, but for all those who will recognize in her voice and singing the timeless ability to move, persuade, and transform.

James Porter
Herschel Gower

Notes

1. Fabian 1983.
2. Coser 1988.
3. Shepherd 1987.
4. See, e.g., Koskoff 1987, Bowers 1989 and 1990, Bowers and Bareis 1991, Solie 1993, Herndon and Ziegler 1990 and 1991.
5. Stephanie Smith 1975.
6. Linda Williamson 1985.
7. MacColl and Seeger 1977 and 1986.
8. Whyte 1979.
9. Stanley Robertson 1988.
10. Court 1985, George Gmelch 1977, Sharon Gmelch 1986.
11. Clifford 1986.
12. Dundes 1964, Toelken 1969.

Introduction

The compass of this book ranges across several fields: biography, folklore, oral history, ethnomusicology. The data too are drawn from heterodox sources. As a consequence, an interdisciplinary approach to singing as the central, transforming feature of one person's life seemed not only appropriate but essential. And while the study has involved a certain amount of interpersonal (as well as interdisciplinary) research over several decades, the result is not a descriptive ethnography, nor is it a "historical" account in the ordinary sense. Singing, songs, and performance are a central concern, but in a broader way our analysis is involved with the notion of transformation, as a practitioner from an oral tradition adapts to the "modern" world. Performance analysis, in other words, is simply a means to an end. As a philosophical basis for interpreting cultural praxis (the human imposition of a new, artificial order on the natural one), this stance involves a hermeneutics of musical behavior—i.e., the focus on meaning and its negotiative channeling—and is influenced by both phenomenology and critical theory.[1]

The Central Figure

In appraising Jeannie Robertson (1908–1975), a traveller woman from the Northeast of Scotland, we have constructed the study around a tripartite scheme: first, her life history (and her own "life story"); second, her songs, arranged in thematic groups; and, third, framing commentaries in the introduction and conclusion. In inscribing her life, we follow a practice of biographical technique in anthropology and folklore that goes back to the 1920s.[2] It is evident, however, that we cannot remove ourselves from the process of narration. In our strategy, Jeannie and others had to speak at vital moments in the narration of her "life history." To some extent, such extracts from an "oral autobiography" lend to the account more the complexion of the "life story."[3] That is, the framework of the "life history" allows at the same time for the incorporation of her "life story." The two narrative modes, Jeannie's subjective one and our more "objective" one, are intertwined. Their "truths" are interdependent.

In this way we picture the changing situations with which Jeannie interacted as a "public" singer of traditional songs. But it is not as simple as that. A tougher goal was to capture the subjective experience of the woman, singer, and tradition-bearer who was recognized nationally and internationally for twenty years. This pursuit meant sifting through extensive data on her life, family history, environment, and transition to a "semiprofessional" career. Indeed, the range of song and prose material Jeannie recorded after her 1953 "discovery" moved Maurice Fleming, the contemporary Scottish writer, to observe in *Scots Magazine* in April 1965 that the autobiographical segments alone comprise "almost certainly the longest record of spoken Scots in existence." While quite as much has been recorded from other travellers since then, Jeannie's accounts of her life and experiences are still valuable for the past they construct and enliven.

Jeannie Robertson was born into a traveller world that, although structurally complex in terms of kin and family relations, was still relatively homogeneous culturally. Recalling the trials of World War I, her oral account of that world is valuable in that, first, it restores to her people their past in a written documented form; and, second, it provides an experiential view of the human relationships embedded in that past.[4] These relationships in turn are conveyed through language that, in its mixed morphology, signifies cultural change: regional Northeastern forms mingle with urban slang and everyday English.[5] We felt it crucial to quote freely those passages in Jeannie's direct speech that capture the essence of a person, place, or event. And while these and the song texts as rendered on the page may seem static, even in Robert Garioch's ingenious orthography, they perhaps function effectively as communicative symbols by being placed at strategic points in the narrative of Jeannie's life. The contexts of her youth, of her apprenticeship in learning traditional songs, of her experience as a wife and mother, and of her influence on the Folksong Revival in Britain during the 1950s and 1960s frame all the eighty recorded songs presented in this book, about two-thirds of her active repertoire. They give an idea of the depth and range of her repertoire as a whole. The reasons for her earlier and later style of singing are brought out in the analysis, however, rather than in the descriptive transcriptions.

We are aware of the hazards of privileging "folk" material at the expense of a singer's entire repertoire. But in Jeannie's case, the number of nontraditional songs was small (e.g., "Once in Royal David's City," "Flow Gently, Sweet Afton," and one or two others), but we consider as "folksongs" American "cowboy songs" such as "The Trail to Mexico" and "The Hobo's Lament."

Even if we allow that in her youth pop songs, hymns, and other nontraditional items may have been part of her fund of songs, in middle age, Jeannie, conscious of her mother's legacy, either relegated these firmly to the background or neglected them entirely. In her case, repertoire adjustment was prompted by a consciousness of local interest and of her own aesthetic preferences.[6] To some extent, we can regard her conservatism as conforming to external views of what a traveller repertoire of traditional songs should be. With this in mind, we have tried to avoid idealizing Jeannie either before or after she captured public attention. Awareness of this problem led us to see her always against a ground, in specific contexts, and to compare her with other singers, living and dead, traveller and nontraveller, Northeastern or otherwise, some of whom experienced a similar transition to public recognition in the Revival and post-Revival period. "Traveller culture," in any case, cannot be reduced to a number of individual personalities, nor is it a homogeneous totality. It displays the same strains and tensions found in the wider society of Lowland Scotland.

The title of this book suggests two things: first, change in an individual ("emergence"); and, second, the power of a traditional voice to transform—not only to transform songs through the singing of them, but also to transform the modern world and our perception of it ("transformative"). In Jeannie Robertson's case, this power was manifested both in public arenas (concert halls, revival *ceilidhs*) and in sound recordings (commercial discs, field tapes). It exists primarily on three levels: *material*, in selecting, arranging, modifying, and crystallizing her repertoire for concert programs according to criteria of variety, balance, and contrast; *contextual and performative,* by merging into the postwar Folk Revival and consequently influencing the values of a wider Anglophone community by her singing; and *subjective,* transcending contextual shifts through adaptive strategies of self-transformation, so that, in creating new attitudes toward meaning and value, the individual "becomes" collective, the modern traditional, the literary oral.[7]

The subjective level is perhaps the most complex to grasp, for at its heart lies the traditional ability of the traveller singer, not just to cast a spell over the listeners, but to change their whole perception of the material world. Subject becomes object and vice versa, with the dissolution of duality in perceiving self as "partly known and partly knower, partly object and partly subject," as William James put it.[8] The philosopher Merleau-Ponty asserted that "the relationship of subject and object is no longer that *cognitive relationship* in which the object always appears as constructed by the subject, but is a *relationship of being*, through which, to use a paradox, the subject is his body, his world, his situation, and in a certain sense enters into *interaction* with it."[9] Hermeneutic understanding—the relation of meanings to one another—is especially suited to transcending the subject-object dichotomy, an effort of some importance in probing a life history and understanding its changing contexts. Meanings, especially in the postmodern world, are dependent upon negotiation and reflexive discourse—the interplay of subjective interpretations of the world—for communication and identification.[10]

The three levels suggested above are constantly framed, however, by two powerful dialectical relationships: first, the interplay of Jeannie's actual world and her performative powers; and second, the interplay of her performances and the external world. Thus the material, contextual, and subjective levels can be understood only within these larger communicative and intersubjective frameworks. On the second dialectical plane, that of performance, Jeannie was able to resolve dichotomies in the "folklore process" (e.g., the conventional idea that it is communal, traditional, or oral rather than individual, innovative, scripted). Poised between worlds, she faced and negotiated the outer, potentially hostile one with cognitive repertoire intact. Though her audience changed, she maintained this integrity, along with other Lowland Scottish traveller singers (e.g., Belle Stewart, Jane Turriff, or Duncan Williamson) who, beginning in the early 1950s, found themselves caught up in a popular, international fascination with their cultural legacy and performative powers. Jeannie, Belle, Jane, and Duncan belong to the generation born around World War I, whose children and grandchildren, since the closing of the gap between travellers and Lowland society after World War II, now find themselves in an exposed position.

Interpreting a Life

Our approach to Jeannie's life needs some clarification. Her life story provides its own dramatic momentum, but it would be foolish to pretend that transcripted accounts did not involve subjective cutting and pasting in both the recording situation and the later editorial process.[11] Constant verification, confirmation, or negotiation of incidents has been part of this reconstructive process. Chronology and historical accuracy are one thing; the drama of separate events another. Nevertheless, although the texture of Jeannie's voice and her expressive gestures are impossible to recreate on paper, the force of her personality bursts out in raw dialect, with crackling humor and graphic visions. Her speaking, while never as powerful as her singing voice, is modulated to a different end, that of "narrative" economy rather than "lyrical" distension. Our task has been to make this texture of Jeannie's life world as intelligible as its chronology, and to interfere as little as possible in the candor, affect, wit, or even embroidery with which she shaped individual scenes in recollection.[12] Like a series of receding boxes distorted by time, space, and multiple perceptions, these accounts should not be read too closely as "facts." But they communicate more than a "virtual reality" because they are deeply felt and intensely "present." Meanings are always experiential, drawn to an immediate, communal past and a personal sense of richness or loss. Our frame is intentionally one that seeks to uncover, reveal, and intimate rather than just recount— that is, to achieve a balance in both diachronic and synchronic dimensions. If intelligibility involves such balance, then it is its own justification. Finally, while songs and singing within the multi-episodic life story form the main foci of this study, the life-story frame does not preclude the importance of single episodes in Jeannie's life. These last reflect or embody themes central to the problem of the personal narrative as a genre.[13]

The Travellers

Since the Middle Ages in Scotland, travellers have been singled out as a special group of nomadic families set apart from settled communities by a habitual movement that, since World War II, no longer has been universally or invariably practiced. The travellers differ from both Romanies and the settled population, and may have their origins in a medieval Celtic tinsmithing caste, though this cannot be proven conclusively. In Gaelic they were known as *cairdean*, ironworkers who in ancient times went from clan to clan making weapons.[14] In Lowland Scotland, travellers were commonly called tinkers or tinklers, a term of abuse probably derived, like *zingaro*, from skill in metalwork and one they strongly resent. Because they preferred a nomadic life, there is a long history of discrimination and ill-treatment. Local residents often drove them from their traditional campsites because, as hawkers and traders, they were accused of leaving litter, living in tents and caravans without proper sanitation, poaching, and habitual drunkenness. With increasing awareness of their plight on the part of local authorities since the 1970s, various remedies have been proposed.[15]

Travellers are found in all areas of Scotland, including the islands. Some have settled into local housing, but the greatest concentration is in Central Scotland (Strathclyde and Tayside regions). The Scottish Secretary of State maintains an Advisory Committee, founded in 1971, that submits three-year reports on travellers, and its official estimate is that there are five hundred families. "Family" is defined as a unit for whom housekeeping and cooking is done communally; this can include those living in more than one caravan (a covered vehicle) or house and may include more than two generations. Their home area, designated by an ancestral burial ground, is a matter of deep attachment.[16]

Many travellers, however, normally lived in towns only in winter, migrating to the country in spring (hence the name "the summer walkers"). They were welcomed in the country during the warm months for several reasons. They were newsbringers, hawkers, peddlers, fortunetellers, entertainers, fiddlers, pipers. The isolated crofter in the upland glen was less inclined to resent their presence than inhabitants in populated areas. The men traditionally were recognized as blacksmiths, farrowers, and tinsmiths. They wormed the cottar's dog and collected herbs and leeches for medicinal purposes. The women sold soft goods (cloth, yarn, and spools of thread) or artificial flowers, hornspoons, and baskets they had woven. Travellers were readily taken on as cheap seasonal labor in the harvesting of crops or fruit in farming areas, and occasionally in the fish trade at seaside villages when catches were abundant.[17] Berry picking, potato lifting, and pearl fishing were among the traditional tasks done for pay.[18]

Travellers' physical characteristics are said to be indistinguishable from those of the rest of the Scottish population.[19] But in some cases a dark, Romany cast of features and hair color is evident. Betsy Whyte tells of her clan's belief that one with such coloring (black eyes, black hair, dark skin) was "evil or bad in some way,"[20] a belief that conforms to the psychology of dark and fair in other parts of Europe.[21] To some extent, travellers are the northern counterparts of the eastern and southern European Gypsies, although their origin is less certain and they profess no kinship with Gypsies. One study finds 25 to 35 percent usage of Romany in vocabulary, if one excludes English and Scots words used in exactly the same way as by the settled population.[22]

The social organization of Scottish travellers, both Highland and Lowland, has parallels among travelling groups in Ireland and other parts of northern Europe.[23] Common surnames like Robertson, Stewart, Macgregor, Whyte, or Williamson in different counties point to different branches of a single clan, and, while separate branches may claim no connection, travellers often trace common ancestry for these branches. They may be regarded as a group because of an elaborate network of blood kin and can also be divided regionally, ethnically, by social class, by occupation, and by family structure.[24] This diversity has often prevented them from organizing to protect their rights and make their cases to local councils.[25]

While travellers can to some extent be referred to as a "group," the lack of integration at the "clan" level means that they were not at all homogeneous in social structure, nor were they an economically deprived class. As a corollary, travellers have different expressive forms: some families might cultivate special types of song, such as parody, or clusters of tales told by previous generations. The competitiveness that has become part of the travelling existence interacts with a sense of individualism, and jealousy of more materially secure families outside the clan can be fierce.[26] Yet the reason for feuds, some of them involving violence, is often a perceived insult or ethical transgression, and the cause of an individual is taken up as the cause of the family. Some families have a recognized long-standing hostility towards one another, and all contact is to be avoided.[27] With the allegiance to one's family goes loyalty to expressive forms held within that family; thus family structure is an important clue to song maintenance and performance.

Travellers, though, define themselves as much by what they were not as by what they were. They were not "flatties" or "scaldies" but a distinctive group, historically separate, in their social organization and cultural life, from the main population of Lowland Scotland. Travellers can be seen, in fact, as marginal. This marginality results from partitioning or dichotomizing the world, dividing it in a way that yields no intermediate situation or confusion.[28] In this state of marginality, the traveller is also "the stranger" (but not the foreigner or alien), a social type with vulnerable community status.[29] At the same time, others have stressed the stranger's iconoclastic, sacrilegious role: the stranger contests the very distinctions which for "ordinary" people are attributes of the universe itself rather than of their views of the world.[30] It is not just that the stranger's existence blurs the coveted clarity of the "we/they" division; he challenges not one but all the distinctions which make up the intelligible world.[31] Thus, for obvious reasons, ballads that involve the stranger have been popular in the traveller repertoire.[32]

Lowland traveller structures and institutions, then, such as kinship, education, social control, and language, have been penetrated and influenced by the larger Anglophone social complex, influences derived from Scotland, England, and North America.[33] As to language in particular, everyday English and Anglicized expressions absorbed from books, the media, and outside visitors (including scholars) have entered local or dialectal traveller speech to such an extent that basic cultural conceptions sometimes have been affected: "auld sangs," for instance, have become "ballads" and "folksongs" through contact with academics and students. Among more traditional families, traveller cant, a living marker of group identity, continues to accrete words from Romany and other languages.[34]

As a marginal group ("strangers") in a complex society, bound by ties of kinship, reciprocity, and ritual, travellers conform closely to the concept of a small-scale, traditional community of the type cited by folklorists and social anthropologists. Change, however, mainly in the guise of forced legislation on settlement and education, along with intermarriage with nontravellers, has begun to overtake them and effect interaction with the wider society. Tensions already present in traveller society and within individual families have become accentuated with the slow but steady erosion of traditional *praxis*. The different cases of Jeannie, her daughter Lizzie Higgins, and her nephew Stanley Robertson illustrate this partial closing of social and cultural gaps.[35]

The closing of gaps and merging of contexts, as a cultural process, is central to assessment of travellers such as Jeannie, who grew up in the old, almost entirely oral culture of the traveller in the Northeast. Travellers always have been a marginal group in Scottish society, since they tend to value freedom from the economic norms of settled society—the bourgeois trappings of property and material security (some, a small minority, are nevertheless well-to-do). Their role has been as transmitters and transformers of a potent oral culture that transposes harsh yet vital experience into the creative forms and symbols of dramatic ballad and magic tale. With increasingly coercive legislation concerning housing and education imposed by the Welfare State, their lives after World War II entered a critical phase. Material poverty and cultural riches have given way to dependence on Social Security and the erosion of their interdependent communal network.

Social Structure

Traveller families normally were founded when a couple married, though a ceremony did not always accompany the marriage. A young couple would begin to cohabit, often in a tent of their own, or they could elope, as Jeannie and Donald Higgins did. There seems to be no particular preference for varilocal or uxorilocal settlement. In recent times, church and registry office weddings have become accepted, especially because of the state welfare benefits that accrue. According to one source, church marriages in the past were staged in order to collect money and gifts from impressed "flatties" or "scaldies."

Typically girls were wed by twenty and men by twenty-two or twenty-three. A young male might select a girl for his spouse on condition that she not be a lineal ascendant or descendant. Cousins frequently are chosen, and marriage often occurs between double cousins (cousin status from both mother's and father's side). Belle Stewart's mother and mother-in-law, for instance, were first cousins; such a relationship was a common basis for marriage.[36] Traditionally, after marriage, the couple becomes independent, with their own residence. Men may cooperate economically with fathers and brothers, or daughters with their mothers and sisters. Despite early problems in Belle Stewart's marriage, the family was close-knit.[37]

Division of labor within the family was the rule; women took care of domestic chores and men the means of transport (horses, trucks, or automobiles). Whereas horse trading was once important, men now deal in used cars, scrap metal, and second-hand furniture, or take seasonal work on farms and play bagpipes for paid entertainment. Women had traditional occupations that complemented those of the men: flax pulling, peat stacking, pearl fishing, harvesting, milling, potato lifting. They often would hawk goods door-to-door, using a basket not just for "soft goods" (haberdashery) but also as a symbolic object to gain sympathy from women householders, a strategy sometimes reinforced by having a child with them. Jeannie took her young son Jeemsie along on these outings, and it is even common to borrow children within kin groups for this purpose.[38]

Children are usually baptized at birth, as parents believe that this will protect the health of the child. Later, however, they do not usually go to church or Sunday school. Travellers have an elaborate system of nicknames and adopt ones for their children that often outlast childhood.[39] Reared with affection by their parents, traveller children receive basic schooling (reading, writing, arithmetic) through formal education, but their public education usually does not go beyond this rudimentary level. There are two reasons for this: hostility on the part of other children (and teachers), and the nomadic or seminomadic mode of traveller living, which allows families legally to have their children attend school for only half the normal period. Even those travellers with settled homes would leave in the spring on their exodus to the country, returning only after school had begun in the fall. The Compulsory Education Act of 1944 (amended in 1972) stipulates that children between five and sixteen must attend school regularly, yet the Caravan Sites and Control of Development Act of 1960 prevents travellers from camping on sites other than those provided, and the paucity of such sites means travellers must move constantly.[40] While this situation has had a seriously detrimental effect on the academic level of traveller children in comparison with others, in traveller society formal education beyond the basic level was not regarded as indispensable; it was more important to learn how to contribute economically to the family. Boys learned trades in metal and cars, girls the strategies necessary to sell knickknacks to flattie women.

Among travellers the older generation is respected, even at such an advanced age that individuals can no longer contribute in a material way to the group. Some traveller women were robustly independent even at an advanced age: Tina Stewart of Fetterangus, one of Jeannie's cousins, continued hawking goods until she was over eighty.[41] Relatives prefer not to see older travellers hospitalized except when in dire need, and placing the elderly or the handicapped in special institutions is resisted. To some degree, hospitals are regarded with suspicion. One reason for this distrust is the old belief in burkers, the eponymous descendants of the infamous Burke and Hare team of body snatchers operating in Edinburgh in 1827–29, about whom there are many tales among travelling folk. The burkers, significantly, usually were accompanied by "noddies" (doctors) who acted as their employers, and abduction by the team was associated, in travellers' minds, with a quite specific location in Aberdeen or Perth.[42]

Marriages with "scaldies" or "flatties" continue as younger travellers (such as Stanley Robertson, Jeannie's nephew) seek to negotiate their way into an economic system that conflicts with traditional traveller values. Older travellers, on the other hand, forced into handouts and housing "like wild birds in cages," hated the compulsion of the Welfare State.[43] Legal marriages have increased nevertheless, for the practical reason of claiming welfare. There are fewer close-kin marriages, though the first-cousin marriages referred to above are not uncommon. Arranged marriages have declined, and it seems more usual now for a traveller man to marry a nontraveller woman (the pair then choosing to return to traveller life, or not) than for a traveller woman to marry a nontraveller man. The increase in exogamy seems to have been in the city rather than in the less impersonal environment of the small town or village.[44] The process of change seems to be more rapid than before World War I, especially in the face of external legislation and internal defection. Younger travellers who maintain ties to their parents' world and traditional praxis thus are at odds with those of their generation who feel a need to abandon the old way of life as destructive and demeaning. The "nonconformists," already caught in the web of nontraveller institutions, motivations, and desires, are placed in direct conflict with their peers.

Gender and Music

The relationship of gender and musical behavior is part of the larger problem of the biology of music making.[45] Furthermore, gender cannot be divorced from other elements of an individual's identity: for instance, age, class, or ethnicity. In itself, gender as a concept is closely linked to sexuality, desire, and difference, on the one hand, and to personal authority and social power on the other. Complex questions thus arise in the relationship between gender and musical behavior, and some of these have been posed in recent studies.[46]

All the issues cannot be dealt with here, but we may explore two prominent ones. Invariably, in any society or community, ideology and power relations are asymmetrical.[47] That is, men control the public sphere, including music making, and deal with the outside world.[48] Women are discouraged from public performance because their sexuality, as central to their identity, affects their musicality. While this does not lead to tension in every society, young women's public musical behavior often is limited because of their sexual attractiveness, to which performance draws attention. In many societies, older women, in contrast, assume a special musical or social role imbued with power and status because they are no longer seen as childbearers or as sexually potent.

Among travellers, male violence was one way of controlling a woman's behavior, including musical behavior, and is documented in various sources.[49] (For examples, see Betsy Whyte and Linda Williamson.) It is not surprising, then, that most female singers among the travellers were recognized as singers only in their postmenopausal years, when they had more opportunities to perform.

The gender ideology that motivated such role-playing was that of the heroic male. This reflection of masculine insecurity was the product of a history of political failure, religious repression, and, most of all, personal inadequacy in the face of constant challenges from flatties, other clan members, or their own women. Many traveller men, however, must have rejected this ideology as both foolish and futile, and Donald Higgins, Jeannie's husband, was one of them.

While still a young woman, Jeannie Robertson was recognized in her family and clan as a remarkable singer. But it is not coincidental that she became known to the outside world in her late forties; she was by that time mature, sure of herself, and, after Jeemsie's death, prepared for any eventuality. Donald did not interfere in her emergence, for his musical talents were of a different kind. However mature, Jeannie's style of singing was to undergo a transformation of a more radical kind over the years 1955–61. The factor of age, then, modifies gender-related musical behavior in significant ways. Contact with the outside world facilitated the transformation of Jeannie's singing style, as consciousness of her traveller identity reinforced difference. The "we," "wir folk," in Jeannie's accounts construct a personal positioning within her own cultural and social group. Her singing style and, even more, her choice of repertoire are saturated and conditioned by a complex of identities: woman, mother, traveller, oppressed minority; Stewart, Catholic, Aberdeenshire native.

Gender-related behavior can be tied to specific contexts, such as the campfire circle, Jeannie's house in Aberdeen after World War II, and the arenas of the Folk Revival. In the first of these contexts, the campfire circle, Jeannie was still learning a style and repertoire until her teens. The egalitarianism of the traveller circle continued this process until she, as a mature woman, was married and able to host small gatherings at her home. The death of Jeemsie was a devastating blow to her, and the pathos that emerged as a hallmark of her big ballad singing began to overshadow the heroic side of her repertoire. "Harlaw," as it were, the communal battle for survival, took second place to "Son Davit" or "The Moon Shined on My Bed Last Night," the personal struggle for love and affection. As the recording studio and concert stage separated her from her audience, the intimate and personal took over and began to privilege the female over the male heroic ideal.

Life stages, then, can produce dramatic changes in a person's expressive needs and powers. Physical change, more marked in women than men, makes transformations in artistic performance easier for women than for men. This cannot be emphasized sufficiently in the case of Jeannie Robertson, who, having found her voice in middle age, crystallized her experience in a repertoire that was both appropriate and sufficient to articulate that experience. Some portions of her repertoire could be described as men's songs, but even these speak of concerns that were close to her people's experience: outlawry, imprisonment, social rejection. Any "purifying" of her repertoire, such as jettisoning popular or nontraditional songs, was minimal and was effected quietly to make room for an emergent persona. This was the persona of the traditional singer who had learned to value a legacy inherited largely from her mother, upon whose heroism Jeannie modeled her own image of how a traveller woman should and could behave. Thus, in a traveller context, the concept of "heroism" cannot be ascribed only to males. The conclusion must be that complex webs of reciprocity, age, group consciousness, and interpersonal value systems constantly modify the "difference" issue in gender studies.

Cultural Practice and the Individual

Unlike the more abstract term "culture," "cultural practice" involves the notion of actively shaping a subjective world. The products of cultural practice on the individual level are of special importance because they reveal the subjective meanings of those who produced them. Socially, cultural practice consists in the intersubjective meanings by which individuals create the world they live in, which itself is riddled with conflicts and ambivalences.[50] Music making, singing, and narrating supply a performative means of making these conflicts and ambivalences intelligible and, what is more, meaningful. The travelling people of Lowland Scotland until recently have preferred, for reasons of group or at least clan solidarity, to maintain performance as a communal act—a choice that in turn generates the variations in form and style characteristic of an oral culture.

Like "culture," "tradition" is polysemic. Tradition most recently has been represented through seven distinct notions: as the lore of particular social groups, as the cultural canon of a folk society, as a process implying the transmission of cultural heritage, as an organic mass or repertoire, as culture (for some anthropologists), as an abstract system of knowledge that generates actual performance (*langue* versus *parole*), and as performance.[51] Tradition, then, has been viewed as both content and process. It has signified the process of handing down the material, as well as the quality people attribute to the subjects that connote either the process or the material (see, e.g., Holbek).[52] Specific traditions, as manifestations of traditionality, may well be invented for ideological reasons, but they also evolve through communal habit or perception.[53]

Traditions of the latter kind (e.g., singing, narrating) are founded, at least among marginal groups such as the Lowland travellers, on fairly precise collective, internally negotiated notions about the past. Through their enactment in song or prose, they reflect the value assigned particular events, people, or places that are experientially "known" or recognized as "true" in a symbolic sense. Even here, though, invention and innovation are cultural; the invented product is new and must be transmitted through time and space before it becomes a tradition. The "invention" of culture and of tradition, moreover, contains within it an ironic sense that, once invented and rooted in speech usage, these concepts take on an "inventive" role—i.e., they give rise to new transformations of themselves.[54]

More concretely, tradition is also closely involved with group identity. S. N. Eisenstadt has remarked that traditional societies or communities share in the acceptance of tradition, the "givenness" of some actual or symbolic past event, order, or figure as the major focus of their collective identity. "Traditionality" not only serves as a symbol of continuity but also prescribes the limits of creativity and innovation and is the major criterion of their legitimacy.[55] More concisely, traditionality is a valuative means of structuring collective experience. How traditionality is located for travellers, in and through the medium of singing, is one of the topics of this study.[56]

Some scholars have proposed that contemporary folk traditions are devised, adapted, or formally schematized for the modern world.[57] The origins of this notion of "folklorism" and of its core representation, musical folklorism, lie in critical attitudes in industrialized central Europe.[58] As a concept, musical folklorism suggests that the face-to-face interaction of primary group performance is ending, for such reasons as ideology or tourism; thus it posits the demise of authentic "folk" practice. The dichotomous conception of "folklore versus folklorism" has been a difficult one to substantiate in rural areas of Europe. Even in the context of folk festivals, younger "revival" musicians and singers encounter older, "traditional" performers on an informal as well as a formal, competitive basis.[59] In any case, the process of adaptation, change, or transformation of folklore is a complex one that cannot be described in terms of either linear development or an idealistic either-or proposition. The adaptation of traditional genres and idioms to novel circumstances is nothing new, and the process should be seen as a dialectical one.[60]

As traditional singers, including travellers, emerged from their communities during the British Folk Revival of the 1950s and 1960s, they encountered new audiences in unfamiliar contexts. These situations could conceivably be called "folklorism," yet the presence of such singers and musicians, and their informal interaction with young Revival performers, blur the boundaries of the concept. While reciprocal singing by turn normally was not part of the concert situation, exchange did occur in more intimate late-night *ceilidhs* in hotel rooms or in singers' homes. A range of contexts for cultural communication thus was available. The dialectical relationship of "traditional" and "revival" music making was renewed and set dynamically in motion through these encounters. The result was a fertile exchange of musical ideas. Traditional singing style, however, often began to take on a more personal character. This development was a mark of increasing adaptation to, and immersion in, a populist, enthusiastic, starstruck, semicommercialized world of popular "folk music."

Community Value and Artistic Judgment

Jeannie Robertson passed over the threshold of the traveller community into a world that, while by no means alien in terms of speech and superficial cultural patterns, had a history of hostility toward travellers. Therefore more than one set of values must be accounted for. Traveller social, cultural, and moral values can be differentiated in several respects from those of the populace in different Lowland Scottish regions. These attitudes related to property and material goods, as well as to music and song. Travellers have been confronted by legislation that compelled them to abandon their nomadic lifestyle and behave like urban proletarians, with whom they had virtually nothing in common. Over the past few generations, then, they began to merge with the settled population.

Given this development, we cannot make a rigid distinction between a "pure" traveller's set of beliefs and values and a nontraveller's, except among the older, more traditional segments of the traveller population. Clan and family rivalries, well documented among travellers, meant that skilled individual musicians might be recognized only among their immediate kin. But the contemporary fame, *outside* their community, of singers such as Jeannie, her daughter Lizzie, and her nephew Stanley; Belle Stewart and her daughters Cathie and

Sheila; Jane Turriff; Betsy Whyte; Duncan Williamson; and others has led to internal traveller reassessment of such individuals, often in ambivalent terms. They may be admired or envied as singers while being evaluated differently as persons belonging to a certain clan or family.

The term "community" therefore needs to be redefined, for it cannot any longer be understood to refer to a homogeneous social grouping (i.e., Lowland travellers), nor can it signify still the limited number of opinions expressed by a sampling of interested parties. "Community" is now closely bound up with cultural identity: travellers in the Northeast and in Central Perthshire, through intermarriage and compulsory schooling, have come closer to the cultural norms of Lowland society than at any time in the past fifty years. A "traveller" identity among many of the singers mentioned above exists alongside a "Scottish" and perhaps a "Northeast" identity. Differences in gender and occupation add further layers of complexity in analyses of taste and cultural values. "Community," then, can be recast primarily as a complex of overlapping Lowland groups, traveller and nontraveller, with cultural features in common. The individuals in these groups define themselves primarily through a hierarchy of personal and social identities (e.g., woman, housewife, traveller, singer, Aberdonian). "Community evaluation," therefore, refers to a relatively narrow range of overlapping assessments culled from individuals related to Jeannie, as well as from nontraveller singers and others involved in the Revival.

Jeannie's daughter Lizzie, married to a nontraveller, experienced the transition to the wider world of the Revival. She could recount the former contexts in which Jeannie sang—egalitarian, noncompetitive gatherings of kin and acquaintances in domestic surroundings. There, among others who could sing old songs, Jeannie was recognized as a fine singer, as was her little Jeemsie.[61] Lizzie saw her mother's voice as being suited to "big classical ballads" while viewing herself more as "a lyrical singer, in a lighter vein," and modeling her delicately inflected melodies after her father's piping style.[62] Even if Lizzie's description is colored by terms derived from academic fieldworkers and even if her piping songs are not all "in a light vein," her family's perception of Jeannie's singing is significant. For her part, Jeannie's view of her own style carries aesthetic weight when she contrasts her "high" (loud) voice with that of her mother Maria before her.[63]

Stanley Robertson, Jeannie's nephew (also married to a nontraveller), came to admire his aunt's singing and learned from her strict tutoring how best to sing an old song: "Sing it right, sing it proper, and sing it real." Careful imitation of her style was the key to a satisfying performance.[64] A nontraveller like Ray Fisher, who studied with Jeannie in order to find her own individual voice, distinguishes between her own sense of traditionality in singing and that of Jeannie, the difference being the transmission of songs within the family. Ray developed her style in spite of, as much as because of, her mentor.[65] Jean Redpath, another Lowland nontraveller who has since forged a career as a singer in Scotland and North America, met Jeannie at Revival concerts. To her, Jeannie's age and personal maturity were central factors commanding both song material and audience. For Jeannie's generation, the songs had an "immediate and direct application for them, and that's why it comes over so powerfully." Differentiating between Jeannie and Lizzie, Redpath called Jeannie "the Queen of Tragedy" and Lizzie "the Mistress of the Poignant." Jeannie would "hit all the tragic chords. Lizzie would move me to tears faster. . . . Each style has something emotionally moving to recommend it."[66]

Recognizing the essential bonds between songs, singing, and experience, a young songwriter, Andy Hunter, wanted to learn from Jeannie's family. To him, Jeannie's people had a basic understanding of life and of human nature which he had not met before, and this came through in the songs, the stories, and the music to be heard in the prefab in Hayton. Jeannie taught him as a young singer to translate this understanding into his singing and left him with "this gift of recognizing authentic music, folk music, and recognizing the human qualities in it."[67] This means of crystallizing a repertoire, by selecting diverse songs for personal treatment, has affected Lizzie's performances, too; many of her listeners have confessed that her singing, and the emotional release that it offered, purged them of materialism, taking them "through a vortex."[68]

The image of the vortex is one of the few symbolic expressions that travellers have used to describe the aesthetic effect of songs. Jeannie once referred to a song's giving satisfaction in terms of "it's a fine air and a good story," while Lizzie has alluded to the lack of decoration in a melody as being "like an egg without salt." These and other proverbial expressions suggest both a range of aesthetic values and a shared sense of function and purpose in cultivating oral traditional genres. The sense of "taste" in a traditional community is an aesthetic one, but it is also bound up in the experiential reality of traveller life—a crucial point that leads discussions of "aesthetics" away from purely formal considerations toward the sociology of art.[69] As is well known, associations can form an important part of style; Jeannie and Lizzie were reminded of their mother and father, respectively, when they sang. Travellers frequently link songs, especially old songs, to the people who sang them.[70]

Learning a song from a singer particularly identified with it might imply that the source "owned" the song, in the sense that others would not sing it in her or his presence. Jeannie's family, however, did not adhere to the strict ownership of songs, no matter from whom they had been learned. Though they would recognize special skill in the performance of songs, such a concept ran counter to the traveller idea of freedom from possessions. Largely a non-materialistic group who valued nature and the open road, travellers would often give away items of value like gold rings, earrings, or brooches. They had the pleasure of owning and wearing something but then would give it to someone else, so that they too could have that pleasure.[71] As outside influence seeps into traveller values through intermarriage, this may be changing. The notion of property rights and the vexed laws of copyright have begun to reach into and transform traveller culture.

Aesthetics

Traditional singers like Jeannie see an equilibrium between the melody and the narrative text or lyric set of words. Fullness or semantic completeness of text, on the other hand, was not as mandatory for Jeannie as it was for Granny Riddle in a comparable tradition. Jeannie was not compelled to amplify a song text even if it seemed "incomplete." In such cases, fidelity to tradition and to memory accounts for the number of "fragmentary" texts among her songs (about 14 percent). But the concept of incompleteness is, or has been, one held by scholars rather than by singers, who are, on the whole, less disturbed by it. Jeannie's notion of completeness was not confined to the semantic wholeness of text, for songs were complete when they made artistic sense to her. She normally recorded piecemeal texts in private recording sessions rather than in public concerts, where her image of herself as a "singer" took precedence. Struggling to recollect the verses of "Son Davit" for Hamish Henderson and Peter Kennedy in 1953, she overcame memory problems to make the song her most celebrated one, singing it on almost every public occasion. The stimulus brought by outside recognition is the key to her relearning ("memorizing," "re-cognizing") songs and her readiness to move out from the confines of the traveller circle.

Some have contended that, for prose storytellers, the important point in successful performance is the attitude of the narrator rather than faithfulness to a received "text." A good memory is only one of a storyteller's talents, and close adherence to the text is not itself a guarantee of quality.[72] One song collector was told by a singer that she knew perhaps five hundred songs, but appeared to sing from her repertoire almost automatically, with no inclination to alter anything; because of her phenomenal memory, she did not need to patch songs, but she was not sufficiently critical to reshape them.[73] This problem affected another singer from the American South, Marybird MacAllister, who would sing snatches of half-remembered songs as readily as more "complete" texts.[74] In contrast, Almeda Riddle would rarely sing such fragments. Her longing for coherence and consistency often coaxed her into changing the verbal stuff of a song. Where Marybird's repertoire indicated a wider range of influences and responses, Granny Riddle's was more of a piece because of the intelligence she brought to her texts. Memory for verbal texts, then, can dominate a singer to the extent that creativity is absent, although memorizing a text is clearly not the same as remembering a song.[75] Lack of recall, on the other hand, at times can spur the reshaping of traditional materials.

For Jeannie, memory played a less obvious role. She would make small modifications to text and air of a song until it seemed right to her in balance and tone. Rather than "editing" a text, she remolded the entire song as an exercise in individual taste. This occurred with songs she had learned in later life as much as with those learned in childhood (e.g., "Lovely Molly" [62 in "The Songs, Annotated," below]). The learning and absorption of material were subject to her emotional preferences and aesthetic standards. Where this did not occur, as in the North American or Harry Lauder songs, a lack of conviction was evident. She felt uncomfortable with songs that were not part of her identity or experience. In pastiche folksongs such as "Flow Gently, Sweet Afton" or "The Flower of the County Down," she could produce a stylistically acceptable performance that lacked the intensity and persuasiveness of her traditional songs.

Jeannie's ideal instrument for singing such songs was a "high" or "loud" voice. With this instrument, she immersed herself in the ballads; when she sang a "big battle song," for instance, she visualized the swords clashing, much as the epic singer Avdo Mededovic saw in his mind every piece of trapping on a horse when he sang. He visualized the scene or action, and from that image he formed a reflection in his song.[76] That singers feel such identification with events, places, or emotions is a well-known phenomenon, reflecting the experiential "truth" of songs.[77] Cecil Sharp tells of a Kentucky woman who assured him, when he told her the historical facts behind "The Death of Queen Jane" (Child 170), that the song must be true because it was so beautiful.[78]

If, in Jeannie's conception, the explicit plot of a song was deficient, she might fill it out with a prose explanation, sometimes in chantefable form—part song, part speech—like one rendering of "Lord Lovat" (77 in "The Songs, Annotated," below). More often she would rehearse the plot when she had sung the song through, as in "Young Emslie" (67) or "The Moon Shined On My Bed Last Night" (65). Lizzie could also explain "Proud Lady Margaret" in detail.[79] As children, Jeannie and her contemporaries were often told the "story" of a song before it was sung. This may account in part for Jeannie's gloss on the action of "Son Davit."[80]

Such examples suggest the presence of a deeply rooted aesthetic sense. Yet the category of "the aesthetic" that separates art from other aspects of social life is a social-historical construct and therefore "arbitrary."[81] The concepts of "aesthetic experience" and "aesthetic value" are particularly problematical, in that defining and discussing the latter inevitably involves the former. Evaluation, which should be distinguished from "value," further involves taking a position on the nature of the aesthetic. But whose aesthetic? And who is evaluating what or whom?

Kenneth Goldstein set out to ask "key people" in various Anglophone communities on both sides of the Atlantic to name the best singers in their respective regions.[82] Posing such questions, of course, involves judgment on the part of such "key" persons; answers were, perhaps unsurprisingly, similar and directed to a single criterion in all regions: the extensiveness of repertoire. Other criteria were length of songs, completeness of texts, diversity of song types. Judgment was rarely based on the nature of songs or vocal quality, though in one instance a Newfoundland singer was described as having a "big voice."[83] We may note here the use of the term "big ballad" by travellers, a term that was introduced into their conceptual vocabulary by fieldworkers.[84]

Goldstein concludes that the ability to perform long songs and tales at extended sessions was a prized talent. The singers and storytellers with large and diverse repertories became the "best" performers in both Old and New World contexts.[85] But we might argue, on the other hand, that "big is best" is indicative of richness of experience and artistic talent rather than mere size, and that qualitative judgment is as essential as quantitative in small, traditional communities. What is more, "big" is metaphorical and projective, standing (like "high" for "loud") for such concepts as "full," "grand," or "replete" rather than simply for size, though that is clearly an encompassing element. "Smallness," on the other hand, as a contrasting term may refer more to the reality of everyday life, to quotidian behavior in a folk society, even to pettiness, whereas "big" refers to the world of the imagination, to the wealth, nobility, and grace evident in the heroes and heroines of the "big ballads." That is, rather than being simply literal, "big" is associative and projective. Its aesthetic dimension involves the quality, as much as the quantity, of communicated experience. If that were not so, in the Northeast singers (such as Jimmy MacBeath) with larger repertoires than Jeannie would have been considered superior.[86]

We would further argue, with Alan Lomax, that singing is an act of communication. The singers in North America with whom he worked often stressed the need to sing "in a loud, clear voice" so that the words were plainly understood. A good singer was one who remembered all the words. The themes, moreover, of parting and of masculine heroism so dominate the ballads of the eighteenth- and nineteenth-century expansionist British world as to form a single theme: ballads were tales of separation anxiety.[87] This judgment is too sweeping, although parting is certainly a major topic in ballads as the British Empire recruited cannon fodder for its foreign wars. Along with other songs of social and familial conflict, ballads that tell of separation crop up frequently in Jeannie's repertoire. Still, the aesthetics of popular expressive forms can hardly be evaluated apart from the critical, involving processes of communication and social value.[88]

These processes are intimately linked, in turn, to those of artistic meaning and cognition. The artistic process of singing and communicating learned, adapted, and modeled by Jeannie Robertson involved mastery of a symbol system, or set of meanings, in which both her own and traveller experience were embedded. These learned representations reside, though, not just in the texts or music of her songs but also in the style of performance that overarches them, since it encompasses a range of intelligences and behaviors that lie outside the "text" or "product."[89] These signs and symbols tell of dominance and coercion by the larger society as well as of conflicts within traveller life, and any study of traveller cultural practice should include the fullest reading of such representations. Because this cultural practice consists of signs (bodily gestures, artifacts, music and singing, language) and symbols (concepts used in the cognitive construction of the human world that perform the function of representation), the expressive symbols that appear in traveller culture form part of a wider symbol system representing identity, values, and world view. On occasion, they overlap with the symbols of the majority culture of Lowland Scotland. By and large, they dramatically communicate what is important to a traveller's view of the world: union with nature; the triumph of love over adversity; the inevitability of fate; and freedom from legislation, from imposed material values, and from institutionalization.[90]

Meaning comprises fields of signification that can be arranged hierarchically according to interpretive purpose: performative, contextual, musical, generic, historical fields, and so on. There also may be other, more abstracted meanings of a folksong, such as that understood by the singer, or reader, on reflection (the "epistemic" meaning). Yet the principal set of meanings are those conveyed in the enactment, in the singing situation, because the material and symbolic meanings of the song have been chosen by the singer as an act of will. These meanings may be the "inherent" ones that derive from collective experience, while idiosyncratic associations, which also can be part of aesthetic experience, are "delineated" meanings.[91] In a concert situation, both kinds may be operating at once. At any rate, Jeannie's own shifting perception of meaning began to affect her style and move it from one embedded in intimacy and community toward one associated with universality and transcendence. The transformative nature of this shift is the key to changing levels of meaning in the songs and in her singing of them.

Orality and Literacy

Jeannie's active repertoire was a mixture of songs learned from oral tradition and from written sources, especially from broadsides and chapbooks. These sources, however, often came to her through the medium of orally performed versions by other singers, and she freely adapted to her own artistic purposes both orally transmitted and written textual material. Maria, Jeannie's mother, had many songs, however, that Jeannie admitted she never learned—for instance, "The Loch o' Shallin." Whether she did not learn a song because of aesthetic preference or memory problems is difficult to determine, but the importance of the tune never was in doubt. For Jeannie, as for her daughter Lizzie and other traveller women such as Jane Turriff, the tune was central to learning a song.[92] Yet story and melody had to balance each other—a concept similar to that held by the Ulster singer John Maguire.[93]

The opposing of orality to literacy tends to presume certain absolute conditions in different societies and periods, i.e., purely oral or literate. An unfortunate byproduct, moreover, has been terms like "oral literature" (or "oral poetry") that superimpose one opposition on another without resolving the dichotomy. Some folklorists have preferred the term "verbal art," which, however, normally has referred to the analysis of prose narrative rather than song.[94] At any rate, "orality" and "literacy" often are misplaced in studies of other folklore genres because of their wholesale adaptation from the influential work of Albert Lord in *The Singer of Tales* (1960). There, the goal of understanding Greek verse, and Homer in particular, involved field studies of modern Yugoslav epic singers, all illiterate, who constructed their lengthy epic songs under a rubric of formulas (meaning conventional lines, half-lines, and phrases) while performing. This technique enabled them to recall episodes of the tale as they sang, and such formulas parallel the refrains and commonplaces in West European ballads.

But there the parallel ends. Balladic style aims at concentration of narrative, while epics aim at its expansion. The ballad is strophic, divided into stanzas shaped by a rounded melody, whereas the epic is stichic and its melodic line falls within a narrow, repeated compass. Ballad singers in Western Europe were not always male, nor invariably specialists in their own society. The ballad tradition in Scotland, as David Buchan has observed in the case of Anna Brown, was mainly a woman's province.[95] The traditional ballad audience was small, communal, and mixed; while the epic singer, if he were Moslem (as many in Bosnia were), performed to an all-male audience in coffee houses during the feast of Ramadan. The epic singers certainly were illiterate when Parry and Lord recorded them, whereas ballad singers, living in a society generally literate since the eighteenth century, did not hesitate to use printed texts from broadsides or chapbooks to supplement oral tradition within the family. Such differences stem from divergent historical developments in Western and Eastern Europe since the Middle Ages.[96]

Yet it is problematical to see any society or its culture in terms of dualities (e.g., oral/literate, urban/rural) that purport to explain social or psychic differences.[97] There is no distinct oral poetic style, since formulas, parallelism, prosodic style, and repetition are widely distributed in oral, literate, and intermediate traditions. The same is true for music, in that it is difficult to isolate traits that characterize oral tradition only. The historical processes by which such features become meaningful to the practitioners of a tradition are important; these meanings are of a complexity that cannot be reduced to orality nor to its supposed traits, such as dominance of the ear rather than the eye or the nonlinear nature of performative forms.[98] Instead of emphasizing traits, we should focus more critically on the intersubjective communication that orality establishes and indeed aims at. The latent power of Jeannie Robertson's singing style lies in its intersubjective, transformative character.

Traditional Singers and Singing

The present research follows on a handful of studies on source singers in Europe and North America.[99] Bronson's seminal essay on Anna Brown (1747–1810), the minister's wife from Aberdeenshire who supplied F. J. Child with nearly three dozen texts for *The English and Scottish Popular Ballads*, is chiefly concerned with the problem of textual recreation.[100] Since Bronson's monograph was written, Lord's influential book on Yugoslav epic singers has posed the question of whether singers in the British and American tradition memorize (the texts of) their narrative songs.[101] Linda Williamson found some Perthshire travellers who improvised melodically and textually, often depending on the particular song and audience, but this is now a rare practice, even among travellers.[102] Except among certain traveller families, improvisation has not been the dominant practice, at least since the eighteenth century and the coming of general literacy in Scotland, despite David Buchan's valuable study of Anna Brown's ballads. Hers appear to have been learned, and most likely memorized, from several different sources rather than improvised on demand.[103]

From analyses of oral narrative songs by Lord and Buchan, it seems evident that important questions of production and transmission of song materials can be tested by reference to the singers themselves and their concepts of learning, usage, and transmission.[104] A number of studies have begun to explore in greater depth the concepts of the individual performer. There has been, first, a reaction against the stereotyping of "traditions." Second, scholars such as Phillips Barry firmly believe that the individual singer should be studied, because experience and psychological states can color and alter song texts which are then, presumably, transmitted with those changes intact.[105] This process of working outward from the singer is quite different from that envisaged by the "culture and personality" anthropologists. Notably, the scholar sees tradition not in the abstract but as a definable process based on the study of transmission from individual to individual, family member to relative, and so on. The context of these transmissions must be analyzed; since change has rapidly overtaken rural culture throughout the English-speaking world, this process has tended to transform communicative situations as well as methods of recreation and transmission.[106]

Jeannie Robertson, as a singer in this Anglophone, strophic song tradition, was caught between rapidly shifting worlds and was compelled to negotiate transformation of the contextual level noted above—namely, that of unfamiliar audiences in concert situations. How was she able to do this? The answer emerges in the concluding analysis, where the understanding of performative contexts and genres and, even more, of transformative acts on different levels and in different social situations is worked out. The last notion, that of the transformative enactment, suggests the active power of Jeannie's singing. It also suggests the ways in which she was able to mold aesthetic ideals to a profoundly palpable communication in specific contexts, so as both to affect her view of herself, and to stimulate self-appraisal in her audience: this is the way life is, how I (we) have experienced it, how I (the singer) have compressed it into (ritualized) communicative form, listen (learn, and know). Besides being the life story and songs of an individual, this book attempts to relate and explain a process of subjective transformation through intersubjective means. As authors and editors, we therefore are implicated in the subjective and intersubjective process of storytelling. In a sense, Jeannie's words are our words. Yet, on a more searching and profound level, Jeannie was, and has become, over the years of association, the narrator of our lives and of our involvement in traveller song culture. She is the narrator who set the entire study project in motion, determined its nature, and brought it to a conclusion in this book. Accordingly, it is Jeannie's book and, we believe, her legacy.

Notes

1. See the discussions in Brenkman 1987 and Marsh 1988. Zygmunt Bauman 1973 describes *praxis* as "turning chaos into order, or substituting one order for another—order being synonymous with the intelligible and meaningful" (119). In adopting this stance, we note at the same time the confluence of disciplines in our thinking: (1) the parallel existentialist tradition from Buber to Merleau-Ponty, esp. in relation to intersubjectivity; (2) sociological insights from Weber, Mannheim, and Simmel through Schuetz and Berger, in particular concerning marginality, minorities, and their conflicts with society; (3) the dialectical sociology of the Frankfurt School (Adorno, Horkheimer, Marcuse) and their musicological offshoots; (4) the work on liminality and ritual, from van Gennep through Victor Turner and others involved in social enactments; (5) folkloristic work on performance and communication; and (6) ethnomusicological studies of cognition. Historically, several lines of thought derive from Wilhelm Dilthey and his insistence that: we can make sense of another's actions because we ourselves are actors; to the extent that we know ourselves through introspection, we are equipped to know another; and to the extent that we discern the meaning of another's lived experience, we come to apprehend the meaning of our own. Understanding, wrote Dilthey, is the rediscovery of the "I" in the "Thou" (Rickman 1961: 67, 113, 120).

2. See Langness 1965, Langness and Frank 1981.

3. Titon 1980.

4. See Thompson 1978, Vansina 1985.

5. Aitken 1981, Henderson 1983.

6. See Kenneth S. Goldstein 1971 and 1991.

7. To some extent, these levels correspond to the semiotic dimensions of *syntactics* (the relation of signs to one another), *semantics* (the relation of signs to their contexts), and *pragmatics* (the relation of signs to their interpreters); but the emphasis here is less on the abstract patterning of signs, signifiers, and signifieds than on the human, transitive agency of the singer, and on performative events that led to a transformative sequence of change. See Todorov 1969.

8. William James 1892: 178.

9. Merleau-Ponty 1948: 143f.

10. Watson 1976: 101.

11. In this regard, hermeneutics, the reflexive search for meaning, can bridge the gap between inscriber and the subject of the life history. It provides an interpretive frame that is essentially discursive and reciprocal. A phenomenological approach, on the other hand, seeks to understand the nature of her subjective experience as a phenomenon in its own right. For such interpretation, there is a need to span the chasm that separates our context of intellectual operation from that in which the object of interpretation lies embedded (Watson 1976: 98). In the bridging lies the need to question our preunderstandings and establish a dialectical relationship with the phenomenon under inquiry. We move back and forth between different contexts until we understand in the light of our own preconceptions, but in an altered context in which the

unfamiliar has become in some way familiar to us (Gadamer 1972: 275–83). Ricoeur sees the relationship of understanding and explanation as one that involves moving from an initially vague, hypothetical understanding through explanatory structures to a more comprehensive understanding (cf. Reagan and Stewart 1978: 149–66, Marsh 1988: 182). The goal in the hermeneutical sense, at any rate, is a synthesis in which the investigator, while never totally abandoning her or his own pre-understandings or the context of his or her own thought, now understands the life history or life story in a qualitatively different way, incorporating something of the text's context of reference and merging it with her or his own (Watson 1976: 104).

12. The concept of the life world as Edmund Husserl envisaged it is central, as the basis of meaning, to phenomenological interpretation. Our everyday world is an intersubjective world of culture, in which we are bound to others through influence and work, understanding them and being the object of understanding for others. It is a universe of significations or frameworks of meaning that we must interpret, and of interrelations of meaning we institute only through action in this life world. It is a world of culture, too, because we are always conscious of its historicity, which we encounter in tradition and habit, and which is capable of being examined because the "already-given" refers back to one's own activity or to that of others, of which it is the sediment. The human being born into this world, and naively living in it, is the center of this world, and it has significance and meaning, first of all, by or for him or her (Schuetz 1967b: 465–66). But when, in the "life story," the individual reflects on his experience, this may transform what Husserl called the "natural attitude" into the "phenomenological attitude," by which the individual makes his ongoing experience an "intentional" object of inquiry, something intended as given rather than given. It is essential that the investigator be aware of preconceptions and assumptions in her or his thinking, in order to approach directly the objects of phenomenal consciousness in the other person. Hermeneutics and phenomenology together, then, explicitly recognize the text such as the life history (or "story") as a subjective product equal in importance to the investigator's whole subjective bag of preunderstandings. Thus the meaning of the life history we want to interpret is revealed not by imposing external constructs but by accommodating the foreign frame of reference that brought it into being, the individual's culture and tradition (Watson 1976: 100–101). The concept of the life world, however, as the basis of all meaning, demands modification in practice. While the life world is built around the ego, it is connected to others through relationships that are articulated in various degrees of intimacy and anonymity; the ego and these relationships that it institutes can change. There is a real danger, as Schuetz warns, of transforming the fullnesses (*Füllen*) of the life world into a social science typology (1967a: 470–71). In the case of a life world that underwent major change, we avoid the tendency to idealize and formalize. Change, embodied in a series of real events, counters the static conception of the life world that idealization can bring about. Even Max Weber, with his notion of "ideal types" as analytical instruments for the intellectual mastery of empirical data, saw a potential danger in applying them in practice (1949: 106). Here, too, as subjective agents seeking to interpret this process of change, we can bear in mind Weber's caution not to confuse such "ideal types," or theoretical constructs, with the true content of reality, and to distinguish between the

comparative analysis of historical data and the imposing of value judgments upon them on the basis of extraneous ideals (Weber 1949: 59–112).

13. Cf. Clements 1980, Dolby-Stahl 1977 and 1985.

14. Cf. Maslow 1962.

15. Gentleman and Swift 1971 are generally dependable on the Scottish travellers' social and economic problems. They cite earlier works, including Farnham Rehfisch's early (1958) unpublished study in the School of Scottish Studies, "The Tinkers of Perthshire and Aberdeenshire, 1958." See also Rehfisch 1975, Spence 1955, and *Scottish Studies* and *Tocher,* passim. A unique account of a traveller family and its kin during the 1930s is Betsy Whyte's autobiographical *The Yellow on the Broom* (1979). Like Linda and Duncan Williamson's collaboration on Duncan's *Traveller Horsieman* (1989), Whyte's book presents a view of traveller life written from the inside. The Williamsons' collaboration has produced collections of tales for children (*Fireside Tales of the Traveller Children, The Broonies, Silkies and Fairies, A Thorn in the King's Foot*).

16. See Gentleman and Swift 1971: 113, 118; Linda Williamson 1985: 4.

17. Cf. Neat 1978.

18. MacColl and Seeger 1986: 10–14.

19. Gentleman and Swift 1971: 57, 84.

20. Whyte 1979: 51.

21. See Berne 1959.

22. See Clement 1981.

23. Cf. Barth 1955, George Gmelch 1977, Heymowski 1969, Rehfisch 1975.

24. Gentleman and Swift 1971: 93.

25. United Kingdom, Scotland, Secretary of State, Advisory Committee on Scotland's Travelling People 1982: 45.

26. Gentleman and Swift 1971: 93.

27. Ibid.: 56.

28. Zygmunt Bauman 1973: 133.

29. Cf. Simmel 1971 [1908].

30. Schuetz 1967b: 95–96.

31. Zygmunt Bauman 1973: 130.

32. See Shields 1986.

33. Clement 1981.

34. MacColl and Seeger 1986: 41.

35. Cf. Stephanie Smith 1975.

36. Porter 1985: 312.

37. MacColl and Seeger 1986: 10.

38. Rehfisch 1975: 280–81.

39. MacColl and Seeger 1986: 21–23.

40. Ibid.: 17.

41. Ibid.: 122–23.

42. See Porter 1978.

43. Whyte 1979: 174.

44. But see Munro 1984: 214 for a different perspective on this issue.

45. Cf. Blacking 1992. Blacking, however, does not address the issue of gender in his summary. See, rather, Sarkissian 1992.

46. Herndon and Ziegler 1991, Koskoff 1987. Most recent studies have tended to single out for analysis the status of women in Western societies, especially their artistic accomplishments. Women composers have received a greater share of attention in these studies than recreative artists, for the very good reason that women's creations often were downplayed or ignored in favor of a male-centered creative tradition (cf. Solie 1993). Female singers (the Jenny Linds, Maria Callases, or Bessie Smiths) traditionally have received greatest attention from male commentators, perhaps in compensation for having mastered interpretive rather than compositional abilities. But this is, of course, a result of privileging composition as an activity separate from that of performance, a concept challenged by Albert Lord in the light of epic singing by Bosnian (male) guslars in the twentieth century. The distinction that elite art makes between composition and performance has historical roots in the Romantic era, with its adulation of the individual artist, and rarely holds good for traditional societies. In such communities, the process of making songs or music is, after all, closely bound up with communicating reciprocity rather than with creating an aesthetic object. That is not to say, of course, that traditional societies are without aesthetic notions (see below).

47. Carol E. Robertson 1987.

48. Nettl 1983: 335.

49. E.g., Gentleman and Swift 1971: 59, Munro 1984: 211.

50. See Berger 1967. In recent times, the terms *culture, tradition,* and *folklore* have been supplemented in academic discourse by *cultural practice, traditionality,* and *folklorism,* signaling thereby a revised view of how traditions operate and adapt to change. *Culture,* for example, has been a contestable notion ever since E. B. Tylor invited social scientists over a century ago to study "the condition of culture," and the term has been defined in countless ways (Cafagna 1960). To be meaningful, definitions of culture have come to be framed in terms of both social context (the arena of its activity) and an intersubjective mode of understanding (the negotiable discourse essential to its interpretation). In this sense, culture is better seen not as some kind of category of sociological inquiry but rather as a mode of *praxis* (or practice) in which knowledge and interest are one (Zygmunt Bauman 1973). *Cultural practice,* while elaborating upon the polysemic *culture,* is still an imprecise term, but introduces the active notion of shaping a subjective world.

51. Ben-Amos 1934.

52. Cf. Holbek 1987.

53. Hobsbawm and Ranger 1983.

54. See Wagner 1975.

55. Eisenstadt 1969: 453–54.

56. Conscious of this "affirmative" sense of traditionality, we can insist that cultural traditions also involve domination of one class by another. Walter Benjamin (1969), recognizing that an interpretation of culture and a critique of society were modes of understanding that depend on each other, sought links between them. His argument that barbarism and civilization are interwoven in Western traditions challenges cultural

studies and suggests that all cultural interpretation must be, at the same time, an ongoing critique of society. The challenge was taken up by the Frankfurt School, from Adorno, Marcuse, and Horkheimer to Habermas, and in the phenomenological tradition of Husserl, Heidegger, Merleau-Ponty, Ricoeur, and Gadamer. The former, neo-Marxian view contrasts sharply with the latter tradition in insisting that questions of cultural preservation and transmission be linked to social criticism. Because Lowland travellers have stood at the outer margins of society, they constantly must be seen in the context of a need on the part of the local populace for both social domination and cultural dependence.

57. See Moser 1962. The term *folklore*, too, has both positive and negative senses in popular usage. Richard Dorson, in coining the term *fakelore*, attempted to separate the genuine from the spurious, esp. advertisers' inventions such as Paul Bunyan (Dorson 1956). But others have pointed out that, even if the term refers to commercial motives in cultural invention, the invented product can enter and undergo a transformative process by which *fakelore* turns into folklore (Dundes 1984, Gailey 1982, Gailey 1989, Newall 1987). Others have attacked the whole concept of *folk* as a bourgeois invention (e.g., Keil 1978). Without acknowledging Dorson's parodic neologism, Harker 1985 proposes *fakesong* to denote the popular song products mediated by, or appropriated by, bourgeois collectors and editors in Britain from the eighteenth century on.

58. Cf. Baumann 1976, Klusen 1967.

59. See Porter 1985.

60. Cf. Bausinger 1986a, Heimann 1977.

61. Stephanie Smith 1975: 23–24.

62. Munro 1970: 73.

63. Gower 1983: 134.

64. bid.: 145.

65. Ibid.: 140.

66. Ibid.: 141.

67. Ibid.: 142.

68. Stephanie Smith 1975: 103.

69. Cf. Wolff 1983: 20.

70. Linda Williamson 1985: 62.

71. Whyte 1979: 152.

72. Cf. Degh 1969: 166.

73. See Wolf 1967: 104.

74. Abrahams 1970: 13.

75. McCarthy 1990: 7.

76. Lord 1956: 125.

77. Halpert 1964; cf. Coker 1972: 191f.

78. Sharp 1932, 1: xvii.

79. Stephanie Smith 1975: 181–83.

80. Porter 1976 and 1988.

81. See Bourdieu 1979. While this is true, others have argued that a concept of the aesthetic needs to be rescued both from the claims of a radical sociology of art which would equate aesthetic value with political worth, and from the total relativism into

which aesthetics might be led by the self-reflexivity urged by the social history of the arts and of criticism (Wolff 1983: 21).

82. Kenneth S. Goldstein 1991.

83. Ibid.: 168.

84. Adopting a "star singer" approach in his sampling-oriented fieldwork, Kenneth S. Goldstein 1991: 169 notes that Sara Cleveland from Brandt Lake, New York, sang the only reported version in North America of Child 52, "The King's Dochter Lady Jean" and referred to it as a "big ballad." But she disliked the song and declared that she sang it only for her scholar friends. Yet Sara also noted that her Child ballads (some 12 in number) tended to be longer than other British ballads in her repertoire, usually telling more complex stories through greater use of dialogue than other ballads (Goldstein 1991: 169–70).

85. Ibid.: 173.

86. Other factors clearly enter the picture in evaluating singing: gender, traveller and non-traveller identity, regional preferences within the wider Revival. In her study of a traditional East Suffolk community, Ginette Dunn emphasizes the performative nature of aesthetics in local singing. The recognition of performers as "good" is the primary critical standard in the tradition, but there are secondary standards related to vocal delivery and vocal acceptability: pronunciation should be clear, musicianship sound, and clarity essential for a "good performance" (Dunn 1980: 205–10). A relaxed strength of voice is a recognized asset, and many old men lament having lost the ability to sing with feeling. The ideal combination is strength of voice linked with sympathetic feeling and a kind of power (associated with masculinity) that is restrained yet produced in a relaxed way. The aesthetics of traditional songs and singing thus are tied closely to the social structure and to gender relationships within the community, and cannot be considered apart from such factors (Dunn 1980: 214–27).

87. Lomax 1967: 213–14.

88. Aesthetic experience and value, of course, also need to be considered in relation to artistic meaning and cognition. In the cases of music and song as human systems of meaning, some kind of emotional reaction is involved. Symbolic forms like music and poetry arouse strong responses both emotionally and cognitively. Emotion and cognition need not, however, be opposed to each other. Following Suzanne Langer's allusion to "a vast and special evolution of feeling in the hominid stock" (1967: xvi), some scholars have argued for a focus on the cognitive features of emotion. Mihaly Csikszentmihalyi 1978, for example, has observed that the making and experiencing of art constitute a process in which cognition and emotion are intertwined, and that the conflicts which art attempts to master cannot be encoded by the unambiguous symbols that reason relies on. Like other forms of knowledge, art is an adaptive tool by which we master forces in the environment in order to survive in it. Artistic cognition models experiences that are ambiguous, and must therefore use codes that are multivalent, changeable, and holistic but highly specific.

89. The debate as to the meaning of *text* is a convoluted one that involves different understandings of the term in different disciplines. In folklore, D. K. Wilgus 1973 suggested broadening the word to include not just the verbal but also the musical component in any song—i.e., the transcribed music would also be part of the "text."

The influence of literary criticism, esp. that of Barthes, Derrida, Kristeva, and other French writers involved in deconstruction, has meant that almost any conceptual schema, as an object of study and interpretation, can be called a "text"—even a person. Social scientists, less bound to fine literature and the art of writing, generally have been reluctant to admit the sophisticated arguments of the deconstructionists into their fields. This is partly because the deconstructionists privilege writing as a medium, and partly because of folklorists' belief in the traditionally strong link (thought by such as Derrida to be fragmented) between signifier and signified in oral traditions. See Hawkes 1977: 145–46.

90. These are often expressed as themes rather than in specific images. The difficulty of the term *symbol* has led to the substitution of *meaning system* in order to avoid confusion between internal meanings and external signs (d'Andrade 1984), though *meaning system* itself describes imprecisely the range of meanings possible in a specific situation. Discussion of meaning involves the mediating power of symbols or "meaning sets," as instruments primarily of cognition and secondarily of communication. While linguistics has made progress in explaining the semiotics of language, some recent work has discarded the notion of music as a secondary modeling system based on language. A system of signs, or musical semiotics, should proceed only from the primary reality of text-music as sound (Orlov 1981). One scholar regards music as more appropriate than verbal language for revealing the purely structural requirements of a symbolic system, and has argued that the processes of sharing become as crucial to the semiotics of music as the sonic product that is the focus of analysis (Blacking 1981). The cultural meaning of music, in other words, has to be shared and negotiated to be at all "meaningful." Whether a traveller singer's nontraveller audience, of course, could share or negotiate this system of meanings is a moot point. Further, the "meaning" of a song is dependent more upon the communicative ability of the singer, and the audience and context of performance, than the separate parts (music, words) of the "text." That in traditional songs, too, the tune is often at odds with the words is immaterial. "Meaning" derives from the communicative criteria applied by the singer and by the audience, as the former conveys a particular message to the latter at a specific time and place, and under the rubric of active feedback. Meaning, in other words, is primarily performative, since the gestural and sensuous elements of the singing communication, as well as the present account of it, must be taken into consideration. This does not mean, of course, that disembodied songs in print can have little or no "meaning." It is simply that the communicative chain has been weakened.

91. See Green 1988.

92. Porter 1978: 18; Stephanie Smith 1975: 52–53.

93. Morton 1973: 10.

94. See Bascom 1952, Richard Bauman 1984 [1977].

95. David Buchan 1972.

96. The arguments that have materialized since Lord 1960 was published need not be recounted here, though Jones 1961 and later David Buchan adapted Lord's findings to the analysis of balladry (see Friedman 1983). David Buchan's study of Anna Brown (1972) and McCarthy's later study of Agnes Lyle (1991) have lent weight to the notion

of formulas "memorized" and "remembered" by ballad singers, formulas that are melodic as well as verbal (Andersen 1985). Melodic formulas have been studied in terms of "tune families," genetically related melodic structures that incorporate "formulas" such as whole phrases or partial phrases (Bayard 1950 and 1954, Cowdery 1990). Analysis clearly must take into account the conservative building blocks that both types of formulas exhibit. Yet to discuss these separately, rather than as fused in performative unity, is to miss the artistic impulse, the creative, singing gesture that binds them together. The temptation to deal with the verbal and the musical materials as if they were divorced from each other, as well as from the singer's performance of them, is a strong one that reflects disciplinary training and the established boundaries of academic fields. These boundaries must yield to the greater imperative of understanding the traditional creative process.

It has been argued that, in understanding communicative, artistic orality in a culture as primary as that of Jeannie's, we should attend to sounds rather than words, to mnemonics and formulas rather than propositions and proofs. Thought and expression in traveller culture could be described, in one formulation, as: additive rather than subordinate, aggregative rather than analytic, redundant, conservative, close to the human life world, agonistic (involving interactive struggle), empathic and participatory, homeostatic, and situational (Ong 1982). The import is that, because words are sounds, proceeding from the human interior, they manifest human beings to one another as conscious interiors, as persons. The interiorizing force of the word, and even more of song, relates in a special way to the sacral, the ultimate concerns of existence. On psychological and physiological levels, interiorizing corresponds to shared somatic states and the rhythms of interaction that transform commonly experienced sensations into externally visible and transmissible forms (Blacking 1977: 9). Jeannie's singing had an effect of this kind on her listeners.

97. Finnegan 1980.

98. Feld 1986.

99. Every singer must be discerned against a ground consisting of other singers in the same or a contiguous tradition; otherwise, the sense of a collective well of language, style, and idiom is lost. The Scots-English ballad tradition is widely diffused but admits a limited range of themes (Wilgus 1970) and aesthetic models (Glassie 1970). Studies in the song traditions of individuals in Britain and Ireland have succeeded those of Anna Brown in Bronson 1969b and David Buchan 1972. Some of these are analyses of a historical repertoire: that of Miss Reburn (Gardner-Medwin 1976), Andrew Crawfurd (Emily Lyle 1975), Charles Leslie (Mary Ellen Brown 1985), and Agnes Lyle (McCarthy 1991). Others deal with living singers on various levels of complexity (commonly life, repertoire, style, social occasion): Joe McCafferty (Shields 1982), John Maguire (Morton 1973), Lizzie Higgins (Stephanie Smith 1975), Belle Stewart (Porter 1985). More rarely, some studies have involved families: the Turriffs of Fetterangus (Porter 1978), the Stewarts of Blairgowrie (MacColl and Seeger 1986), the Fisher family of Revival singers (Stephanie Smith 1988). Three collections of songs from recent oral tradition, with notes on individual singers (a fair number of them travellers), may be cited: Kennedy 1975, MacColl and Seeger 1977, and Munro 1984. These can be supplemented by North American studies: of Almeda Riddle and

Marybird McAllister (Riddle 1970), Sara Cleveland (Kenneth S. Goldstein 1968), Larry Gorman, Lawrence Doyle, Joe Scott (Ives 1964, 1971, 1978), Dorrance Weir (Glassie 1970), Paul Cox (Szwed 1970), Andrew Jenkins (Wilgus 1981), Rena and Buna Hicks, Hattie Presnell, Lena Harmon, and Bertha Baird (all, Burton 1978). Such research guards against presenting a picture of the singer or composer as unique, idiosyncratic, quirky, or, in a bourgeois sense, "exotic." In general, the studies noted represent a tradition, in its variant regional clusters, of mostly domestic themes that was fragmented by 1700, revitalized by antiquarians and hawkers of eighteenth-century broadsheets, and subsequently diffused by local and, in Scotland and Ireland, traveller singers through performances in the mass media and in folk clubs in the post–World War II Revival.

100. Bronson 1969b.

101. See esp. David Buchan 1972, McCarthy 1990.

102. Linda Williamson 1985: 262f.

103. Cf. Andersen and Pettit 1979, David Buchan 1972, Nygard 1978. This conclusion does not apply tox the tunes, Anna Brown's singing of them, or the performance aspects of these songs, although tentative attempts were made to capture her singing in staff notation in the eighteenth century (Bronson 1969b). Lord 1960, in describing modern epic singers such as Avdo Mededovic, an illiterate butcher and ex-soldier who could improvise songs thousands of lines long, also addressed questions of learning and the context for the performance of heroic songs. Lord's main emphasis was on the technique of oral formulaic composition as a means of explaining the recreation of lengthy epics and the verbal material in particular. Ballad scholars initially found this suggestive for the analysis of ballad style as a textual construct, but rejected the idea of improvisation because of the close structural identity of plot and text, if not tune, in British-American balladry (Friedman 1983). Traditional singers in Western Europe have evolved a shorter strophic verse and the self-contained melody that contrasts markedly with the character of stichic epic songs (i.e., a tendency to compress rather than expand). Whereas Lord stressed the primacy of the story in epic singing, with the music being simply a formalized vehicle for the progression of plot, episode, and theme; in Western Europe singers usually have conceived of the "song-story" as a genre in which the semantics of story and the framing, ritualizing melody are balanced against each other. The relation between *logos* and *melos*, between verbal matter and melodic curve, is more evenly divided than in the epic, where the concentration and skill of the singer is placed on the syntagmatic narrative element. This simultaneous melding and tension in performance of two different communicative media—words and music—were primary factors in Jeannie Robertson's attitude to and control of her songs.

104. See David Buchan 1972: 5.

105. Barry 1961: 75.

106. See Henderson 1980.

Part I

The Life of Jeannie Robertson

As told by herself, her family,

and a number of her friends

1. "The Bonnie Bunch o' Roses": Traveller Kith and Kin

Jeannie Robertson was "discovered" by Hamish Henderson in the city of Aberdeen in 1953 and immediately hailed by him and the American folksong collector Alan Lomax as "a monumental figure in twentieth-century folksong."[1] In *Folk Revival,* an assessment of the folk music movement in Britain published four years after her death, Fred Woods called Jeannie "the acknowledged Queen of traditional singers."[2] The English folksong authority, A. L. Lloyd, dubbed her "a singer sweet and heroic." Simultaneously, almost, with the early recordings of her ballads and songs, she began recording recollections of her family and early life as a traveller child. She also recounted her years as wife and mother selling sundry goods from door to door in the Northeast territory of her seminomadic relatives.[3] Jeannie gave Henderson an account of her life, a chronicle of her family, and a clan odyssey of the open road, leading him to recognize that this dark-eyed, dark-haired, heavy woman of forty-five was one of her clan's most significant communicators of its tradition.[4]

Jeannie was the youngest child of Donald Robertson and Maria Stewart, born about 1870 and 1880, respectively, both of traveller stock. Before Jeannie's birth on October 21, 1908, her mother had had four other children: William, Robert, David, and Elizabeth Mary Ann. Donald and Maria were related through earlier unions of the Robertson and Stewart clans, but there is no record that they were ever legally married, even though they were accepted in traveller society as husband and wife. A grandson, Stanley Robertson, has noted that, "because my granny and granddad were not married, there was a bit of controversy over the surnames of the children. My father [William] and his brother Robert were registered Robertson. All the rest were called Stewart but known as Robertson."[5]

As they were growing up, then, David, Elizabeth Mary Ann, and Jeannie were known as Stewarts. Jeannie's marriage certificate, dated September 3,

1927, lists her as "Christina Jane Robertson (formerly Regina Christina Stewart)."[6] At age nineteen, therefore, when about to be married, Jeannie altered her first name and officially took the surname Robertson, even though the same document gives "Donald Stewart, Pedlar" as her father. It is not entirely clear when "Regina" became "Jane" and then became "Jeannie," but it was Hamish Henderson who, some years later, suggested that Robertson was a more appropriate name than Higgins for a Scottish traditional singer, even though she had been married to Donald Higgins for twenty-six years when Henderson met her.

Stanley Robertson, who is a Mormon and thus a serious genealogist, has noted that William, Robert, David, Elizabeth Mary Ann, and Jeannie "were full-blooded brothers and sisters" and that "it's hard to write about one's relatives, especially when they intermarried so closely without actually being wed sometimes. Everyone is full cousins or second cousins, double cousins or in-laws—except my mother [Elizabeth Brookes McDonald], who was only a third cousin of my father. You speak about Royalty intermarrying!"[7] Stanley provided the genealogical information for appendix A, which traces Jeannie's lineage. Maria Stewart's younger children by her marriage later to James Higgins are included there as well.

During her early years, Jeannie experienced the kind of life her people had known for centuries. She got to know the string of campsites traditionally used by them in spring and summer, along the banks of the Dee and Don rivers flowing eastward through Aberdeenshire to the North Sea. When barely into her teens, she would leave the parked caravan of her mother and stepfather at the camp and set out on foot with her pack crammed with soft goods, bits of cheap jewelry, and drams of perfume and head for the back glens:

> So many vans goin' aroon nowadays has done the packman out. We lived in Aberdeen six months oot o' the year an' traveled the other six in a caravan. My ain father bein' dead, we always traveled with members of my mother's family, the Stewarts. When we come to one of the campin' grounds, there wes other families—maybe no relation to you, but travellers too.[8]

Jeannie's traveller identity was a telling cultural mark in a conservative, rural Northeastern society that was either ambivalent or openly hostile toward her people. The settled rural dweller in the Northeast reinforced his own identity through callous prejudice. But as Jeannie and other traveller singers became celebrities, as public knowledge of traveller life and behavior increased, as legislation and intermarriage with nontravellers gradually forced the travellers reluctantly to conform to the ways of the settled population, prejudice toward them diminished. At the same time, however, traveller identity was threatened.

Because of Jeannie and others of her generation, internal accounts of the traveller worldview first became available to a wider public; thus, too, traveller identity was recognized and validated, even though assimilation continues to threaten the newest generation (i.e., these singers' grandchildren).

When Jeannie grew internationally famous through public performances, records, and published interviews, visitors flocked to her door. She became a mouthpiece for the Robertson and Stewart families, a group of headstrong hawkers who refused to stay in city or village for any length of time, when the clean air of the country was there for the taking. Jeannie told of feet that itched to explore the wide, lonely glens, the salmon streams between Deeside and Donside, the deer trails upward into the Perthshire highlands:

> You would leave Aberdeen an' you'd go by Coulter. An' from Coulter you'd go to Banchory—an' maybe there wes camps between them places, lovely camps, an' then from Banchory maybe up to Aboyne an' to Ballater and Braemar—all these places. I've walked in one day fae Braemar an' went richt oot owre the Devil's Elbow an' then to Blair an' four miles above Blair to St. Fink. That wes thirty-eight mile in one day.[9]

Jeannie was young and strong at that time and took pride in the freedom provided by her trade. An endless assortment of Robertson and Stewart relatives, as well as Camerons on her father's side and Croalls and MacPhees on her mother's side, afforded shelter and company on the road. She drank in their stories, music, and songs around the campfires. From the older people Jeannie heard many tales, some of them about her own father, a professional soldier who had died when she was only a few months old:

> My father, Donald Robertson, was very handsome. We aye had his photograph, wi's full Highland dress on an' his pipes. He was a sodger—in the artillery. He wes overseas for years in South Africa an' India an' aa that places, ye see. He wes on the guns. I've heard them speakin' aboot it. My father wes in the Boer War, ye see. Through aa the Boer War. Sae ye'll ken he wes ten years older than ma mither.

According to family tradition, Donald Robertson was born about 1870 and at age thirteen ran away from home to join the army. A muscular lad for his age, he was persuaded by his friend Jimmie White to enlist. The two youths were sent into Aberdeen by their fathers, according to the story heard by Jeannie, to sell a horse; but, having done so, they spent part of the money on drink and used the rest to go to London to sign up for duty overseas. When they returned to Scotland after several years, Donald and Jimmie took to the road again; and soon Donald, then twenty-six, met sixteen-year-old Maria Stewart in a nearby camp:

> Ma father wes like masel', aafie fine skin. Fair skin wi' aafie rosy cheeks. Ma mither wes the same, ye see. An' he'd big black een. Fine featured. Bit he wesnae black like me. No. Bit a lot of his brithers an' family wes. It rins through the folk. Whit wes black wes black, jet-black. An' whit wes auburn wes auburn. Ma father wes a dark chocolate-auburn. He was a big, strappin', handsome man. He had to be, because thir wisnae a wummin under the sun bit whit said it. He wes fine-backed too. Broad-made, broad shoulders, an' weel-built. An' ma father wes one o' the finest on horseback. An' he used to—on market day, an' him hauf-drunk—hing on by his heels. His heels would be on the horse's back an' his mooth tae the grun'. He'd be pickin' the hankies up an daein' aa the tricks fir a bottle o' whusky. Fir a bottle o' whusky he used tae dae it to let the men see him. Ma father belonged tae the Leochel Cushnie on Donside. Ma mither was born in Ballater in Gairnside.

Maria Stewart's mother, Mary Croll, who was descended from "show people," disapproved of Donald Robertson's courtship of her daughter. She had in fact selected Jock Higgins as a more suitable husband for Maria, just turning sixteen.

One day, having dinner at a farmhouse after helping with the harvest, Mary Croall made a remark about Donald and his wild ways to her hostess at the head of the table:

> She criticized ma father, an' held up Jock Higgins, God rest his soul! An' tother woman turnt an' said to ma grannie, "Weill, weill, Mrs. Stewart, aabody's nae the same," she says. "Bit God," she says, "I hiv to tell the truth. For mesel', I'd raither hae a drunken man aa week," she says, "as long as he's sic a bonnie man as Donald Robertson on Sunday."

In spite of Maria's mother's objections, the union took place, and the couple kept to the roads in summer, in the winter taking a house in Aberdeen. In time there were born to them sons William, Robert, and David, then daughters Elizabeth Mary Ann and Jeannie, born three years apart. Other periods of military service followed for Donald Robertson, yet while he was away, Maria managed to keep the family together in Aberdeen or on the road in summer. The wives of the other travellers remembered Donald as a dashing soldier in Highland dress when he came home on leave. "Ye ken this, lassie," one of them confided to Jeannie in later years, "yir father wes sic a bonnie man, God help me, I cud hae rin awa' wi' him mysel'."[10]

Though Jeannie, born in 1908, could not recall her father, she could

Fig. 1. Donald Stewart Robertson ("Soldier Donald"), the father of Jeannie
Robertson. Courtesy of Stanley Robertson.

describe through the accounts of others his looks, daring, and well-known strength. He was also a hard drinker. "My father wes a guid man, bit he had a weakness o' drink, bein' sae lang in the army, I suppose. Ma father cud earn money, bit he cudnae keep it. That wad be jist the worst o't." Donald Robertson was again in service in 1909 when he died. Maria at age twenty-eight was left with five children, Jeannie being the youngest and only eight months old when the news of his death spread quickly among the travelling people. "Ma father wes only turnin' thirty-eight when he died. An' in the army. He went below the dyke when he wes in barracks. Fell owre the dyke. An' he died as a result o't." As a child, Jeannie knew a number of her father's brothers and sisters, her numerous Robertson kin. They seemed a family singled out for sudden, violent deaths:

> There wes sixteen in 'is family an' there wes seven o' them died when they wes little. An' Jeemy and Geordie died when they wis jist young. An' then there wes two lassies. One had a lang heid o' reid curly hair. An' aafie heid o' hair she had. She wis marrit til a country man. He sellt fush. Called him Fush Davie. An' they'd baith haen a drap—in that days the women took a drammie—an' she wes killt in the road. The lang reid curly hair wis lying aa awre the road.

Jeannie knew of other such incidents among her kin, their weaknesses compounded by intermarriage. To her, their problems with alcohol were familial: if the weakness could be traced to both sides of the family, she felt it was a case of "one marriage bringin' two strikes against the wean." She seems early to have developed a realistic outlook on the world and a kind of stoical wisdom as she observed her elder brothers and her many traveller relatives. Living among them, she saw people who were not "institutionalized" in the formal sense but who nevertheless habitually made capricious decisions that imperiled their very existence.

As she recounted her family history, the dark moments were sometimes offset by a wry comic remark. She could see that her brother Davie (nicknamed "The Iron Man" because of his prowess in weightlifting at country fairs) was cast in the same heroic but reckless mold as their father. He had tried to join the army at fourteen, posing as eighteen; by seventeen, he had thrown a man out of a Gallowgate pub in Aberdeen and assaulted policemen in the Spa Bar. He made a name for himself as a self-taught swimmer who could cross the Dead Man's Hole on the River Ericht at Blairgowrie, carrying first Jeannie and then Lizzie on his back.

> Davy wes always desperate. I mean he's been in a lot o' trouble jeest for fightin' and cairryin' on. But he's been a kind o' a black sheep, you see. Well, you know,

he feels it too. An' yet he cudnae help hissel'. Nancy Whisky wes his favourite since he wes fifteen years o' age an' frae that day to this he's a daily drunkard.[11]

Davie had a lot of songs that Jeannie remembered only in part and he could sing entire, but Davie "wes hard to find sober long enuch to gie 'em to me." When Davie sang some of the serious songs, however, he was inclined to parody them in a comic style:

> When Davie sings a sang—a battle sang or onything like 'at—at the bits where he killed them with the sword, Davie gaes through all the actions o' drawin' the sword an' lickin' the bluid off the swords. He wes doin' that in the hoose one night an' he put everyone to lauchin' and I took such a sore fit o' lauchin' that I had a pool o' tears below my eyes on the floor, an' Davie lookit an' said, "God help me, I sung sae sweet that my puir wee sister's greetin'." He didnae ken I wes lauchin'.

Davie was the family clown, the trickster and satirist, a black sheep given to mockery and, when liquor was present, violence. Volatile, mercurial temperaments in men and women alike are well known in traveller society, and one could argue that cynicism was a key factor in Davie's talent for sung parodies.

On her mother's side, there were numerous Stewarts to care for Jeannie and for Maria's other children after Donald Robertson's death; Maria had three sisters and four brothers who taught the youngsters the traditional trades of travellers, along with songs and tales. The children began to recognize themselves as part of a transient community with its own standards and values. Maria's mother and father, William and Mary Croll Stewart, helped out when the caravans camped near Atholl or when the travelling clans assembled in summer to work in the berry fields at Blairgowrie. The children got to know the Stewarts of Huntly and could hear their great-uncle John Stewart playing the pipes in his Highland dress and listen to stories about the day he left the Blairgowrie Games with three first prizes. They also heard their aunt, Margaret Stewart, who was celebrated in the community for her fine singing voice and vast collection of songs inherited from her mother.

As a community sharing surnames like Cameron, MacGregor, MacDonald, and MacPhee, the travelling folk worked out a system of "adopted" names or "by-names" to avoid confusion among individuals with the same name:

> See, there wes lots o' Donalds. My father was one. An' they cried ma father "Sodger Donald." He wes a sodger. So it wes "Sodger Donald" or "Granny's Donaldie." 'At wes a chap brought up by his granny. Anither Donald was cried "Shepherd" or "Shepherdie." He liked tae tak a drink. Sometimes he'd tak a drink an' lie amongst the sheep aa night. An' his folks wondered what had come

across him, an' he wes lyin' up there on this hill among the sheep. The sheep wes aa roon' aboot him, bit he wasnae a shepherd. They only cried him that. An' then "Ginger Donaldie." O whit names! Funny names. Well, with all these same names ye need some way to tell one fae the ither.

The frequency of "adopted" names occurs also in the Highlands, where "by-names" or lineal designations often are a necessity: *James son of John son of James*, for example.

From the time Jeannie could remember, her mother was a singer recognized among the travellers from Aberdeen to Perth. Maria's father Willie Stewart likewise was a fine singer who encouraged his granddaughter:

He wes a great big man an' weighed about seventeen stone. Nae big-bellied, bit fine-made. An' 'e likit a dram, aye, at the end o' the week. An' it wes mostly at any little gatherin's—mostly at them—when 'e wes drunk 'at he wad sing. At that time 'e had a second wife an' she used t' like the auld songs too. An' mony's the braw shillin' the twa o' them used t' gie me for t' sing. I wes ma grandfather's favorite. Ye cud never pit 'im aff singin'. Cud never pit 'im aff hearin' sangs. "Bonnie Charlie's nou awa'/Safely owre the friendly main. . . . " 'At wes 'is favorite o' aa. He used t' sing that yin wi' me. O, 'e cud sing that yin wi' me. O, 'e cud sing 'issel, he cud.

Maria inherited a portion of her songs from her father and some of her talent for self-dramatization from her mother's people, the Crolls, who dressed up, put on shows at fairs or at the Blairgowrie Games, and passed the hat among the spectators.

Maria, the widow with nut-brown hair and five children, made a striking figure as a hawker in her brightly-painted wagon with its elaborate fittings:

She wore her hair in a middle shed. It was pure nut-brown an' wes in waves. Natural waves. She didnae pit it lang hair. She jist had it tae her shoulders, an' it hung in short curls, aa wavy, an' curly, fae the top. An' she had grey eyes. An' reid cheeks, an' fair skin.

In 1914, at the outbreak of World War I, James Higgins, Maria's second husband, was a member of the reserve and was called back into service. His stepdaughter Jeannie, then six years old, remembered the tremors of excitement when the declaration of war reached their caravan:

When the hue-an'-cry gaed oot, all reservists wes tae report immediately. So my stepfather had tae report. I mind fine that he'd t' rise an' leave ma mither an' ging

Fig. 2. Maria Stewart Robertson Higgins, mother of Jeannie Robertson.
Courtesy of Stanley Robertson.

awa' there an' then. An' we had only landed at St. Fink hill that very nicht before tae pick the berries. Aye, he'd t' catch the train at Blairgowrie. I mind he wes aafie excitit beciz he wes leavin' ma mither an' us behind an' him an' my mither wisnae long mairrit. So ma mither got a house in Blairgowrie an' we lived there about a year. Then ma mother left the hoose an' we went back to oor ain part of the country—Aberdeenshire. We travelt by train. An' ma two younger brithers, Bobbie and David, wes along with Lizzie Ann an' me an' the first of the second family, Andra. My oldest brither, Willie, had already joined up. He wes seventeen an' in by this time.

The effects of the 1914–18 war were to remain with Jeannie through the new deprivations of World War II.

Maria found a house in St. Andrews Street and put the children in school while she ran a small shop, drove her wagon called "The Bonnie Bunch o' Roses," and hawked for a living. Then, the following year:

Ma mither shifted from St. Andrews Street to wir big hoose in Gallowgate. It had four lovely big rooms an' the big shop in the front firbyes. Ye see it wes nothin' for ma mither to fill it full o' stuff. . . . it was a second-handit shop, a pawn shop. It had ivry new stuff and old stuff, ivrything, because she went roon the toon an' bocht an' also from ither people comin' in. An' maybe ma sister Lizzie—she wisnae very old, bit she still wes three years aulder gin me—she cud ging to the shop an' see til it. Bit ma mither wes always hame by a little eftir the dinner hour an' folk kent when to git her in, ye see. She just sellt in the shop in the eftirnuin.

More than forty years later, Jeannie retained vivid memories of the Gallowgate and the period around 1916 when she attended school there:

The shop wes across from Kitson's the big china shop, which is all down now. Thir used to be the big barn at the top o' the street. An' 'en, thir wiz a big landin' tenement—ye know whit I mean by a landin' like this—then thir wes the big baker's shop, then thir wes ma mither's shop. An' then thir wes anither shop ma mither had too. She went owre an' took the ither shop. . . . she giv up wan an' gaed into the next shop for a while. . . . an' then—well, eftir that it wes grocers' shops, fruit shops, an' tattie shops, an' bars. It was aa in the Gallowgate. It's a long time ago I'm speakin' aboot. The Gallowgate wes a thrivin' place 'cause ye'd Spring Gairden, Young Street, Berry Street, an' Stable Close—aa that streets wes aa gaun off it. See? It wes a real busy place at that time.

Maria sang a song about the Gallowgate, a part of which stuck in Jeannie's memory:

O the Gallowgate's the place fir me (bis)
Fir its fightin' women
An' greetin' weans
An' the Gallowgate's the place fir me.

This fragment pictures women like Maria, small, alert and physically courageous when aroused.

Among traveller relatives, the story is told of how Maria, a week after the
birth of her fourth child, Lizzie Ann, came to blows with a woman dubbed the
Terror of the North:

"Weel lassie," Mither says. "I never was feared of nae woman in my life. I was a
wee bit windy," she says, "but still I wudnae show it. Ma bad temper wudnae let
me show it! The Terror fought a clean fight, an' I fought a clean fight wi' her. The
woman had bonnie hands that was scientifically learned, ye see, but I had fat she
didnae. I had a terrible strength, wi' naething but the power o' bad temper."[12]

There were other incidents when Maria was unwilling to give quarter and
faced the world with little more than her two fists and the "terrible strength" of
her arms.

Yet the children respected Maria for her scruples as much as for her physical
power. She did not use foul or blasphemous language, for example, and though
she could neither read nor write, she spoke with a dignity that imprinted itself
in their memories:

She wes very religious. She nivir lay doon in her bed without prayer. . . . an'
couldnae sign her ain name. . . . she'd aye pit a cross. This wes wan thing, she'd
her own belief in God, an' naebody would iver change her. An' although Lizzie
cursed—ma sister Lizzie—she wes a different wummin firbyes ma mither, entirely different aathegither. . . . ma mither wes high-tempert an' wes feart at
nuthin', bit she wudnae tak the Lord's name in vain, curse, swear, or blaspheme,
na. To Lizzie she'd say: "God bless iz, an' mercy, wummin. Git oot o' here, ye
sinful wummin!" She cudnae bear that—if Lizzie had took God's name in vain.
An' I dinnae like it either, na, I dinnae like blaspheming the Lord's name.

Those who knew Maria well agree that she and Jeannie were very similar in
their outlook. Maria not only became a model of social behavior for her
daughter but also influenced her singing style:

I sing verra like ma mither, but she hudnae sae high a voice as what I have. She
wes a guid singer and a true singer, bit nae sae high—down lower. Yes, ma
mither sung a lot o' sangs—three times mair than fat I can mind. Three times
mair.

Several years after Maria's death, Jeannie described her family's use of song. Maria would sing to her and the younger children, whether in a camp or by the hearth in their Gallowgate tenement:

> My mither cudnae sleep as her sons and her husband wes oot in the First World War an' she cudnae sleep because she wes worried. An' she used to sit up till aboot two in the mornin'. Her an' her brother used to sing the songs thegither, an' I used to listen, an' I got interested in the ballads an' the folksongs. I started to learn them at that time. The auld sangs went frae mooth tae mooth in these days. They never learned them off paper, that's certain. An' nae ma mither—she cudnae read nor write.

Traveller children were brought up in a culture in which songs and tales were not simply entertainment but rather were guides to everyday action. Stories and ballads became cognitive maps to traveller history.

In the chaos of World War I and the hardships of their daily lot, Maria and her family found in songs an outlet for anxieties as well as a mode of learning from and about past events. Through symbols charged with affect and through performative communication, these songs not only validated traditional values but also heightened social solidarity in a period of stress. Individuals among the travellers came to be known for their musical or narrative talents, often feeling personally responsible for fulfilling their assigned role of cultural guardian:

> My people lived in the caravans an' tents. Through the day they went oot sellin' their wares an' their soft goods an' at nicht after the supper they used to sit round the fires an' we'd have a little sing-song or a bit o' music. They cud play— bagpipes, fiddles, accordions, or mouth organs—an' they cud all sing. I was askit to sing an' of course I wud sing a few sangs what the people askit, what the people likit me to sing, an' it wes the ballads that they askit. An' some o' the older people wud sing. An' some o' the ones aboot my age that wes guid at the auld sangs. That's how we passed the time.

"Passing the time" does not adequately portray the communal activity to which Jeannie refers. Travellers were excluded from a society that placed value on progress, novel technology, and material security, and they were regarded as anomalies in modern, post–World War I life. They persisted in defying the norms of progressive capitalism and the privilege of the landed gentry. At the same time, they refused to identify with the passivity of the urban proletariat. Circling on the fringes of the larger culture while much of the modern world, caught up in materialistic "progress," moved in the opposite direction, the travellers were viewed as parasites or wastrels. They seemed as disposable as the outdated tools of the Northeast farm servant. As a pocket of cultural "anarchy" that moved seasonally from place to place, traveller society held to norms based on family and clan ties and clung to an archaic familial code.

Travellers also maintained a belief in intuitive powers, in the preternatural, as well as in conventional religion, all without doubts or feelings of dissonance. They continued to respect their warriors, athletes, singers, musicians, and poets. Their beliefs were a potent feature of their everyday life and a part, ultimately, of their visionary and somewhat animistic outlook. In spite of conflicts with the law or with social reformers, sanitation engineers, or missionaries, the "traveller way of life," despite its drawbacks, represented a potential for freedom in the modern world. Theirs was a freedom not of "disposable time" nor of coercion, as Marxian arguments might have it, but a freedom validated by traveller custom and tradition. Jeannie's narrative confirms this quality again and again.

Other internal accounts confirm the traditional value placed on freedom and the world of nature. Betsy Whyte, ten years younger than Jeannie but also the child of travellers, in her autobiography recounts life on the road during her youth, emphasizing the excitement she felt when the group had escaped the city. The sensuous sights and sounds of nature completely enchanted her.[13] Stanley Robertson, Jeannie's nephew, describes the paradisaical refuge that the countryside became for his family as they made their "exodus to Alford" to work in the flax fields, escaping the hated city and the prejudice of the scaldies:

My little brother and I sat on the back of the cart, surrounded by all the things we most valued in our lives. . . . my sisters and other women folk trekked along the road, the great excitement in their voices mellowing and flowing in the gentle breezes. . . . Songs rent the air and so did stories of the past. . . . The men stopped for a smoke or to take tea provided by the womenfolk along the route. . . . Everything was wonderful!

To the country people we passed we may have seemed a strange migration, but to us this was a journey to a better land—where we would be at home again with the natural elements to whom we belonged—and where for generations we had been a part of that creation and at home within it. . . . and so as we were now far away from the eye of the scaldies, we felt a deep sense of privacy and a feeling of pure freedom.

Our first stop at Echt was wonderful: a very warm evening with a red sky, and while all around us was the fine smell from the fire of withered broom (and we sat at last, at ease in our natural home), . . . we could begin now to listen to piping, fiddling, accordions, singing, and best of all—the master storytellers.[14]

These descriptions are revealing, not only for the liminal context of campfire at dusk for the celebration of music, song, and narration, but also because they confirm that travellers are not a stereotypical "oral" culture. Ample evidence exists that many could supplement oral versions of songs with written and printed variants of the texts, sometimes composed or copied by themselves. Jeannie did this, as did Jane Turriff and the Stewarts of Blair. The act was an index of respect for the authority of the written word by a culture that was, however, basically oral. Moreover, travellers traditionally have respected the quality of formal education in Scotland even when they were reluctant to submit their children to it.

As for the songs, a written version indicates a respect for print and for the authentic or "correct" version. This trait has been shared by the Northeast population at large since literacy gradually became universal in the nineteenth century.[15] As participants in a marginal culture that found itself halfway between orality and literacy, traveller singers could determine for themselves the origin and form of songs (and especially song texts). Yet in the social obligation of performance, these "origins" mattered less than the conviction of the singer about the appropriateness of her or his sung version. As Jeannie grew up, she absorbed not only the modes of performance but also the resources available for the songs she preferred. Instinctively, she went about practicing mastery of the modes while she selected the song texts—oral and written—that most appealed to her. The next-to-last stage of cognitive and performative accomplishment was to be complete by the time she had reached her teens.

2. "The Lady o' the Lake": Childhood and Courtship

Just before World War I, Jeannie was six and attending school in the Perthshire town of Blairgowrie. She met there a boy of seven by the name of Donald Higgins, son of Jim and Christina Higgins. The families knew each other; in fact the boy was a grandnephew of Maria, Jeannie's mother, and therefore was considered a third cousin to Jeannie. She described their first meeting:

> It was at the old Rattray school. An' thair I first saw Donald—fourteen months aulder gin me. An' then as kiddies we wes thegither. An' we left thair, an' I nivir saw him fir, och, he must ha' been aboot twelve anyway. At that time we nivir wes sweethearts. Na. We wes relatit tae each ither, bit nae sweethearts.[1]

Their paths crossed from time to time in the camps or back in Aberdeen. At one point the two families lived in adjoining houses in Union Street, but only for a few months before Maria moved to a better house in Denburn and Donald's family went to the village of Pitsligo. His father at that time was a tinsmith, having learned the trade from his father before him. At Denburn, meanwhile, Jeannie celebrated her last two years at St. Mary's Catholic School, enjoying a close relationship with the teaching sisters, of whom she spoke warmly for the rest of her life. She considered herself a Catholic even though she seldom attended mass in later life and did not participate in the church sacraments. Donald was never a convert.

It was not until Jeannie was nineteen and Donald a little over twenty that they were thrown together again and the courtship began:

> Wir people wes living in company—Braemar—on the market-stands at Braemar—an' Donald, he—widnae stop. He made advances an' things an' ach weel, thir wir a wee bit o' a rowie, ye see, an' things got up. He really did rin eftir me. An' he wudnae tak no fir an answer. He widda gied through fire an' watter then. Nothing cud stop him, ye see. An' he wes tellt that he hudnae tae. . . . tae follie eftir me so much an' things.

The origin of the conflict, according to Jeannie, was in the attitude of the families. Donald was told bluntly by his father Jim Higgins that a marriage between him and Jeannie would be illegal, since Jim by that time had taken Jeannie's older sister Lizzie Ann as his second wife, Donald's mother having died at the age of thirty-seven (see appendix A). Certain incest laws were held over their heads. Donald's grandfather, grandmother, and several of his aunts also opposed the marriage, arguing that if Donald married Jeannie, his own father would be his brother-in-law. But Donald rejected his family's counsel and was willing to take a chance on the legal ramifications. Set on claiming Jeannie, he persisted, and Jeannie's later view of herself at this time reveals a touch of vanity:

> Donald widnae keep awa'. He widnae tak nae tellin' frae them. An' coorse, though I say't masel,' I wes jist aboot as fine a lookin' lassie as what wes amongst them at that time. I wes only nine stone four an' wi' skin as white as the driven snow, an' cheeks like a perr o' roses. An' I wes nae small or little featured—big dark eyes—an' ma hair wes as black as the pickaninny. I wes really well-lookin'. An' it didnae maitter whaur I went, aye people peyed attention to me an' ma looks an' things. . . . I had nae want o' fellows trying to marry me an' things, bit I always kept ma heid above the watter. I always kept masel' decent an' respectable. I cud haud ma heid up to the world an' can still dae't.

Family strife continued for some weeks in the Braemar camp because of Donald Higgins' avowed intention of marrying Jeannie. Set against him were his father, his stepmother (Jeannie's sister Lizzie Ann), Jeannie's mother, and Jeannie's stepfather. But this opposition only brought the two closer together:

> If they hadnaea spoke, if they just hadda tellt us quietly, I think it widnae maybe come to oniething, bit ye see they startit to boss us aroon' an' show their authority. It only made the situation worse. They startit to boss us an' kick up holy murder an' fight an' quarrel. They wir jeest at each ither's throats. An' they ordert Donald awa like a collie dog, ordert him awa frae the camp. 'At wes an aafie thing to dae. An' of course he had to ging awa', but he roared back, he says, "I'll follie—I'm nae carin' whaur yese ging," he says, "I'll follie, an' yese cannae keep me back." He left an' went intae Aberdeen. We went o'er the Devil's Elbow and through Glenshee an' intae Blairgowrie. Then Donald tellt his tales o' woe to some of them there, ye see, whit had happent. God knows aa what he said, I dinnae ken. Bit it disnae make nae odds. He did come to Blairgowrie—barely a week ahin it—an' then I slept wi' his sister, wi' Jeannie, an' he used to steal doon and come intae the tent wi' me an' Jeannie.

This deception did not last. As the families were camped on St. Fink's Hill, on what they called Laird Stewart's place, three and a half miles from Blairgowrie, Donald entered the camp openly and declared himself:

> When he turnt up they said, "Here he goes! Here he goes! Here's the Divil hissel' comin'! An' by God, he steppit in as brave as oniebody could step in. He steppit in tae this big encampment of people. His father said to me, "Jeannie, ye must keep him away from about ye." I says, "I cannae dae that. That's nae whit I can dae in the open country. An' it disnae maitter whit happens, he'll follie me." They wir askin' something impossible. So I says, "I cannae dae it." So my stepfather—God rest his soul an' Heaven be his bed—he liftit his hand an' he hit me a hard smack across the face. A damnt hard smack across the face. Aye—my stepfather. It wesnae a canny yin, it wes a bloomin' sair yin, an' I nivir did nae wrang fir tae git it. So of course that made me sair wi't, ye see, an' Donald kent the moment to step in. I didnae like the idea o' gittin' a slap across the face fir nuthin'. An' a damnt hard smack it wes. So this did something to me. I turnt rebellious, an' I said, "If he wants tae try an' win me, I cannae kill him for it. He'll dae it in spite o' me an' you an' aa ither body."

Then and there Jeannie knew that Donald was the man for her: his valor was proving it.

At the time, Jeannie was earning good pay picking berries in the Blairgowrie fruit fields. She remembered being sympathetic to Donald because "he'd nae mither or naebody." When he came to her, he stuttered out his proposal:

> "I havenae got nuthin'," he says, "I've nae money. I havenae got money. But the best thing tae dae is come on. We'll rin awa' thegither an' we'll git marrit in Aiberdeen." So w' me gittin' insultit in front o' the folk an' hit fir nuthin', I jeest walkit awa. The two o' iz gaed on. We left the camp in the efternuin, in front o' them. Aye, we walkit oot, an' the whole encampment wes seethin'. The very fire wes fleen fae thir mooths. An' we jist turnt wir backs upon them an' walkit oot an' walkit doon the road. We took a bus a certain distance o' the road fir fear o' them folliein' us. Took the bus til Forfar an' then the train frae thair t' Aberdeen.

Years later, after a quarter century of marriage, Jeannie recalled the early life and hardships of the lad she eloped with to Aberdeen in 1927:

> Donald had a hard life. Considerin' the life that I had to his, I had a lady's life. He'd a dog's life. A pure dog's life. Aye, he lukit fir a livin' frae he wes aboot twelve. His father took a good drink an' aa, ye see, an' aa this bairns wes left an' he wes jist a lonely young lad an' he had them to look eftir. Na, thir's nae gettin' awa fae the fact, him and Isaac an' the rest o' them aa had a terrible life. I nivir wantit fir nothin'. I nivir kent whit it wes to go wi' bad boots or shoes upon ma

feet. I nivir kent whit it wes to want a perfectly *good* diet. A good diet. Nair nir whitiver I wes able to eat. We could aye share wi' ither folk. I nivir kent whit it wes to go dirty, or kent whit it wes no' to be weel-dressed. I used to be sae well-dressed as a lassie they used to cry me the Lady o' the Lake.

In Donald's family there were nine children desperately needing help. As the eldest, Donald tried to look after his younger brothers and sisters: Jeannie, Kristy, Jocky, Isaac, Jimsey, Davie, Willie, and a baby who died soon after its mother. Three of the boys, Donald, Jocky, and Jimsey, had what Jeannie called "the hibber." They stuttered badly. Though Isaac the younger brother escaped the affliction, Donald stuttered for the rest of his life, especially when under pressure. He could sing, diddle, and recite without any signs of the impediment, but his speech remained affected in ordinary conversation to the end of his days.

When Jeannie and Donald got off the train in Aberdeen with marriage in mind, they went first to the Gallowgate to stay with Donald's aunt and uncle, Jeannie sleeping with the aunt and Donald with his uncle. It was too late that day to have the banns read, but next day they had this done at St. Mary's Cathedral in Huntly Street, where Jeannie had wanted to be married. Her mother meantime had made inquiries as to whether it was legal for them to marry, and was told that it was:

> The man went on an' told her: "It's quite legal fir them to merry. It's no' like two sisters marrying a father an' a son afore—an' brithers an' so forth like that. It's quite legal." Well, we'd the banns in, an' jist went on wi' the merrige—carrit on. "Well," ma mither said, "I'm no gaun to interfere. They've done the deed— they've run awa thegither—an' fir aa thit I ken, aa the harm that could be done it's done." It wesnae, of course, bit nivirtheless, ye cudnae convince people. Bit thair ye are. We wes marrit in St. Mary's Cathedral. Oor two bairns wes baptized there too—Jeemsie and Lizzie. Isaac's a Catholic, bit Donald wesnae—Donald wes a—isn't it a Presbyterian ye cry them? Aye, his family wesnae aa Catholics.

The marriage certificate shows that Jeannie and Donald were married at St. Mary's on September 3, 1927, "after publication according to the forms of the Roman Catholic Church."

Jeannie and Donald returned to his uncle's house at 170-½ Gallowgate after the wedding and sublet a room. They were nineteen and twenty, respectively, and had music, a shared tradition of travelling, and a deep attachment to each other. "We lived quite happy," she recalled, "even though that wes the time that depressions were. We didnae owe oniebody nuthin', cud pey wir rents an' gae t' the pictures ivry night. An we'd plenty to eat. What mair wes a body needin'?"

There were *ceilidhs* in the neighboring homes or behind the shops in the Gallowgate when the travelling families gathered on holidays or during the long winter evenings.

Donald had taught himself to play the pipes when he was only ten or eleven years old, and he practiced every day. His mother asked him to try the piping competition at Stonehaven when he was sixteen, wearing a worn suit and carrying an old set of pipes that belonged to his father. He was permitted to enter the Games without the customary Highland dress because the son of a "gentleman" had been entered wearing plus-fours:

> So therefore them that wes in Highland dress cudnae keep Donald out or else they wid hae had to pit the young chap oot wi' the plus fours. . . . So Donald had to play amongst the men. An' I'll no' get awa frae the fact—whit's in the book— Donald had the two firsts. He got a gold medal, a gold and silver medal, an' so much money. Then Jockie Higgins cam' in first fir the puttin' o' the stone. Aye thair's nae gettin' awa fae the fact, an' the people roun' aboot the place wesnae very weel pleased. They cried til 'em in the Northeast o' Scotland 'at the hawkers went in an' took the first fir the pipin' an' the first fir the puttin' o' the stone. They wirnae very well pleased.

Having always felt themselves at the bottom of the social ladder, travellers who entered organized games and piping contests used these to demonstrate their superiority in strength and musical skill. Winning with the pipes, even in an ill-fitting, hand-me-down suit, or bringing home a medal for twirling the stone were strategies for building self-esteem and celebrating an egalitarian spirit.

Piping especially was an art prized among the men (more rarely, women also have been known to play the instrument), and many travellers enlisted in the Third Gordons regiment because the Pipe-Major was Robert Reid, one of the finest teachers and exponents of piping in the country. Donald Higgins had been kept out of the military because of a weak constitution. But he persevered with the pipes, always with Jeannie's encouragement, and the two took pride in celebrating the music they had learned within the traveller community. The autumn and winter months of 1927 were among the happiest they ever knew.

3. "A Gift o' Some Kind": Jeemsie, Lizzie, and Second Sight

After staying with Donald's aunt and uncle and hawking in the city, the young couple felt the call of the open road the following spring. With them went young Willie Porson and his wife Margaret, a Higgins by birth and therefore a relative:

> We wes livin' in this wood on a middle road that taks ye from Kincardine O'Neil down til . . . Banchory. Well, we wes livin' in this wood an' it wes very warm an' there wes plenty firin'—we'd plenty food an' things—warm camps and warm beds—an' the ither lassie an' her man had a little dog—a collie kinna dog. He'd keep the watch. Bit I wisn't feelin' too well, ye see, because I wes aboot five or six month wi' ma bairn. I had nivir been very well carryin' the child. Though I had been a strong lassie, I wes nivir well carryin' the children.[1]

One evening during the encampment Jeannie felt so tired that Margaret Porson suggested she go into their camp (tent) to get warm. She fixed Jeannie a hot drink and put her to bed. After an hour or so of heavy sleep, Jeannie was awakened and told that the dog's barking was a warning of men stalking in the woods, and they must run for their lives. Their fear was sharpened by the knowledge that Jeannie's uncle Willie Stewart had been molested in this same place. "They shot his horse an' attackted his wagon an' he'd a wife an' a guid few bairns in the wagon. They riddilt his wagon wi' shots."

The two couples fled the spot, Jeannie and Donald carrying nothing but their clothes and bedclothes tied in a pack. Like other travellers, they thought of the "Burkers," so-called for the criminals Burke and Hare, who in the nineteenth century had murdered a number of indigent but innocent people and sold their bodies for medical research.

> We'd tae leave ivrything! Aa wir pans, pots, dishes, spoons, knives, ivrything. Camp an' ivrything. An' the dog, it wes gaen mad. At that time I wes quite light

made even if I wes nae weill. I says til Margaret, "Fear," I says, "'ll lend wings to my feet. I'll rin," I says, "when I ken thir's oniebody eftir me!" Of course Donald wes made like a needle an' nuthin' wrang wi' him. An' aa we had packit wes bed-cloes. Hudnae a bowl or a cup or a drop o' tea. Not even a teapot or a kettle.

Who were these stalkers? Local authorities often accuse travellers of departing campsites and leaving behind heaps of rubbish, including the broken parts of wagons and the bodies of rusting automobiles. Sometimes residents took the law into their own hands in cases of trespass, as happened with Jeannie's uncle.

During their flight, the two young couples hid in a quarry when they saw car lights approaching in the distance:

> We got right down in the back o' the rocks, the dog an' aathing. A car gaed by, an open car wi' the hood back, an' we coontit thim wirsel'. To be precisely, thir wes seven men. An' ivry man had soft hats on their heid an' waterproof coats on. Now, they lookit fir us an' we nivir gied a move.

After the car disappeared, they walked into Banchory to a campsite that had been a traditional refuge for travellers, one of the many recognized grounds on which they could camp and feel at home. "Ye were allowed to bide in thair as long as ye likit. Naebody ivir touched ye or lookit at ye. Naebody ivir touches ye in none o' the roads—nae that kinna wey oniewey." They believed that the seven men in the open auto were possibly poachers "daein' the Dee" and who, breaking the law themselves, wanted no witnesses to their crime. In the prob-able case of a traveller encampment, the men's search for victims to persecute included the use of an automobile, in those days a symbol of social superiority.

> We wir in their road. An' us bidin' thair fir a whilie, they saw we werena gaun to ging awa, that we wir plantit thair maybe fir a month or two. So they had to git us out o' the road. An' why did they follie us in the car? That's the bit that I cudnae get owre. An' then again, why did my uncle git the same thing in the same place a few years a front o't, an' them to use guns?

Frustrated and sick at heart, the four realized they had no protection under the law. As Betsy Whyte has confirmed in her autobiography, police in the 1930s were barring entry to many traditional campsites; her mother was driven to remark, "God pity them. . . . They would deprive us of daylight if they possibly could."[2]

After a night in Banchory, Jeannie and Donald returned in daylight to the campsite in the woods, recovered their belongings and made their way, tired and defeated, back to Aberdeen. This seemed the only choice for them at the time because Jeannie, who vowed she would never camp in the deep woods again, was regularly ill with her first pregnancy.

Taking a small flat in the Guestrow ("a very historical place") they were living there when the first child was born two weeks prematurely, on June 5, 1928, at 8:00 A.M. An hour or so after baby Jeemsie's birth, Jeannie was taken to the hospital with complications of enclampsia that resulted in memory loss for several months. The doctors worked with her, as many as seven at a time, but for days she hovered between life and death.

> I wes seriously ill when I had ma son. They nivir thought I wid live. In fact I wes that far gone I'd the reid screens roun' me an' it wes only the nearest o' ma kin that wes gettin' in to see me. It was 'clampsia fits that I had wi' childbirth. I wes thirty-six hours in fits and three days unconscious.

For the rest of her life, she could recall vividly a vision she had while lying in hospital at the point of death:

> I wes a deith's door an' queer things happened when I wes there. The first time that I ever cheated the grave, the Lord come for me. I wes dyin', an' there wes no hopes for me. When I wes in this state—wes given up, wes dyin'—I lookit up a brae an' the sun was shinin' at the top o' it. . . . an' near half-way doon the brae, it wes cold, dreary, an' dark-lookin' weather. But in the top the sun wes vivid and shinin' bonnie. An' I lookit up this brae an' I saw the Lord in a white goon upon him—a long white goon o' a flimsy kind o' stuff. I saw him so vivid I'll nivir forget it. An' I thocht he beckit me to come up the brae til him.

As her vision intensified, she thought the Lord was begging her to approach, and the temptation to do so led her halfway up the hill, but she realized that if she went all the way she would die.

> Na, but I didna gae up the brae. But I lookit doon at the fit o' the brae, an' I seed my man standin' there. Donald wes young at the time. I was only 20 and he was 21. He wes greetin'. So I lookit up and I said to the Lord, "God bless me, you're a bonnie man." I says, "Look, I can hardly stand the temptation. But I dinnae think I'm gaen to ging up to you at a'. I'm gaen to gae back the road." An' I rin doon the brae as quick as I cud to resist the temptation o' the Lord.

When she opened her eyes, Donald and the hospital sister were standing by the bed, and she could hear the sister telling Donald to get her to talk:

> An' I said, "God bless me, here ye are. I've come to ye. I wes almost awa' wi' the Lord, a bonnier man than ye'll ivir be, an' a better man." An' my man said to me, "Of course, he's a better man than ivir I'll be." An' awa' I wes again. I mind naething after that.

Weeks later, Jeannie told all this to the visiting minister when he asked about the actual experience of dying. He suggested that it was the Devil who had come to her in the form of the Lord, and that he was trying to tempt her. This interpretation provoked a sharp answer from Jeannie: "So I lookit intae his face an' I said, 'Don't try to change my mind noo. To me it'll always be the Lord, nae the deevil.' Then the meenister lost his heid speakin' aboot it tae me, an' he nivir come back to my door again." She had seen the Lord herself and would always bear witness to the great temptation.

Jeannie's extended illness brought on such a deep depression that her family despaired of her recovery. She sensed her loss of memory when Donald's sister brought a maternity robe to the hospital:

> I'd lost ma memory of ma past life an' asked her who gev me the lovely dress. Bit it wes ma own guid dress an' I hed pit all the fancy silks an' embroidery on it masel' before the bairn wes born. I cudnae mind ma past life an' I got a wee bittie frightened when she said, "You put aa the fancy work upon it." When I got back home she kept coachin' me ivry hour we had tae wirsels an' speakin' aboot this an' speakin' aboot that—an' wir past life—things that we'd done when we wir kids. "Ye must mind, ye must mind," she hammert it in ma heid. An' I tried an' tried—an' jist walkt up an' doon the floor tryin' tae git ma memory back.

In spite of her sister-in-law's patience and the gradual return of her physical strength, Jeannie's memory seemed damaged for good, no matter how hard she tried to remember. After three months there was no improvement, only spells of mental exhaustion and depression:

> One night I begun to greet. I greet wi' vexation because I cudnae min'. I got workit up in a terrible state an' it wes a queer thing—something happent tae ma memory an' I felt things beginnin' to crowd in upon me by the thoosans. Aathin' wes crowdin' up in ma mind. Aa the years o' ma past life begun to crowd in. Terrible. I held ma heid 'n walkit up an' down the floor. I wes beginnin' tae mind . . . ivrything now. Even tae the night I took ill. I suddenly remembert finishin' the fancy work upon the frock when I wes in labor. I wes overcome wi' the excitement. So Jeannie run an' made a drop o' tea an' I took a tablet to soothe me doon. She says, "Now naebody kent—they're none the wiser." An' I says, "But sangs—ma sangs—they too wad hae aa been gaen. . . . the very same as ivrything, if I'd nivir got ma memory back."

With her recovery Jeannie began to enjoy the baby, a "bonnie bairn—very handsome." She sang the old songs to him to lull him to sleep, and recited the jingles that Maria had chanted to her and the younger children round the campfire or at home during the war.

Jeannie was greatly attached to this first child, and as he grew to boyhood, he resembled her more and more. When she was fifty-seven, she looked back and remembered:

He'd long dark dusty ringlets an' the bonniest face that ivir oniebody lookit upon. Ye see, he wes aafie lassie-lookin'. He'd a fine roun' facie. His skin wes like ma ain skin—as white's white—an' ma cheeks is as reid as roses yit, an' I'm fifty-seven past. The bairn—he'd the same complexion. Donald wes tan-skinned, bit nae me. I'd an aafie fair skin compared to ma ain darkness. It wes unusual, an' ma laddiekie wes the same. He'd a big dimple in his chin the same as masel'—I'd aye a dimple that gaed in thair an' on wan cheek. An' a perr o' gret big dark eyes. An' he wes aafie refined in the face. Aafie refined. Bonnie-faced an' the lovely skin.

Jeannie's love for Jeemsie did not lessen with time, and there was further idealization as the years passed.

Fifteen months after Jeemsie was born, Jeannie gave birth to a girl whom she and Donald named Elizabeth Ann and called Lizzie. Jeannie was ill at this birth, too, and recovery was slow. Lizzie was born at home in the Guestrow flat; as a toddler beginning to talk, she would refer to her home as "the Gush" [the Guestrow]. Her parents often called her "Lizzie tae the Gush" as a by-name. Just as Jeemsie had his mother's coloring, Lizzie looked like her father and as a child worshipped him, inheriting from him an instinctive love of pipe music.

With the help of her mother, sister-in-law, and other kin living either in the Guestrow or the Gallowgate, Jeannie continued to work part-time after she was strong enough to return to hawking. Her children became part of her public life as soon as they were able to accompany her on her rounds. When Jeemsie was too young to go on foot, she would carry him proudly in a pack:

I aye took ma bairn wi' me, an' people into the big hooses in Aberdeen wad tak ma bairn oot o' ma' oxter an' tak him awa, maybe amongst the rest o' the people in the hoose, to let them see him, he wes sic a bonnie bairn. I've heard people sayin' whit's tae me wes stupid. . . . "Why is it 'at youse people on the road have such lovely children?" Many's an' many's the time ma bairn wes tooken frae me an' tooken through the hooses. An' ivrybody thit aye lookt upon him aye said, "O God! Whit a bonnie bairn! Ken? An' I aye thocht it wes unlucky that ma bairn wes admired too much. An' I didnae—wir folk didnae believe in that. They think it's unlucky if a bairn is admired too much.[3]

Such adulation for Jeemsie was an ominous and distressing sign for the young mother brought up in the traveller tradition.

During her stay in the hospital after Lizzie's birth, Jeannie was given the nickname "Doodum" and voted the best-looking patient in the ward. In spite of the traveller taboo against beauty contests and the representation that one human being is superior to another, Jeannie accepted the judgment of her hospital peers with little comment, except to say:

I wes sittin' up noo in bed an' me lookin' bonnie on the bed an' things like that. It wes a big ward, a surgical ward full o' women, an' they cried me the best-lookin' wan in the ward. Didnae worry me, God help us. Aa that I wes worrit aboot—I wes aye feart o' takkin' somethin' else—that wes whit wes botherin' me. Gettin' one o' thir ills. They had to dae somethin', I suppose, to pass the time away.

Jeannie suddenly developed pneumonia and was dangerously ill for several days. Suddenly she felt a great choking sensation overwhelm her when she begged for water, but it was denied her by the nurse in charge, who gave the excuse that she must wait until the ward sister came on duty. The sister left a dish of mouthwash by the bedside, never imagining what her patient would do with it:

She says, "Where did you spit it out?" Ye see? She thought me being that ill maybe I'd spat it oot aboot the bed. I says, "It's nae spat oot," I says, "it's doon thair—swallowed it. You widnae gie me nuthin'. Widnae gie me a drink. . . . widnae gie me nuthin' when I'm chokin'." An' she says, "Are ye any the better," she says, "of swallowin' that? That may do ye harm, I don't know, because it's an antiseptic mouthwash. That could do ye harm." "Ach well!" I says, "if it diz me hairum," I siz, "it's nae ye to blame. It's masel to blame. I drunk it."

Although she did not repeat the intake of mouthwash, Jeannie despised hospital routine all her days—the noise, the lack of privacy, and daily baths.

From the aftermath of pneumonia, Jeannie began a slow recovery and was finally released from hospital. As each spring came, she and Donald would take young Jeemsie and Lizzie in the caravan, moving to the country to sell their wares. Donald, never robust, was frequently ill during these early years of marriage. The stuttering became more pronounced, and the young husband succumbed to periods of nervousness and bleak depression. At one point, stricken with diphtheria, he was hospitalized for several weeks:

He wad hae been aboot twenty-five, twenty-six, an' it wes the very first time thit ivir he took sic a thing, an' he really wes ill wi' diphtheria. Thir wir a bad epidemic o't broke oot in Aiberdeen at that time an' my wee laddie Jeemsie cairrit the germ in his nose, an' yet nivir took it hissel'. Lizzie nivir took it, or I nivir took it. Donald wes chokin' when he gaed awa. See, he wadnae get the doctor in or allow me. He'd nae belief in doctors at that time. An' a lot o' poor folk hadnae. An' his throat wes very bad. So Dr. Lindsay removed him to the hospital right away and he wes a good while in hospital, near two month. That wes aboot 1934 or '5. 'Twis the time o' the Depression.

Exposure to all kinds of weather for a good part of his life made Donald's slight frame thin and vulnerable. "He was nivir fat. Ye see, he'd a slim bone," as Jeannie put it.

Recovering from diphtheria, Donald got a job that winter in a sawmill in Aberdeen. But with further exposure, he developed a cough that alarmed Jeannie because of its severity, and she begged him to see another doctor. He refused: "Ye're beginnin' to imagine things now. Ye're beginnin' to imagine that I've got a deadly disease." Jeannie insisted, "I'm nae imaginin' ye have a deadly disease. Ye have a deadly disease. An' ye're needin' to be catcht an' saved in time—there might be savin' in ye if ye wad only listen to me."

After further pleading by Jeannie, Donald agreed to an examination. He was placed in hospital with tuberculosis and remained there, bedridden, for some months with odds against a recovery. Jeannie's instincts had been right—more accurate than Donald's or those of the doctor who first examined him. It was characteristic of her to speak up and voice her convictions in a time of crisis. Like Maria, when aroused she could speak with a fiery tongue that kindled action. Donald went into hospital for treatment, and Jeannie, with her children at her side, prayed hard for his recovery.

Baptized a Catholic, Jeannie had both children baptized in the Catholic faith. At times she could be critical of other churches if she suspected double standards or insincere piety on the part of their members, but she was not otherwise critical or condemnatory. Her faith was very personal, but it was also typical of the traveller spectrum of religious experience:

> I'm maybe not a guid Catholic, I maybe don't go to chapel very much, but within myself I am really religious. I don't go about preachin' to the folk or Bible-thumpin'. But within myself I have a great belief. I have seen a lot from my childhood, an' I've went through a lot, an' I wouldnae like tae tell ivrybody—but I have a gift o' some kind. Yet I wouldnae ivir dabble in witchcraft or mak second sight mair or bigger than it is. An' that's the God's truth, though I should nivir leave this chair, an' I'm neither mad or nothin' else. I'm as wise as aabody in the town of Aberdeen, an' that's true.

Jeannie's accurate perception of Donald's illness and the need for treatment suggests the faculty known among travellers as "second sight." Her extrasensory ability and her visionary Catholicism mingle in her narrative, above, of a handsome Christ as spiritual seducer when she was near death. Other narratives of hers display a mixture of the real and the visionary.

Jeannie first suspected her extrasensory ability when she was five years old. Later, at sixteen, she dreamed about a small boy in the flats next door and awoke from a heavy sleep to see a small white coffin coming out of the back of her bed, passing over her face. Agitated, she told her mother and stepfather what she had seen, but they insisted she had seen the coffin only in her dreams and there was nothing to be afraid of. They had seen the child the day before, and he was quite fit. Jeannie repeated, though, that while the rest might have been dreamed, the coffin was not.

By this time she had become distraught and was growing ill—as is the case with others who have second sight and are physically affected by what they see. Jeannie was put to bed with tea and aspirin and admonished to stop her foolishness. Maria left the flat for a good part of the morning before she returned to Jeannie's bedside with unhappy news about the Hutchinson lad:

> I'll no' forget whit she said. "Now I'll tell ye something," she says. "Jeannie you did see the coffin." An' when she said that . . . it made me worse. She says, "You did see the coffin. An' the bairn is deid." God bless us, I cudnae get it outa ma heid. . . . So I said, "Well, mither, I seed others before they died. . . . will ye believe it nou?" "Well," she says, "it's a giftie—ye must be born wi't. You cannae help it." "But," I says, "I'm feart. I'm feart tae tak it again. . . . When I ging t' my bed ony nicht, I'm aye feart t' sleep. For fear I see something again." She says, "Well, you hiv a sort o' second sight an' you see them." An' 'at's right enough.

In several of her recorded conversations Jeannie refers to other visions that foretold tragedy and to community events that she knew about in advance. She was, like most others with second sight, an unwilling medium and interpreter of signs. "It's a gift," she said ironically, "I jeest wish the giver wad tak it awa." When someone once asked, "You've got the gift, Jeannie? I believe the gift is yours," she replied, "I cry it nae gift. I cry it a rotten curse upon us that has it."

Unwelcome insights in her later life foreshadowed events that Jeannie came to look upon as inevitable. While Donald was hospitalized, she was alone with the two small children and had to provide for them, but she never lost hope that Donald would recover. She was comforted by having the children beside her. Left with little else, she had their company and affection during the economic gloom of the mid-1930s. Even a hand-to-mouth existence during this period called for all her resourcefulness, and she displayed the kind of iron will necessary to survive.

4. "The Flure o' Ma Family": Jeemsie

Jeannie had long felt uneasy about the way young Jeemsie was admired. By the time he was six, she sensed that he was almost too handsome and perfect a child to live. But he was a joy to her as she filled her pack with soft goods and sold them from house to house in the glens and villages around Tarland. She and Jeemsie had forged the same strong bond that Donald and Lizzie were developing at the same time.

When Jeannie was twenty-six and Jeemsie a lad of seven, they set out to spend the day selling in the country. In the afternoon, just above Tarland, they met the remarkable Mrs. Martin. Jeannie often told how she found out that Mrs. Martin also had certain powers, and how that particular day would be forever stamped on her memory:

> I was all dressed up because I sold soft goods. An' sellin' soft goods ye've got to be
> . . . nice putten on . . . We went up a glen, just a little glen, just a mile outa
> Tarlan' . . . An' I went with my big thing of soft goods to sell, an' my little boy
> was with me. An' I had been doin' well at the farms before I came to Mrs.
> Martin's house. . . . I was at one or two houses before I went tae her . . . an' this
> two little, kin' o' auld-fashioned thackit cottar houses wes thair on the roadside.
> An' when I went to the first door it wes a woman about forty, but she didnae tak
> anything. But I went to the next door an' this is the first time I'd saw Mrs.
> Martin. She wes a big, jet-black-haired, black-eyed Highland wumman. She cud
> belong tae Inverness or someplace near Inverness. At that time she wudda been a
> wumman about . . . between sixty and seventy.

Mrs. Martin took a long searching look at the twenty-six-year-old Jeannie and asked her straight out why such a bonnie young woman would sell such goods around the doors. Jeannie assured her that she was making an honest living, and Mrs. Martin bought a few small things. But the dark eyes unnerved Jeannie because of the way Mrs. Martin looked at her.

After a few minutes, Mrs. Martin asked Jeannie if she liked rabbit, because she was just at that moment cooking one. She gave Jeannie the rabbit to take to the camp, as well as some sugar, tea, and eggs, inviting them at the same time into her house for tea and something to eat. A bit later, she told Jeannie that if she went to the houses at the top of the hill nearby, she would sell her whole pack of goods. Jeannie thought this strange because the cottars up there were poor and usually did not buy anything from her. Mrs. Martin also assured her that she would get milk from the woman in the small farm across the way, a woman whom Jeannie knew would rather throw her milk to the pigs before she would sell it to travellers. As a final word, Mrs. Martin asked Jeannie if Jeemsie would stop on the way back so she could wave good-bye to him from her window.

> So I nivir said nothing, bit I'd a strange feelin'. I said, "That's funny that wummin . . . askin' ma bairn to stop at the windae . . ." "Bit och," I siz, "she's an elderly wummin. An' God help us!—she's maybe fond of bairns, an' she's been very good to me . . ." Jeemsie wes really a bonnie bairn. As bonnie a face as ivir onie a bodie lookit upon. . . . he wes kindly natured too. Ma laddie had a godly lookin' face too. . . . my son was the flure of ma family. That's the Gode's truth . . . An' very, very intelligent. He wes a very, very clivir boy at school. . . . An' now, I always thought he wes too clivir. Too good fir tae live long. Bit it nivir entert my mind til eftirwards.

There was a chill between her shoulders as she and Jeemsie climbed the hill.

As Mrs. Martin predicted, the woman at the farm treated Jeannie kindly, buying something from her and giving her two pints of milk in her pail and a half-dozen fresh eggs. At the top of the hill, Jeannie sold boys' blazers, shirts, and other goods and lightened her load, just as Mrs. Martin had said. On the way back, Mrs. Martin asked to say good-bye to Jeemsie, who had run off after a stray rabbit he spotted. Jeannie called the boy back:

> "The lady wants tae say good-bye tae ye, Jeemsie." I says, "Wave til her," I roart til him. So of course he stood still an' he turned round til her, an' she pit her hand up like that an' waved til him. Ye see! An' she spoke kindly words. An' he pit up his hand an' he waved til her. It wes my poor bairn bidding farewell til her forivir. That wes the last time she seed him. That's the God's truth. Bit I didnae know at the time. Bit I'd a queer feelin', I cudnae help it. An' it bit on me, a queer feelin.'

Coming home Jeannie told Donald and Isaac, who was living with them by this time, of her premonition, but they scoffed. So Jeannie let the matter drop.

The change in other people's attitudes in the months that followed struck Jeannie as strange:

"Ivrybody wes so kind, so lovin' and so good tae me," I said, "folk thit widnae gie a kind word." Ye know! An' I cudnae git ootowre the change. So it aye bade in the back of ma mind. Well, that winter passed an' my bairn died comin' the New Year followin'. He wes eight past by that time. An' he dieit on the Christmas week, an' he wes burriet the day before Hogmanay, an' he wes eight years and sivin months.

This was a loss she could not outlive—a severe loss to her as a mother, to the clan, and to the tradition of folksong.

A year after Jeemsie died, Jeannie was in Mrs. Martin's neighborhood again and went to her door. She found a woman who looked older but who complimented Jeannie on her appearance as she gave her a long look and asked her why her son was not with her.

"No, Mrs. Martin. You ken fine," I siz, "I haena my son. An' you ken my son will nivir come back this road wi' me again." "Well," she says, "lassie, I cud hae tellt you that, the last time when you were here. I kent your son wesnae long fir this world." An' I says, "Whit wey did you ken that?" She says, "Because yer bairn had too godly a look aff his face, an' also . . . his soul wes shinin'," she says, "in his eyes. . . . An' when I lookit at him, I kent," she says, " yer bonnie wee laddie wesnae lang fir this world. An' that's what wey . . . I wantit to bid him farewell."

Later, curious about this remarkable woman, Jeannie discovered that the folk round about were terrified of Mrs. Martin. She had scared a local youth who had tried to make a fool of her, causing him to be ill in bed for a month, and had told the local doctor attending her dying mother-in-law that she would eventually die from drowning. This did happen when the woman, struggling from bed to find her relatives outside the house, fell into a ditch filled with water.

Aftir that I've been til her door siviral times. But she startit to speak about . . . well, I took it to be like Spiritualism cairry-on an' things. But I turnt an' I said til her, "Tell ye the God's truth, Mrs. Martin," I says, "I haven't a very strong heart." An' I siz, "God forgive me! bit I dinnae want to see nothin' comin' back from the dead. My belief is, if thir daid," I says, "let them rest." An' I says, "I dinnae want mines to come back, God help iz! to this weary world. . . . Ye see, I've a weak heart, an' I don't think I could stand the shock. It would maybe kill me."[1]

Jeannie was as convinced of her own powers as she was that Mrs. Martin had foreseen Jeemsie's death. But she adamantly refused to capitalize on her gift or to explore spiritualism or the occult arts, for she disapproved of them. Though ready to acknowledge the validity of such phenomena, she had a strong moral sense, guided by Maria's convictions and precepts, that did not allow her to be drawn into such occult practices.

When Jeannie, Donald, and the two children returned to Aberdeen after the first encounter with Mrs. Martin, Donald was taken ill while working at the sawmill that autumn and had to be hospitalized for tuberculosis. He had been there three months when young Jeemsie, now eight years old, fell ill, and Jeannie faced a major crisis. Jeemsie had contracted influenza just at the time Donald was taken to hospital, but he seemed to Jeannie to be on the verge of recovery because she was feeding him well and his weight was stable.

What appeared to be influenza, however, was diagnosed in December as meningitis, and the boy lay desperately ill during the Christmas holidays:

> The doctor said he didnae even hae a hussle at his chest. Bit it jest workt quick—went up the back, ye see, up the spine an' intae the heid. An' I'm sure when he wes lyin' dyin' he hadnae lost very little wecht. . . . He wes jeest a wee picture when he wes lyin' dyin'. Ye wadnae think nothin' wes wrang wi' him. Ye wad jist think he wes lyin' sleepin' there in the hospital. He wes eleven days in when he died.

The recollections crowded into Jeannie's head when she thought back, in 1962, on the birth and brief span of years of her son's life. He had been born

> on the fifth of June . . . on a mornin' o strong sun. . . . I jist had to suffer all the pains o' childhood—no chloroform, nae nothin'. Not one thing tae ease yer pain. The only thing 'at they gied to me wes they tieit a big leather belt affa the doctor's middle on to the bed—it wes iron beds at that time—it was aul'-fashiont maternity ye dependit upon in the time of the Depression. I lost ma memory and the next mornin' I didnae ken that I had sich a thing as a son. At the hospital they said, "You had a baby when you came in here. You had a son. An' he's not too little, not too little." So they took him ootowre an' pit him to the breast. An' I lookit doon an' saw this wee bairn—wesnae fat or nothin'—wes poorly-lookin', see. I lookit doon upon the poorly wee bairn.

Her protective instincts were called up, weak and depleted though she was, for the boy was premature and poorly equipped for survival.

When Donald was told of Jeemsie's death at age eight, he asked the doctors at his hospital to grant him leave for one day so that he could be with Jeannie and attend his son's funeral. At first they agreed, but just when he had put on his suit, they changed their minds. Donald, by nature docile and still quite sick, refused to be thwarted. According to Jeannie, having been given sixpence by a man in the ward for his bus fare, he "throwed the sister doon upon the bed" when she tried to stop him and ran out the back door "an' over the big dyke [stone wall]."

Donald found Jeannie at her mother's house in Pittodrie, beside the beach, and as he entered the mourners were shocked to see a walking ghost come through the door:

> He jeest had his slippers on an' his suit. An' it wes driftin' high win' an' snow. Beneath the suit was only a suit of pyjamas. He jeest cam' in through the door as they wes takin' ma son's coffin in through the door at the same time. I remember that. An' ma boy wes buriet the day before Hogmanay. He dieit in the Christmas week—wes eight years and sivin month. He wes big fir his age an' ivir sae bonnie—til the very last he wes ivir sae bonnie.

Donald stayed with Jeannie for a few days and then returned to hospital.

When Jeannie became fully aware of their loss, her grief was so great that she again went into shock. Her nervous system could not stand the nightmares of the past three months. She was in such a daze that

> fir ages eftir that I had to be led in an' oot the buses an' aathing . . . it struck me here—that's yer nerve center—aye. Fir lang, lang over a year I'd be the same as thir wir a ton in the back o' the neck. It cam' on whan I got that shock, whan I gaed in an' seen ma bairn blind . . . lyin' blind wi' meningitis.

Jeemsie's death brought two further crises: Donald's diminished chances of recovery, and Jeannie's sudden disregard for, and hostile attitude toward, their daughter Lizzie. "I'd nae time for ma lassie eftir that—isn't it funny? An' she wes the youngest. . . . Whit a queer, strange feelin' cam' owre me. . . . Lizzie wes jist sivin past an' I cudnae be bothered wi' her. Isn't that funny? No time fir her."[2] By this time, the forces of tragedy had taken their toll on all four members of the Higgins family. Illness, death, emotional strain, and the economic insecurity of the Depression made 1936 a year that those who survived it could hardly forget. The relationships in the family changed in ways that were to influence the musical expression of Jeannie and especially Lizzie.

In talking about her early childhood before Jeemsie's death, Lizzie Higgins Youlden told Stephanie Smith that when she was four and Jeemsie five, he was found to take easily to ballad singing, while she was more attracted to her father's piping. When Donald inspected their hands, it was she, not her brother, who had the "crookit crannies" that traveller tradition associated with great pipers:

> Goin' back hundreds an' hundreds of years . . . the clans looked at their newborn baby boys to see if they had the mark of great pipers. My father had the two mis-

shaped crookit crannies, an' the mis-shapen second fingers as well . . . It's a rare gift o' God, you can put it like 'is.[3]

This trait, the misshapen fingers, symbolized the alignment of the two children with the respective parents: Jeemsie excelled in ballad singing, Lizzie at adapting pipe decoration to her vocal style. Much as she loved piping, she did not consider it a woman's art and declined instruction. Donald, on the other hand, longed for his son to show an interest in the pipes and bought him a child's set when he was six.

Lizzie remembered the *ceilidhs* that were held in their home. At an early age, Jeemsie would sing a ballad learned from his mother, but she herself was hopelessly shy as a child, and even as a young woman she refused to sing except in private.[4] As a child she had to be coaxed to sing in company. Until she was seven, she was aware of competing with her brother, and after his death she faced the discouraging business of singing in competition with her mother. But over the years, having been constantly exposed to her family's songs and the singing of other travellers, Lizzie worked at and perfected a sizable repertoire of traditional songs and a personal singing style quite distinct from her mother's.

Lizzie's style is colored largely by bagpipe melodies and bagpipe decoration. Jeannie's fondness for the ballads her mother Maria taught her stood in contrast to Lizzie's love of her father's pipes:

> Pipes is one of the most beautiful music a person can listen til. But they've got to love it, they've got to understand it . . . They're soulful in a lament . . . they bring your soul—they drag your soul out o' ye. If it's laments an' pibrochs an' things, if it's for dance tunes, it fires up your blood till you dance an' carry on. It can be a happy thing. . . . When I sing this pipin' stuff, I dinnae see that audience . . . Because I'm comforted from right inside ma soul. An' ma soul's bleedin'—I always see a mist. . . . I'm that involved, the pipin' an' singin' in my voice becomes as one. . . . I hear a voice. I think 'at's mine. But yet it's nae a part o' me. I seem to be awa' fae't. I've no control over it. Somehow there's a wee connection sayin' it's my voice, it's me, it's a beautiful thing that's happenin' to me. At's what my father used to experience when he played the pipes.[5]

But no such musical and emotional responses as those between Donald and Lizzie were to take place between Lizzie and her mother. The ghost of Jeemsie was to keep them apart for some years to come.

5. "Intil the Country": Renewal and Discovery

In 1939, at the beginning of World War II, Jeannie was thirty-one, Donald thirty-two, and Lizzie ten. With Donald's health precarious in the years before and Lizzie's schooling to consider, they made up their minds to stay in Aberdeen, try to find regular work in shops or hawking door to door, and thus forego the freedom of the open road. But bomb scares in the city changed their minds:

> For a few years before the war come on, we didnae go out. Donald didnae like campin' very well. But when the war did start, a haill street o' people wes killed an' it wes only a matter o' a few yards awa' fae us. The haill street wes cleaned oot. That wes Charles Street that wes right across frae oor auld hoose. Well, Donald said, "You're goin' to go to the country, because we cannae stay here." Nichts he wesnae gettin' rest. An' it wes funny, but I cudnae bide in the hoose when the sirens went. I had a smothery kind o' feelin' wi' a terrible fear. So Donald said, "I'm gang to the country an' not jeest set here an' be blewn to dust."[1]

Industries and shipyards were the targets of German planes. The open countryside was never more appealing to those who knew how to cope.

The decision to return to the country in wartime Britain still involved hazards and uncertainty. The family had to have means of support.

> I said, "Well, we cannae jeest rise an' run. Ye need some money. Or maybe we'll live frae day to day, wantin' for nothin'." But then we hadnae money tae gang intil the country. An' if ye're gaun tae the country, you ned a hame if it's cauld weather. But him no' bein' too strong either, Donald wes beginnin' to be—I suppose he wes gettin' workit up wi' nerves an' things. My boy wes deid by this time an' my girl Lizzie wes jeest a bairn in school. So I said, "We'll gang tae the country"—after the next bombs had killed forty people.

They had no money to buy a caravan, but they decided to leave the city where they felt they had turned soft. They were weary, too, of the hubbub in the city with the air raids. Donald left one night early to put up a tent for Jeannie and Lizzie.

> He didnae get far. He went oot by Coulter. That's nae far fae Aberdeen. It's a good few miles but nae far. Within another day or two we went into Banchory an' stopped near the mouth o' a big forest and built a hut oot o' wood an' covert the roof with a tarpaulin cover, like fat you see at the stations. You cud buy them at that time. Then we got a canvas to cover the floor an' carpets. It was jeest quite comfortable. Of course, you couldna have no blazin' fires on the outside. Aebody had a fire on the inside, so you cud sit comfortable on the inside, hear stories, an' a sang, an' a bit music. An' yet when we were inside, ye were covert up because the trees sheltert ye.

Jeannie's people had always known what to do when the weather was cold, and their resourcefulness protected them.

> An' now we werena afeard of the bombs. We heard them, mind you. We cud stand there an' look doon an' see Aberdeen gettin' bombed onie nicht, ivry nicht. So we lived there during the winter in the hut an' when the summer come on, by this time we bought a horse an' harness an' a float. An' then we went awa' through the country in the float. By then the fine weather wes in an' we workit at government work—pulling flax. . . . An' then we saved up the money—I didnae work all the time at the flax, I workit on my ownio—an' what money that we saved we bought this wagon.

This was an adventure for young Lizzie and a return to the years of their youth for Jeannie and Donald.

Life in the fine new wagon gave Jeannie a renewed pride in her domestic life. Her description of the caravan reveals her love of bright decoration and color.

> Well, you slept in your caravan. It was jeest like a house. We were the last caravan that wes up an' doon the Deeside an' it wes made at the Tollcross of Glesca an' there werena a bonnier thing in the place fat it wes. Beautiful thing it wes. Big, four-wheeled, owre top pure green. It wes fat we called a bow-toppit wagon— nae a square wagon—it wes bow-toppit. Then you had a bed made intil it, a full-size bed. An' below you opened up doors and there wes another bed—that wes for the family—you had a full-size bed in the top—a little wee windae at the back where there were bonnie wee curtains on top. You put the same curtain material through over the top of the front o' your bed—beautiful done—an' wer bunks were alang the side o' the wagon—at your feet—an' wers were eggshell

beautiful—bonnie, bonnie glossy paint—pure eggshell-blue painted. It was all eggshell blue in the inside. Then we had a fire. We had a beautiful big overmantel in the wagon an' you had a beautiful fireplace, an' then fittin' in the fireplace was a Queen Anne stove.

Jeannie elaborated on the beauties and conveniences of her caravan, and especially on the colors and qualities of the workmanship:

The wagon wes beautifully painted—yeller, green, an' red—it wes all beautiful designs an' horses' heids an' things, an' the big hubs on the wheels was solid brass. Well, a man that took pride in his wagon—the hubs o' the wheels—you would see yer face in it. The two big lamps at the front—great big beautiful lamps—would be worth a fortune today. Solid brass. Ivry wee bit o' fancy thing on aboot the wagon wes aa brass.

She also insisted on standards in keeping the caravan neat and clean, standards opposed to the stereotype Flatties hold of the travellers:

You keep your place clean to suit yersel'—if ye dunnae keep it clean, then ye're lazy, there must be something wrang wi' ye. . . . I've seed the bairns [Lizzie and nephews] in the bed an' me in the wagon settin' an' me ccokin' the men's supper. An' then when we come to this place, the supper wes ready. But ye cannae dae that wi' a camp. You've got to pull an' mak yer supper an' carry on to the place that we want to live in. Aye, I could cook as I wes movin' in this wagon.

Her pride was boundless when she remembered the bright caravan and all its amenities.

Traveling to escape bombing in the city also took them away from urban amusements and commercialized entertainment. Lizzie recalled that as a child she often went to the "fillums" with her parents. In the city, too, they experienced such novelties as the phonograph and the wireless radio. Lizzie especially missed entertainments of this sort during the war when her family took to the road, for whatever "entertainment" existed was provided by travellers themselves and their relatives.

A few weeks after Jeannie and Donald built their wooden hut, Isaac Higgins joined them in the country, and the two brothers played their pipes again in the evenings. Isaac, who had been in the household since he was sixteen, had a float of his own.

Music and singin' wes the only thing we had to pass the time by. Men maybe playin' the pipes—maybe aboot poachin' for rabbits because rabbits wes good at that time—but when they give them that disease [myxomatosis, to control excess proliferation] we wadnae look at them again. . . . But for years an' years in the war the beasts wes guid an' ivrything wes rationed—even to a bit o' biscuit, a can

Fig. 3. A traveller's caravan. From a calendar, c. 1967. Origin unknown.

o' beans wes rationed, a can o peas, your sugar . . . the very biscuits, the very sweeties. . . . Things to sell were scarce enough. If you could have got the stuff, we'd be well off today. But what you did get, you could sell it. The people in the country wes glad to get a body comin' to their door.

They had the caravan about three or four years before they sold it, the only one on the road after the war because wagons were going out of fashion.

It is significant that traveller families began to be reunited during the war period. In a real sense it was this return to the old ways that sparked the modern Folksong Revival in Scotland, for old songs and tales were recalled in a period of social upheaval, and singing under the stars was resumed while the cities of Britain were being leveled by Nazi bombs.

Yes, mony's the time you might see seven or eight families at the camp. You had got to have somethin' to pass the time by. You had no pictures, no dance hall—not that I wes ivir in a dance hall in my life. Amongst my people there wes fiddlers, accordion players, squeeze box players, mouth organ players, pipe play-ers, an' sometimes a lot of very good singers. It's funny that I nivir learned no songs after people later. The younger people at that time wes singin' mostly up-to-date songs, cowboy songs or somethin' like that. Unless it wes some auld body. I've sung mony a time around a campfire. That wes when I was jeest at my very level best. Wi' a big fire and a cup o' tea and somethin' good goin', we could sing aa the better.

By 1945, when the war ended, Jeannie was thirty-seven. She was recognized already among her own folk travelling up the Dee and down the Don as the finest of the women singers in their circle. With her rich voice and heroic delivery, she knew many of the "auld sangs" of her mother Maria, her aunt Margaret Stewart, or the travellers who traversed the roads between Aberdeenshire and Perthshire in summer.

She and Donald sold the fine bow-topped wagon that had been their home during the war years and went back to Aberdeen to live in a Gallowgate tenement. Donald worked when his health allowed. Jeannie helped Maria in her little store until Maria fell ill and died in 1952. For a time, Jeannie undertook day work or looked after her two nephews, Wee Froggie and Colin, in her home at 21 Causewayend. She, Donald, and Lizzie shared the ground floor flat, with its single cold-water tap, with Isaac. They would go to the Castlegate market to pass the time and visit with travellers who came to sell their wares on market days. Jim Higgins, father of Donald and Isaac, kept a stall there. They would also invite relatives for tea or the odd dram and some singing and piping.

In 1952, the American folklorist Alan Lomax arrived in Britain to record and edit an anthology of British folksong. Contacting Peter Kennedy, A. L. Lloyd, Ewan MacColl, Hamish Henderson, and others, he came at a time when the English Folk Dance and Song Society was starting to foster regional interest from its headquarters at Cecil Sharp House in London. In Scotland, the University of Edinburgh, stimulated by a similar postwar renewal effort, opened its School of Scottish Studies at 27 George Square; from 1951, it sent collectors into both the Highlands and Lowlands in search of traditional material of all kinds. The development of the magnetic tape recorder, patented in the United States and Germany in the late 1920s, was a major benefit to these collectors and to the establishment of permanent archives for research.[2]

In the gray northern city of Aberdeen, where Gavin Greig and his collabora-tor the Reverend J. B. Duncan had assembled one of the great folksong collections of the pre–World War 1 period, Jeannie Robertson Higgins listened to the radio as she was preparing tea:

I heard Hamish Henderson an' Alan Lomax on the wireless speakin' aboot auld sangs. But I nivir seed 'em. We nivir seed folks like that. At the time we wes livin' at 21 Causewayend an' I wes puttin' oot the supper when I heard them discussin' the sangs. An' I says, "That man's speakin' aboot auld sangs." Jeest like that. I wes impressed at listenin' to them. So I said to Donald and Isaac, "If those men only kent to come to Cassieend, I cud give them a good few auld sangs." I still nivir forgot them.

Hamish Henderson made it his business, in the search for songs and singers, to be at the Castlegate market in Aberdeen. He knew travellers when he saw them, according to Jeannie, and passing through the stalls and chatting with the folk he met there, he began to quiz them about any singers. One of the men he talked to was Bobby Hutchinson, for whom Jeannie had often sung the "auld sangs."

"If you want a puckle o' auld sangs," he said to Hamish, "go up to Jeannie Robertson"—he nivir even said my married name—"at 21 Cassieend. You cannae go wrong." So Hamish comes up an' the knock comes to the door an' there's this great big man in a beautiful Highland dress. O, he wes beautiful-dressed that day, real military-lookin' he wes. But I said, "I'm too tired to think aboot singin'. I'm that tired I'm ready to collapse. I cudnae sing for naebody today." But Hamish wes nae easy to put awa'. I wadnae put him awa', mind ye. God forgive me, I nivir put naebody awa' frae my door in my life—let him be rich or poor. So I says, "If you like you can come back at night when I'm no' so tired—say aboot maybe eight or nine o'clock, whichivir is suitable to you, but I cudnae sing in the meantime."

Undaunted, Henderson pressed Jeannie to allow him a few minutes of her time:

"Couldn't I just come in for three or four minutes?" he said, "O, look, I'm gang to let nae ither body come in an' tak my mind off my rest. I must get a rest." He lookit at me an' seed I wes jeest the picture o' health an' had mysel' aa dressed, for at that time I was awfu' particular. But mind you, I wes well enough at that time an' I lookid very young for my age. I wadnae gae ill, an' the very first thing in the mornin' I was aye decked up to the ninety-nines. They used to cry me the Lady o' the Lake, and that's the God's truth. I likit mysel' aye lookin' nice. It wes keepin' Wee Froggie and Colin, my sister-in-law's bairns, that day that had been greetin' and gettin' on my nerves that had really made me ready to fa' doon to my bed. But Hamish got the boy—who was jeest past five at the time—to sing til him. A bonnie wee laddie. My brother's bairn he wes—you see Donald's sister married my brother. And after the bairn had sung siviral of Auntie Jeannie's sangs, Hamish stayed on to tea an' I sung for him steady till two o'clock in the morning. I nivir got my rest—nae rest that day, you see. An' that's the God's own truth if I nivir rise from this chair.

Hamish Henderson's ability to engage the interest and attention of singers is explicit in Jeannie's account, and it is through his warmth and enthusiasm that most of the fine singers in the Northeast became part of the Folksong Revival of the 1950s and 1960s. A graduate of Cambridge University and a veteran of Field Marshal Montgomery's North Africa campaign in World War II, he took to living with travellers in their tents, keeping their hours, making them feel at ease in front of a tape-recorder and microphone.[3] He arranged *ceilidhs* in Jeannie's little tenement house in the Gallowgate, standing the crowd to re-freshments as the recording went on. New singers would wander in, and Jeannie's house became a center for hearing the old songs that were threatened by commercialized pop music.

A number of traveller singers were included in the LP recording of British folksongs that Alan Lomax and Henderson brought out in 1954. That record, which contains Highland and Lowland material along with English, Welsh, and Ulster songs, reinforced to travellers not only the worth of their song heritage but also the validity of their singing style in comparison to other related styles throughout Britain.

Another significant development took place through radio. The Scottish Home Service of the BBC had hired George Bruce of Aberdeen as a program director and, at this time early in his career, Bruce planned and produced a series with the title "Scottish Life and Letters," the aims of which were far-reaching.

Bruce felt confident that the dissemination of traditional songs by means of radio was a valid end in itself. He scheduled frequent programs dealing with the traditional arts, with particular emphasis on music and song. It was this program that introduced Jeannie Robertson to a nationwide Scottish audience and brought her ballads to a younger generation of radio listeners. With this broader exposure, she began to be sought out by complete strangers: non-traveller singers, folklorists, those involved in some aspect of the Revival, and the merely curious. Her singing was gaining her admirers far beyond the Gallowgate.

Soon after Henderson had spread the word on the radio about the wealth of songs, tales, piping, diddling, wonder tales, memorats, humorous tales, and the like to be found among the travellers in Aberdeenshire and Perthshire, other collectors began to search out the travellers. Peter Kennedy, for one, compiled a series of tapes for the English Folk Dance and Song Society and for the BBC

Fig. 4. Jeannie Robertson and Hamish Henderson, c. 1954.
Courtesy of School of Scottish Studies.

Archives in London. A nephew of Maud Karpeles, the woman who had accompanied Cecil Sharp on his Appalachian collecting trips, Kennedy aired some of the most impressive recordings of Jeannie. During this period there was close collaboration between Henderson, in 1953 appointed a Research Fellow at the School of Scottish Studies, University of Edinburgh, and other fieldworkers in England and Ireland. The sociological studies of Farnham Rehfisch, for example, grew out of interest in the travellers during the 1950s.

Jeannie was forty-five at the time of her "discovery," and she continued to sing her songs as she had always sung them, though new audiences and unfamiliar arenas such as the concert stage and recording studio began to affect her style and delivery, especially of the "big ballads." But like all the older traditional singers in Scotland, she generally sang without instrumental accompaniment. She still felt uneasy trying to fit her free rhythms to that of a pipe chanter, squeezebox, or guitar. Her individualism, formerly submerged in a communal environment, emerged full-blown as she became the concentrated focus of attention from outside her traveller circle.

Like other singers such as Belle Stewart or Jane Turriff, Jeannie was capable of adapting her own words to an old tune or devising a tune for words she found in a book or in one of the broadsides published by the small press at Fintray.

Aye, I cud make a tune for some of those ballads or sing them to an auld-fashioned air. I could put ma ain air to them if I didnae like the air they named. I have sangs that I put the air til masel'. Aye, here's a poetry called "Cruel Fate" that Burns wrote to his Jean when he wes planning to go to the West Indies an' they wes to be parted for guid. I didnae have a tune to the words, so I made up my ain, like I have for siviral. I'll tell ye the God's truth. I got the words but there wes no air til it. It's in the Burns book without an air. By the God's truth the air's mine. I can make up airs, I can. It's only a small two verses an' I saw it in a Burns auld, auld song book—a big auld song book, lang, lang ago, when I wes jeest a lassiekie. But there wes no air attached til it. So therefore I put a hauntin' kind o' air til it mysel'. My mother sung a lot o' Burns's songs. You see, us people goin' oot, many's an' many's the auld, auld books o' Burns we've pickit up. At school we sung "The Banks o'Doon" to one air, but the air that I sing to it now wes from a man I heard singin' it an' I fancied it. I likit his air better.

And on several occasions Jeannie was known to sing what she avowed was a "traditional sang" and then slyly admit she had composed it while washing up.

The process of recreation and composition in traditional songs involves several kinds of aesthetic activity: recognition of a completeness, meaningfulness, or "fullness" (or lack of these), not just in a text or tune but also in a performance; the search for and construction of the component parts; the joining of words and air; the forging of a singing style appropriate to sharply different situations. Jeannie's observations on composition, re-composition, and adaptation suggest that, as a singer, she arrived at a working combination of the verbal and musical elements before she would sing, even in front of her traveller relatives. She could grasp the possibilities of her song tradition on each of its levels: text, tune, performance, context. From her words, one can see the tradition as a merging of a communal traveller tradition and a wider, popular Scottish tradition based on Burns' centrality as a folk poet and folk composer-recreator. Jeannie developed, if on another social level, a sensibility like that of Anna Brown in absorbing foreign linguistic elements. Yet she could also demonstrate a sturdy Northeast sense of independence when "realizing" specific songs in the face of different audiences.

6. *"The Pleasure of Scotland": Fame*

After the broadcasts of Henderson's first tapes by the BBC Scottish Home Service, the Aberdeen and Edinburgh newspapers sent reporters to interview Jeannie, and she began to see her name frequently in print. In the cramped flat at Causewayend, sitting regally in an overstuffed armchair with a cage of her chirping budgerigars behind her, she would enthrall visitors with stories of her premonitions of tragedy or ribald anecdotes about Robert Burns as seducer and wit. Her sure sense of the grand and the heroic, as well as the comic, was governed by a gravity, a dignity that put aside any hint of parody or self-mockery.

In a few months, she was asked to appear at folk clubs in Glasgow and to sing at festivals catering to young audiences eager to experience their heritage of traditional songs. Heavy on her feet by now and slow of gait, she would get herself ready for these appearances as best she could, considering her limited means and inexperience in handling "public" stage appearances. The jet black waves of her hair were as tight as they had been when she was younger, and she parted the curls across the front of her head, combing a "bonnie fringe of bangs" down her forehead. Her teeth, never comfortable, were a frequent source of irritation, and she often sang without the lower plate.

Students in Scotland's first folk club, stimulated by enthusiasts like Norman Buchan, Maurice Blythman, and Ewan MacColl, invited Jeannie to come to Glasgow in fall 1953 to sing at a *ceilidh* they were staging. The group passed songs among themselves, the mark of a good evening, everyone contributing her or his piece. Among the members were two young singers, Ray Fisher and Andy Hunter, who were pursuing further education in the city. Both had musical talent and had been struck by Jeannie's voice on the tapes played to them earlier by Hamish Henderson.

Ray Fisher retains a vivid recollection of her first meeting with Jeannie and its ultimate influence on her own career:

Norman Buchan was trying to show Jeannie and the other older singers what was happening in Glasgow at the time and he asked me to sing. Very sheepishly, I sang "Jeannie My Dear Will You Marry Me?" Jeannie Robertson came up to me afterwards, and she said to me, "O, that's one of my songies you're singing," she says, "and you're no takin' it oot richt," she says. . . . and I said, "Ooh." To "tak it oot" means to vary the emphasis and timing. Thus the implication was that I was not singing it right, and she proceeded to illustrate her proper fashion. And Jeannie sung the entire song after I'd sung it. . . . talk about upstaging! Nevertheless, as a result of what she said, "I think you'd better come to Aberdeen," I went and stayed with her for about six weeks. I learned a tremendous amount about Jeannie's songs, her singing, and Jeannie herself. (Glasser 1974)

With her readiness and accessibility, Jeannie dissolved the barriers between urban and rural, traditional and revival, because she was able to stimulate enthusiasm and understanding. She made urban singers like Ray and her brother Archie feel at home with a song repertoire that was not an authentically "traditional" one learned in the domestic circle of their own home. But this was for Ray the beginning of a collaboration and a lasting teacher-pupil relationship.

Jeannie's version of the way Ray sang at first and how she improved with instruction completes the picture:

She wesnae takin' it oot richt. She wesnae singin' the words richt an' she wesnae restin' whaur she should rest, I thocht. She wesnae pittin' the richt feelin' in 't. Bonnie singer and lovely voice, but singin' like an egg withoot salt. Thir wes nae taste til it. She had to ken the feelin'.[1]

During her time with Jeannie, Ray learned the song "Ainst Upon a Time," but Jeannie knew only three verses. Ray thereupon wrote another five verses of her own. The results of this "collaboration" appeared in the journal *Chapbook* (volume 3, no. 1) in 1966, with the following note: "Ray Fisher learned the original of this song from Jeannie Robertson—the traditional verses are 1, 5, and 7, which form Jeannie's version—and expanded it into its present form, 'to tell a more coherent story.'"

Jeannie's "lyric" version, with its emphasis on the devil-may-care attitude of the singer, became, in Ray's refacimento, a "ballad" with an explicit narrative. It is quite possible that Jeannie's variant may once have had such a narrative, though this is hard to prove. Some reasons for transformation from ballad to lyric have been identified by Coffin (1977), and, indeed, Jeannie herself recognized the possibilities of recomposition, though in her case it was mostly with the tune rather than the text.

Those who heard Ray Fisher sing under Jeannie's influence, then, would be able to mark her absorption of Jeannie's style, as much as of the particular song text and tune. "Yes," Ray would reply, "you mimic because you admire. Any student will take guidelines from the master." But today Ray Fisher has forged her own personal style and aesthetic:

> You adapt and find a bit of yourself instead of just a reproduction of the original. I cannot forget Jeannie's singing, but I sing the songs my way now. Jeannie was such a proficient artist that she communicated the material, the sensitivity, and the understanding she had. I would like to think I retain some of this in my singing. . . . but I am not a traditional singer: I am a singer of traditional songs. I interpret what traditional singers have done, the difference being that the traditional singers have their songs handed down within the family. (Glasser 1974)

Though Ray's idea of tradition may seem an idealized one, she studied the repertoire to which Jeannie exposed her, adapting it through her perception of herself and her own personality—a process she also had absorbed from Jeannie's example.

In 1953, Jeannie made her first visit to London, where she and a well-known Irish singer were guests of Alan Lomax. Lomax invited them to appear on a television show he was producing, and later they were to sing at the Bedford, a club that had become a successful night spot for folk musicians as the Revival took hold. Jeannie unfortunately did not take to the other singer:

> She wes a fine cratur an', to lots o' folk, she might hae been sensible enough. But tae me she wesna. She wanted tuppence o' the shillin'. . . . or maybe it wes my different wey, at that time. Course I wes very, very refined an' aafie quiet at that time. She was aafie *bold*, an' *present*, an' no shame nor nothing. *Not* one *ounce* o' shame. An' one funny thing: she gaed on an' on an' she widnae sit doun an' she widnae stop singin'. . . . na, na, she didnae want nobody t' sing but her. She'd not *one bit* o' shame. She'd nae sense o' shame like anither body. She wes like the toon's clock: she'd a face all round.

While the two singers were in Lomax's apartment, an incident occurred that caused Jeannie some embarrassment. Lomax had bought a bottle of special whisky as a prophylactic against his singers' catching a cold:

> But it wesnae a cauld that I took—it wes worse. But we got plenty o' this, ye see. But Alan says, "You take a glass of that." An' I took a wee glassie like this, but she, she glassed an' she glassed, an' she glassed an' I says, "I'll put the bottle awa' now." An' I'se tried tae tell her, ye see. She couldnae understand me speakin', y' know. No. "Please, for God's sake," I says. "You're only supposed to take one

glass o' whisky oot o' that. . . . He tellt me, " I says, 'that's a bottle o' *special* whisky 'at's ordered for the night." I says, "For his ceilidh the night, ye see." An', there'd be a lot of the BBC folk comin' down for a ceilidh. Well, Alan Lomax gied awa' for about twenty minutes an' when he came back the whole bottle wes shot. She had it *drunken* before he had the breakfast made. An' I tried an' tried, but na—it wes too much of a temptation til her. An' aye she said tae me, "Och, I can't help Alan Lomax. I'm wantin' a wee drap o' the cratur."[2]

Jeannie had her own view of her Irish companion's singing at the Bedford later:

She disnae sing like me, looking straight on, an' maybe haen a peek at the face. She sings looking up an' doon. She sings wi' her mooth roun' intil her ear. Min' you, the woman's a bonnie singer. She can sing an' play her banjo. Ye see, it's jeest she'd her own weys o' singin'.

Avoidable or not, the rivalry was obvious to Lomax and the promoters.

Jeannie's health problems altered the course of events just after the dress rehearsal for the show:

"I'm nae ill," I says. "There's nothin' wrong wi' me." See when the pain passed over I wes aa richt again. But for that second that pain struck me, it wouldha tooken a horse til its knees. I went tae ma room. I took a tablet. An' I says, "Och," I says, "I'll be aa richt. Whit could've happened." An' I thought it's maybe jist a *severe* rheumatic pain across ma kidneys. . . . ye see. The tablet pit me tae sleep richt enough . . . for aboot a good hoor an' a half. *Sound* sleep. An' I wakit up—I wes aboot climbin' the wa's. I thought I had a nightmare. . . . An' here I wes sufferin' the awfullest pain, an' O God Almighty. . . . O, terrible. . . . An' I walkit the floor from two o'clock in the morning until nine o'clock. An' I nivir went fur any ither people t' help me. . . . I wes sufferin' the agonies o' Hell, an' I couldnae dae nothin tae help masel'. So, the first one to enter wes the Irish woman. "God," she says, "I wes wonderin' what wey you werenae up this mornin'," she says, "early," ken. An' then she says, "O, what's wrang?" So I says, "Well," I says, 'there's something far wrong," I says.

Lomax sent immediately for a doctor and Jeannie was taken to hospital where her illness was diagnosed as peritonitis. She was well cared for, but this setback prevented her from appearing on British television for the first time. Jean Ritchie, the Kentucky singer who had earlier traveled to Aberdeen to swap songs with Jeannie, looked after her in the London hospital and with Lomax's help escorted her to the train when she was well enough to return home. Still weak and disoriented, she fell into her own bed and remained there for several weeks through a slow recovery.

Fig. 5. Jeannie Robertson on the steps of the Gallowgate flat,
1955. Photo by Herschel Gower.

During the Edinburgh International Festival in late August 1956, Jeannie
appeared at the Assembly Hall in a Scottish musical revue written and directed
by George Scott-Moncrieff and called "Pleasure of Scotland." Her ample figure
was draped in folds of plaid, and she seemed uncomfortable walking down a
flight of steps singing "The Battle of Harlaw." Later in the show, she sang
another ballad, "Son David." She charmed the audience with two of her songs,
and backstage she found flowers from the United States in her dressing room.
When "Pleasure of Scotland" closed at the end of the festival period, she was
guest of honor at a party given by Sir Compton and Lady MacKenzie. Every-
body wanted more songs, more of Jeannie. She sang "what auld songs they
askit" for the rest of a long evening at the MacKenzies' townhouse in fashion-
able Drummond Place.[3]

Such occasions brought out her wit and humor, and her rejoinders could be pointed and telling. At the opening night of "Pleasure of Scotland," the Lord Provost of Edinburgh, in keeping with official protocol, was seated with his wife in the front row. As Jeannie sang the lines from "Son David," she could not help noticing the disparity in the ages of husband and wife. The next evening she was approached by the provost at the Festival Club, a favorite rendezvous for both performers and audiences. He mimicked the song and condescendingly remarked, "Well, Jeannie Robertson, how's the blood on David's sword tonight?"

Jeannie's response to this was to come the next day, at a concert of folk music. When her time came, she stood directly in front of the provost with his young wife and sang all the stanzas of "An Auld Man Cam Coortin' Me," emphasizing the final line of its refrain, "Maids when you're young never wed a auld man." Recalling this, Jeannie remarked with perfect good humor, "Ye ken, I flang it richt in his face."[4] Her performance of the song, in which a woman scornfully relates courtship by and marriage to a dotard, transformed its rueful humor into a satirical tit-for-tat that was not lost on audience members.

In 1961, Jeannie was invited to sing at a folk festival in Chicago and tour some university campuses. But three weeks far away from home and family did not appeal to her, and she made a variety of excuses, some real, some perhaps imagined, to avoid commitment. She cited fear of a transatlantic flight or of seasickness if she went by ship. Donald had been ill for a year after several spells with his nerves and was not well enough for her to leave him. Because the halls in Edinburgh in which she had sung had been overheated and she had trouble getting her breath, she was afraid that the universal central heating in America would harm her health. All offers to cross the Atlantic received polite replies in Donald's hand but contained excuses that were clearly Jeannie's.

Later in 1961, Jeannie, now fifty-three, was invited to London by the singer and folksong scholar Ewan MacColl to take part in a program on Independent Television (this was while television in Britain was still only black and white). Among the participants were John Laurie, the actor, singer Isla Cameron, and MacColl himself. Jeannie's account of this occasion catches her mood and the self-image she had developed by this time, a self-image that came into question under the force of mass media manipulation:

We had wir breakfast in a very fine big posh place, the best of ivrything, an' then I met the two young ladies that does ye up. The director says, "I don't think you'll have tae do a lot tae Jeannie because her color's natural an' ivrything, ye see." He meant to say my color an' my face an' things wes natural an' things. But when it really came to be, it wes me that needed the *most* makeup.

First thing, aa the red in ma cheeks had to be done oot because they said it would come out dark, show a dark shadow in ma face. This natural dark shaddas in here. That had to be aa painted out wi' a sort o' creamy colored paint. An' it wes a young lady with a little easel, an' little brush, an' a whole dose o' different colors. . . . After that, the lady for ma hair. Well, she took about a half an hour to do ma hair up. Ma hair, she thought, wes a bitty too high in the front. She lowered it down, ye see, an' then, I got the shock o' ma life, as I'd no grey hairs in ma heid at that time. . . . An' tae *me*, looking in the mirror, I lookit, it lookit tae me like ma hair wes completely grey at the front. An' this, I resented this bit, ye see. . . . I says, "Ye've made ma heid grey. Whit ye daein' this for?" She says, "No, no. . . . you'll come out jet black . . . But we've got to do this to tone the color of your hair down a wee bittie, as it's jet black an' we've got to tone your hair down." An' then I turned round and I said, "God bless me," I said. "The man at television said I wes needin' little makeup. When it comes tae be," I says, "I'm the one 'at's needin' aa the makeup."

Well, when I lookit masel' i' the mirror, I said if I come out like this folk'll tak me for some Oriental body. I thought, I wes as like a Chiny or a Japany as ivir I seed. But funny, when I lookit into the monitor tube I wes a bitty amazed to see that I jist lookit ma natural sel'. Then when I lookit at masel' singing, I says, "O, God bless us aa, surely ma face is nae sae peetiful." . . . I'd aa sweated, ye know, and I lookit at aabodies' faces, ye see . . . meaning as much, "Is that me really singing? Do I sing in front o' folk like that?" I wes singing "My Son David" and here wes me singing but . . . ye didnae see ma hands or a'ing like 'at an' ma hand micht hae just been like 'at, but O, the *peetiful* face. . . . I felt embarrassed tae start again. . . . But he said, "Jeannie, nivir mind that, that's your gimmick. Just you carry on the way you were doing before. Dinnae alter."

Jeannie's horror at her transformation into, in her eyes, an unnatural figure was followed by a request that was to have an even more radical effect on her singing:

There wes three heid young men an' they wes all ranging aboot the same age an' the one 'at wes on television with us, he came in aboot an' he said, "Now Jeannie, ye'll have tae cut out three verses of 'My Son David.' Cut it down to six."

"Bless us . . . it's a bitty sudden," I says. "Jeest at the minute 'at we'll be on television," I says, "in nae time an' I've tae cut oot three verses," ye see. . . .

An' then, it wes funny, it wes maybe the way I lookit or whit I did, he put his hand on my shoudder, ye know, he says, "We're very sorry, Jeannie, but we've *got* tae do this. In fact," he says, "it's a *shame* to cut out the three verses. . . . of such a *lovely* song an' it must hurt you to do this . . . We've got to do it for time. Could you do it? . . . You would know the best places tae cut out a verse, here and there. . . . But ye'll still have a wee whilie . . . for to rehearse it over without the three verses."

Well, it wes funny. I cut out the three verses which I knew widnae be missed, an' then I sung it over, a matter o' twice. An' I had it—the six verses, ye know. So they were aafie well pleased. I mean it wes funny—jist wi' that understanding an' kindness that this three fellas showed. . . . It wes nae bother at aa. It was *absolutely* no bother. An' the heid chap wes tall, nice built, wi' aafie broon curly hair.[5]

So the real Jeannie, under commercial demands, gave in under the pressure of a handsome young producer and a timed format. Her self-image was altered by a television monitor.

Even though Jeannie happily, if naively, carried away pleasant memories of commercial television producers, the experience in London alerted her to the fact that the world outside Aberdeen was ruled by tight schedules, compromises, and uncertainties. She was persuaded to throw out three verses of a favorite song, and her image of herself in the monitor shocked her into questioning her confident self-regard. Even the comfortable flat in northwestern London where she stayed was foreign to her, disconcerting. Finding herself a total stranger, she refused to venture outside on her own.

Yet it was during this same visit that Jeannie was applauded by celebrities in the world of the London stage. She sang at the Mermaid Theatre on July 21 in a festival program of one week that featured a sizable assembly of actors, poets, and singers. During "Poetry at the Mermaid," she sang her big ballads, holding her own in such company as Dame Flora Robson, Dame Edith Evans, and Sir Ralph Richardson, who were reading poetry and scenes from plays.

Later, for several evenings at the Edinburgh Festival of 1961, she sang at The Howff, a crowded coffee bar and nightclub housed upstairs in a Royal Mile tenement just across from St. Giles' Cathedral. Among those who came to hear her after their own late-night shows ended were the French chanteuse Juliette Greco and Cleo Laine, the London-based jazz singer with a large following. But Jeannie, performing for this urban and vaguely Existentialist audience, remembered mainly the stifling heat and cigarette smoke that made her want to cough with each breath.

Jeannie was reluctant to sing far from home after the bout with peritonitis and the second uneasy trip to London. When she and Donald were invited to the Soviet Union, he was eager to accept, but Jeannie turned the offer down because the journey was too long and their sponsors wanted them to stay for up to a year. Jeannie also had a strong feeling that she was being compromised

Fig. 6. Jeannie Robertson, 1955, two years after being discovered
by Hamish Henderson. Photo by Herschel Gower.

and asked to "denounce" her religion ("throw yer religion awa") and become a
Communist:

> They didnae ask me outright to become one, but they wes—aye, a nod's as good
> as a wink til a blin' horse. I got that feelin'. . . . Ye see, none of our people wes
> nivir political people or nivir wes intae anything like that. "Well, I'm very sorry,"
> I says. "Bit ye see I'm maybe no' a very guid Catholic, bit I'm very guid within'
> masel'. I winnae throw mud on ma religion fir naebody."

However mistakenly Jeannie may have interpreted her sponsors' intentions,
they finally gave up trying to persuade her to visit Russia and the Soviet
Union.[6]

In March 1964, Jeannie and Donald were asked by the Honorable Gareth
Browne of the Guinness family to perform in Dublin. The journey to Ireland

seemed less forbidding to them than going to North America or Russia because, for one thing, many of their Lowland traveller kin had traveled to and from Ireland, and, for another, they had learned versions of Irish songs and Irish tunes over the years. The magnet that Ireland and Irish cultural modes held for travellers never has been adequately explained, but the informal, spirited, nonmaterialistic coloration of Irish rural life seems to have appealed to them, despite their rambunctious encounters with Irish travellers (see Barnes 1975, Porter 1985).

With some difficulty Jeannie and Donald made their way south to Edinburgh and then to Greenock on the west coast for the steamer crossing to Belfast. The overnight trip was rough, and they were afraid the boat would never reach port. After a sleepless journey and some misgivings, they were met by their Irish hosts and gradually made to feel at ease. Having endured a week of singing at Irish festivals and attending *ceilidhs* at houses in and around Dublin, they returned to Aberdeen weary and drained. Their hosts, as elsewhere, had been generous and hospitable, but there never seemed to be enough time for a proper rest between one folk club performance and the next ceilidh.

During this period of the early 1960s, several clubs had been set up and were flourishing in the larger Scottish cities (Munro 1984). By 1965, there were twenty-five scattered from Inverness to the Borders, from Aberdeen to Dumbarton. They were somewhat loosely organized under the Federation of Scottish Folk-Song Clubs, whose official publication, *Chapbook*, begun in 1964, was edited by Arthur Argo, great-grandson of Gavin Greig and organizer of the Aberdeen Club. Argo observed that "the increase in the number of folk-song clubs has been little short of phenomenal" and announced the roster of singers for the Aberdeen Festival of November 1965: Archie Fisher, Hamish Henderson, Norman Kennedy, Jimmie MacBeath, Pete Seeger, and others. He also pointed with pride to the fact that in Causewayend ("the street where Jeannie Robertson used to live") the Aberdeen Club had acquired a six-room house for workshops and library. The main meetings on Sundays still were to be held in the Royal Hotel in Bath Street.[7]

By this time, Jeannie, Donald, and Isaac had left 21 Causewayend and taken a prefab house at 22 Montgomery Road, where they had more room, a fridge, and a modest garden. All three performed at the Aberdeen Club on Sunday evenings and saw a lot of young Arthur Argo. By this time, a dozen years after Hamish Henderson's first visit to Causewayend, Jeannie would sing the songs that had made her famous, while Donald or Isaac alternated on the pipes or played the pennywhistle or mouth organ. Jeannie engaged these young audiences with narratives—wonder-tales about Silly Jack or anecdotes about Burns, whose tongue could puncture bourgeois complacency:

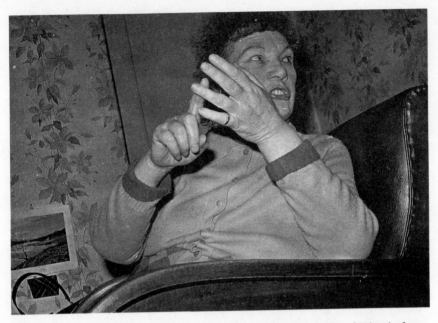

Fig. 7. Jeannie Robertson lays it on the line, c. 1961. Courtesy of School of
Scottish Studies.

You see, there wes a great lady called Lady Matilda. An' as far as I heard she wes a
poet too. But she wes very wealthy an' had a big castle-hoose an' plenty o' money
an' ivrything. So, the only thing I can't tell in my story is where she come from.
But she said she wad like to have Burns come to her hoose an' that she wad send
for him. She kenned a lot aboot him. She heerd aboot 'im being a great poet an'
she also heerd that Burns cud mak up poetry aboot ye by jeest lookin' at ye. . . .
Especially if ye did somethin'.

So she sent for Burns and Burns did come to this big fine castle-hoose an' this
Lady Matilda had it full o' gentry, you see, an' they wes all settin' in the big
beautiful hall, settin' round it, but the middle o' the floor wes empty. So when
Burns come in at this door she pit a drink intil his hand an' he wes nae dressed
to come in amongst the gentry because at this time he wes jeest a poor man, he
wes jeest a plooman, an' he wes dressed like a plooman when he did come intil
the hoose. He had his auld guttery-sharny boots on, no' very weel dressed. . . .
An' all in a sudden she gathered hersel' up in the front o' Robbie Burns an' she
gaed flyin' right frae one end o' the hall tae the other end, an' as she wes flyin'
she wes imitatin' the cock crowin' an' flyin'—both at the same time. She imi-
tated the cock cryin' oot "Cock-a-loo-ra-loo" an' she wes fleein' way up the hall.
Now Burns lookit after that a wee bitty surprised, you see, an' then she gaes up

tae the end o' the hall where there wes another door, she flew right up tae the door. Burns lookit at her for a minute or two, an' he still had his glass o' whusky an' he said:

> Matilda tae the door she flew,
> To imitate the cock she crew.
> She cried jeest like the little sinner:
> You wadda actually thocht the cock was in 'er.

So that wes Burns's wee bit o' poetry aboot Lady Matilda.[8]

No transcription can capture the gusto of Jeannie's oral style or the ripeness of her language. In her bawdy tales, in particular, there was neither salaciousness nor any suggestion of the furtive, off-color joke. Burns would have been proud to see himself as hero in this sexually frank anecdote, and there is no question that many travellers lionized him not only as poet but as lover and, as here, wit (Brown 1984).

One evening in 1966, when Jeannie was singing in the Crombie Hall, Aberdeen, a young actor who was concurrently making a name for himself with a one-man show, "An Evening with Robert Burns," sat in the audience. To some, John Cairney had become Burns incarnate, through his physical likeness to the poet and his ability to deliver the poems, dialogues culled from the letters, and anecdotes with a convincing Ayrshire inflection. On his night off, Cairney made his way to Crombie Hall to hear some of the "source singers" (as *Chapbook* called performers like Jeannie) who were keeping a tradition alive, albeit in a public hall in the bustling commercial city of Aberdeen.

In spite of the stark wooden seats, Cairney, first curious and then charmed, jotted down an account in verse of Jeannie Robertson and her story of Burns and Lady Matilda:

> For Jeannie Robertson at Crombie Hall
>
> This nicht cam I wi' mony mair
> Tae lippen Jeannie sing
> And sat there in my widden sate
> That never boastit spring.
> I little thocht
> That thus enthront
> I'd see the evenin' thro'
> But on the first note frae her lips
> I scarce believed it true
> That from such comely mien and stance

Such magic sound should pour
Tae lift me up
Frae my hard seat
Tae follow Jeannie's soar.
Soon all about me was forgot
In the echoes of her voice
And I was held
Imprisoned—
But a captive now, by choice.
She told about Matilda
What Burns said
When he met 'er
But for the tactic phrase he used
Well—perhaps—less said the better:
But one thought stays
An' a' nicht lang
I know't will surely linger
If Burns is the writer
Of Scotland's songs
Then Jeannie is surely her singer.

with respect
JOHN CAIRNEY[9]

Afterward he presented her the poem she had inspired, and the lines on the crumpled sheet of paper were one of her proudest keepsakes to show to visitors. She treasured her memories of "the well-faured actor laddie with bonnie manners and a fine-spoken voice."

7. "An' I Nivir Sung Better": London and the MBE

By 1960, Jeannie had drawn the attention of scholars from around the world, including Bertrand Bronson of the University of California, Berkeley, who began publishing some of her song variants in volume 3 of the masterwork, *The Traditional Tunes of the Child Ballads*. Over the twenty years of her life as a public singer, Jeannie was recognized by a host of major academic figures. Just as important, she inspired a generation of revivalist singers who were searching for an exemplar with solid traditional roots. Both camps were attracted to her, with good reason.

Jeannie maintained an artistic and personal authority always, and its first base was her house in Aberdeen's Gallowgate. Young singers followed her to the prefab at 22 Montgomery Road and to the council house at 90 Hilton Road, Woodside. These houses she shared with her husband Donald, her brother-in-law Isaac Higgins, and young singers such as Ray Fisher and Andy Hunter, who came to listen and learn. "God forgive me," Jeannie would repeat to callers, "I nivir put naebody awa' frae my door in my life—let him be rich or poor." Many contended that it was she who transformed the Revival by channeling its direction away from bookish sources toward the vital spring of oral tradition nurtured by the travellers. Though she was not the only traveller singer with influence, her singing of narrative songs impressed all who heard her few commercial recordings.

Herschel Gower's Recollections

I feel it is appropriate for me, as Jeannie's biographer, to speak in the first person and record here some recollections that will help to characterize the singer and her times. I began listening, in autumn 1954, to the tapes Hamish Henderson had made at the School of Scottish Studies. As I sat there day after day listening to that miraculous voice, each tape was better than the last. Although I had just come from Nashville and had lived all my life in Tennessee (behind me stood seven generations of Scottish forebears in North America), I never had heard anyone like Jeannie. No voice as rich as hers, no story as heroic in the telling as the ballads she sang. For six months I sat and listened and hoped that the real Jeannie might come down to the school or put in an appearance at a festival in Edinburgh. Neither occasion took place that year, but already I admired the singer and what she represented far beyond the level of a casual meeting at a folk club or an Edinburgh ceilidh.

It was not until the next year and the renewal of my Fulbright grant that I was able to go up to Aberdeen to visit Jeannie, Donald, and Isaac. At the time, they were living at 21 Causewayend in the Gallowgate. I was welcomed by the three of them for a long session of singing and playing that first night and was asked to come back the next for a ceilidh they would put on with kinfolk and traveller friends. Jeannie was in her prime as a singer, and I still remember her with a half-filled teacup, standing at the mantel, singing the ballads.

The house at 21 Causewayend was fast becoming a school for young singers, and students were experiencing Jeannie's generosity and open door. Accompanied by my friend Russell Hart from Harvard the next evening, I drank in the house, its atmosphere, and the ceilidh that they arranged for us. We entered directly from the street into a small front room, the large bed to the right filling half the room and Isaac's pipes sprawled on the cover. We moved straight ahead to the kitchen. The sink was in the far left corner of a room measuring about ten by twelve feet, one light bulb hanging from the ceiling center, the stove on the left wall. A window on the back wall was open at the top; I remember it well because at midnight Isaac was persuaded to get his pipes and play. I eyed the open window, wondering who in that crowded neighborhood would be able to sleep.

Jeannie stood at the back left corner, her right hand on the sink as she sang. Who else sang? Wee Willie, I think, and Tommy Campbell, and a traveller named Albert. Then there were long and—for Hart and me—very ardent debates about which tune fitted "Gypsy Laddie" best. Call these "aesthetic" though we may, they alternated with Jeannie's careful accounts of the people of the stories: the Gypsy Laddie was known, and Jeannie had spoken to people who *knew* the family long ago. Her songs were authenticated in the way that James Hogg authenticated his tales: he had a real if indirect link with the persons involved, and he knew the places. Specific place always has had authority in Scottish lore and folk traditions generally; they are more concerned with "truth" than with historical "facts." Songs often are the means of expressing this "truth" (Halpert 1964).

Fig. 8. Hamish Henderson, Jeannie Robertson, John MacInnes, and Jock Whyte, a basketmaker, c. 1958. Courtesy of School of Scottish Studies.

But Jeannie had a marvelous mobility of attitude, too. She could have had little sense of "historic" time, so that "long ago" could designate half a century and five centuries, without distinction. Yet she could also trick and tease collectors. I remember what a sly way she had of recalling how she handled "Aalun" Lomax, how superbly patronizing she could be in speaking of him and Hamish Henderson and others. Then there was her trick of singing us a song she thought we might not have heard, and afterwards admitting that she had composed it the day before while doing the washing-up. That's the Burns analogy: fiercely loyal to authentic tradition, and at the same time passing off her own songs as traditional, without realizing that they *were* "traditional" and "authentic" because it was she who made them. She did not know that she was giving instruction to scholars with doctorates from Harvard and Vanderbilt.

We also heard the Buchan fiddler with no teeth, yet how he could play! And the wee man, dressed in soiled working clothes, who was the soul of dignity and concerned hospitality. The evening was a true ceilidh: most people contributed their song, their playing, or their part to the debate. Yet there stood Jeannie, planted solidly in the corner or leaning on the mantel, the matriarch in control, sipping only one teacup of whisky throughout the evening.

Finally, Hart and I both came away with the realization that the ceilidh had been arranged for our visit, that these people perhaps had not all been together for several months. The city, and their urban lives, kept them apart. We were thus present for a rare and vital renourishing of tradition—not just of song, but of story and debate as well. As we walked back through the gray granite streets of Aberdeen at 1 A.M., we knew this was one of the unique nights in our "academic" experience, because never in our experience had poetry and song had such force as for that group we sat with and listened to that evening.

Although travellers sometimes used the language of cant and told jokes in a thick dialect that was hard for us to penetrate, they were always open, interested in who we were and why we had come. In a country where legal whisky is so heavily taxed that it is beyond the reach of many working people, our contributions in that line were reverently accepted. Nor were we armed with tape recorders to make away with their songs, however much we would have liked a record of that evening. They thought they could trust us, and they could; after all, we had come "a lang mile" to get there.

Over the years I kept going back for summer visits—not as a song collector, since Hamish was doing all that with the greatest skill and success. I went back to the houses where Jeannie, Donald, and Isaac lived in Montgomery Road and Hilton Road as a friend, admirer, and fellow traveller in the old ways. I met Lizzie, too, and we were bound by the same themes in art and song that Yeats wrote about. Between reunions, I kept in touch by letter and got news from returning Americans who were as captivated as I had been. I urged Jeannie to accept some of the invitations she was receiving every year to sing in North America. I promised her in one letter, I recall, that I personally would cool down the concert hall in Chicago, bring it down to Aberdeen norms, so that she would run no risk of being felled by central heating. Not even that gesture, however, could bring her from Scotland. Money failed, too; the pace so far from home was not hers.

We did put one formal program together—Jeannie singing, I introducing her songs—at Gladstone's Land, a former Royal Mile tenement, during the Edinburgh Festival in 1967. There were two morning appearances at 11 o'clock, too early for a night person like Jeannie, but once she got started, she sang with conviction before an international audience in the small crowded hall. I know she tried very hard, but I accepted the fact then that Jeannie never was meant to go commercial. Having accepted it, I came to appreciate her more and more every time I saw her. This was especially true when my wife Dona and I invited her to stay in our Edinburgh flat during her two appearances before the staid Saltire Society. During her time with us, we felt we had an international celebrity as our guest, for her young admirers trooped up the stairs to the second floor flat in Forrest Road, and she held court under our roof into the small hours. Often it was daylight that roused them and sent them packing.

During this stay, Jeannie talked a lot about second sight and her ability to foretell the future or to predict certain turns of events in the lives of people close to her. She told us how she experienced a vision of her cousin Bill Robertson's death in Australia, an event thousands of miles removed from Aberdeen. On another occasion, she encountered the ghost of a friend who had taken her own life. In yet another long story, she faced the figure of a very old woman in whose bed she was sleeping while staying with friends in Edinburgh. She discovered later that the bed had been bought by her hosts at an auction and, according to Jeannie, the old lady, who recently had been buried, was not yet ready to give up her comfortable resting place in that bed. Nor was she willing to permit Jeannie a peaceful night's sleep in it. So Jeannie sat locked in the bathroom the remainder of a sleepless night.

Jeannie reported apparitions, ghosts, practitioners of black magic, and certain portents of death. She gained a reputation for accuracy in telling fortunes with cards and predicting events in the personal lives of callers. Because of her brooding sense of tragedy and the signals she received that foretold doom, she never seemed able to cut herself off from the supernatural or to divest herself of the gift that was also a curse. With sardonic humor she informed us, "I'm neither *mad* or naethin' else. I'm as *wise* as oniebodie in Aberdeen."

Even in her sixtieth year, Jeannie's perceptions were still sharp. If anything, they seemed to us clearer than ever. Dona and I were delighted to put her up in the modest flat and have the chance to hear her stories. When she arrived, she thoughtfully presented us with a black satchel of gifts brought by train from Aberdeen: kippers, fresh butter, two haggises, eggs, and several blood sausages. "Maybe this flat'll be lucky for youse," she said noncommitally, "maybe it'll be lucky." Those were her words when we showed her to her room. Little did we know what she was feeling in the air.

Musically, Jeannie's visit to Edinburgh was a success; the Saltire Meeting Rooms were packed every morning for her singing. As we walked down the High Street at noon one day, a young woman recognized Jeannie and stopped us to ask for Jeannie's autograph on the back of a Festival program. Jeannie squinted at the paper, took the pen that the woman handed her, and with some labor drew out the letters of her name on the paper. She was silent in the face of praise, obviously pleased, never ruffled. On the other hand, she did not feel comfortable in our flat. She seemed to sleep poorly, kept her bedside lamp burning till daybreak, and stuck pins in the wallpaper beside her bed. "Maybe this flat'll be lucky for youse," she said again, and with the appearance of relief boarded the train for Aberdeen with her satchel after four days with us.

Curious about Jeannie's second sight, Dona and I began to ask among our colleagues at the School of Scottish Studies about other occupants of the flat. One friend was thoroughly familiar with it because his parents had lived in the flat just above us. "A madwoman had yours for a while," he reported, "and gave all kinds of trouble on the stairs till she had to be put away, poor old dear. But long before she was removed, my parents shifted to quarters that were more peaceful."

Six months after this piece of background information was revealed, we went up to Aberdeen to pay homage to Jeannie in a BBC broadcast called "Oor Jeannie," written and produced by Arthur Argo. One evening when Jeannie was out of the room, Dona asked Donald about Jeannie's second sight and if indeed she had been unhappy in our Edinburgh flat. Donald candidly told us what he knew. He said that Jeannie had returned to Aberdeen somewhat shaken after being with us in September and was quite uneasy about "the presence" she felt in the flat. She thought there was something evil about it but had wanted to spare us any suspicion. She had indeed been glad to get away, Donald said.

"Oh, yes," Dona replied. "We know more about it now. We were told a crazy woman occupied the flat before we did and gave her neighbors all kinds of trouble. Was it that madwoman that Jeannie sensed was still around?" "No," said Donald. "It was no . . . no . . . not exactly that." As if trying to decide if he in turn should spare the two of us, he paused and lit a cigarette, his hand shaking. "It's all right, Donald. You can tell us," I said. "You see, we had to give up that Forrest Road flat in January. So tell us—we'd like to know what Jeannie felt. We've moved to Moray Place."

Donald was seized with the hibbers and stuttered out the words painfully. "Jeannie cam . . . cam . . . back an' sai . . . sai . . . said tae us that she . . . she . . . she . . . thought it wes someone that might have committed suicide." About this time, Jeannie returned to the sitting room and verified what Donald said. She went on to explain that she did not hold her uneasy feelings against us while in the flat, and she and Donald both assured us that Jeannie felt it poor form to complain about things of this kind in light of the hospitality she had received. Then she reiterated her hope that the flat had proved lucky for us. We assured her that it had been, all told.

Fig. 9. Donald Higgins, c. 1958. Photo by
Hamish Henderson.

This story does not end there, however. Back in Edinburgh after the taping in Aberdeen of "Oor Jeannie" and while living in our new flat in Moray Place, we had the same colleagues to a farewell dinner party. The recent conversation with Jeannie and Donald was introduced towards the end of the evening. "It was not the crazy woman that Jeannie sensed in Forrest Road," Dona said. "She felt there had been a suicide. That's why she burned her light all night." The Edinburgh couple then looked rather guiltily at each other, and the husband confessed, "We tried to spare you the suicide." His wife added, "We spared you all those bloody details while you were still sleeping in the flat." All four of us laughed, though somewhat hollowly. The husband admitted,

Fig. 10. Jeannie Robertson and Dona Gower, 1968. Courtesy
of School of Scottish Studies.

"Jeannie was right. The madwoman's husband gassed himself with the burners
in your kitchen. We only wanted to spare you." "Well, thanks, of course,"
Dona said. "But I'm glad to be able to report to Jeannie that she was right from
beginning to end."

We were in Moray Place in spring 1968 when Jeannie received a letter from
London saying that her name had been placed in nomination for MBE (Member of the British Empire). She was asked to reply if she would accept the
award, and further to keep the contents of the letter confidential until the press
announcements on Sunday, June 9. She was to be named in the Queen's
Birthday Honours List as a Member of the British Empire in her sixtieth year.

In less than a week, the news of her honor had spread through traveller communities on the open road from one end of Scotland to the other. In Jeannie their art of song finally was being recognized. Hamish Henderson invited us to go up to Aberdeen to help with "Oor Jeannie," the salute devised by Arthur Argo to be taped in advance and broadcast on Monday, June 10, after the formal announcement of the Queen's Birthday Honours.

We were delighted to go, particularly after Donald's letter to us about Jeannie's recognition:

> Jeannie is not keeping too well. She has bad days and not so bad days. Everybody is overjoyed about Jeannie's MBE, but don't know when the Queen has her birthday. We will have to wait till they send her another letter when to come to London. Jeannie is taking it very calmly. She is a canny Scot, as you know. Some said it was like a fairy tale come true.[1]

Jeannie was still calm when we assembled at the BBC studio and put together testimonials of praise by Hamish Henderson, Ray Fisher, Arthur Argo, and others. Pete Seeger sent a glowing tribute by tape from New York.[2]

The moving force behind the MBE was Norman Buchan, MP, who in 1953 had invited Jeannie to Glasgow to sing for his high school pupils. He kept promoting her records as representative of the singing tradition in the Northeast of Scotland, whence his forebears had come. As a teacher in the poorer schools of Glasgow, he had wanted to find some way for his students to bridge the gap between folk traditions and the distractions of modern urban life. Jeannie and the older songs of Scotland filled this gap, because they were direct and universal in their appeal.

Buchan knew he had the solution when he first heard Jeannie at the Edinburgh People's Ceilidh as far back as 1953:

> She had a big voice and extraordinary repertoire. She was very much a woman of presence and conscious of herself as a performer. She was in the grand tradition—not only as a singer but an individualist and a "makar" at the same time. She was the tradition and the individual talent. She had a natural dignity and held her audience by the "bigness" of her singing. She was always inside the song and moving it out to her listeners.[3]

With the keen attention of Buchan and his wife Janey, Jeannie sang in the Glasgow schools and sparked interest in a tradition that had been eroding over the postwar years with the boom in commercialized entertainment. At Glasgow University, Jeannie had sung to a joint meeting of honors students in English literature and in music. Professor Robin Orr, composer and head of the Music Department, said that he had not been aware that Jeannie's type of

Fig. 11. Hamish Henderson, Jeannie Robertson, and Herschel Gower taping "Oor Jeannie," June 1968. Courtesy of School of Scottish Studies.

singer still existed in Scotland. When he received her first recordings, he had said, in effect, "We realize that we modern musicians can do things differently, more complexly, but we can't do anything better than this." Orr was all the more impressed when he heard her sing to his university classes.[4]

Norman Buchan began writing a column on folksong for the *Edinburgh Evening News* and was one of the first to discuss Jeannie's songs in print, setting out the words and music to what he felt were choice examples of her repertoire. Then, in 1962, he published several of her songs in *101 Scottish Songs*, a pocket-sized volume intended for a popular rather than a scholarly audience. His aim was to recapture the tradition, or at least an important part of it, and give it back to the people.

What else could Buchan do for Jeannie? In 1967, he was a minister in the Scottish Office during the Labour Government, looking after home affairs, and in this position he received letters from time to time proposing certain individuals as nominees for honors by the Queen. "I made no nominations at the time because I don't really like the Honours system very much. But in Jeannie's case I thought it would be appropriate. It would mean a lot to her personally and would be helpful to the travellers in every possible way. So I spoke to the permanent secretary—the head of the Civil Service in Scotland—and he put the nomination forward."[5]

Buchan was greatly pleased when it was approved and sent his congratula-

Fig. 12. At the taping of "Oor Jeannie," a BBC program
honoring Jeannie's receipt of the Member of the British Empire
(MBE) award by the Queen. June 1968. Courtesy of School
of Scottish Studies.

Fig. 13. Ray Fisher, Jeannie Robertson, and Herschel Gower, 1968. Courtesy of School of Scottish Studies.

tions to Jeannie on the Sunday the Official Honours List was published. For the first time in British history, a member of the travelling clans was to be decorated by a reigning monarch. Knowing Jeannie, we all felt an encouraging turn of events, as official recognition was directed not only to Jeannie as an artist and an individual but also to the history and circumstances of her people. It was also intriguing to speculate on how Jeannie and the Queen would address each other when they met at Buckingham Palace on the following December 3.

Norman Buchan helped with the December arrangements after the date was officially set. He arranged for a party afterward at the House of Commons and asked Jeannie to tell the guests about her conversation with the Queen.

> I said to her, "Jeannie, what did the Queen say to you?" Jeannie said, "The Queen said: 'Fat did you get it for, Jeannie?' An' I said, 'For ma services to Scottish folksong, Your Majesty.'"[6]

Later Donald, who had accompanied Jeannie to London, wrote to us with an account of the ceremony.[7]

Jeannie was looking her best, wearing a Robertson tartan dress made especially for her in Aberdeen. Their prosperous friends Bella and Bobby Hutchinson offered to drive Donald and Jeannie to London, and they left Aberdeen by car three days early, since the journey took eight and a half hours and it was important that Jeannie rest before the investiture itself. After Sunday and Monday to themselves in London, they all went to Buckingham Palace at 10:30 A.M. to see 150 others waiting like them for their honors. To Donald, the inside of the palace was "like a fairy tale or a scene from one of Jeannie's big ballads." When Jeannie's turn came, the organ began to play the tune "Rose in a Country Garden." The Queen shook her hand, gave a broad smile when she heard Jeannie's answer to her question, and pinned the medal on her Robertson tartan dress.

Afterwards, Jeannie and Donald went to the House of Commons for the party arranged by Norman Buchan:

> I invited some interested people—Iona and Peter Opie, for example, who wrote *Language of School Children*.[8] It was a small gathering and we laid on some drinks. But in the House of Commons you can't have songs, you can't have music. They won't even allow a Burns night there. So we couldn't have Jeannie singing. [Might Scottish songs have prompted a rebellion?] I made a little speech about Jeannie and she stood up and said she wouldn't answer but thanked me very much and sat down. But having sat down, she started to talk non-stop. She told lots of instances when she was singing at various places under conditions that were far from ideal. After telling each story, she ended up saying, "An' I nivir sung better." On one occasion she'd broken her teeth—at least developed a crack. So somebody rushed them off to the dentist for a bit of glue and temporary repair and got them back to her just before she was to go on stage. Again she reported, "An' I nivir sung better."[9]

If Jeannie was not allowed to perform in the House of Commons, she made up for it by singing at the other two parties to which they were invited and putting in an appearance on the Dave Allen Show on December 8.

Summing up Jeannie's career and her qualities as an individual, Norman Buchan later commented:

> I think she was monumental in two senses. First, in what she brought to folksong—monumental in her sources and the number of songs. The matter of abundance. Second, she was a big singer in voice, style, feeling. She carried weight when she sang. Her lyrical songs were great in their own way. Everyone seemed to agree that when Jeannie sang we all knew it was important. This was something that mattered. So this was how she got the Revival under way. . . . The quality of being a *singer of truth* was never dissipated in Jeannie by being a "performer." She had a tragic sense that reached greater depth than we usually plumb today. Tragedy is vitiated in the modern world by appalling commercial journalism. Many singers who've gone commercial have a lot of drive and flexibility but phony ways. They sing songs for *show* and not for *truth*. There was nothing phony about Jeannie. She believed in art, not trappings.[10]

Fig. 14. Arthur Argo, the great-grandson of Gavin Greig; Donald Higgins, piper and husband of Jeannie; Jeannie Robertson Higgins; Herschel Gower; Ray Fisher, one of Jeannie's best singing students; and Isaac Higgins, piper and brother-in-law of Jeannie. This photo was taken in June 1968 in Woodside, Aberdeen, after the taping of the BBC's "Oor Jeannie." Photo owned by Herschel Gower.

At the same time, we know by count that Jeannie's repertoire was not unique in its number of songs and their sources. Indeed, other less celebrated singers had more songs and sources that were just as authentic. Rather, it was Jeannie's artful manipulation of repertoire that gave the impression of range and virtuosity, even to her most critical observers. With creative fluency, she breathed on ancient words and music and created art.

Bobby Hutchinson, who with his wife had driven Jeannie and Donald to London, was quoted as saying that "Jeannie's MBE is the greatest event in traveller history since the mustering of the clans at the 1745 Uprising under Prince Charles Edward Stuart." It was Bobby, once a traveller himself, who had directed Hamish Henderson from the Castlegate Market to Jeannie's house fifteen years before. Like many others, he saw cause for celebration among the travelling clans as he and Bella drove Jeannie and Donald up the M1 motorway away from Buckingham Palace and back to the grey council house in the granite city of Aberdeen.

8. "A Fine Air and a Good Story": Aesthetics

Because Jeannie's taped autobiography is rich in personal and social detail, we can find embedded in it some "native" evaluation of songs and singing. We know more about the circumstances of her life than about those of her famous predecessors, Mrs. Brown of Falkland, Motherwell's Agnes Lyle of Kilbarchan, Scott's Mrs. Hogg, and Gavin Greig's Bell Robertson, all women with notable song repertoires and strong views about the oral culture and the singing tradition to which they belonged. We learn a great deal from Jeannie's statements about her learning and acquisition of songs, what particular songs meant to her, and how songs and singing were valued by her community; and we deduce her notions of the aesthetic relationship of words and music. This is significantly more than we know about the eighteenth- and nineteenth-century informants.

Except for the testy replies she gave to Sir Walter Scott about printing ballads, Mrs. Hogg is almost as anonymous as Sir Philip Sidney's famous blind crowder. Her son James Hogg left only the briefest memoir of his mother, and it answers none of the questions that interest scholars today.[1] David Buchan's study of Anna Brown's repertoire and his studies of Bell Robertson of New Pitsligo and James Nichol of Strichen (all, 1972) have brought a new awareness of the Northeast singer's art and its centrality in a historical context. Mrs. Brown was a literate and highly conscious artist, blessed with a good memory, according to her father. She reveled in the emotions she associated with songs she had learned in childhood from her aunt, mother, and a maidservant in her mother's family, the Forbeses of Disblair in Aberdeenshire.

Alexander Keith, Greig's editor, in an appendix to *Last Leaves of Traditional Ballads and Ballad Airs,* noted that Bell Robertson was the most voluminous transmitter of ballads in the history of ballad collecting; her contributions to Greig, both ballads and folksongs, numbered 383 items (1925: 289). What

Bell Robertson had to say about these items might have filled many revealing pages, for she, like Anna Brown, was literate and articulate. Although she was not a singer and only recited the ballad texts, Bell was obviously aware of the value of her mother's and grandmother's songs. She wrote to Greig in 1908, enclosing what she called "fragments and other odds and ends of minstrelsy":

> I have given you a lot I never would have thought of had the sole objective been to select songs for a book, but in Scotland the study of our national life through them can only be attained by careful consideration of every bit, for even a straw will show how the wind blows, as the saying goes. I am interested in the snatches. I think they are not bits of song but just the overflow of some singer whose heart was full of some feelings that must have outlet, just as the birds sing.[2]

Adding his own terse postscript on these "wise words," Greig printed "snatches" of this kind in his newspaper column for the *Buchan Observer*. But then Bell Robertson as interpreter passes more or less into anonymity. Greig took her songs, printed his note of thanks in the *Observer*, and reserved the right of exposition and criticism for himself.

Agnes Lyle of Kilbarchan contrasts sharply with both Mrs. Brown and Bell Robertson. As the collector William Motherwell's most prolific singer, she performed, and Motherwell recorded, twenty-two songs, some of them with tunes. Drawn to express traditional attitudes toward luxury, sexuality, and death, she could be vehement in her overall style and range of themes, revealing a consciously radical vein that departs from notions of balladry's "objective" tone. While Anna Brown preferred to sing ballads with a romantic and magical content, Agnes Lyle seasoned the patriotic emphasis of her ballads with a vein of personal cynicism. Whereas Mrs. Brown acquired in her youth, and refined over the years, a ballad repertoire that was fairly uniform in its structuring of plot and character, usually featuring a triangular love story told through dialogue, Agnes Lyle knew and sang songs of different kinds as a part of everyday life and hardship in Scotland of the 1820s. Her style was freer, less consciously "artistic," more in tune with the struggle for existence that a weaver's daughter encountered, less bourgeois in its insistence on neatly packaged structures (Andersen 1985, McCarthy 1991).

Why were these notable singers all women? The easy answer is that, in most local European song traditions, it has been the women who—because of their domains of child-rearing, cleaning, cooking, mending, and domestic tasks—have developed ways of realizing their artistic potential and fulfilling themselves through music: lullabies, dandling rhymes, counting-out ditties. The men in a generally poverty-ridden rural Scottish economy, if they were cottars, farm laborers, or even small landholders, were absent much of the time, engaged in seasonal or part-time labor. The yeoman culture of their ancestors, of a texture comparable to that in other parts of Lowland Scotland, has been sketched by David Buchan for the Northeast (1972) and William McCarthy for the Southwest (1991) in their individual studies of balladry's historical and economic context.

But why would women in a rural culture that had been generally passive since the mid-eighteenth century want to sing heroic ballads that in other parts of Europe were reckoned more or less exclusively the province of men? For one thing, men were usually instrumental specialists; and in a part of Scotland not given to rhetoric but instead to a certain sparseness and economy of conversation, it was the women who to a large extent assumed roles as narrators, raconteurs, and singers of "historic" events. This role was, however, a flexible one that could ebb and flow with the particular kinship structure, economic situation, and the personality of a particular family, as well as with the gender and artistic bent of its individual members.

In her own family, Jeannie largely took over the responsibility of maintaining a repertoire that had serious, weighty ballads as its fulcrum. Her view of the events in these ballads reflects not only a dramatic sense of the actions and characters but also a tendency to telescope time. According to her, the song of "The Battle of Harlaw" pictured a palpable, actual, "historic" conflict, as she replied to Hamish Henderson:

HH: And, Jeannie, have you ever heard any stories about "The Battle of Harlaw"?

JR: Yes, what I've always heard is that the Hielan' men wouldha' won at the Battle o' Harlaw had they stayed put an' fought on. But . . . but they lost when they saw their leader fall, MacDonald. There wes terrible bloodshed. They say the roads wes running for days with blood—like water—after the Battle o' Harlaw.[3]

The music ritualizes this notion of a memorable event by means of its march tempo and undertones of lament for the Highland cause. This battle of the year 1411 has, however, become indelibly overlaid in the minds of travellers with the calamity of the Battle of Culloden in 1746, fought not far off in a fading Stuart bid for the British throne (Buchan 1968). Remembering the fierceness of the Highland clans who stormed out of the darkening glens, canny Aberdeen burgesses and lairds sided with Cumberland and his redcoats, just as their forebears had resisted the Lord of the Isles. But travellers, mindful of their Highland kin, identify as much with the Gaelic-speaking warriors as with the domesticated Lowland burghers and cottars whose material victories, since the eighteenth century, have been accompanied by their historical suspicion and oppression of travellers.

In other conversations Jeannie identified the songs she learned with a sagacity embedded in past-ness, the wisdom that comes from legitimizing tradition. In her value system, the art of singing carried within it a dominion of respect for the experiential "truth" of tradition: nothing else could convey this respect and truth so completely. The people in "Mattie Groves" were real to her and had a code of honor she recognized. "Lord Darnley," she commented, "was a fair man. He let little Mattie Groves have the better sword." Place names were also real, not because the events actually had occurred there, but because they were associated with precise experiences: emotional or familial conflicts, even the learning of songs. This fixity of experience, realized and recreated in the act of singing, is different in quality from the codes channeled by a printed song text which, however denotative the actions or images may be, are essentially abstract and associative rather than concrete and interactive. This performative process is not just the objectification of experience via singing communication, but the experience relived and shared, reflexive more than responsorial.

Jeannie often referred to the practical uses of poetry and song in her own life and in the lives of her people. Because singing was fundamentally oral and communal, it was not simply entertainment. It communicated value and meaning, but it also released intergroup tension, expressed social concerns, educated the children. Every song, or rather every singing of it, was like Robert Frost's view of a poem, "a stay against the confusion of the world." The Robertson family could take the old ballad measure and give form to the daily struggle for survival while weaving baskets, mending pots and pans, currying horses, putting a new wheel on a float, or even roasting a poached deer over an open fire.

For travellers, the relationship between singing and narrating was a fluid and organic one (see Williamson 1985). There are many instances on the autobiographical tapes in which Jeannie comes to the end of a stanza, launches into a spoken explanation of the action that has taken place, and then, without a pause, returns to singing. Not a moment is lost in thinking, in making transitions, in consciously returning to pitch, in distinguishing speech from song. Lucy Stewart of Fetterangus, another traveller singer, moved from one medium to the other in this way, as did Duncan Williamson and several others (Goldstein 1961; Henderson 1975, Williamson 1985, Tannen 1988).

Conventional genre distinctions break down under such contextual pressures. The act of singing performs a ritualizing function, lifting and abstracting the material context to another, more ideal world; then switching back to narrative wrenches the audience back to face its quotidian surroundings. The effect of this is to move the listener rapidly back and forth between ideal and reality, between an imagined world and a palpable one, between reason and emotion, as it were from a color film to one in black and white, all accomplished with performative momentum and a sure sense of drama.

Again, the aesthetics of traveller song mean the quite indispensable presence of music. Jeannie could not conceive of a ballad without its tune:

HG: Do you have any opinion about this—which is more important, the tune of the song or the text of a song?

JR: Do you mean the words or the tune? Well, to tell you the God's truth, I like them baith. If the words are good, I like the words. When I wes a bairn, I wadnae learn a sang off my mither—she'd plenty o' sangs—if the air wasnae bonnie. I didnae like it, though the words wes guid. When I was a bairn the air caught my fancy first. I learned the air first, an' I think if you get the air o' a sang, the words are nae ill to learn. The words or idea would come second. That's my opinion. An' once you get the air in yer heid, then ye can easily learn the words, it doesnae matter who has the ballad. You know how lang it took me to learn "Lord Donald"? It's the longest sang I've got. I learned it from a young chap in one night's time. But it wasnae only because o' the air wi' it. It appealed to me as a good story.

HG: Why do you think so many people ask for "Lord Donald"? Is it because of the air or because of the story?

JR: Because it's a fine air an' a good story.

HG: The question that I'm really trying to get at is what do you think makes some songs more popular than others—the story or the music?

JR: The music an' the story. It's got to be a combination of both.

HG: If it had to be that one was more important than the other, which do you think is the more important?

JR: Well, the words, I suppose appeal tae people, an' I suppose if it's a bonnie air it appeals tae people. Both o' them. (JR, interviewed by HG, Edinburgh, 3 September 1967, audiotape in HG's personal files)

Jeannie, further, could not recite poetic lines with equal artistic or dramatic skill. When she was interviewed in 1953 by the American singer Jean Ritchie, Jeannie told how she first learned the words of the song "Mary Hamilton" from an old lady in Perthshire who did not sing the ballad but said it "jeest like a poetry." She then proceeded to recite the verses in a self-conscious, sing-song way.[4] The ballad text could not be separated from the tune without violating her unified concept of "the song Mary Hamilton" as she had reconceived it in performance terms. This close association, for traditional singers, of the structural elements in song was noted by Cecil Sharp, whose English informants were, conversely, unable to sing the tune without the words.[5]

Andy Hunter, though, recalled that Jeannie often had more than one tune for a song and would make a conscious choice about which to sing:

> She had two tunes for "Little Matty Groves"—a big one and a short, thumpy one. Once at a festival when someone requested her to sing "Matty" at the opening of the program before she was warmed up, she said to us under her breath, "Dammit, I'll no' start off with my big tune first an' be here five minutes longer!" So she sang the short one first. That's how she built up a program to a climax. The big guns came last when she was all warmed up and the audience completely with her, expectant.[6]

Public performances could vary a great deal with her mood and the makeup of the audience. She would not be confined to an announced program but linked song to song with elements of surprise for the listener.

Not essentially a student of songbooks and the printed word, Jeannie would occasionally resort to them to fill in forgotten verses or those she had not learned from her mother. In her early years, she had picked up a few Harry Lauder songs, a half-dozen music-hall pieces, and a handful of cowboy or "sentimental" ballads of American origin, mainly from gramophone recordings. But neither print, the gramophone, Tin Pan Alley songs, London musicals of the 1920s and 1930s, jazz, nor Hollywood movies appear to have affected the basic repertoire that she had received orally from family and friends. If she ever did incorporate popular urban songs into her repertoire, these were no longer in evidence after 1953. This development argues strongly for the notion of a powerfully resonant performance aesthetic inculcated through mimesis at a formative stage in her upbringing; it also indicates self-appraisal, a recognition of her own strengths as a singer, and selective paring of repertoire to what she felt was valuable for her as a performer and for the professional collectors at her door.

Jeannie was prepared for recognition when it came, and we must infer that she had to some extent crystallized this repertoire by middle age. She was already aware of the significance of her songs for the world outside her traveller community; but other problems of responsibility, external to actual repertoire, crowded in. How was she to handle this song tradition? How guarded should she be, how open? What legal assurance was there in the matter of copyright law, contracts, fees, royalties? Though travellers are known to be traders, swappers, and bargainers, Jeannie made only meager sums of money from her public singing or record albums.

Fame came to Jeannie not because she sought it, but because a postwar generation, anxious to salvage "fragments against the ruins," was hungry for the values she represented in her person and her songs. This hunger was also a reaction against a society moving rapidly to embrace materialistic goals and to legitimize a music industry involved in commercial exploitation. In contrast to the professional performer, to whom success meant public acclaim and financial gain, Jeannie's personality and her life were tightly bound to the songs as entities both experiential and aesthetic in character. These songs, and her narratives, embodied a code of experience by which she lived and through which she interpreted life—seeing life as what Thomas Hardy called a "salt and pepper" mixture of the tragic and the comic. The breadth of her vision allowed her to accommodate to the vicissitudes and currents of her own life and to make the best of her situation. What she offered to the searching young people who flocked to her house and concerts was the stability of tradition and community, legitimized through her songs and, more particularly, her singing of them. In the final reckoning, the contracts, fees, copyright laws, and royalties of a legalistic society were only secondary matters.

9. "Farewell to My Jean": A Singer's Legacy

Like Ray Fisher, there is another younger singer from Fife who has forged a career both in Britain and in North America. Jean Redpath recalls the early 1960s and acknowledges Jeannie Robertson's influence. Redpath was studying English at the University of Edinburgh, had sung "respectable music like Brahms" as an adolescent, but was not singing at all until she heard Hamish Henderson lecture on Scottish folksong and play some tapes of Jeannie Robertson. These sessions conjured up songs Redpath had heard as a child growing up in Fife. Later, Jeannie came down from Aberdeen to sing at the University Folksong Society, and Jean Redpath heard her perform in person. To Redpath, Jeannie was always in command because of her age and personal maturity; she knew who she was, and she was sure of her expressive material.

Jean Redpath studied Jeannie's tapes and records and listened to her at *ceilidhs* when no one moved a hair during a stirring ballad. Later, she was able to compare Jeannie and her daughter Lizzie as singers, identifying their contrasting styles: Jeannie as "the Queen of Tragedy" and Lizzie as "Mistress of the Poignant." Jeannie could capture the tragic mood, but Lizzie could move her to tears faster, Redpath concluded; each style had something emotionally moving to recommend it. We have noted how Lizzie modeled her style on her father's pipe playing.[1] We can infer, therefore, that Redpath admired Jeannie greatly, but, because of her age, she evolved a personal style that was closer to that of Lizzie Higgins.[2]

As a young man of twenty, Andy Hunter studied Jeannie's style and learned to adapt it to his own singing. He never forgot the impact she made as an interpretive singer. Besides believing in the "truth" of the narrative, she knew how to dramatize the action and dialogue, placing emphasis on certain phrases and thereby altering the pace, slowing or heightening it, so that she avoided the monotony of a steady, predictable meter. She could trick her audiences into going along with her narrative by changing tempo, catching the foot-tappers out as many as two or three times in a single stanza, Hunter observed. No thumpety-thump.[3]

Accompanists too were caught off guard. Most of them gave up and let Jeannie maintain her own rhythmic patterns. Norman Buchan, as one of Jeannie's sponsors, described an incident when she was staying with his family and taping songs for her first LP record. Someone suggested that a bit of guitar background would make the record more attractive to a general audience. Buchan and his wife Janey knew the professional guitarist Josh MacCrae and invited him to the recording session. Although he was an admirer of Jeannie and sympathetic to the task in hand, MacCrae saw that his guitar was just a distraction. Jeannie was an individualist, unused to accompaniment, and the problem finally was solved, if only partially, when the producer put Josh in a closet with a mike and earphones, while Jeannie sang outside, unencumbered. It came through as background accompaniment, with Josh playing only an interval filler here and there.[4]

The loss of her son Jeemsie had been a continuing trauma for Jeannie. She had expected that Jeemsie would learn the old songs and that she would teach him as Maria had taught her. Her singing of "Son Davit" in later years took on the tone of a lament for this loss. But young Andy Hunter, who first met her at the Glasgow folk club, came in time to fill, at least partially, the role of the young boy she and Donald had lost. Though born in Glasgow, Hunter had experienced a semirural environment as a boy. During holidays in the country, he found a ready, discerning audience at barn dances, Hogmanay parties, and *ceilidhs*. The older folk sang bothy ballads for him. His grandfather was a good speaker of Scots, using Ayrshire dialect, and, as a great admirer of Burns' lyrics, he wrote poems celebrating local events. He was also a trained singer.[5] Andy inherited a voice of strong quality from relatives on both sides but little in the way of traditional song.

The Glasgow folk clubs sparked his interest, especially with the appearance of traditionalists like Jeannie, Jimmie McBeath, and the Stewarts of Blair. After finishing school, Hunter went into an accountant's office as an apprentice because he was not sure that he was interested in a university degree. After some soul-searching, he decided to apply for admission to Aberdeen because it was the "most Scottish" of the four ancient, major universities. Having already visited Jeannie and Donald, he would use his spare time to study tradition among the folk who had somehow retained their ways and traditions longest.

To young Hunter, Jeannie's people had a philosophically realistic view of life, of people, and of human nature that he had never encountered elsewhere. This came through in the songs, the tales, and the music that he came to hear in the prefab in Hayton. Travellers could instantaneously communicate their

Fig. 15. A pet monkey, Jeannie's nephew Isaac Higgins ("Wee Froggie"), and
Andy Hunter. Aboyne, 1964. Courtesy of School of Scottish Studies.

knowledge of other human beings. Jeannie, who taught Andy to translate some
of these insights into his singing and his music, left him with the gift of
recognizing the basic qualities inherent in authentic folk music.[6]

While he never actually lived with Jeannie and Donald, Andy Hunter was
never out of their house. As a kind of adopted son, he got to know the
members of the traveller community, caught onto their cant language, and
learned about their daily lives, their codes, their ways of trading and dealing—
all this in addition to learning their songs and modes of singing. He went with
them to *ceilidhs*, was accepted as a promising singer and piper, and was encouraged to sing his own songs to a perceptive audience. In a gesture of heartfelt
generosity, the prosperous traveller Bobby Hutchinson bought him the first set
of quality pipes he ever owned, making him this gift when he was a student
with very little means.

In 1964, Andy accompanied Donald, Isaac, "Wee Froggie" (Jeannie's
nephew), and others of the clan to the Braemar Games, which scheduled a
competition for pipers, to which many travellers habitually throng. The night
before, there was a fight at a bar in Aboyne. Out of the incident, which he
observed at close hand, Andy made a ballad which he entitled "Aboyne Games"
and which he later sang to Jeannie's great approval. It appears that Isaac
Higgins, Jeannie's brother-in-law, well known as a piper and a recognized
authority on pipes and piping, was asked by a certain Alec McPhee to judge

the quality of McPhee's new pipes when they met in a bar. Isaac began to try them out, obliging McPhee and trying to form an opinion. But there were Stewarts from Lumphanan in the bar as well, and they had not only competed in the games that day, but had lost. Badly disgruntled, they retreated to the pub when rain began to fall, and drinking proceeded apace.

At length, one of the elder Stewarts—the father, in fact—took McPhee's chanter in his hand and declared it no good. Alec McPhee asked him to stop his talk. With that, Alec was grabbed by three Stewarts and tried to fight them off. Finally they cracked his head against the bar, left him on the floor, and ran off. Isaac, however, took hold of the pipes, tuned the drones for Alec McPhee, his face streaked with blood, and Alec played "John MacFadyen" on his instrument as he paced slowly through the pouring rain in bloody triumph outside the pub. The following day, thirty of the McPhee clan turned out in force at Braemar for a revenge battle with the Stewarts, but their adversaries failed to appear, missing the Games for the first time in fully fifty years, according to Hunter's song.

When Andy first sang "Aboyne Games" to Jeannie, Donald, and Isaac, the ballad was greeted with serious approval. Jeannie reasoned that once tempers cooled, they could all laugh about the incident. So she went so far as to urge Andy to go to Lumphanan and sing his ballad to the branch of Stewarts who had failed to show up for the donnybrook with the McPhees. Andy prudently declined. The song itself sharply etches the kind of incident that occurs between travellers when the code of conduct is broken. It was a breach of traveller ethics, a violation of manners, to insult another man's pipes. The last note belonged to the battered, bleeding Alec McPhee as he stood outside the pub soaking in the rain, defiantly playing his pipes:

> But noo my sang is ended, and I'll hiv ye bear in mind,
> The Stewarts are not all like this; there's plenty guid and kind.
> But drink gings roon a bodie's heid in gills and quarts and pints,
> But drunk or sober, *never misca' anither gadgie's pipes.*[7]

The "adopted" traveller had caught the spirit of the clan code in words and music.

From Jeannie and the travellers in Aberdeen, Andy Hunter learned that their people resented being called tinkers but did not mind "summer walkers" or "ga'n-aboot people." Most of them lived in houses in winter, carried on their trades in town, and normally obeyed the legal requirement of a hundred days school attendance per child. But spring and summer meant leaving the city for the country. Hunter also observed their code of behavior, in which honor was central. Jeannie's mother Maria Stewart felt she had been insulted by the woman called "The Terror of the North," and in terms of the code, it was necessary to do physical battle with her, just two days after Maria had given birth to her fourth child. Travellers would fight not only with "scaldies," or nontravellers, but also, as is known, with their own people when the code of honor was violated. But despite an apparent similarity to the "honor and shame" societies often thought to be typically Mediterranean, traveller groups also have been affected by the surrounding culture, increasingly so in recent years, and therefore, at the end of the century, do not always follow the old ways.

Andy Hunter, then, had tutoring not only in musicianship but also in traveller ways of seeing and thinking. He paid attention, adapting their integrity in his own affairs. Jeannie often gave him advice about singing and what it could do for him. "Andrew," she once said, "if there's money in it, tak' it. If there's guid money in it, tak' it quick." In her later years, she came to see singing as a means of making some extra money, and she had a separate little bank account for her earnings from royalties and concerts. Apparently it never amounted to very much. The Scottish edition of the *Daily Mail* newspaper in 1959 quoted her as saying that her fame had brought her little money: "I had not thought of growing rich. . . . but I would like to make enough to keep my invalid husband and myself in comfort." Donald had a small pension as a result of meningitis during World War II. Isaac continued to hawk or go about on his bicycle to sell or barter. His role, essentially, was that of the traveller who went to the country, brought news, told stories, and sold from his pack. He was given farm products by those who enjoyed his company. According to Andy Hunter, it was Isaac who brought in the extras that kept the household going.

Hunter also came to recognize how much Jeannie and her kin loved pretty objects, small pieces of jewelry and trinkets or a finely turned-out set of bagpipes. They liked to own such things for a while and then barter them or turn them into cash. The odd piece of jewelry or a silver fork were not acquired and stored out of sight; the game was to get it, fondle it for a while, and then get rid of it. Travellers are confirmed traders, swappers, bargainers. They had to travel light in order to survive. Yet circumstances never blinded them to an appreciation of rich apparel and superior craftsmanship. The women often would give a brooch or a pair of earrings to a favorite friend or relative when they parted at the breaking up of a camp.

This trait emerges in the story told by Hunter of how old Jim Higgins, father of Donald and Isaac, kept a stall in the Castlegate until he reached an advanced age. His chief possession when he died was a handsome set of pipes, highly decorated with chased silver and ivory. Nothing else of much value was

Fig. 16. Isaac Higgins (center, with dog), Andy Hunter (right), and
Robbie MacGuire (left) in 1966. Courtesy of Andy Hunter.

left in the house. Donald, the eldest son, was to get the pipes at his father's
death. So when old Jim died, Donald took the pipes and made arrangements
to bury his father. He came to young Hunter with a proposition. He offered to
trade Hunter his own pipes (quite a good set) for Hunter's pipes plus £25.
Hunter agreed, handed over the pipes Bobby Hutchinson had given him, and
managed to raise the required cash. With Andy's pipes to turn into money and
the extra £25 in cash, Donald was soon able to bury his father. Old Jim's pipes
stayed with Donald, then, and did not leave the family. Moreover, Jim Higgins
presumably was at peace knowing that his son Donald would be playing the
silver and ivory pipes he had left him. And the funeral director was satisfied
with the cash flow.

Soon after this, Donald came down with a heavy cough and began to lose weight rapidly. Jeannie had three strokes which affected her right side and impaired her speech. She entered hospital for several weeks. On March 17, 1971, Donald wrote to friends: "She is getting a wee bit better since coming home. I am looking after her although I am not too good myself. But God is good and he will see us through."[8] Yet Donald seemed far worse than Jeannie when Andy came to pay his respects that spring. Suspecting that he had cancer of the lungs, Donald told Hunter that his father's pipes had been cursed—old Jim had died of cancer—and that he had burned the fine set of pipes since they last met. Before doing so, however, he had first stripped off the silver and ivory and sold them to make Jeannie more comfortable in her weakened condition. "The bonnie things you get are not meant to last for aye," Donald confided to Hunter.[9] The "adopted" son already understood.

On July 25, 1971, Donald Higgins died of cancer, after a painful illness stretching over many months. The *Aberdeen Evening Express* of July 27 noted his death and ran a photograph:

> Mr. Donald Higgins, one of the finest solo pipers to come out of Aberdeen, died in the City Hospital today aged 64. He began playing the pipes at the age of 10 and was still entertaining his family and friends up until a few weeks ago at his home at 90 Hilton Road, Aberdeen. With his wife Jeannie (63), who is herself an internationally known balladeer, he played at most of the major centres in Britain. He won his first awards for piping at the age of 16 at the Netherly Games, near Stonehaven, and went on to win numerous distinctions in competitions throughout Scotland. Ten years ago he played before a packed Royal Albert Hall at a Folk Festival, and two years ago he accompanied his wife to Buckingham Palace where she received the M.B.E. for her contribution to folk music—the first folk singer to be so honored. In addition to playing in solo competitions he was for a time bandsman with the Gordon Highlanders. Mr. Higgins, who had been in failing health for the past year, went into hospital a few weeks ago. He is survived by his wife and his daughter Lizzie.

Lizzie wrote to America about her father's final days:

> He died parilized and Blind, the Doctor told me he had a huge Cancer on the Brain and on both Lungs, he lived 6 months over his time they had giving him. . . . Jeannie is taking this very brave. . . . they had a piper at his grave to play for him, and this was very Sad indeed.[10]

Many came to pay their respects to "Donty" Higgins, the soft-spoken piper, a staunch friend with the manners of a gentleman. He was a faithful correspondent to all who wrote to him and Jeannie during the twenty years of their recognition by the world outside. In spite of his early hardships as a traveller's son, his family problems, and his almost constant illness, Donald did not die a bitter, self-pitying man. When he taught Andy Hunter "The Laird o' Drum" at a ceilidh in Montgomery Road, Andy could see that the song reflected Donald's dignity and high moral standards. Donald once had read to him from a newspaper how the Perthshire travellers were the poorest of all travellers and how they lived out all winter and had a severe alcohol problem. They needed help with housing and wages, the article said. But Donald objected, "Andy, the solution for my people is not money and new houses. My people need moral help." Donald felt this very keenly, and the sentiment in some songs like "The Laird o' Drum," with its egalitarianism, corresponded to his convictions.[11]

With the lone piper playing as the coffin was lowered into the earth, the wracked body of Donald Higgins was buried on the green sloping hillside of a large marble-dotted cemetery close to the sea in Aberdeen. He died concerned about Jeannie's health but proud that Lizzie, with her ear for pipe music, had come into her own as a singer, had made an outstanding LP record, and was regularly receiving offers to sing throughout Britain.

In the meantime, Lizzie, whose first marriage had ended in divorce, had made a second marriage to Brian Youlden and went on working "in the fush." Her deft physical skills were widely admired among the other workers in the fish processing plant in Aberdeen. Soon her speed and dexterity in her chosen job earned her the nickname of "the fastest knife alive," as she sliced the catch that came down the trough. She was also a singer increasingly sought after on the folk club circuit.

In the evenings and on weekends, Lizzie looked after her mother and her uncle Isaac, who lived on at 90 Hilton Road after Donald's death, while maintaining her own household. Jeannie had stopped singing in public because of her impaired speech. When academics and professional song collectors came to her door, she would talk about her songs and hum an occasional air. Lizzie supplied the answers when her mother's memory faltered. As always, the household was hospitable: Isaac would rise, disappear for a while, then return with a tray of tea and sandwiches for visitors. They were never found short of simple hospitality.

Among those who came as a regular visitor was young Stanley Robertson, Jeannie's nephew, son of her elder brother Willie. Stanley recalled his aunt in sunnier days when they all had camped alongside the brown rushing water of the River Dee:

She was always dressed in a red cardigan tied with a brooch at the neck. She had beautiful black hair which she wore high, with ringlets coming down over her forehead. She was a very attractive, Gypsy-like woman.[12]

Fig. 17. Stanley Robertson, Jeannie's nephew and student,
c. 1984. Courtesy of Stanley Robertson.

As Stanley grew older and more committed to music, his admiration for his
aunt grew. He came to recognize her awesome side, too, for he found she could
often be critical:

> If I was asking her for a ballad—asking her to teach me—she was very, very
> strict, very, very hard. "All right, laddie, I'll learn you this song, but I want you to
> sing it right, sing it proper, an' sing it real." If I did not sing it *exactly* as she told
> me, I was in trouble. She would say, "Noo, listen again an' listen careful." By the
> time she was through she'd put *you* through.[13]

One can only guess at the critical terminology equivalent to Jeannie's "right,"
"proper," and "real."

It was during the final year of her life that the relationship between nephew

---

and aunt grew closer, the mutual respect greater, the ties of kinship and singing stronger than ever. Jeannie gave Stanley, for his children, a little set of boy's pipes that had belonged to Jeemsie, and continued to teach him more songs.

> Her last song she taught me was called "The Moon Shone on My Bed Last Night." She was very ill. This was about six or seven weeks before she died. I went by her house on a cold day—it was January—and she said I want to teach you this song. Her speech was very erratic and her health very bad. Her legs and arms were very sore because of the gangrene.[14]

The years of diabetes had taken their toll.

Andy Hunter recalled the details of his own final visit to Jeannie on March 13, 1975:

> She knew she was dying. Her physician was Stuart Begg, who was very good to her and tried to look after her. She always had a daily health visitor who came to see to her needs. But the end was near at hand. Yet on her death bed she was talking about getting more songs on tape and recorded for posterity. She was absolutely committed to the world of poetry and song.[15]

Andy stayed by Jeannie's bedside and held her hand:

> It was the first time in my life I'd been so close to death and I was talking to her. She knew that I was acutely upset and she sensed so well how I felt that she said, "Andy, awa' to the ben o' the hoose." So I left her room and went and sat with the others. She was still in full command and she died three or four hours later.[16]

She was determined to spare all of them the final throes of her passing.

On the morning after Jeannie's death, Lizzie and some of the other women covered the windows of the house with white sheets, referred to as "white blinds" by the family, so that visitors would know they were entering a house of bereavement. Lizzie telephoned Jean Crawford, wife of Tom Crawford, professor of Scottish literature at Aberdeen University, to tell them about Jeannie. Mrs. Crawford helped with some of the details, registering the death and visiting the undertakers to make funeral arrangements. During this time, Lizzie stressed her mother's bravery toward the end, the quietness and nobility of her passing. Her body was returned to the house in her coffin, which was placed in a bedroom cleared of most if not all of the furniture. A large cross, of which Jeannie was very fond, remained on the wall. She was clad in a blue shroud.[17]

Tom and Jean Crawford, who on good days had taken the ailing Jeannie for outings in their car, also helped in other ways, as did Jeannie's nephew Donald Higgins, who selected pallbearers from the family and the worlds of academia

Fig. 18. Jeannie Robertson and her daughter Lizzie Higgins,
c. 1965. Photo by Herschel Gower.

and Folksong Revival. Her pupil Ray Fisher remembers being called during an
engagement in England and boarding a train for Aberdeen late at night. Ailie
Munro of the School of Scottish Studies, who had made a study of Lizzie's
songs, left Edinburgh for Aberdeen. At the house, Lizzie grasped her hand and
said, "Thank God you've come." They all had a cup of tea, and the mourners
overflowed into the road.

Jeannie was lying in her coffin in the bedroom at the back. The priest,
Father John Copeland, came in and consecrated the room. The Rosary was
said with Peter Holden giving the responses. Then Father Copeland made a
few simple remarks about Jeannie and her special place in her family and the
community. Although she didn't come to Mass, she always considered herself
a Christian and a Catholic.[18]

Among the pallbearers was Andy Hunter, who helped take the coffin out of
the house and place it in the hearse. The mourners observed the old Scottish
custom, even in a motorized age, of the men walking behind the hearse. Only

the men followed it, first at a walking pace, then running as the vehicle gathered speed. As the hearse finally drove away, the men returned to the cars, joined the women, and rode to Trinity Cemetery near the seashore by Pittodrie where Donald was buried. Hunter recalled the effect this scene had on him:

> Bobby Hutchinson and his son and the other male members of the family fell in behind the hearse. I had a split decision to make when I saw them all moving off. I knew I ought to be there with them. I felt that close to Jeannie. So we all went down the road for a token hundred yards before getting into taxis and cars.[19]

At the cemetery, young Donald Higgins arranged that the pallbearers should be changed as they moved from the cemetery gates to the grave. Then Father Copeland committed the body to the earth, with travellers, friends, and admirers of Jeannie in solemn attendance. There was no piper, no music. Later, several of the mourners mentioned to Andy Hunter that they had supposed he would bring his pipes. He said he had assumed one of the relatives would play Jeannie's farewell:

> If I had been asked I would have played "Farewell to Lochaber, Farewell to My Jean" because that was the song she used to get Donty to play on the pipes. I've often thought if there's ever a ceremony at Jeannie's grave, with the placing of a headstone, somebody ought to play that tune.[20]

But at the end the pipes were mute and the voices silent around the grave. Symbolically, as well as in fact, Jeannie's music was stilled, and any other at such a moment might have seemed ill in the silence.

On March 15, 1975, *The Scotsman* ran a notice of Jeannie Robertson's death with a fine photograph of a younger, smiling Jeannie in her prime:

> Jeannie Robertson, one of the best known singers of traditional Scottish songs and ballads, has died at her home in Aberdeen. She was 66. Miss Robertson had played a major part in the resurgence of interest in Scottish folk culture since the Second World War. Born in Aberdeen, she learned much of her vast store of unwritten songs and stories from her parents, who were Northeast travelling people.
>
> She was "discovered" in her home city in 1953 by Hamish Henderson, of the School of Scottish Studies of Edinburgh University, who was collecting and recording examples of the oral Scots tradition. Later she sang to a meeting of the English Folksong and Dance Society in London, and soon after that she began to acquire a worldwide reputation among specialists in folk culture. Her first records were made for use in the United States, where much of the interest in her output is still concentrated.

Fig. 19. Jeannie Robertson, Hamish Henderson, and Isaac Higgins, c. 1973. Photo by James Porter.

Hamish Henderson said in a tribute last night that Miss Robertson "had a vast repertoire of songs, ballads, and stories, and was unique in reshaping and recreating them with a powerful, creative intelligence. Some of the ballad performances which she recorded are amongst the finest which the Scottish ballad tradition has produced. She was a storyteller of genius, and spoke a form of Lowland Scots which was almost eighteenth century in character. She was a poet in song, a virtuoso at the art, and an artist of the first order." Miss Robertson appeared at the Edinburgh Festival, and throughout Great Britain, once sharing a concert programme with Maria Callas and Sir Thomas Beecham. However, she never took up any of the numerous invitations to sing in the U.S. or the Soviet Union. She received official recognition for her work in 1968 when she was presented with the M.B.E. Miss Robertson was married to Donald Higgins, a well-known piper, who died three years ago. She is survived by her daughter, Lizzie Higgins, who is herself a prominent traditional singer.

Fig. 20. Jean Redpath, of the next generation of singers.
Courtesy of Jean Redpath.

After the funeral, close family and friends returned to the house, where Lizzie, who had not been able to bear going to the cemetery, and other female relatives served tea and sandwiches. There was whisky for those who wanted it. Hamish Henderson, discoverer, promoter, friend, and perpetual admirer, proposed a moving toast to her memory.

A bit later, Andy Hunter remembers that Isaac Higgins took down the M.B.E. scroll off the wall and handed it to Bella and Bobby Hutchinson. "'I thought Lizzie would be getting that," Hunter said to Bobby. But Bobby said, "Don't worry. That's all been settled.'" It was Bobby who first sent Hamish to Jeannie, and it was Bella and Bobby who took Jeannie and Donald in their car to London for the M.B.E. ceremony. Lizzie was convinced in her own mind that there was a curse on the M.B.E. award, and she wanted someone else to have the scroll. She was following traveller tradition in doing away with the cherished possessions of the dead.

As Andy Hunter got up to say goodbye and take his leave, a bereaved Isaac rose from his chair, clasped Andy's hand, and said, "I can't allow this to happen. I can't allow you to go for your train without saying first that you have been a member of our family." Andy nodded his gratitude for the gesture, for the years of friendship and tutoring. Then they all said "Cheerio," and he knew without looking back that he was leaving the house forever.[21]

In one of the many conversations with Hamish Henderson in 1953, Jeannie looked back to an exchange she had with Maria many years before:

> My mither said t' me before she died: "Sing my songs tae everybody," she says, "I want the *warld* t' hear them." I wasnae gotten known at that time. I says, "What wey am I gien t' let the *warld* hear them, mither? I'm askit t' sing at nae place, but the hoose here. Or maybe amang wir ain people." Funny idea, she had, an' she said, "Will ye sing my songs, min', Jeannie?" she says. An' I promised her that day. I said, "I'll sing them to the best o' my ability—whenever anybody requires t' hear them."[22]

Jeannie kept that promise, but she did more. In her sixty-six years of singing, entertaining, instructing, haranguing, and sometimes jousting with folklorists or those ready to patronize her, she embodied and ennobled the traditions she learned. Her life and her art ultimately merged in a way that validated communal and traditional means of living, seeing, thinking, feeling, and singing. She passed these means like a legacy to a younger generation that was yearning, in an alienated world, for peace, wholeness, and understanding.

Notes: Part I
The Life of Jeannie Robertson

1. "The Bonnie Bunch o' Roses": Traveller Kith and Kin

1. Alan Lomax to Hamish Henderson, 31 Dec. 1953, Archives of the School of Scottish Studies, Univ. of Edinburgh, Scotland.

2. Woods 1979:16.

3. Gentleman and Swift 1971. See "Introduction," n. 15, *supra*.

4. The tapes on deposit at the School of Scottish Studies, Univ. of Edinburgh, have been catalogued and indexed, as have those made by Peter Kennedy for the BBC, copies of which are in his personal collection. A fair number of tapes are owned by individuals (or their estates), including Andy Hunter, Norman Kennedy, and the late Arthur Argo.

5. Stanley Robertson to HG, n.d. [ca. Oct. 1979], HG personal files, Dallas, Tex.

6. On file at the General Register Office, Edinburgh, as are the birth certificates of her children.

7. Stanley Robertson to HG, n.d. [ca. Nov. 1979], HG personal files, Dallas, Tex.

8. Unless otherwise noted, direct quotations from Jeannie's autobiographical reminiscences are taken from transcripts by Robert Garioch of tapes recorded by Hamish Henderson and on deposit at the School of Scottish Studies. The transcripts are in the personal files of HG and JP and are based on the following tapes at the School of Scottish Studies, Edinburgh: SA 1962/72–74; 1964/154; 1965/168–72; 1965/177. (The year the recording was made comes first, then the identification number assigned the tape.)

9. Jeannie Robertson, interviewed by HG, Edinburgh, 3 Sept. 1967; tape in HG personal files, Dallas, Tex. Every reasonable attempt has been made to transcribe Jeannie's speech accurately, although a detailed study of diction and intonation is beyond the scope of this study.

10. Other stories about her father were published in Henderson 1979a, based on SA 1965/172.

11. A longer version of her reminiscences of Davie was published in Henderson 1979a, based on SA 1961/41 and SA 1954/98.

12. For a longer version of "The Terror of the North," transcribed from SA 1961/41, see Henderson 1979a.
13. Whyte 1979:144.
14. Stanley Robertson 1988:16.
15. See David Buchan 1972.

2. "The Lady o' the Lake": Childhood and Courtship

1. All direct quotations in this chapter are edited from SA 1962/72 and SA 1964/154.

3. "A Gift o' Some Kind": Jeemsie, Lizzie, and Second Sight

1. All direct quotations in this chapter are edited from SA 1962/72, SA 1965/170, and SA 1965/171.
2. Whyte 1979:159.
3. This attitude toward children is referred to in ibid.: 62–63, 104, 108.

4. "The Flure o' Ma Family": Jeemsie

1. Edited from SA 1962/74 and SA 1965/177.
2. The foregoing direct quotations are from SA 1965/177.
3. Stephanie Smith 1975: 22.
4. Ray Fisher reported being in the Higgins house when a song collector asked Lizzie to sing. She shyly refused. Persistent, the collector finally obtained a recording by agreeing to let her take the microphone into the bedroom and close the door while he and the machine remained outside. Ray Fisher, interviewed by HG, Whitley Bay, Tyne and Wear, England, 2 Mar. 1979; tape accidentally erased.
5. Stephanie Smith 1975: 53.

5. "Intil the Country": Renewal and Discovery

1. Jeannie's recollections of the war years and the appearance of Hamish Henderson at her door in 1953 have often been recorded. The version here is edited from a long taped interview with her by HG, Edinburgh, 2 Sept. 1967; tape in HG personal files, Dallas, Tex. Parts were published in Gower 1968.
2. Munro 1991.
3. MacNaughton 1991.

6. "The Pleasure of Scotland": Fame

1. From SA 1965/77.
2. From SA 1962/73.
3. Hamish Henderson to HG, 17 Dec. 1956; in HG personal files, Dallas, Tex.

4. Andy Hunter, interview by HG, Edinburgh, 24 June 1979; tape in HG personal files, Dallas, Tex.

5. SA 1962/168–69.

6. From SA 1962/74.

7. *Chapbook* (1966): 2.

8. For a discussion of this tale and its relationship to other apocryphal stories about Burns, see Gower 1968b, Mary Ellen Brown 1984.

9. Printed in *Chapbook* (1966).

7. "An' I Nivir Sung Better": London and the MBE

1. Donald Higgins to Dona and Herschel Gower, 15 May 1968, HG personal files, Dallas, Tex.

2. "Oor Jeannie" was recorded at the BBC studios in Aberdeen on Wednesday, 5 June 1968, and broadcast on Monday, 10 June 1968, from 10:30 to 10:59 P.M., Scottish Home Service.

3. Norman Buchan, interviewed by HG, Glasgow, 24 June 1979; tape in HG personal files, Dallas, Tex.

4. Ibid.

5. Ibid.

6. Ibid.

7. Donald Higgins to Dona and Herschel Gower, 18 Dec. 1968; HG personal files, Dallas, Tex.

8. Iona Opie and Peter Opie 1959.

9. Norman Buchan, interviewed by HG, Glasgow, 24 June 1979; tape in HG personal files, Dallas, Tex.

10. Ibid.

8. "A Fine Air and a Good Story": Aesthetics

1. Elaine Petrie 1983 discusses the traditional informants in Hogg's family.

2. Greig 1963: 34; see other references to Bell Robertson, *passim*.

3. From SA 1953/247.

4. See notes on "Mary Hamilton" (74 in "The Songs, Annotated").

5. Sharp 1965: 25f.

6. Andy Hunter, interviewed by HG, 27 June 1979; tape in HG personal files, Dallas, Tex.

9. "Farewell to My Jean": A Singer's Legacy

1. Munro 1970, Stephanie Smith 1975.

2. Jean Redpath, interviewed by HG, Edinburgh, 27 Dec. 1978; tape in HG personal files, Dallas, Tex.

3. Andy Hunter, interviewed by HG, Edinburgh, 27 June 1979; tape in HG personal files, Dallas, Tex.

4. Norman Buchan, interviewed by HG, Glasgow, 24 June 1979; tape in HG personal files, Dallas, Tex.

5. Andy Hunter, interviewed by HG, 27 June 1979.

6. Ibid.

7. The full text of "Aboyne Games," with music and several of Andy Hunter's other songs, appeared in *Chapbook* 5, no. 2 (1968). His version of "King Fareweel" appears in *A Collection of Scots Songs* (see School of Scottish Studies 1972), while his "Baron James McPhate" is included in Norman Buchan 1962. Andy was a regular contributor to *Chapbook* and wrote a short but significant essay on song writing in modern Scotland.

8. Donald Higgins to Dona and Herschel Gower, 17 Mar. 1971, HG personal files, Dallas, Tex.

9. This attitude of travellers is echoed in Whyte 1979: 108, 131, 151.

10. Lizzie Higgins to Dona and Herschel Gower, 31 July 1971, HG personal files, Dallas, Tex.

11. Andy Hunter, interviewed by HG, 27 June 1979.

12. Stanley Robertson to HG, 17 July 1979, HG personal files, Dallas, Tex.

13. Ibid.

14. Ibid.

15. Andy Hunter, interviewed by HG, Edinburgh, 27 June 1979.

16. Ibid.

17. Jean Crawford of Aberdeen to HG, 5 July 1979, HG personal files, Dallas, Tex.

18. Ailie Munro, interviewed by HG, Edinburgh, 26 June 1979; tape in HG personal files, Dallas, Tex.

19. Andy Hunter, interviewed by HG, 27 June 1979.

20. Ibid.

21. Ibid. Andy Hunter studied languages at Aberdeen and is now a lecturer in French at Heriot-Watt University, Edinburgh.

22. From SA 1962/74.

Part II

The Songs, Annotated

Songs in Part II

Songs of Childhood

1. O Jeannie My Dear Would You Marry Me?
2. Goodbye Mama, Goodbye Dada
3. I Ken Whaur I'm Goin'
4. Ten O'clock Is Ringing
5. Up and Doun the Street
6. Rub a Dub Dub
7. What's Poor Mary Weepin' For?
8. Come Up an' See My Garritie
9. Tammy Doddle
10. Soo Sewin' Silk
11. I'll Sing to Ye a Story
12. He's a Bonnie, Blue-Eyed Laddie

Songs of Freedom

13. I'm a Rover and Seldom Sober
14. The Gypsy Laddie (Child 200)
15. MacPherson's Farewell
16. Johnnie the Brime (Johnie Cock, Child 114)
17. Jock Stewart
18. Brennan on the Moor (Laws L7)
19. Yowie Wi' the Crookit Horn
20. Davie Faa (The Jolly Beggar, Child 279)
21. The Beggar Laddie (The Jolly Beggar, Child 279)
22. The Beggar Man (The Gaberlunzie Man, Child 279 Appendix)

Songs of Social Conflict

23. Tullochgorum
24. Jimmie Drummond
25. Twa Recruitin' Sergeants
26. The Handsome Cabin Boy (Laws N13)
27. Harlaw (The Battle o' Harlaw, Child 163)
28. The Bonnie Hoose o' Airlie (Child 199)
29. I Hae ae Bit Son
30. The Golden Victory (The Golden Vanity, Child 286)
31. The Deadly Wars
32. MacCrimmon's Lament

Songs of Love Affirmed

33. The Gallowa' Hills
34. Bonnie Glenshee
35. The Fair o' Balnafannon
36. Bonnie Lass Come Owre the Burn
37. Tak' the Buckles Frae Your Sheen
38. Rolling in the Dew
39. The Laird o' the Denty Dounby
40. The Laird o' Drum (Child 236)
41. I Will Lay You Doun
42. Carrbridge Castle (The Lady of Carlisle, Laws O25)
43. O Haud Your Tongue, Dear Sally
44. A Pretty Fair Maid (Laws N42)
45. Cruel Fate

The Humors of Love

46. The Laird o' Windy Wa's
47. The Bonnie Lassie's Pleydie's Awa'
48. The Braes o' Killiecrankie
49. The Thorn Bush (The Cuckoo's Nest)
50. A Dottered Auld Carle
51. The Overgate
52. The Bonnie Wee Lassie Who Never Said No
53. Cuttie's Weddin'
54. Roy's Wife o' Aldivalloch
55. Maggie A-Milkin'

Songs of Love's Ironies

56. Ainst Upon a Time
57. Brush Ye Back My Curly Locks
58. Hap an' Rowe
59. The Lassies in the Cougate
60. The Banks o' Red Roses
61. Three 'Stralion Dragoons (Trooper and Maid, Child 299)
62. Lovely Molly
63. Bonnie Barbara O (The Bonnie Lass o' Fyvie)
64. Green Grows the Laurels
65. The Moon Shined on My Bed Last Night

Songs of Love Denied

66. When I Was Nou But Sweet Sixteen
67. Young Emslie (Edwin in the Lowlands Low, Laws M34)
68. The Butcher Boy (Laws P24)
69. Bonnie Udny
70. I Made Up My Mind (The Trail to Mexico, Laws B13)
71. Far Over the Forth
72. She's Only My Auld Shoes (The False Bride)
73. I Wish, I Wish (Love Has Brought Me to Despair, Laws P25)
74. Mary Hamilton (Child 173)

Songs of Fraught Relationships

75. Willie's Fate (Willie's Fatal Visit, Child 255)
76. The Twa Brithers (Child 49)
77. Lord Lovat (Lord Lovel, Child 75)
78. Mill o' Tifty's Annie (Andrew Lammie, Child 233)
79. Lord Donald (Lord Randal, Child 12)
80. Son Davit (Edward, Child 13)

About the Songs

Jeannie's songs can be grouped by theme, as they are here: childhood, freedom, social conflict; love affirmed, humorous, ironic; love denied, fraught relationships. That is, the songs fall into thematic segments that are familial and domestic yet keyed to elemental experience, even in historical songs. These thematic groupings should always be seen in relation to Jeannie's sequencing of individual songs in her concert programs, since she imposed variety and contrast on her active repertoire. The songs are to be understood, then, in relation to her performance of them, not as artistic products abstracted from use and communication. While this active repertoire was to some extent shaped by external factors, in the end Jeannie herself was responsible for choosing and perpetuating the songs she sang.

Two main criteria guided our selection of eighty songs from Jeannie's repertoire for inclusion here. First, we wanted to give a full representation of traditional, orally transmitted items; and, second, we wanted thematic variety within the framework outlined above. Under these criteria, we excluded songs of music-hall origin (Harry Lauder songs, for example) and hymns or carols ("Once in Royal David's City") but not non-native songs of traditional character (e.g., "I Made Up My Mind" [or, "The Trail to Mexico"], 70 below). Also excluded are "arranged" songs, such as "The Snowy Breasted Pearl" or "Flow Gently, Sweet Afton." The traditional songs included here give a fairly "pure" picture of Jeannie's repertoire. The picture, however, is one that follows her own conception of value, at least in her years of public singing.[1]

The grouping of the songs follows broad thematic patterns and is not intended as a system of classification, native or otherwise. The sections are arranged to emphasize major topics in Jeannie's repertoire of traditional songs. The first group, *songs of childhood*, was learned when Jeannie was little, from her mother ("O Jeannie My Dear Would You Marry Me?") or on the playground ("I Ken Whaur I'm Goin'," "Up and Doun the Street," "Rub a Dub Dub"); or later, from Donald ("Tammy Doddle"). Some of these are widespread throughout the English-speaking world, and some are more local in flavor or are tied to the streets of Aberdeen. Texts and melodies generally are simple and direct. The images reflect a child's view of the world and of familiar objects, as well as spontaneous emotional responses to these: cups and saucers, porridge, dolls, fruit and candy, laughing, weeping, dressing up in bright tartan. The emergent sexuality of some images (e.g., physical deformity, wearing the opposite sex's clothes, fruit and candy) is always couched in comedic or optimistic rather than fearful terms.

The second group, *songs of freedom,* expresses stronger feelings concerning social relations, limning traveller experience in the guise of outlaw, robber, or drunkard. "I'm a Rover and Seldom Sober" is the prototypical traveller refrain, but the song also reflects a tradition of amorous night-visiting widespread over rural Britain and Ireland. Ballads certified by Child 1882–98, such as "The Gypsy Laddie," "Johnnie the Brime," "Davie Faa," and "The Beggar Laddie"; or by Laws ("Brennan on the Moor") jostle local Northeastern compositions ("Yowie wi' the Crookit Horn") or traveller *braggadocio* ("Jock Stewart"). Yet the notion of the free individual in conflict with conformist society, standing against brutal suppression or institutionalization, unites this group. A song such as "MacPherson's Farewell" was popular with travellers, not only because of Burns' interest in MacPherson's execution and his version of the song in *The Scots Musical Museum* (James Johnson 1788), but also because of local associations and the story of its half-Gypsy hero, whose capture in 1700 has been detailed by Lucy Stewart of Fetterangus.[2]

The third thematic group, *songs of social conflict,* raises the issue of political freedom in particular, as well as that of factional strife. Like "Yowie," "Tullochgorum" relates to eighteenth-century Whig and Tory politics, though Jeannie, far removed from such historical wrangles, had other ideas about the song's "Whig an' Tory" refrain.[3] Cant terms surface in "Jimmie Drummond," a male traveller complaint against injustice. Jeannie's "Twa Recruitin' Sergeants" continues a popular localization of the song, with its promise of release from drudgery and domestic cares in Queen Victoria's service. "The Handsome Cabin Boy" belongs in the group of songs about female warriors, and women in men's apparel, that forms an important topic in nineteenth-century broadside ballads.[4] With "Harlaw," "The Bonnie Hoose o' Airlie," and "The Golden Victory," Jeannie celebrates three historical events, often blurred in fact but dramatically "present," while the others of this group mourn the effects of war and emigration on an already wretchedly poor society.

The large group of *songs about love* is necessarily subdivided. Those dealing with the positive outcome of love (*love affirmed*) range from the lullaby-like "The Gallowa' Hills," incitement to travel to "Nature's realm," and the widespread "Rolling in the Dew," to the *noblesse oblige* seduction and marriage of

"The Laird o' the Denty Dounby" and an ultimate profession of egalitarianism in "The Laird o' Drum." The theme of seduction is basic to "I Will Lay You Doun" and "A Pretty Fair Maid," the text of which has stanzas identical to those of "Green Grow the Laurels" (64). Irish elements are perceptible in the first of these songs and in "O Haud Your Tongue, Dear Sally." Jeannie found "Cruel Fate" in a book of Burns' lyrics and put an air of her own to it. This song in particular speaks to Jeannie's personal ideals of love: the indissolubility of love's union, the impossibility of parting.

The *humors of love* group presents comic or bawdy texts: the collapsed bed of the promiscuous "Laird o' Windy Wa's"; the impotence of an old suitor; the erotic symbolism of "The Bonnie Lassie's Pleydie's Awa'," "The Thorn Bush" ("The Cuckoo's Nest"), and "Cuttie's Weddin'"; and the racy adventures of "The Overgate" and "The Bonnie Wee Lassie Who Never Said No." Sexual frankness spills over in "The Braes o' Killiecrankie" and "Maggie A-Milkin'." Most of these are set to strathspey or dancelike tunes that emphasize their airy, devil-may-care character. Imagery confirms this mood: collapsed bed, lost plaid, disheveled frump, lost maidenhead, aged suitor, pub crawl, middens— all are redolent of sexual delight or catastrophe.

A darker strain appears in the next group of songs, in which *love's ironies* are explored. Jeannie learned "Lovely Molly" from Hamish Henderson, then taught it to Lizzie, who recorded it. Jeannie added "Bonnie Barbara O" to her repertoire late, possibly because it was sung often during the Revival. A note of regret, of sorrow or pain reflecting personal experience, enters into songs such as "Ainst Upon a Time" and the richly evocative "The Banks o' Red Roses." "Brush Ye Back My Curly Locks," on the other hand, is more sexually challenging than sardonic. The symbols mostly speak of unwanted pregnancy or lovers' forced partings. The theme of "The Moon Shined on My Bed Last Night" seems to form a bridge between Jeannie's satirical songs and those which show a girl's resolve in following her true love. This was the last song she taught to Stanley Robertson before she died.

The penultimate group deals with the negative side of love relationships (*love denied*), often specifying separation and loss or even murder and death. "When I Was Nou But Sweet Sixteen," in its tone of regret, forms a bridge from the foregoing group. "Young Emslie" and "The Butcher Boy," from broadside tradition, convey the horror of a sweetheart's murder, with its images of foaming brine, knife, lily-white hand, handkerchief, candlelight, flames of hell, gallows, and roses. "Mary Hamilton" is the story of infanticide, whose refrain became, over the centuries, a prototype for "goodnight songs," i.e., songs—such as "MacPherson's Farewell"—reputedly composed by condemned felons. "I Made Up My Mind" (also called "The Trail to Mexico" and one of the few "cowboy" songs Jeannie continued to sing), together with "Hobo Bill," "Bonnie Udny," and "Far Over the Forth," deplores the banishment or loss of a loved one. The harsh realities of love surface in "When I Was Nou But Sweet Sixteen," "She's Only My Auld Shoes," and "I Wish, I Wish."

The final set of songs concerns *fraught relationships*, songs with weighty themes especially well suited to Jeannie's grand and somber treatment. All are ballads with Child's imprimatur: "Willie's Fate," "The Twa Brithers," "Lord Lovat," "Mill o' Tifty's Annie" (at twenty-one stanzas, Jeannie's lengthiest ballad), "Lord Donald," and "Son Davit." In performing these songs, Jeannie focuses upon fratricide (76, 80) or the rupture of a love match by heartless or willful behavior (75, 77, 78)—events not uncommon in traveller experience. Her texts often are shorter than those from other singers, yet her concentration of treatment, the solemn focus on a central desperate act, compensates for narrative fullness. Where an argument perhaps could be made against such compensation, as in "Willie's Fate," the melodic and narrative echoes of parallel ballads such as "Lord Lovat" provide a symbolic richness and contrast against which her performance may be assessed.

As a whole, Jeannie's songs, whether from the Child canon or not, tend toward the dramatic rather than the narrative, the mythic rather than the legendary. They deal more with elemental passions or reactions in a short, traumatic moment than with quasihistorical events. Even items with conventional narrative sequencing, such as "The Golden Victory" (30) or "The Butcher Boy" (68), are pushed toward compression and dramatic exchange between characters. To that extent, they reflect a depth of experience on the part of the singer that has little to do with the nuts and bolts of narrative logic and everything to do with emotional intensity. This intensity is evident not only in performative tone and style, but also in the density of commonplace phrase and metaphoric image, of iterative line and melodic phrase. The final effect is, and was when Jeannie sang these songs, overwhelmingly Aristotelian, charged with a terror and a pity that, even today, long after the living voice fell silent, leave an indelible mark upon those who listen to her recordings.

Transcriptions of the Songs

The transcriptions of the songs are both descriptive and prescriptive, to use Charles Seeger's terms (1958). That is, they combine description, in conventional notation, of major variations in melody and rhythm with a prescription that reflects Jeannie's preferences in these two aspects. This prescription can also be drawn upon, of course, by those who want to learn the songs. The tunes generally have been transposed from their original pitch in order to keep the tunes readable within the confines of the staff. The preferred type, in larger notation, is statistically derived from all sung verses in a single recorded performance. The relationship between the descriptive and prescriptive types is indicated by the use of large and small note-heads. The melodic and rhythmic gestalt thus produced forms a model capable of being grasped by a competent reader. It also conveys, in a short space, an idea of Jeannie's variations in melody and rhythm. Transcription of the texts, similarly, does not describe any one particular singing. Rather, it provides a crystallized text from the range of recorded variants, with variation in words, phrases, or lines being noted when it occurs.

Recorded Versions of the Songs

In the listings of recorded versions of the songs below, if no artist is specifically mentioned, the reader may assume that the artist is Jeannie Robertson. The School of Scottish Studies numbering system is used for many entries in these listings. SA denotes the Sound Archive at this school. Thus, for example, "SA 1954/105" signifies "Sound Archive, year 1954, reel 105."

1. O Jeannie My Dear Would You Marry Me?

O Jeannie my dear would you marry me?
O Jeannie my dear would you go?
O Jeannie my dear would you marry me?
Whether you're willint or no?

I've a pottie for bilin' my porridge,
An' a skillet for bilin' my whey,
I've a set o' new cups and saucers
Aye, an' a kettle for bilin' my tay.

1. O Jeannie My Dear Would You Marry Me?
"A little strathspey," as she called it, this was the first song Jeannie heard from Maria. Ewan MacColl, who picked it up from Jeannie in 1957, describes it as a game song "for bouncing the ball on the ground and cocking the leg over" (*Singing Streets,* Folkways disc 8501, 1958). The sexual connotation of household utensils adds a symbolic layer to verse 2. The tune is printed in MacColl and Seeger 1977: 164, as that for "My Father Was Hung for Sheep Stealing," sung by Maggie McPhee, but it has a demonstrably longer pedigree. Chappell 1858–59 (553–55) has it with the title "Give Ear to a Frolicsome Ditty; or The Rant," and comments (2:359) that there are two ballads in existence and a third in the Roxburghe Collection entitled "Mark Noble's Frolick, &c, 'to the tune of The New Rant.'" The air is in one of the many editions of Playford, *Apollo's Banquet,* with the name "The City Ramble," and in a number of ballad operas. In Mrs. Centlivre's comedy *The Platonick Lady* (1707), one finds it as "Give Ear to a Frolicsome Ditty"; and, in *The Beggar's Opera,* it is called "Have You Heard of a Frolicsome Ditty?" About fifty years later, it turns up in Ritson's *Bishoprick Garland* as the tune of "The Hare-Skin." Its "Saddle to Rags" congeners often seem close to the "Rosin the Bow" tune complex (cf. Bronson 1959–72, 4: 282– 302). According to J. H. Dixon 1846: 126, it is the tune to which the northern

"Saddle to Rags" is sung; cf. also Kidson 1891: 140–42. James O'Neill included it in *The Dance Music of Ireland* (1907: 88) under the name "Open the Door for Three," a tune Capt. Francis O'Neill (1910: 14) mentions as being in the manuscript collection of Timothy Downing, a gentleman farmer from Cork. "Open the Door for Three" (or "Winifred's Knot") is in Playford, *The English Dancing Master*, and variants of it are found in Scottish collections such as the Macfarlan MS (1740), *An Evening Amusement* (1789), *The Caledonian Muse* (1795), and Davie's *Caledonian Repository* (1829). Joyce 1909: 37 publishes a song, "Kitty, Will You Marry Me?" to a different air. A close Irish relative, "Lá 'gus mé teasdal amwänar," appears in the *Journal of the Folk-Song Society* 6 (1921): 278 with a note by Lucy Broadwood, who includes it in Broadwood and Maitland, *English County Songs* (1893).

Recorded versions: SA 1954/105; 1959/76/82; SX 1959/2; Jazz Selection JES 1; Ewan MacColl, Topic 12T41.

Additional references: Gower and Porter 1977: 78–79.

2. Goodbye Mama, Goodbye Dada

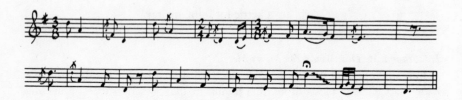

Goodbye mama, goodbye dada,
Goodbye to all the rest;
Goodbye mama, goodbye dada,
For I love dolly best.

2. Goodbye Mama, Goodbye Dada
This may have been one of the first songs Jeannie learned, when she was five years old, in Blairgowrie. The tune's second phrase is perhaps a borrowing from "Mary Hamilton" (74 below), which Jeannie also heard while in Blairgowrie.

Recorded versions: SA 1954/103.

3. I Ken Whaur I'm Goin'

I ken whaur I'm goin',
  But you're no comin' wi' me;
I've a lad o' my ain,
  But ye daurnae tak' him frae me.

He wears a tartan kilt,
  He wears it in the fashion;
An' every time he turns aroon',
  You'll burst your sides wi' lauchin'.

3. I Ken Whaur I'm Goin'

A song Jeannie learned in the playground as a child, this is probably a direct parody of the Irish text collected by Herbert Hughes in *Irish County Songs* (1909; see also O'Keefe 1955: 85). The earliest Scottish parodic variant in print is *Sandy Candy* (William Montgomerie and Norah Montgomerie 1948: 114), though it has probably been current for a long time:

I'm gaein in the train
And ye're no comin wi me;
I've got a lad o ma ain,
An' his name is Kilty Jeemie.

Jeemie wears a kilt,
He wears it in the fashion,
And every time he twirls it roon,
Ye canna keep frae laughin'.

The editors mark this variant "Dundee," but Jeannie's text was picked up in Aberdeen. The air, generally known in Scotland as "The Massacre of MacPherson," or "Phairson Swore a Feud" (see Ford 1899–1901, 2:152–55), is a later adaptation of "Bobbin Joan" (or "John," "Joe") found in Playford, *The English Dancing Master* (1650) and Playford, *Musick's Delight on the Cithren* (1666). It is called "New Bob-in-Jo" in *Mercurius Democritus* (1652), and many songs of the post-Restoration period used it. Gay found a place for it in *Polly*. Another variant, entitled "Lunnun is the Devil" is in *Davidson's*

Universal Melodist (Davidson 1847: 303). In Ireland, the air is commonly known as "Courtin' in the Kitchen" (cf. Healy 1965: 88–90). O Lochlainn 1939 adapts it not only under this name (64–65) but also for "The Piper's Tunes" (22–23; see also O'Canainn 1978: 102–3).

Recorded versions: SA 1954/101; 1960/110; SX 1960/2 (with Lizzie); Selection JES 8; Prestige International 13006.

Additional references: Chappell 1855–59, 1:291.

4. Ten O'clock Is Ringing

Ten o'clock is ringing,
Mother let me out;
My love is standing waiting
To take me out a walk.
First he gave me apples,
Then he gave me pears,
Then he gave me sixpence
To kiss him on the stairs.

My love's a bonnie lad,
My love's a dandy,
My love's a bonnie lad,
Sweet as sugar candy.

4. Ten O'clock Is Ringing

Close variants of the text are to be found in William Montgomerie and Norah Montgomerie 1948: 112, Ritchie 1964: 97–98, and David Hammond 1978: 11. Many others have been recorded in North America. The Montgomerie version is marked "Berwick" in reference to the border town:

> Eight o'clock bells are ringing
> Mother, let me out;
> My sweetheart is waiting
> For to take me out.
>
> He's going to give me apples,
> He's going to give me pears,
> He's going to give me sixpence,
> And kisses on the stairs.

Hammond's Belfast collection contains "Five O'clock Is Striking" to a different tune:

> And five o'clock is striking,
> Mother may I go out
> My true love is awaiting
> For me without
>
> First he brought me apples
> Then he brought me pears
> And then he gave me sixpence
> To kiss him on the stairs
>
> I would no' take his apples
> I would no' take his pears
> I gave him back his sixpence
> When he kissed me on the stairs

The incipient sexuality of the images of apples, pears, and sugar candy is common to most versions. Five o'clock, eight o'clock, and ten o'clock are all "liminal" times: end of daily work (tea time), middle of a (summer) evening, midmorning break, or school recess. While these times need not be taken literally, they broke up the day for both children and adults. See also Legman 1968: 82–83 on the connection between clocks and male potency.

Recorded versions: SA 1954/100; Prestige International 13006.

Additional reference: Abrahams 1969: 100, 140.

5. Up and Doun the Street

> Up and doun the street.
> A window made of gless;
> Isn't our Maria
> A bonnie lookin' lass?
> She can dance, and she can sing,
> She can show a weddin' ring;
> Fie, fie, fie for shame,
> Turn your back to the wall again.

5. Up and Doun the Street

Jeannie's comment on this children's song was, "Yes, we used to go—play a ring, you know, go in a ring. And the one that was taken out was put in the center of the ring." A version of the song appears in *Gammer Gurton's Garland, or The Nursery Parnassus* (enlarged edition, 1810). Iona Opie and Peter Opie 1951: 399 lists analogs. Ewan MacColl sings a variant on *Streets of Song* that he learned in Falkirk as a child (with "Isn't oor wee Jeannie" in the third line). William Montgomerie and Norah Montgomerie 1948: 78 prints another set of verses from Lanark:

> Up streets and doon streets
> And windies made o glass,
> Isna Maggie Tocher
> A nice young lass?
>
> Isna Angus McIntyre
> As nice as she?

When they are married
I hope they will agree—
Agree, agree, agree.

Clean sheets and blankets
And pillow-slips and a,
A little baby on her knee
And that's the best of a.

These correspond closely to the text of Northall 1892. The search for a mate and the security of family in the third stanza are offset by the sexual dangers of verse 1. There, the sometimes hazardous search for a mate is reflected in images of the cityscape, with its endless streets and windows of glass.

Recorded versions: SA 1954/101.

Additional references: Gomme 1898; Halliwell 1843: 51.

6. Rub a Dub Dub

O rub a dub dub, three men in a tub,
A butcher, a baker, a candlestick maker,
They all went into the garden
Where Mary found a farden,
She gave it to her mother
To buy an Irish brother,
The Irish brother died.
Up in the mountains high,
A low showd an' a high showd
Tae mak' the pussy dee.
One two three,
Ma mither catch'd a flee,
An' put it in the teapot
Tae mak' a suppie tea.

6. Rub a Dub Dub

Described by Jeannie as a ring game song, this children's item combines two separate songs in the context of swinging. "Rub a Dub Dub" first saw print in 1798, in the second volume of the *Christmas Box* (analogs are cited in Iona Opie and Peter Opie 1951: 376). It became associated with swinging in the nineteenth century, when it seems to have joined with "I Went Down the Garden" (*Folklore* 1895: 202; Gomme 1898, 2:222–24). Halliwell 1860 gives as a riddle: "I went into my grandmother's garden/And there I found a farthing/I went into my next door neighbour's/There I bought a pipkin and a popkin/A slipkin and a slopkin/A nailboard, a sailboard/And all for a farthing" (the answer is a tobacco pipe). Northall 1892: 360, giving these words for "Rub a Dub Dub," specifies them as accompanying swinging. The verses in Montgomerie and Montgomerie contain elements nearer to Jeannie's text:

> As I gaed up the garden,
> I fund a little farden,
> I gied it tae ma mither
> Tae buy a little brither.
>
> Ma brither was a sailor,
> He sailed across the sea,
> And a the fish that he could catch
> Was ane, twa, three.

Another hand (Tom Scott's) has added, as a note to the original transcription of Jeannie's words, "We used to sing the end: 'She roasted it and toasted it/And had it for her tea.'" The images of swinging, small coins, and fish (or pipe by substitution) suggest the sexual concerns of the prepubescent child.

Recorded versions: SA 1954/101; 1960/114; Caedmon TC 1225/Topic 12T198; Folktracks 067.

Additional references: Abrahams 1969: 22.

7. What's Poor Mary Weepin' For?

> What's poor Mary weepin' for?
> Weepin' for, weepin' for?
> What's poor Mary weepin' for
> On the golden frosty mornin'?
>
> Because she wants to see her lad,
> See her lad, see her lad;
> Because she wants to see her lad
> On the golden frosty mornin'.
>
> So she buckled up her tails an' away she run,
> Away she run, away she run;
> She buckled up her tails an' away she run
> On the golden frosty mornin'.

7. What's Poor Mary Weepin' For?

Jeannie sang this to the same tune as another childhood item, "Mother Mother May I Go?" which is not included here. "Golden frosty morning" is an engaging transformation of the usual "cold and frosty morning." An analogous text from Berwick is printed by Montgomerie and Montgomerie 1948: 82, with the first verse:

> Oh, what is Jeannie weeping for?
> A-weeping for, a-weeping for?
> Oh, what is Jeannie weeping for,
> All on this summer's day?

Ewan MacColl, who learned the song as a child in Salford, describes it as a ring game song: "A dance drama. Girl kneels in the centre of ring. The other girls join hands and sing. A small boy is pushed into the sing during third verse ('I'm weeping for my lover') and is wept over by 'Mary.'" The order of verses is fluid (*Singing Streets*). Chilton 1965: 10–12 prints the tune to the words of "The Lost Child." In Kennedy 1951: 28, the tune is called "Buffalo Girls" or "Old Johnnie Walker."

Recorded versions: SA 1960/114/229; SX 1960/2; Prestige International 13006; Ray and Archie Fisher, Topic 12T137.

Additional references: Abrahams 1969: 128; Udal 1889: 202-64; Gomme 1898, 2:46–62; Sutton-Smith 1972: 23–24.

8. Come Up an' See My Garritie

> Come up an' see my garritie,
> Come up an' see it nou;
> Come up an' see my garritie,
> It's a' paintit blue.
> A crackit cup and saucer,
> A chair withoot a leg,
> A humpy-backit dresser
> An' a aul' bowdy bed.

8. Come Up an' See My Garritie

An example of this vivid song is included in Ritchie 1964: 115. Ewan MacColl, who learned a version from his father in childhood, sings it on *Streets of Song* to a different tune in the same rhythm and meter:

Come up and see my garret
Come up and see it noo;
Come up and see my garret
For it's a' furnished noo;
A second-handed table,
A chair withoot a leg,
A humpy-backit dresser
And an auld iron bed.

The grotesque images emphasize the comic sexual overtones of the text, and relate it to other songs of coupling and disaster such as "The Laird o' Windy Wa's" (46).

Recorded versions: SA 1954/100; 1957/107; SX 1958/5.

9. Tammy Doddle

Tammy Doddle is a cantie chiel,
　Fu' cantie an' fu' croosie;
The fairies liked him unco weel
　An' built him a wee hoosie.

An' when the hoose was all built up
　An' finished but the door,
A fairy man cam' skippin' in,
　An' danced upon the floor.

He whiskit up, he whiskit doun,
　He loupit and he flang;
He friskit up an' friskit roun',
　An' croon'd a fairy sang.

The fairy whistl'd loud an' shrill,
　An' in cam' a' the gang;
So pair wee Tammy Doddle
　Wis mis-smother'd in the thrang.

9. Tammy Doddle
Variations exist in the transcribed texts for Jeannie's and Lizzie's renderings of this song, which both may have learned at different times from Donald. Alternatively, Jeannie may have learned a slightly different version when young (see Hall 1975: 47–48; Stephanie Smith 1975: 254–55). Lizzie's third stanza runs:

He loupit up, he loupit doon,
　He friskit an' he flung;
Till puir wee Tammy Toddles,
　Was malmaist among the thrang.

This seems to be a medley of Jeannie's third and fourth verses. *Croosie* (Lizzie's *coussie* according to Smith, *couthy* according to Hall) has a meaning similar to that of "canty"—namely, brisk, lively, cheerful (*crouse* in Webster). Lizzie explained the song when introducing it to an audience of the Edinburgh Folk Song Society in 1973:

> It's a wee Scots fairy song. . . . well, Tammy Toddles he wisnae deformed. An'—because he was so small up in the Highlands, big, brawny Highlanders cast him out o' society. So the only thing he could do was go an' build a wee shack himself in the woods, ye know? An'—he bult this wee shack, so he'd no friends or relations or anything like 'is. Anyway the fairies took a likin' til 'im. An'—'at's the song. Just a little short thing wi'—sweet, short an' bonnie. (SA 1973/174; Stephanie Smith 1975: 254).

How much of this explanation is Lizzie's own and how much is her father's is difficult to guess. Yet it reflects something of the continuing belief, half-humorous and half-ironic, in the power of the "wee folk"—a belief that enters more usually into the traditional narratives of travellers. Another transcription of Jeannie's singing is in Henderson 1972: 178.

Recorded versions: SA 1957/44; Lizzie Higgins, SA 1973/174; Topic 12TS260.

10. Soo Sewin' Silk

Soo sewin' silk
Fa fou fa fou
Soo sewin' silk
An' the young one's churnin' milk
An' we're a' blind drunk
An' the jolly man's fou.

For it's loose chasin' puss
Fa fou fa fou
Loose chasin' puss
Roun' the barn an' the hoose
An' we're a' blind drunk
An' the jolly man's fou.

10. Soo Sewin' Silk

These two traditional verses known by Jeannie derive from an old song often called "Wha's Fou?" or "I Saw an Eel Chase the De'il." A version of it, from the singing of Arthur Lochead of Paisley, is in Buchan and Hall 1973: 41. Kinloch published a longer text in his *A Ballad Book* (1828), the ninth stanza being:

> I saw a sow sewing silk
>   Wha's fou, wha's fou?
> I saw a sow sewing silk,
>   What's fou, now, my jo?
> I saw a sow sewing silk,
>   And the cat was kirning milk,
> And we're a' blind drunk,
>   bousing jolly fou, my jo.

Donald, Jeannie's husband, felt that Jeannie's verses could be expanded. Andy Hunter then took up the idea and composed four more stanzas that Lizzie now sings (Stephanie Smith 1975: 259). Jeannie's variant was first printed in *Chapbook* 5 (2): 14–15.

Recorded versions: SA 1960/110/200/209; SX 1960/2/9; Prestige International 13006; Folktracks FSA 067; Lizzie Higgins, SA 1973/174; Topic 12T160; The Clutha, Topic 12TS242.

11. I'll Sing to Ye a Story

I'll sing to ye a story, I'll sing to ye a sang,
  Wi' ma fa fa ma deedle come a dandie O;
But it's a' damnt lees frae beginnin' tae the end,
  Wi' ma teerin oorin eerin ansie O.

There wis a aul' miller an' his name wis Gibbie Reid,
  Wi' ma fa fa ma deedle come a dandie O;
As I come by the mill door he wis sittin' on his breeks,
  Wi' ma teerin oorin eerin ansie O.

He had his bonnet on his erse an' his breeks upon his heid,
  Wi' ma fa fa ma deedle come a dandie O;
Five-an'-twenty Hielan'men chasin' at a loose,
  Wi' ma teerin oorin eerin ansie O.

It cockit oot its horns like only hummel cou,
  Wi' ma fa fa ma deedle come a dandie O;
"O watch," said the hinmost een, "it'll stick us a' through,
  Wi' ma teerin oorin eerin ansie O.

But up come the hinmost een an' snatched it on his piece,
  Wi' ma fa fa ma deedle come a dandie O.

11. I'll Sing to Ye a Story
This "upside down" song is of the same order as "Soo Sewin' Silk" and other parodic
rhymes (cf. Opie and Opie 1959: 87–97). Another text is in Montgomerie and
Montgomerie 1964: 110 with these stanzas, the first being:

> Four and twenty Highlandmen
> Were riding on a snail,
> When up came the hindmost
> And trampit on her tail.
> O, the snail shot out her wee bit horns,
> Just like a hummel cow,
> "Hech!" quo the foremost, "we'll all be stickit now!"

As in a number of these Lowland traditional songs, Highlanders (and their dress) are
regarded as risible. See the poem from the Bannatyne MS, "How the First Hielandman
was Made by God of an Horse Turd" as an example of this attitude, though the view
could be qualified, depending on the narrative mode and context (ballad, lyric, satirical
song, or children's rhyme). A transcription of "Fower an' Twenty Hielan'men," sung by
Maggie Stewart, Aberdeen, is in *Tocher* 14 (1974:): 239.

Recorded version: SA 1956/2; Maggie Stewart, SA 1954/97.

12. He's a Bonnie, Blue-Eyed Laddie

For I will dress you in tartans
  And ribbons sae braw,
'Cause your daddie he's a soldier
  In the bold Forty-Twa.
He's a bonnie, blue-eyed laddie,
  He's the flooer o' them a',
An' he jined yon gallant regiment
  Ca'd the bold Forty-Twa.

12. He's a Bonnie, Blue-Eyed Laddie

This fragment, which Jeannie used to hear when she was "very, very young" alludes to the Forty-Second Black Watch Regiment, also celebrated in "The Gallant Forty-Twa," a short piece printed by Greig 1963: 158; see also David Hammond 1978: 36–37. The fame of the Forty-Second has lent itself to songs of *braggadocio* like John Strachan's "The Stoutest Man in the Forty-Twa" and even to songs quite different in tone, such as "McCaffery" ("I left the homestead in full content to join the Forty-Second Regiment"), in which the regiment mentioned is more likely, in fact, to be the 47th Loyal Lancashire (Dallas 1972: 171–72).

Recorded versions: SA 1954/104; 1960/200; SX 1958/2; 1960/2.

Additional reference: Shuldham-Shaw and Lyle 1981: 171, 514.

13. I'm a Rover and Seldom Sober

Refrain:
O, I'm a rover and seldom sober,
    I'm a rover of high degree;
An' when I'm drinkin' I'm always thinkin'
    How to gain my love's company.

This very nicht I am ga'an tae ramble,
    This very nicht I am ga'an tae roam;
This very nicht I am ga'an tae ramble
    Intae the airms of my ain true love.

He steppit up to her bedroom window,
    An' knelt doun gently upon a stone;
He whispered through her bedroom window:
    "My darling dear, do you lie alone?"

She raised her head from her snow-white pillow,
    Placed her hand on her lily-white breast;
Saying, "Who is that at my bedroom window,
    Disturbin' me at my long night's rest?"

"It is I, 'tis I, lass, your ain true lover,
   Open the door, lass, an' let me in;
I'm wet and tired frae ma lang nicht's journey,
   An' mair than near drenched tae the skin."

She opened the door wi' the greatest o' pleasure,
   She opened the door an' she let me in;
We baith shook hands and embraced each ither,
   An' wished that mornin' would never come.

13. I'm a Rover and Seldom Sober

Jeannie did not sing this song often in public, although Arthur Argo used it to introduce the BBC tribute to her in 1968. Hers and other recorded versions resemble that printed in Buchan and Hall 1973: 96 from the singing of James Grant of Aberdour. The text of Jeannie's song has affinities with that of Cecilia Costello (née Kelly), born in Birmingham of Irish parents. This song encompasses the notion of the revenant lover who must disappear when the cock crows (see Vaughan Williams and Lloyd 1959: 52). Costello's second and third stanzas are close to the poetics, if not the diction, of Jeannie's equivalent verses. Lloyd 1967: 193–94 offers a nineteenth-century broadside text by T. Birt of Seven Dials to demonstrate the fluid character of the textual tradition, which includes verses normally strung together in "Died for Love." Many scholars believe that the song text is the detritus of a revenant ballad in which the lover seeking entrance to his sweetheart's chamber is in fact a ghost ("The Grey Cock," Child 248). In some cases, the progenitor song is assumed to be Child 77, "Sweet William's Ghost." Shields 1972b argues persuasively that the introduction of ghostly elements in such ballads may be attributed to post-Romantic fashions. Scottish texts in recent times seem to stem from the same broadside or chapbook influence, composed out of a bothy background in combination with the more earthbound idea of night visiting.

Recorded versions: SM 1968/3 (BBC Program "Oor Jeannie"); Cecilia Costello, Caedmon TC 1146/Topic 12T161; Robert Cinnamond, Topic 12T269; Davie Stewart, Topic 12T293.

Additional references: Kennedy and Lomax 1961.

14. The Gypsy Laddie (Child 200)

Three Gypsies came tae oor hall door,
   An' O but they sang bonnie, O;
They sang so sweet and too complete
   That they stole the hairt of our lady O.

For she cam' tripping down the stair,
   Her maidens two[1] before her O;
And when they sa' her weel-faur'd face
   They throw'd their spells oot owre her O.

When her good lord came home that night,
   He was askin' for his lady O;
The answer the servants gave tae him:
   "She's awa' wi' the Gypsy laddies O."

"Gae saddle tae me my bonnie bonnie black,
   The broun it's ne'er sae speedie O;
That I may go ridin'; this long summer day
   In search of my true lady O."

For he rode east and he rode west,
   And he rode through Strathbogie O;
And there he met a gey aul' man
   That wis comin' through Strathbogie O.

For it's "Did ye come east or did ye come west,
   Or did ye come through Strathbogie O?
And did ye see a gey lady,
   She wis follyin' three Gypsy laddies O."

For it's "I've come east and I've come west,
    An' I've come through Strathbogie O;
An' the bonniest lady that ere I saw,
    She wis follyin' three Gypsy laddies O."

"For the very last night I crossed this river
    I had dukes and lords to attend me O;
But this night I must put in my warm feet an' wyde
    An' the Gypsies wydin' before me O."

"Last night I lay in a good feather bed,
    And my own weddit lord beside me O;
But this night I must lie in a caald corn-barn
    An' the Gypsies lyin' aroond me O."

"For it's will you give up your houses and your land,
    And will you give up your baby O?
And will you give up your own weddit lord
    And keep follyin' the Gypsy laddies O?"

"For it's I'll give up my houses and my land,
    And I'll give up my baby O;
And I'll give up my own weddit lord
    And keep follyin' the Gypsy laddies O."

"For they are seven brothers of us all,
    We all are wondrous bonnie O;
And this very night we all shall be hanged
    For the stealin' of the earl's lady O."

14. The Gypsy Laddie

The connection between Jeannie's air and that for John MacDonald's "Rovin'
Ploughboy" bothy song is made plain on *The Muckle Sangs* disc. A transcription of the
tune is included in Bronson 1959–72, 4:495 (see also Dallas 1975). It is not unlike the
tune in Greig and Keith 1925: 128 recorded from a Fyvie singer in 1906. The octave
leap in the melody may be significant in accounting for its presence in North American
tune variants—that is, it is an identifying feature in tracing tune relationships. Bronson
has made a convincing case for regarding "Lady Cassilis' Lilt" (from the Skene MS of
before 1630) as sure evidence of a link with the House of Cassilis that was traditionally
associated with the ballad plot (*Traditional Tunes*, 3:198). This other melody was not

transcribed until the early nineteenth century (Dauney 1838: 228). The first printed copy is in Barsanti's *Collection of Old Scots Tunes* (1742). Distinguishing aspects of Jeannie's version are: the number of Gypsies (three at the outset and seven at the end, both numbers being found in recorded variants); localization of the action, in the Northeast; and the abrupt switch of narrator, from lord to lady, in stanza 8. Lizzie's text and tune are very similar (Stephanie Smith 1975: 159).

Recorded versions: SA 1953/239; 1955/154; 1959/79; 1960/110; Caedmon TC 1146/ Topic 12T161; Riverside RLP 12-633; Topic 10T52 (12T96); Lizzie Higgins, SA 1970/78; Jean Redpath, Electra EKL-214.

Additional references: Child 1882–98, 4:61–74; Coffin 1977: 119–22; Glen 1900; Greig 1963: 110; Huntington and Herrmann 1990: 509–10; MacColl and Seeger 1977: 39; Shields 1993: 212–13.

15. MacPherson's Farewell

For it's some cam' here for tae buy my fiddle,
    There's ithers tae see me dee;
There wis some cam' for tae see me hang
    On yonder gallows tree.

Refrain:
Sae rantin'ly, sae wantonly,
    Sae daatin'ly gaed he;
For he played a tune an' he danced it roon'
    Below the gallows tree.

But it's gie tae me one tune o' my fiddle,
    An' let me play her free;

Before I let onyone play on her,
I will brak her owre ma knee.

It is place the cause on Peter Broon,
An' let MacPherson free;
All through a woman's treachery.
It's caased MacPherson tae dee.

15. MacPherson's Farewell

It is hardly surprising that this song has been popular among Scots travellers, given its association with the Northeast, with Robert Burns, and with the half-Gypsy outlaw hero of tradition (an account of MacPherson is given by Lucy Stewart in Kennedy 1975: 798). Maggie McPhee, for instance, has the opening line in her version, "I stole from the rich and I gave to the poor," and other variants have been recorded from Jimmy McBeath and Lucy Stewart (Kennedy 1975: 776). With traveller singers, the tune has taken on a rhapsodic style different from the marchlike dotted rhythm of its first appearance in the Margaret Sinkler MS (1710, "McFarsances tesment," *sic*). Other manuscript versions are in the Gairdyn MS (ca. 1729–35) and Macfarlan MS (1740). It was printed by Oswald in *The Caledonian Pocket Companion,* 7:14 (ca. 1755), and by McGibbon in his *Scots Tunes* (1762). Burns' reworking as "McPherson's Farewell" appears in James Johnson, *The Scots Musical Museum* (1788: 117), with the air marked "slowish." Maidment 1859: 29–31 prints an account of James MacPherson's capture and demise on the gallows at Banff in November 1700 (cf. Dick 1962: 175–77). The last person to be executed in Banff, MacPherson is said to have walked the mile or so from prison to the gallows playing this tune on his fiddle. The broadside text composed in 1705 (*McPherson's Rant; or the Last Words of James McPherson, Murderer, To Its Own Tune*) found its way in part into Herd's collection of 1776 but was published in full only by Maidment 1859: 31–34. As for the "Peter Broon" of stanza 3, this refers to Peter Brown of the more consciously poetic "MacPherson's Rant." As a confederate of MacPherson, Brown was freed through the intercession of the Laird of Grant, who "pleads the cause of Peter Brown and lets MacPherson dee" (Ord 1930: 445).

Recorded versions: SA 1952/33; 1957/107; Selection JES 8; Jimmy McBeath, BBC 21533, Topic 12T173; Davie Stewart, Prestige International 25106, Topic 12T293; Maggie McPhee, Topic 12T179.

Additional references: Collinson 1966: 210–12; Ford 1901: 223–26; MacColl 1953: 35; Ord 1930: 443; Seeger and MacColl 1960: 89; *Spin* 3, no. 7; Wilgus 1965: 195–209.

16. Johnnie the Brime (Johnie Cock, Child 114)

Johnnie he raise one Mey mornin',
   Caal' water tae wash hees hand;
Roarin', "Bring tae me my twa grey hounds
   That are bound in iron bands, bands
   That are bound in iron bands."

Hees aal' wife, she wrung her hands,
   "Tae the green wids dinnae gang,
For the sake o' the venison,
   Tae the green wids dinnae gang, gang
   Tae the green wids dinnae gang."

But Johnnie went up through Monymus',
   An' doun an' through some scroggs;
An' it was there he spied a dun deer leap,
   She wis lyin' in a bush o' sprogs, sprogs
   She wis lyin' in a bush o' sprogs.

The first arrow he fired at her,
   He wounded her on the side;
An' between the water an' the wids,
   For his greyhounds laid her pride, pride
   For his greyhounds laid her pride.

Johnnie an' his twa grey hounds
    Drank so muckle o' her blood,
That Johnnie an' his twa grey hounds
    Fell a-sleepin' in the wids, wids
    Fell a-sleepin' in the wids.

By came a silly aa' man,
    And a ill daith may he dee;
He went up an' tellt the first forester,
    And he tellt what he did see, see
    And he tellt what he did see.

"If that be's young Johnnie the Brime,
    Ye'd better leave him a-be;
If that is young Johnnie the Brime,
    Ye'd better leave him a-be, a-be
    Ye'd better leave him a-be."

He went up an' tellt the seventh forester,
    He wis Johnnie's sister's son;
"If that be's young Johnnie the Brime,
    Tae the green wids we will gang, gang
    Tae the green wids we will gang."

The first arrow the' fired at him,
    They wounded him on the thie;
And the saicont arrow they fired at him
    For his hert's bluid bleynt his e'e, e'e
    For his hert's bluid bleynt his e'e.

But Johnnie rose up wi' an angry growl,
    For an angry man was he;
"I will kill a' you six foresters,
    An' brak the seventh one's back in three."

He placed his fit upon a stone,
    And his back against a tree;
And he killed a' the six foresters,
    An' broke the seventh one's back in three, three
    An' broke the seventh one's back in three.

Johnnie he broke his back in three,
    And he broke his collar bone;
And he tied him on his grey meir's back,
    For tae cairry the tidin's home, home
    For tae cairry the tidin's home.

16. Johnnie the Brime (Johnie Cock, Child 114)

Learned from Maria, this was a ballad to which Jeannie was exposed from her earliest days. Between 1953, when she first recorded it, and 1960 or so, she refined her text. Jeannie's later text is printed by Bronson with the tune which, in its minor hexatonic shape, shares that feature with most airs from the Northeast. The earliest recording has the chantefable structure commonly employed by other traditional singers in Scotland and Ireland (cf. Bella Higgins' "Young Beichan" on *The Muckle Sangs*, and Shields' singers on *Folk Ballads from Donegal and Derry*, Leader LEA 4055; see also Shields 1972b). Jeannie's explanation of the plot is printed as an addendum to the singing of the ballad by John Strachan on *Folk Songs of Britain*, volume 5:

> It happened into Monymusk, that's quite true. You send to Monymusk beside Inverurie and you'll find out that Johnnie the Brime was killed there for the sake of hunting venison. Long, long ago you weren't allowed to sing near that place. Johnnie was a desperate hunter for deer, and all the foresters were feared of him, because they could not catch him in fair play, you understand. He was a fine cracksman shot with an arrow. So, as my song tells you, the rest of the foresters wouldn't have bothered him, only the seventh one had a spite towards him— Johnnie was his uncle, you understand. He wanted to get in and tackle his uncle.

The picture of late medieval society resembles that in many of the Northeast ballads. One could speculate on the significance of the uncle-nephew relationship, which in medieval texts traditionally was fraught with rivalry and danger, especially when property rights came through the female line. Yet here the hero is not a wealthy landowner, but an independent yeoman driven to desperate lengths by feudal restrictions on hunting. The "green wids" [woods] are, as usual in the ballads, a locus of danger rather than misfortune, though the latter can often follow the former.

Recorded versions: SA 1953/147; 1960/200; Prestige International 13006; John Strachan, Caedmon TC 1146/Topic 12T161.

Additional references: Bronson 1959–72, 3:3–11; Buchan 1968: 58–67; Child 1882–98, 3:1–12; Coffin 1977: 100–101; Greig 1963: 33: Ord 1930: 467–69; Shields 1993: 211–12; Shuldham-Shaw and Lyle 1983: 232–45, 550–52; *Spin* 5, no. 4: 7.

17. Jock Stewart

For ma name is Jock Stewart, I'm a canny-ga'n man,
  And a rovin' young fellow I have been;
So be easy and free when you're drinkin' wi' me,
  For I'm a man you don't meet every day.

Come fill up your glasses of brandy an' wine,
  Whatever it cost, I will pay;
So be easy and free when you're drinkin' wi' me,
  For I'm a man you don't meet every day.

I have acres of land, I have men at command,
  I have always a shillin' to spare;
So be easy and free when you're drinkin' wi' me,
  For I'm a man you don't meet every day.

For I took out my gun, and my dog I did show't
  All down by the River Clare;
So be easy and free when you're drinkin' wi' me,
  For I'm a man youse don't meet every day.

Come fill up your glasses of brandy an' wine,
  Whatever it cost, I will pay.
So be easy and free when you're drinkin' wi' me,
  For I'm a man you don't meet every day.

17. Jock Stewart

Jeannie, who heard her mother sing this song, added two verses at separate recording sessions after the first in 1952. In the studio, she replaced "coortin'" by "drinkin'." The curve of the tune's first strain, with its leap of a sixth, suggests a general relationship with many Highland and Irish melodic models. In particular, there is an affinity with such tunes as "Caitlin Triall" ("Kitty Tyrell," first published in Cooke's *Selection of Twenty-One Original Irish Airs*, 1793), with "The Last Rose of Summer," with O Lochlainn's tune for "Lambs on Green Hills" (1939: 170) or O Boyle's air for "Eamon an Chnoic" (1976: 33). The song has been associated with Scots travellers in recent times, but Irish influence is apparent. The words seem to echo a ditty in Struthers, *Harp of Caledonia* (1819), untitled but directed to be sung to the tune of "The rock an' the wee pickle tow": "I'm now a guid farmer, I've acres o' land/An' my heart aye loups light whan I'm viewin' o't/An' I ha'e servants at my command/An' twa dainty cowtes for the lowin' o't." The words of "Jock Stewart" may have acquired fresh energy from Irish texts such as that in *Walton's 132 Best Irish Songs and Ballads*, and especially from the refrain:

> Come fill up your glasses,
>> And drink what you will,
> And whatever the damage, I'll pay,
>> So be aisy and free while you're drinking with me,
> I'm a man you don't meet every day.

The song has no connection with the one of the same title in the Greig MS, volume 1. Symbolically, perhaps, this emphasizes the social gap that existed between travellers and the settled population in Greig's time and even today.

The transcription here is from Prestige International 13006. Another transcription of Jeannie's singing is in School of Scottish Studies, *A Collection of Scots Songs* (1972: 29).

Recorded versions: SA 1952/33; 1954/154; 1962/26; SX 1958/2; Prestige International 13006; Robert Cinnamond, Caedmon TC 1163/Topic 12T195.

Additional references: Gower and Porter 1977: 94–96.

18. Brennan on the Moor (Laws L7)

It's of a famous highwayman a story I maun tell,
　His name was Willie Brennan, in Ireland he did dwell;
It was on the lofty mountains where he commenced his wild career,
　Where many's a noble gentleman before him shook with fear.

Refrain:
Brennan on the moor, Brennan on the moor,
Bolder undaantin' stood bold Brennan on the moor.

Brennan met a packman whose name was Pedlar Brown,
　They walkit on together till the day began to dawn;
Til he robbed him of his money, also his watch and chain,
　But he onc't encountered Brennan when he robbed him back again.

Brennan's wife bein' down to town, provisions for to buy,
　She saw her own dear Willie, and she began to cry:
"Come hand to me that tenpenny, you really now forgot,"
　But she handed him a blunderbush from out below her cloak.

He held up the Mayor of London, till he robbed him of his gold,
    And with their horse an' saddles, to the mountains they did fly;
For infantry an' cavalry to catch them they did try,
    But he lay amangst the ferns that was thick upon the fields;
Nine bullet wownds he did receive before he would yield.

"Here's to my dear wife, and likewise ma bairnies three,
    But here's to my old father who's shed many's a tear for me;
But here's to my auld mother who tore her grey locks and cried,
    "O I wish young Willie Brennan in your cradle bed had died."

18. Brennan on the Moor (Laws L7)

"I heard one of my older aunties singing it first. I sung it when I was about nine years of age—I was always taken out in the midst of the company to sing. My people always likit to hear me singing these old kind of songs" (SA 1952/33). Ford 1901: 2:58 observes that the song was very popular with "itinerant vocalists" in Scotland in the middle of the nineteenth century. His tune "The Banks of Sweet Dundee" was given to him by a Mr. Kippen of Crieff, Perthshire, who took it down "from the lips of a wandering Orpheus many years ago." Jeannie's six-stanza text can be compared to Ford's twelve-stanza one and the broadside, possibly printed as the original, given by Healy 1965: 118–19. In Jeannie's first verse, the "Kilworth Mountains" have become "lofty mountains" ("Livart Mountains" in Ford); her second stanza corresponds to Ford's and Healy's third ("Pedlar Bawn" is now "Pedlar Brown"), and her third to Ford's and Healy's sixth. Her fourth is a medley of Ford's and Healy's stanzas 7, 8, and 9; and her final stanza matches the last in Ford and Healy. Healy's penultimate stanza ("When Brennan heard his sentence") is not in Ford. Healy 1965: 119–20 offers some background to Brennan's career: starting as a farm laborer, he robbed a British officer on a dare and had to flee as an outlaw; he was caught and tried at Clonmel in 1804 and condemned to death. The incidents in the song, Healy asserts, are based on fact. Joyce 1909: 379 mentions broadsheets printed by Hay of Cork about 1850, though Joyce's version was taken down in County Meath about 1860. O Lochlainn 1965: 217 heard the song sung in Rathmines Town Hall in 1906. O'Keefe 1955: 25–26, 130, prints a seven-stanza variant that perpetuates the "betrayal by a young woman" motif in Healy's broadsheet ("young man" in Ford), which is absent from Jeannie's version. Jolliffe 1970: 27–33 has a note on the international diffusion of the ballad and the model the text provided for the North American *refacimento* "Charlie Quantrell" (cf. Lomax 1960: 347). There is a mention of how a less usual version, "heard in Scotland," implies that Brennan is a deserter (Jolliffe 1970: 32). Jolliffe's fourteen-stanza text adds the verse with which North American variants often conclude:

They hung Brennan at the crossroad, in chains he swung and died,
    But still they say that winter nights bold Brennan he doth ride;

They say that with his blunderbuss all in the midnight chill,
  Across the Kilworth Mountains rides bold Willie Brennan still.

(1970: 31)

Dean-Smith 1954: 55, Laws 1957: 169, and Kennedy 1975: 725 all list variants. To these may be added versions in the Riddell and Greig MSS.

Recorded versions: SA 1952/33; 1953/198; 1953/236; 1954/105; 1960/202; SX 1958/2; Charlie Wills, BBC 18693, Leader LEA 4041; Robert Cinnamond, BBC 24839.

Additional references: Kidson 1891; Sharp 1932, 2:170–71; Shuldham-Shaw and Lyle 1983: 261–63, 553–54.

19. Yowie Wi' the Crookit Horn

The yowie wi' the crookit horn,
Sic a yowie was never born;
Sic a yowie was never born,
Here aboot or far awa.
What dae ye think, for a' ma keepin',
There cam a-nickin' when I was sleepin',
There cam a-nickin' when I was sleepin',
Stole my yowie an' horn an' a'.

But doun by the bush o' thorn,
There I found my yowie's horn;
There I found my yowie's horn,
But ma yowie wis awa'.
Gin I had the lad that did it,
I wid kill him as sure as I said it;
I wid kill him as sure as I said it,
I wid gie his neck a thra'.

When a' the yowies loup the dyke,
Ate ma kale for a' their might,
Ma yowie never did sic like,
But pickit at the barn wa'.
But doun by the bush o' thorn,
There I found ma yowie's horn,
There I found ma yowie's thorn,
But ma yowie wis awa'.

19. Yowie Wi' the Crookit Horn

Imitating the practice among older travellers, Jeannie sometimes would sing this to a pipe-chanter accompaniment by Donald or Isaac (SA 1952/43). Her "thrusty" men and women she explained in an additional verse on SA1959/16 as "thirsty"—i.e., as metathesis. It is likely that the Rev. John Skinner (1721–1807), pastor of Longside in Aberdeenshire, rewrote the words of a song from oral tradition for his own literary version (Reid 1859), which avoids the implication of illicit distilling (cf. "The Blackbird of Mullaghmore," in Boyle 1976: 48–49, where the bird is the symbol of the hidden still). Lucy Stewart, who as a child learned her version about 1910 from her parents, was quite definite about the ewie's being a pot still (Kennedy 1975: 625). Jeannie's and Lucy's texts are traditional and resemble each other more closely than either resembles Skinner's song, which was printed in James Johnson, *The Scots Musical Museum* (1790: 302–3), set to the tune that Cumming 1780 calls "Carron's Reell or U Choira Chruim." The tune appears with the title "The crooked horn ewe" in McGlashan's *A Collection of Strathspey Reels* (1780). Laing, in his *Additional Illustrations* (1853: 412–13) to *The Scots Musical Museum* prints a text from the Mansfield MS (ca. 1776) which predates Skinner's verses and has little in common with them (or with the two variants from traveller tradition). Later printings all follow the Skinner text, as do Buchan and Hall 1973: 38.

Recorded versions: SA 1952/43; 1955/177; 1959/106; 1960/200; Jazz Selection JES 1; Lucy Stewart, Caedmon TC 1225/Topic 12T198; Bessie Whyte, SA 1975/12.

Additional references: Dick 1962; Ford 1901: 2:87; Moffat 1896: 250; Rogers 1855; Headlee 1976: 249–76.

20. Davie Faa (The Jolly Beggar, Child 279)

There was a wealthy farmer,
Lived in the North Countrie;
He had a lovely daughter,
Who was always frank and free;
An' day be day an' night be night,
She was always in my e'e;
So there was a jolly tinker lad,
Come to this farm house.

"It is have you any pots or pans,
Or caunlesticks to mend?
Or have you any lodgin's,
For me, a single man?"
The fairmer thocht it nae hairm,
The tinker for to keep,
And the lassie she thocht it nae hairm
The tinker's bed to mak'.

But the tinker folliet after her,
And he did bar the door;
He catched her by the middle sma',
An' he laid her on the floor;
He catched her by the middle sma',
And up against the wa';
And it was there he teen the wills o' her,
Before she won awa'.

The bonnie lassie blushed,
An' O she thocht shame;
"It's since you've teen the wills o' me,
Come tell to me your name."
He whispered in the lassie's ear:
"They ca' me Davie Faa;
And you'll min' upon this happy nicht,
Amongst the pease straw."

Six weeks had passed and gone,
This maid grew white an' pale;
Nine month an' better brought
Her forth a bonnie son;
"An' since the baby's born,
I will ca' him Davie Faa;
And I'll mind upon the happy nicht,
Amongst the pease straw."

"For any man who weds my girl,
For he'll get farms three;
For any man who weds my girl,
For he'll get gol' quite free;
For although she's lost her maidenheid,
O wheet the waur is she?"

20. Davie Faa (The Jolly Beggar, Child 279)
See discussion under 21.

21. The Beggar Laddie (The Jolly Beggar, Child 279)

There wis a aul' beggar man.
    An' he wis dressed in green;
An' he wis askin' lodgin's,
    At the place near Aiberdeen.

Refrain:
Nae mair I'll gang a-rovin',
    A-rovin' in the nicht;
Nae mair I'll gang a-rovin',
    Tho' the meen shines ere sae bricht.

He widnae lie in the barn,
    Nor yet intae the byre;
He widnae lie in nae ither place,
    But at the kitchen fire.

"For if ye had been a decent lass.
    As I took you to be;
I wadda made you the queen
    O' a' the counterie."

He put his hand intae his pooch,
    He gied her guineas three;
"O tak' you this, ma bonnie lass,
    For to pay the nurse's fee."

He took a horn frae his side,
  He blew it loud and shrill;
And four and twenty noblemen
  Cam' trippin' owre the hill.

He took a penknife frae his pooch,
  He let a' his duddies fall;
An' he wis the brawest Hielan'man
  That stood amangst them all.

20, 21. Davie Faa, The Beggar Laddie (The Jolly Beggar, Child 279)

Jeannie included two distinct versions of this popular ballad in her repertoire. One she learned from her mother when she was about nine or ten. The other was derived from her mother-in-law, Christine Stewart Higgins of Old Deer, sister of "Crow's Nest Jeannie" of Banchory. Our Jeannie assimilated the latter variant when Hamish Henderson recorded it from her brother Willie in 1954, who had learned it from Donald's mother. On another occasion, however, Jeannie said that she had learned it from her brother Davie, a fact that points up the complex lines of transmission within the family (SA 1969/56).

The weight of scholarly opinion seems to be that the version Jeannie got from her mother, "Davie Faa," is in reality a variant of Child 279 even though the hero is a tinker, not a gentleman in disguise, and the central revelation motif is not present (cf. Stephanie Smith 1975: 142–44). The name *Faa* occurs frequently in texts of "The Gypsy Laddie" (Child 200), and some Burnsian reminiscences can be detected in stanzas 4 and 5 ("you'll min' upon this happy nicht" carries echoes of "Corn Rigs"). The seduction in "Davie Faa," with the sexual symbolism of candlesticks and pots and pans, lend it a more authentic flavor than the bowdlerized "Jolly Beggar." The latter type, with its well-known "gang nae mair a-rovin'" refrain and spacious melodic curve, is grouped by Bronson in his class A (6), immediately after Willie's air and text, both of which it closely resembles. This group of texts first saw print in *The Charmer* 1749: 2:237 and then in Herd 1776. The slightly later *Scots Musical Museum* variant (James Johnson 1790: 266) evidently is connected to the Robertson-Higgins family texts. In the recording transcribed here, Jeannie substitutes "Hielan'man" for "gentleman" in the final stanza (cf. Caedmon TC 1146/Topic 12T161). "Davie Faa" falls into Bronson's class D (28) and is usually linked to the bothy song, "Come Aa Ye Tramps and Hawkers." O Lochlainn 1965: 205 names it "The River Roe," or "The Winding Banks of Erne." The dress of green worn by the protagonist betokens danger or, here, the possibility of transformation into a quite different person. On tinker ballads, and tinkers as sexually potent, see Cray 1992 [1969]: 249–50, Legman 1964: 226–27.

Recorded versions [Jolly Beggar]: SA 1952/33; 1960/202; 1962/75; Caedmon TC 1146/ Topic 12T161; Lucy Stewart, Folkways FG 3519; Davie Stewart, SA 1962/79, Topic 12T93; Norman Kennedy, Folk Legacy FSS-34; Isabel Sutherland, Topic 12T151; [Davie Faa]: SA 1953/247; Jazz Selection JES 4; Lizzie Higgins, Topic 12T185.

Additional references: Bronson 1959–72, 4:213–26; Norman Buchan 1962: 46–47; Buchan and Hall 1973: 97 (Willie Robertson); Child 1882–98, 5:109–16; Coffin 1977: 150–51; Greig 1963: 30, 38; MacColl and Seeger 1977: 34: Shuldham-Shaw and Lyle 1983: 296–302, 559–60; Henderson 1974: 278–80 (Davie Stewart); Wehse 1979: 323.

22. The Beggar Man

(The Gaberlunzie Man, Child 279 Appendix)

O lassie, O lassie, you're far too young,
You huvnae got the cant or the beggin' tongue;
You huvnae got the cant or the beggin' tongue,
And wi' me you cannae gang,
Lassie wi' my tow row ae.

But I'll bend my back, and I'll bou my knee,
I'll pit a black patch on my e'e;
And a beggar, a beggar they'll tak' me to be,
An' awa' wi' you I'll gang,
Laddie wi' my tow row ae.

22. The Beggar Man (The Gaberlunzie Man, Child 279 Appendix)

The older travellers sang versions of this song at the campfire when Jeannie was young. She finally learned it from Maria. Lizzie picked up her slightly different variant from her father (Stephanie Smith 1975: 127). Bronson's large class B includes Jeannie's tune and text (Bronson's no. 41). The first strain of a number of Aberdeenshire airs (e.g., Bronson's no. 29) draws on "O Gin I Were Where Gadie Rins," which was Jeannie's model for "Son Davit" (Porter 1979). The song of the wandering beggar was widely popular in Scotland during the eighteenth century, after its first printing by Ramsay in *The Tea-Table Miscellany* (1724); tunes additional to those in Bronson can be found in the Gairdyn MS (ca. 1729–35), Craig's *A Collection of the Choicest Scots Tunes* (1730), and Oswald's *Caledonian Pocket Companion* (1743–59). In one of the texts in *Last Leaves*, the beggar turns out to be the Laird o' Drum, a figure well enough known from the eponymous ballad to be convenient for the kind of amorous situation around which local traditional songs often are constructed (cf. Greig and Keith 1925: 176–77).

Recorded versions: SA 1954/103; Lizzie Higgins, Tangent TNGM 119/D.

Additional references: Bronson 1959–72, 4:227–49; Child 1882–98, 5:115–16; Coffin 1977: 277; Greig 1963: 30, 38; Greig and Keith 1925: 223–26; Henry 1923–29, 2:312; MacColl 1965: 34; Shuldham-Shaw and Lyle 1983: 303–30, 560–62.

23. Tullochgorum

Come gie's a sang, Montgomery cried,
An' lay your disputes a' aside,
It's nonsense for a man to chide
　　At what's been done before them.
Let Whig an' Tory a' agree
(Whig an' Tory, Whig an' Tory)
Let Whig an' Tory a' agree
　　An' dance this reel Whigmorum;
Let Whig an' Tory a' agree
An' come an' dance the reel wi' me:
　　The Reel of Tullochgorum.

23. Tullochgorum

The Rev. John Skinner adapted words to the old strathspey tune, "The Reel of Tullochgorum," at the request of his hostess, Mrs. Montgomery, while on a visit to the town of Ellon. Taking advantage of a heated political dispute among the guests, he composed some verses to the old air. There is a single sheet in the British Museum (1346 m. 7) dated 1776, and Reid 1859 states that the song was first published in April of that year in the *Scots Weekly Magazine* (cf. Hecht 1904: 86). It was printed with the tune in the Perth *Musical Miscellany* ten years later (see Cook, in Dick 1962: 107). Burns, in two letters to Skinner from Edinburgh (October 25, 1787; and February 14, 1788), wrote that it was "the best Scotch song ever Scotland saw." He said, "I have heard your 'Tullochgorum,' particularly among our west-country folks, given to many different names, and most commonly to the immortal author of *The Minstrel*, who indeed never wrote anything superior to 'Gie's a sang, Montgomery cried'" (Ferguson 1985, 1:167, 1:235). The words of the song have found their way into popular anthologies and into oral tradition. In the full six stanzas printed in Chambers 1829: 41–43 and in Rogers 1855–57, 1:11–13, there are already some minor variations in the text. In the Burns MS (Dick 1962: 51), the third line, for example, is "What nonsense is't for folks to chide" where Skinner's original has "What signifies't for folks to chide," indicating that alterations were already current in oral tradition. Moffat 1895 has a note on the associations of "Whig-mig-morum" in Skinner's eighth line of verse 1. Both Dauney and Stenhouse speculate on the tune's origin. The former traces it to "Corn Bunting" in the Guthrie MS 1675–80 and to "Ouir the dek [dyke?] Davy" from the Rowallan MS 1628 (Dauney 1838: 142, 139). Stenhouse 1853: 282 sees a resemblance to "Jockie's fow and Jenny fain" in Adam Craig's collection of 1730; Glen 1900: 180 denies this connection. The first version of the tune under its present name is in Bremner's 1757–61 *Collection of Scots Reels or Country Dances*. There is a version in the Drummond Castle MS of 1734, and it appears frequently in later collections such as those of Gillespie 1768, Cumming 1780, Aird 1782–1803, and Joshua Campbell 1786. In his manuscript, Greig makes the following observation on the tune's origin: "This famous Reel takes its name from a district on the banks of the River Spey, where the Tullaichghorm, or green hillock, is situated, upon which the people probably assembled to join in the evening dance." What may be the earlier Gaelic words, or a variant of them, are printed in Alexander MacDonald 1922, 29:103; see these in Gower and Porter 1977: 88. David Johnson 1972: 91–92 has an amusing anecdote concerning what must be considered Jeannie's explanation of some words in the song, "Whig and Tory." Unlike printed versions of the tune, in which the final note is the second degree of the scale, Jeannie's orally-acquired variant ends on the third degree.

Recorded versions: SA 1953/197/234/246; 1955/175; 1962/75; Jazz selection JES 1.

Additional references: Buchan and Hall 1973: 57.

24. Jimmie Drummond

For my name it is young Jimmy Drummond,
I'm a man that youse a' know quite well;
I was quickly handcuffed and shackled
    And I was led to poor owld Dan'l's jail.

For I quickly did alter my colours
When I had one round twelve-month in jail;
For I quickly did alter my colours
    When I was led to poor owld Dan'l's jail.

But it's nae mair I'll bing a-chorin'
For I swear to my God 'at's above,
And whenever the hornies[3] bings on me
    They'll have no one to snatch but mysel'.

24. Jimmie Drummond

The composer of this song, according to Jeannie, was a man whose "true name was Jimmie Drummond and he was a far-off relation of my Grannie's. He is supposed to have made the song himself and sung it in jail." The prison referred to in the first two stanzas may be Arran's, Oldham's, Derry's, or, more likely, Dublin's jail. The song is not related to any of the English or North American songs with the title, "Durham Jail." Two recent text variants, with tunes unrelated to Jeannie's or to each other, have been published. One is "The Choring Song," collected from travellers at Saint Fillans, Perthshire, in 1956 by John Brune (Kennedy 1975: 768). The other is "Big Jimmie Drummond," sung by Willie McPhee (MacColl and Seeger 1977: 295–97). The mention of "Erin's Green Isle" in the first of these versions suggests Irish influence, for, as Belle Stewart has related, many Scots travellers went back and forth (SA 1972/235). There is also an echo of the piece in Greig's manuscript entitled "The Deserter" (see Buchan and Hall 1973: 14–15).

For her air, Jeannie adopts the first half of "Rosin the Bow (or Beau)," a tune found widely in Ireland and North America (there are also traces of it in the Hebrides; see Gower and Porter 1977: 98). Hardiman, in his *Irish Minstrelsy* (1831), remarks that

---

"few of our national airs are better known than *Youghal Harbour*," under which title the tune is familiar in Ireland, though other names (such as "Owen Coir") are common (O'Sullivan 1960: 155–56; cf. Joyce 1909: 340, 233–34). It is adapted to "The Boys of Kilmichael" in Healy 1965: 102–4 and O'Canainn 1978: 50–51. The words of "Youghal Harbour," however, are matched to the "Boolavogue" tune by O Lochlainn 1939: 16. Printed as a stall ballad by Ryles of Seven Dials, the song "Rosin the Bow" may refer to "Now Robin, lend me thy bow," a canon published in *Pammelia* (1609).

The theme of "Rosin the Bow" in latter-day tradition concerns a dying fiddler or toper who instructs his comrades how to celebrate his passing, paralleling the general denouement of the "Unfortunate Rake/Streets of Laredo" cycle. The tune, perhaps through association, often has been used for songs with a tone of regret or misfortune, or for parodies of these.

Recorded versions: SA 1952/33; 1962/73.

Additional references: *A Collection of Scots Songs* (1972: 30); Hall 1975: 57.

25. Twa Recruitin' Sergeants

Twa recruitin' sergeants frae the Black Watch,
  Markets an' fairs some recruits for to catch;
An' a' that they 'listed was forty an' twa,
  So 'list, bonnie laddie, an' come awa'.

Refrain:
It is over the mountains an' over the main,
  Through Gibraltar and France and Spain;
Get a feather tae your bonnet and a kilt abeen your knee,
  Enlist, bonnie laddie, an' come awa' wi' me.

O laddie, ye dinna ken the danger that ye're in,
  If your horses wis tae fleg an' your owsens wis tae rin;
An' this greedy aul' fairmer winna pey your fee,
  So 'list, bonnie laddie, an' come awa' wi' me.

It is intae the barn an' oot o' the byre,
  This aul' fairmer thinks you'll never tire;
It is a slavery job of low degree,
  So 'list, bonnie laddie, an' come awa' wi' me.

Wi' your tattie poorin's an' your meal an' kail,
  Wi' your sooer sowen soorins an' your ill-brewed ale;
Wi' your buttermilk an' whey an' your breid fired raa,
  So 'list, bonnie laddie, an' come awa'.

O, laddie, if you've got a sweethert an' bairn,
  Ye'll easily get rid o' that ill-spun yarn,
Twa rattles o' the drum an' that will pey it a',
  So 'list, bonnie laddie, an' come awa'.

25. Twa Recruitin' Sergeants

This version became popular in the Folksong Revival, especially in the clubs, as a result of Jeannie's singing. Lizzie also performed the song at the 1969 Edinburgh Folk Festival (Stephanie Smith 1975: 235). A. L. Lloyd 1967: 253 reported that it returned to circulation in English cities, probably under the influence of Jeannie's or John Strachan's recordings. Words similar to those of the refrain appear in George Farquhar's play, *The Recruiting Officer* (1706). Pointing to the text in D'Urfey's *Wit and Mirth: Or Pills to Purge Melancholy* (1959 [1719–20], 4:319) that is related to the present words, Stenhouse suggests a link with "The Elfin Knight" by way of "Over the Hills and Far Away" tune (1853: 63–64; Bronson 1959–72, 1:9, 1:14–15). The refrain part of the tune here is a transformation of the *Pills* melody, "Jockey's Lamentation," which was selected by John Gay for "Were I Laid on Greenland's Coast" in *The Beggar's Opera* (1728). Alluding to the air as an old pipe tune called "O'er the Hills and Far Awa," Stenhouse 1853 apparently had a manuscript copy "of considerable antiquity." Glen 1900: 77 mentions the presence of a tune, "My Plaid Away," in the Sinkler MS of 1710. The closest melodic variant to Jeannie's tune is Bronson's no. 11 from the Greig MS, 2:25, with the title "Twas in that year" and the refrain "We'll over the hills and far awa'." Although the first published verses date from the time of Queen Anne, reference to the Black Watch Regiment is found in a version printed by Greig 1963: 176, but not in the rendering by John Strachan, which updates the setting to Queen Victoria's era. The early form of the song as a recruiting one is discussed by Winstock 1970. As prize enlisting ground for the British Army's colonial exercises during the eighteenth and nineteenth centuries, the Northeast through its singers developed the song's local character. Central to the theme is the promise of freedom from drudgery and domestic cares. Jeannie's text and tune are in Dallas 1972: 18–20.

Recorded versions: SA 1962/203; Selection JES 4001; John Strachan, Caedmon TC 1164/Topic 12T96.

Additional references: Hogg 1821: 77–78; Kennedy and Lomax 1961; Shuldham-Shaw and Lyle 1981: 178–79, 516.

26. The Handsome Cabin Boy (Laws N13)

It's of a pretty fair maid, to let youse understand,
  She had a mind for rovin' to some foreign land;
  She dressed herself in sailor's clothes and boldly did appear,
  Engagin' with a captain givin' service for a year.

For the wind it bein' in favor and they soon set off to sea,
  For the lady to the captain said, "My love, I wish you joy,
  That we have engaged such a handsome cabin boy."

For his cheeks appeared like roses and his side-locks they did curl,
  And oftentimes the sailors smiled and said he lookit like a girl;
  But by eatin' cabin biscuits his colors did destroy,
  And the wyme did swell o' pretty Bill our handsome cabin boy.

"O doctor, dear doctor," for the cabin boy did cry,
  The sailors swore with all their might that the cabin boy would die;
  But the doctor run with all his might, he was smilin' at the fun,
  For to think a sailor lad would have a dochter or a son.

But when the sailors heard the joke thay a' began to stare,
    "For the child belongs to none of us," a' solemn they did swear;
    "But the lady and the captain they have oftimes kissed and toyed,
    And we'll soon find out the secret of our handsome cabin boy."

For they a' took up a bumper and they drunk success to trade:
    "It's twice unto this cabin boy she's neither man nor maid;
    But if this war should rise again our sailors to destroy,
    And we'll ship some able seamen same's our handsome cabin boy."

Through the Bay of Biscay our gallant ship did plough,
    And that night the sailors they kicked up a bloomin' row;
    They took their bundles from their hammocks and the rest they
        did destroy,
    And it was all through the groanin' of our handsome cabin boy.

26. The Handsome Cabin Boy (Laws N13)

Jeannie's various renderings of this broadside ballad show the same structural fluidity as her text of "Young Emslie" (see Laws 1957: 209). In another performance of the song, she did include the initial line of verse 2 that was omitted on SA 1952/33. In her studio recording in 1958 (JES 8) the final stanza, printed here, was omitted entirely, perhaps for reasons of length or timing. A textual variant from the singing of Jimmie Brown of Muir of Fowlis (Buchan and Hall 1973: 115, basically that of Ord 1930: 160), has the same flexible sequence of verses: verse 1 is almost the same, as is verse 2, except that in Brown's version it is clear that "the lady" is the captain's woman ("wife" is not specified). Brown's verse 3 has "Sae nimbly as this pretty maid, she did her duty well/And mark what follows after, the song itself will tell." At this point, Brown's next stanza is the "Bay of Biscay" one, placed last in Jeannie's version; Brown's third line is "They tumbled from their hammocks and it did their rest annoy." The "doctor" stanza then follows, similarly. Brown's verse 6 concludes, "The lady tae the captain said: My dear I wish you joy/ It's either you or I betrayed the handsome cabin boy." The final "bumper" verses then end both seven-stanza versions. See discussion of the type in Dugaw 1989. Brown's tune is not, however, Jeannie's. The air as sung here is related to variants A and B (Somerset), printed in Horn of Aberdeen for "The Soldier Maid" (Buchan and Hall 1973: 134–35) and commonly known in Scotland and elsewhere as "Johnson's Motor Car."

Recorded versions: SA 1952/33; 1953/195; 1954/72; 1957/107; 1958/182; 1959/107/108; Selection JES 8; Caedmon TC 1162/Topic 12T194; Martin Carthy, Fontana STL 5269.

Additional references: Dugaw 1989; Greig MS 1909–14, 2:61; Ord 1930: 160; Purslow 1965: 32; Shuldham-Shaw and Lyle 1981: 486–87, 544. *Spin* 5, no. 4: 18–19; Wehse 1979: 305–6.

27. Harlaw (The Battle o' Harlaw, Child 163)

As I cam' by the Garioch land,
    An' doun by Netherha';
There were fifty thoosan' Hielan'men
    A-marchin' tae Harlaw.

Refrain:
Singin' diddie-aye-O
Sing fa-la-doh
Sing diddie-aye-O-aye-ay.

"It's did ye come fae the Hielan's, man,
    An' did ye come a' the wey?
An' did ye see MacDonal' an' his men
    As they marched fae Skye?"

"It's I cam' fae the Hielan's, man,
    An' I cam' a' the wey;
An' I sa' MacDonal' an' his men
    As they marched fae Skye."

"It's wis ye near or near enough,
    Did ye their number see?
Come tell tae me, John Hielan' man,
    What might their number be?"

"For I wis near or near enough,
    An' I their number sa';
There were fifty thoosand Hielan'men
    A-marchin' tae Harlaw."

For they went on an' furder on,
    An' doun in by Balquhain;
It's there they met Sir James the Rose,
    Wi' him Sir John the Grame.

"If that be true," said Sir James the Rose,
    "We'll no' come muckle speed;
We will caal upon wir merry men,
    An' we'll turn wir horses' heid."

"O nay, O nay," said Sir John the Grame,
    "Sic things we mauna dee;
For the gallant Grames were never bate,
    An' we'll try fit they can dee."

They went on an' furder on,
    An' doun in by Harlaw;
The' fell full close on ilka side,
    Sic strikes ye never sa'.

The' fell full close on ilka side,
    Sic strikes ye never sa';
For ilkae sword gaed clash for clash
    At the Battle o' Harlaw.

The Hielan'men wi' their lang swords,
    They laid on us full sair;
The' drove back wir merry men,
    Three acres breadth an' mair.

Lord Forbes to his brother did say:
    "O brither, dinna ye see?
The' beat us back on every side,
    An' we'll be forced to flee."

"O nay, O nay, my brother dear,
    O nay, that mauna be;
For you'll tak' your guid sword in your hand,
    An' ye'll gang in wi' me."

For the' two brithers brave,
    Went in amangst the thrang;
They swope doun the Hielan'men
    Wi' swords baith sharp an' lang.

The first strike Lord Forbes gied,
   The brave MacDonal' reeled;
The second strike Lord Forbes gied,
   The brave MacDonal' fell.

What a cry amongst the Hielan'men,
   When they see'd their leader fa';
They lifted him an' buried him
   A lang mile fae Harlaw.

27. Harlaw (The Battle o' Harlaw, Child 163)

Jeannie described the climax of the battle thus:

> Well, of course, the Highlandmen was winnin' that battle. But when they saw
> their leader fa' they lost hert. And of course they liftit him an' they run. But if
> they'd ha kep' on they certainly would have won the Battle of Harlaw. But after
> the battle was fought they said that the blood was runnin' on the roads like
> water, from the Highlandmen. (SA 1953/236)

David Buchan 1968 has argued that this ballad text, far from retaining "very little of
sober history," as Child asserted, must be viewed through the eyes of the Lowland
attitude toward Highlanders, especially because of the change that took place in that
attitude between the battles of Harlaw (1411) and Culloden (1746). Echoes of the later
battle, which set in motion final destruction of the paternalistic clan system and the
Stuart claim to the British throne, run through some texts (e.g., the mention of
Redcoats), and there is a glimpse of the brutality of Culloden in Jeannie's gloss cited
above. If the ballad is approached in this way, free from the preconceptions of historio-
graphical "truth," then the ballad narrative can be seen to reflect the pattern of events
in the battle, though filtered through the Lowland imagination. The modern texts we
have from the Northeast (e.g., Greig and Keith 1925, Greig MS 1909–14) all appear to
stem from the hypothetical full text collected by Alexander Laing, only three stanzas of
which are in Child's B-text (Laing was a chapman who sold chap texts throughout the
area). An older ballad clearly existed, as references in *The Complaynt of Scotland* (1549)
and Drummond of Hawthornden's *Polemo-Middiana* (1684) attest. A tune is in the
Rowallan MS of 1620. Bronson 1959-72 (4:494) with some justification, connects
Stenhouse's folio MS "of considerable antiquity" (1853: 447) to the tune called "Gray
Steel" in the Macfarlan MS (ca. 1740) and to its earlier version "Pitt on your Shirt on
Monday" in the Skene MS (ca. 1625), of around the same period as the Rowallan.
These instrumental variants suggest a song and tune tradition from at least the beginning of the seventeenth century, almost two hundred years before the recorded textual
tradition. Jeannie's tune, the usual one known in the Northeast, follows a jaunty 6/8
pipe march rhythm with short snaps that occasionally lend the illusion of common
time (as in the opening stanza; see Bronson 1959–72, 3:122, variants 10 and 11).

Lizzie uses the same tune for her version of Child 110, "I'm a Forester in This Wood" ("The Knight and the Shepherd's Daughter"; Stephanie Smith 1975: 271).

Recorded versions: SA 1953/236/247; SA 1959/85; 1961/44; SX 1956/4; 1957/1/3; 1958/12; 1960/20; Lucy Stewart, Caedmon TC1146/Topic 12T161.

Additional references: Bronson 1959–72, 4:494; Buchan 1984: 166–68; Buchan and Hall 1973: 132–33; Child 1882–98, 3:316–20; Greig 1963: 11; William Mackay 1921; Ord 1930: 473–75; Shuldham-Shaw and Lyle 1981: 302–13, 527–28.

28. The Bonnie Hoose o' Airlie (Child 199)

For it fell upon a day and a bonnie summer's day,
   When the clans were awa' wi' Chairlie;
When there fell oot a great dispute
   Between Argyll and Airlie.

Lady Ogilvie looked frae her high castle wall,
   And O but she sighed sairly;
For to see Argyll and a' his men
   Come to plunder the bonnie Hoose o' Airlie.

"Come doun, come doun, Lady Ogilvie," he cried,
   "Come doun and kiss me fairly;
For ere this mornin' clear's daylight
   I will no' leave a stan'in stane o Airlie.

"For I wadnae come doun, you false lord," she cried,
   "Nor wad I kiss thee fairly;
I wadna come doun, you false Argyll
   Suppose you dinnae leave a stan'in' stane o' Airlie."

"For if my good lord he was at hame,
   As this night he's awa' wi' Chairlie;
For it's no' Argyll and a' his men
   That would plunder the bonnie Hoose o' Airlie."

"For I have reared him seven bonnie sons,
   And it's the last time they'll e'er see their Daddie;
But gin I had as mony owre again,
   They wad a' be to follow Chairlie."

28. The Bonnie Hoose o' Airlie (Child 199)
Older travellers sang this ballad when Jeannie was young. She regretted not remember-ing "all the verses." Lizzie, for her part, picked it up most probably from hearing Jeannie and Maria sing it, though she also learned a version at school. This polite version did not appeal to her, and on the whole she thought the song lengthy and tiresome (Stephanie Smith 1975: 164). Jeannie's singing contributes marginally more to the story than Lizzie's five stanzas. Ford 1901: 296–99, who prints a longer account of the historical associations than Child, asserts that Forter, not Airlie, is the scene of the dialogue. Jeannie's version, further, moves the action forward to the period of the 1745 Uprising, probably because of the strong support given to Prince Charles Edward Stuart by Lord Ogilvie and his wife (cf. Child 1882–98, 4:55). The Castle of Forter was razed, but not until the Campbells held possession of it for several months (Ford 1901: 169). Jeannie's and Lizzie's tune, the familiar "Loch Lomond" modification from the original, can be added to Bronson's Group B (8–11).

Recorded versions: SA 1952/43; Lizzie Higgins, SA 1970/22; Lucy Stewart, Folkways FG 3519; Belle Stewart, SA 1956/120, Topic 12T180.

Additional references: Bronson 1959–72, 3:191–97; Coffin 1977: 118–19; MacColl and Seeger 1977: 89–91; Ord 1930: 470; Shuldham-Shaw and Lyle 1983: 170–75, 541–42; *Tocher* 21 (1976): 174–75 (Belle Stewart).

29. I Hae ae Bit Son

I hae ae bit son, my gallant young Donald,
    Although I had ten, they'd a' follow Glengarry;
Here's health to MacDonald, and the brave Clanranald,
    For these are the men that would fight for their Chairlie.

I'll tae Lochiel, an' I'll bow an' I'll kneel to him,
    Down by Lord Murray, and Roy of Kildarlie;
There's a brave MacIntosh to the field he will fly with them,
    For these are the men that would die for their Chairlie.

29. I Hae ae Bit Son
These stanzas form the second and third verses of James Hogg's Jacobite-inspired
"Bonnie Prince Charlie" ("Cam' Ye by Atholl?"). Wed to music by Neil Gow, Jr., the
song was published in Hogg, *The Border Garland,* as one of nine songs. Four of these
were set to music by Hogg himself, three "by a friend of the Editor" and two adapted to
old airs (see Graham 1861: 75). The work ran to only one octavo number. According
to J. Muir Wood (Graham 1908: 351), a folio edition of the *Garland* was brought out
some years later (ca. 1829), with three additional songs. In this edition, the music was
arranged by James Dewar (1793–1846), composer of an overture to Scott's *The Anti-
quary* and author of *Popular National Melodies* (1826 et seq.). In Jeannie's variant, sung
to the original tune, the refrain is omitted. In her second stanza, the line in Hogg, "I'll
tae Lochiel, and Appin, and kneel to them," has been transformed, possibly because
Appin was not a place name with which Jeannie or her source was familiar.

Recorded versions: SA 1957/44; Prestige International 13075.

Additional references: Farmer 1947: 420.

30. The Golden Victory (The Golden Vanity, Child 286)

There lies a ship in the North Countrie,
    An' the name o' that ship is "The Golden Victory";
An' the name o' that ship is "The Golden Victory,"
    But we'll sink her to the lowlands low.

For up spoke the captain, an' up spoke he:
    "Is there any man on board who will sink this ship for me?
Is there any man on board who will sink this ship for me,
    Who will sink her to the lowlands low?"

For up spoke the cabin-boy, an' up spoke he:
    "What will you give to me if I sink this ship for thee?
What will you give to me if I sink this ship for thee,
    If I sink her to the lowlands low?"

"For I will give you silver and I will give you gold,
    Besides my youngest daughter if you turn bold;
Besides my youngest daughter if you turn bold,
    If you sink her to the lowlands low."

"I neither want your silver or neither want your gold,
    But I'll take your youngest daughter if I turn bold;
I'll take your youngest daughter if I turn bold,
    If I sink her to the lowlands low."

He bendit his breast with a dagger in his hand,
    An' off he did go for to let the water in;

An' off he did go for to let the water in,
    For to sink her to the lowlands low.

Some was playin' dominoes and others playin' draughts,
    An' the water comin' in gave them all a great styte;
An' the water comin' in gave them all a great styte,
    But he sunk her to the lowlands low.

He bendit his breast an' back he did come,
    Roarin', "Captain, dear captain, it's will ye let me in?
Roarin', "Captain, dear captain, it's will ye let me in?
    For I've sunk her to the lowlands low."

30. The Golden Victory (The Golden Vanity, Child 286)

Maria was the source of this ballad for both Jeannie and Lizzie, who seem to have learned it separately when they were young. In Lizzie's case, it was a number that she sang with her grandmother at family events in the latter's house at 32 Ardarroch Place, Aberdeen (Stephanie Smith 1975: 50, 285n). Ford 1899: 108 relates how John Wilson ("Christopher North," 1785–1854) used to sing it "at convivial gatherings, to the supreme delight of his companions," a fact that led him to suspect Wilson's hand in some recreation of the text. Whether or not this was the case, variations of the ballad plot usually hinge on the fate of the cabin boy who offers to sink the enemy ship (cf. Abrahams 1970: 11, for the plot version of the singer Almeda Riddle, in which the cruel captain's ship is also sunk). In Jeannie's text, the instrument of destruction is a dagger (this stanza is omitted by Lizzie), while the treacherous ending of Lizzie's version is not present in Jeannie's (cf. Munro 1970: 179–81). Jeannie's air is a close relative of that in Bronson, *Traditional Tunes*, volume 4, nos. 33, 34. These belong to a widespread subgroup (Ab) spanning the Northeast, southern England, and Maine and Vermont. An identifying feature is the major mode, often with a prominent seventh degree in accented position. The dominant meter in English variants is 6/8; the others, like Jeannie's, generally are cast in common time. The opening of the Macmath MS variant (55) may indicate a transitional phase between Bronson's Ab, Ac, and Ad subgroups.

Recorded versions: SA 1957/44; Lizzie Higgins, SA 1970/22.

Additional references: Bronson 1959–72, 4:312–62, 511–12; Child 1882–98, 5:135–42; Coffin 1977: 153–55; Greig 1963: 116; MacColl and Seeger 1977: 65; Shuldham-Shaw and Lyle 1981: 83–86; 507–8.

31. The Deadly Wars

For the deadly wars they are past an' blaan,
   An' gentle peace returnin';
It left many's a sweet babe fatherless,
   An' many's a widow mournin'.

I left the line and the tented field,
   Whaur I'm no lang a lodger;
A humble knapsack, it's a' my will,
   I'm a poor but honest sodger.

For a lea–licht hert was in my breast,
   My hands unstained wi' plunder;
An' a' for Scottie hame again
   I cheery on did wander.

I thought upon the banks of Coil,
   I thought upon my Nancy;
I thought upon the bewitching smile,
   That caught my youthful fancy.

31. The Deadly Wars
Burns is said to have written the verses of this song after hearing a poor soldier relate his experiences in a little inn at Brownhill, Nithsdale. As has often been pointed out, Burns was sufficiently close to the *Volksgeist* to capture its spirit and formal expression with equal skill (cf. Keith 1922: 83). He regretted, however, that there was so little of the Scots language in this song that "the mere English singer will find no difficulty" (letter

to George Thomson, April 1793). His original text, of which Jeannie here sings only the first two verses in the form of quatrains, runs to eight octaves, and was contributed to Thomson's *A Select Collection of Original Scotish Airs* (1793). Some reshaping of the words is apparent in her version, but in general, the form, content, and linear development of motifs are maintained. She uses the first half of the popular eighteenth–century tune, "The Mill, Mill O," published in the 1725 edition of Thomson's *Orpheus Caledonius*, though Stenhouse 1853: 225 reports seeing it in the now–lost Crocket MS of 1709. The air was borrowed by Gay for his song, "When Gold Is on Hand," in *Polly* (1729). Christie 1876-81, and Greig and Keith 1925 publish it in association with the ballad "The Earl o' Aboyne" (Child 235). The old text attached to the tune was ribald (see Hecht 1904: 115, 287; Legman 1965: 73–74). Some of the words were introduced in Cromek 1808, the *Reliques*. Ramsay's verses to the tune, in *The Scots Musical Museum* (James Johnson 1790: 250), are no more than a mild bowdlerization of the older text (cf. Dick 1962: 455).

Recorded versions: SA 1960/200; Caedmon TC 1154/Topic 12T196; Prestige International 13006.

Additional references: Christie 1876–81; Greig and Keith 1925.

32. MacCrimmon's Lament

Round Coolin's peak the mist is sailing,
    The banshee croons her note of wailing;
But my aal' blue een with sorrow are streaming,
    For him that shall never return, MacCrimmon(d).

Refrain:
No more, no more, no more forever,
    In war or peace shall return MacCrimmon(d);
No more, no more, no more forever,
    Shall love or gold bring back MacCrimmon(d).

The beasts on the brae is mournfully mournin',
  The brook in the hollow is plaintively mournin',
 But my all' blue een with sorrow are streaming,
   For him that shall never return, MacCrimmon(d).

32. MacCrimmon's Lament

Jeannie learned this song "long, long ago off one of my people" (SA 1954/88). The tune appears to be an adaptation of thematic elements in "Cha till MacCruimean," a *ceol mor* (*piobaireachd*) tune said to have been composed by Donald McCrimmon, a member of the famous family, hereditary pipers to Clan McLeod, who was killed at the Rout of Moy in the Jacobite Uprising of 1745–46. Pibroch songs (sung items deriving from classical pibroch tunes) often have been conserved into recent times, such that they are better known than the original instrumental pieces (cf. Collinson 1966: 195–96), and Lowland travellers came into contact with these through the bagpipe music of their Highland cousins. Versions of the song in Gaelic are also extant; see that of Mrs. Archie MacDonald in the *Scottish Tradition* disc series. Whatever its ultimate origin, the tune here did not appear in print until 1884, in Colin Brown's *The Thistle*. The Gaelic words may or may not have been the work of MacCrimmon himself. His sister is a possible author (cf. Blackie 1876: 199; Humble 1934: 69; Blankenhorn 1977). The words may have entered oral tradition fairly rapidly. Scott versified the basic story for Alexander Campbell, *Albyn's Anthology* (1818, 2:54), with a final verse that Lizzie has added to Jeannie's two stanzas and refrain (Stephanie Smith 1975: 216–20). The version in English most widely sung is that by Blackie 1876: 299–300. These constitute the transitional text of the Higgins-Robertson family variants, plus, in Lizzie's case, the Scott stanzas.

Recorded versions: SA 1954/88/105; 1955/48/154; Topic 12T52 (12T96); 12T181; Riverside RLP 12-633; Lizzie Higgins, SA 1970/78; Mrs. Archie MacDonald, Tangent TNGM 110.

Additional references: A. Campbell 1816–18; D. Campbell 1862; Mackay 1838; Blankenhorn 1977.

33. The Gallowa' Hills

For I'll tak' my plaidie contented to be,
  A wee bittie kilted abune my knee;
An' I'll gie my pipes anither blaw,
  An' I'll gang oot owre the hills tae Gallowa'.

Refrain:
For the Gallowa' hills are covered wi' broom,
  Wi' heather bells an' bonnie dunes;
Wi' heather bells and rivers raur,
  An' I'll gang oot owre the hills tae Gallowa'.

For I say, bonnie lass, it's will you come wi' me,
  To share your lot in a strange countrie;
To share your lot when doun fa's a',
  An' I'll gang oot owre the hills tae Gallowa'.

For I'll sell my rock, I'll sell my reel,
  I'll sell my grannie's spinnin' wheel;
I'll sell tham a' when doun fa's a',
  An' I'll gang oot owre the hills tae Gallowa'.

33. The Gallowa' Hills

Because her son Jeemsie often asked for this song as a lullaby, it became one of Jeannie's favorites. Lizzie, who learned the song from her mother (who in turn got it from Maria), has transposed the second and third stanzas in at least one rendering (Stephanie Smith 1975: 233). The text has an affinity with "The Braes of Galloway," a poem by William Nicholson (1782–1849), published in his *Tales in Verse, and Miscellaneous Poems Descriptive of Rural Life and Manners* (1814), and subsequently by Struthers in *The Harp of Caledonia* (1819) and in Rogers 1856: 65–66. Nicholson, who had been a peddler and cattle drover, latterly became something of a gaberlunzie, playing his bagpipes at convivial gatherings for snuff and whisky. His song may be modeled on a traditional item now lost. Jeannie's first and second stanzas correspond roughly to Nicholson's fifth and first. The direction in Nicholson's works, that the poem be sung to "The White Cockade," suggests that a Jacobite song may lurk in the background (Norman Buchan 1962: 154). Herd 1776: 179–80, in fact, prints a verse of "Rantin,' roarin' laddie" with the "rock and reel" image that Charles Kirkpatrick Sharpe, in his *Ballad Book* (1824), notes is "from Perthshire":

> I sold my rock, I sold my reel.
> And sae hae I my spinning wheel,
> And a' to buy a cap of steel
> For Dickie Macphalion that's slain!
> Shoo, shoo, shoolaroo. . . .

A letter by Sir Walter Scott to Miss Sophia Edgeworth notes that singing a variant set of words to "a very beautiful Irish air." Dickie Macphalion, the subject of this dirge, was probably a Captain of Raparees (Grierson 1935: 90-91). Redfern Mason 1911: 268 characterizes the Raparees as rural guerrilla warriors, being named after the long pike that they used. One was the famous Eamonn a Chnuic, or Edmund Ryan, the seventeenth-century hero from Tipperary. The song "Schule aroon" or "Shule agra" often contains the "rock and reel" line in its English or macaronic versions (cf. Mason 1911: 267). It is possible that Scots travellers came into contact with "Shule aroon" in their Irish travels and adapted the "rock and reel" verse to "The Gallowa' Hills" anterior to Nicholson's poem. There are two tunes and one text in Greig's MS. 1909–14.

Recorded versions: SA 1953/239; 1955/154; 1955/177; 1956/169; 1959/76/77/82/83; 1960/110; 1961/44; SX 1958/5; Jazz Selection JES 1; Lizzie Higgins, private recording by Stephanie Smith, 1969; see also recordings of "Shule Agra" by Peg Clancy Power, Folk Legacy FSE-8; and Elizabeth Cronin, TC 1142/Topic 12T157.

Additional references: Gower and Porter 1977: 80–82.

34. Bonnie Glenshee

Refrain

Refrain:
For it's busk, busk, bonnie lassie,
   And it's will you gang wi' me?
And I'll tak' you tae Glenisla
   Near bonnie Glenshee.

For it's do you see yon high hills,
   Now the're cover'd wi' sna'?
There has pairted many's a sweethert,
   An' we'll soon part us twa.

Refrain:
Sayin', busk, busk, bonnie lassie,
    And it's will you gang wi' me?
And I'll tak' you tae Glenisla
    Near bonnie Glenshee.

For it's do you see that shepherd,
    How he marches along?
With his plaidie all around him
    And his sheep he looks upon?

34. Bonnie Glenshee

"I've heard it all my days. I heard it amongst people that came from Perthshire" (SA 1954/104). Jeannie may well have encountered this song first when she lived as a child in Blairgowrie, on the Perthshire side of the Grampian Mountains. The local landmarks in the text, with its direct and nonliterary flavor, have made the song popular among both Perthshire and Northeast travellers. MacColl and Seeger 1977: 143–44 print a version sung by Charlotte Higgins, who was born in Aberdeenshire but settled in Blairgowrie; she died in 1971. Her text and tune are close to Jeannie's, as are the versions recorded by Belle and Cathie Stewart. Belle, who learned the song from Charlotte, Cathie's mother-in-law, has her text and tune in Buchan and Hall 1973: 111. The use of bagpipes, or "goose" (chorus?), a small set of bag and chanter, by the males of the Stewart family suggests that the air has connections with the pipe march, "The Bloody Fields of Flanders" (cf. Henderson 1965). Greig 1963: 107 printed a rather literary text, "Oh No No," but it lacks the evocative refrain.

Recorded versions: SA 1954/104; 1959/106; HMV 7EG 8534; Belle Stewart, Topic 12TS307; Cathie Stewart, Topic 12T138.

35. The Fair o' Balnafannon

I wis coming from a fair,
From the fair o' Balnafannon;
When I met a winsome dame,
She was as fair as the Annan.
I asked her where she dwelt
As we strode along together:
"On the bonnie mountainside,"
She replied, "amongst the heather."

"I will build you a bower,
Down by the clear fountain;
And I'll cover it owre
Wi' the flouers o' the mountain.

I will range the mountainside,
And the dark glen so weary;
And I'll bring a' my spoil
To the bower o' my dearie."

35. The Fair o' Balnafannon

Jeannie learned this song "from a young man in Aberdeen who died about thirteen years ago" (SA 1954/104). Robert Tannahill's "Braes o' Balquhither" (1815: 116–17) has some relationship to Jeannie's text, though only in the second stanza. The first stanza seems to be part of an independent creation that has analogs in the Greig and Duncan MSS, where ten versions of the text are wedded to tunes different from Jeannie's (Shuldham-Shaw and Lyle 1990). Duncan (362) appends a note to a variant: "The word here given was 'Balminna.' There is a 'Balmanno' in Kincardine and another in Perthshire." Morton 1970: 7 prints a variant text with the first lines, "As I was coming from the fair at Ballymoney-O/ I met a comely lass, she was fairer than Diana-O." This posits a close link with Ulster versions of the song. The complex of songs and texts often supposed to belong to a single "love among the heather" type actually shows considerable variation in style if not in plot. Some are cast in the form of an invitation (e.g., "Braes o' Balquhither," "Bonnie Glenshee"), while others depict an encounter that precedes the invitation ("Queen among the Heather," "Up a Wide and Lonely Glen"). The "invitation" subtype crystallized, during the Folksong Revival, in a variant made familiar by Frank McPeake of Belfast ("Wild Mountain Thyme"; cf. Kennedy 1975: 334). The words formed the model for William Allingham's poem, "Among the Heather" (1877).

Recorded versions: SA 1954/104; Selection JES 4001; Folktracks FSA 067; Lizzie Higgins, Topic 12T185; Betsy Miller, Folk Lyric FL-116.

Additional reference: Shuldham-Shaw and Lyle 1990: 385–93, 567–68.

36. Bonnie Lass Come Owre the Burn

> O bonnie lass, come owre the burn,
> I'm the lad'll dae your turn;
> O dinna ye stand there and mourn,
> And what's the deevil ails ye?
> O bonnie lass, come owre the street,
> I am the faither o' your geet,
> O dinna ye stand there an' greet,
> And what's the deevil ails ye?

36. Bonnie Lass Come Owre the Burn

A more polite version of this song appears in Struthers, *The Harp of Caledonia* (1819) with four quatrains. Together with the three-stanza one, further expurgated, printed by R. A. Smith in the fifth volume of *The Scotish Minstrel* (1828: 26), it probably derives from the words written by the Reverend James Honeyman of Kinneff, Kincardineshire, who died about 1779 (see Blackie 1889). The tune offered by Smith is not the present one, nor does Jeannie's air match those variously entitled "What the Devil ails you?" in Bremner's 1765 *A Collection of Scots Reels or Country Dances* or Oswald's *Caledonian Pocket Companion*, volume 10. A close variant of Jeannie's words is in Greig's MS (2:128) with her tune, under the title "Bonnie Lass": "Bonnie lass owre the street, what gar's ye stare and greet?/I'm the father o' your geet. What the sorra ails ye?". The polite version appears under the title "Hie, Bonnie Lassie" (Shuldham-Shaw and Lyle 1990: 421–22). A text and melody from Northumberland have been published recently (Gwen Polwarth and Mary Polwarth 1969: 18). The air is a near relation of Jeannie's, following the general melodic curve but beginning on the tonic rather than the lower fifth:

Bonny lass come over the water,
  Divn't stand there and guam.
I've come the day instead of the morn,
  What's the divil ails ye?

See also Buchan and Hall 1973: 70 for a transcription of words and tune.

Recorded versions: SA 1952/33; 1959/74/76/82; 1960/200; Jazz Selection JES 1; Prestige International 13075; Enoch Kent, Topic 12T128, TOP 81.

Additional references: Gower and Porter 1977.

37. Tak' the Buckles Frae Your Sheen

Tak' the buckles frae your sheen, bonnie lassie O,
    Tak' the buckles frae your sheen, for your dancin' days are deen,
For your dancin' days are deen, bonnie lassie O.

Tak' the flounces frae your goun, bonnie lassie O,
    Tak' the flounces frae your goun, mak' a frockie tae your loon,
Mak' a frockie tae your loon, bonnie lassie O.

Dae ye min' on Glesca Green, bonnie lassie O?
    Dae ye min' on Glesca Green, when I played on your machine?
Dae ye min' on Glesca Green, bonnie lassie O?

37. Tak' the Buckles Frae Your Sheen
These verses are a later variant of the traditional song, "O the Shearin's No' for You,"
from which John Sim and Thomas Lyle cobbled the sentimental text of "Kelvin Grove"
(see Graham 1908: 285). The words of "Kelvin Grove" first appeared in *The Harp of
Renfrewshire* (1819), the editor of which was none other than the ballad collector
William Motherwell. It seems that Lyle wrote the first draft of the text, while Sim, who
died shortly after *The Harp* was published, made additions and alterations. The tune
was included in R. A. Smith's *Scotish Minstrel* (1821), where it is called "Kelvin Water,"
the original title and words now replaced ("deservedly forgotten" is Graham's comment,
in 1861: 73).

Recorded versions: SA 1955/155; Prestige International 13006; Folktracks FSA 067.

38. Rolling in the Dew

"What wid ye dae if I were to lay ye doun,
  Wi' your reid and rosy cheeks and your curly black hair?"
"I'd be fit enough to rise again, kind sir," she answered me,
  Rolling in the dew mak's a milkmaid fair."

"But what wid ye dae if I were to bairn ye,
  Wi' your reid and rosy cheeks and your curly black hair?"
"For you would be the daddie o't and I would be the mither o't,
  Kind sir," she answered me,
"Rolling in the dew mak's a milkmaid fair."

38. Rolling in the Dew
Jeannie added a third stanza to her singing of the song in 1955, a year after she first recorded it. Her mother's version had "other verses" that she did not at first recall. The tune has cognates in the Gardiner MS 1907 (682, from Hampshire), in George "Pop" Maynard's variant (Stubbs 1963: 191–92), and, more distantly, in the air published in Gainer 1975: 150. A text of the song is included by Ford (1899: 149–50), who remarks that Hugh McAulay of Johnstone told him how he had learned the song "more than twenty-five years ago" from the singing of a girl named Bathgate, "who had quite a host of these simple old wandering songs." An early appearance of the theme is in a broadside (ca. 1660–70) by William Thackeray, with the title *A Merry New Dialogue between a Courteous Young Knight and a Gallant Milk Maid* (cf. Purslow 1972: 135–36). According to Opie and Opie 1951: 281–83, Thomas Tonkin, the Cornish anti-

quary, heard a version sung at Cardew in 1698. The words of this were reproduced by William Pryce in his *Archaeologia Cornu-Britannica* of 1790. In one of the earlier broadsides in the Pepys collection, the tune to "A mery new Jigge" is named "Strawberry leaves make maidens fair." It is possible, then, that a text and tune were known in Jacobean times. Burns, in discussing "The Posie" (*Caledonian Museum*, 373; see Cromek 1808), remarks how he took down a text and tune from a country girl:

> There was a pretty may and a milkin' she went;
> Wi' her red rosy cheeks, and her coal-black hair;
> And she has met a young man a-comin' o'er the bent,
> With a double and adieu to thee fair may.

For associations with Burns and Celtic tradition, see Crawford 1963: 37–46. Ritson 1802: 14 published the song "Laddy Lye Near Me," with the first stanza:

> "What if I lay thee down, lassy, my deary?"
> "Cannot I rise again? Laddy, lye near me,
> "Near me, &c."

The traditional words apparently served as an inspiration for Allingham's poem "The Milkmaid" (Allingham 1877: 134–35). Later traditional variants are listed by Kennedy 1975: 436. To them may be added those in the Riddell MS 1903: 3 and the Greig MS 1909–14, the latter with a tune, "Rolling in the Dew Mak's a Milkmaid Fair," though not the present one. Maggie McPhee's air for "The Bonnie Green Tree" is a close variant of Jeannie's (MacColl and Seeger 1977: 229–30; see also O Lochlainn 1965: 20–21).

Recorded versions: SA 1954/154; 1955/154; 1957/98/107; Selection JES 4001; George Maynard, Topic 12T286.

Additional references: Buchan 1984: 108–9; Gower and Porter 1977; Shuldham-Shaw and Lyle 1990: 203, 546.

39. The Laird o' the Denty Dounby

A lassie was milkin' her father's kye,
    When a gentleman on horseback he cam' ridin' by;
A gentleman on horseback he cam' ridin' by,
    He was the Laird o' the Denty Dounby.

"O lassie, O lassie, what wad ye gie,
    If I were to lie ae nicht wi' ye?"
"To lie ae nicht that'll never, never be
    Suppose ye're Laird o' the Denty Doonby."

But he took her by the middle sae sma',
    He laid her doon where the grass grew lang,
It was a lang, lang time till he raised her up again,
    Sayin', "Ye're lady owre the Denty Doonby."

It fell upon a day and a bonnie summer's day,
    To face the lassie's father some money had to pay;
To face the lassie's father some money had to pay,
    To the Laird o' the Denty Doonby.

"O good mornin', how dae ye do?
    And hoo is your dochter Janetie nou?
And hoo's your dochter Janetie nou
    Since I laid her in the Denty Doonby?"

"O my wee Janet she's no' very weel,
    My dochter Janet she looks unco pale;

My dochter Janet she cowks at her kail
    Since she laid her in the Denty Doonby."

But he took[4] her by the lily-white hand,
    He showed her roun' his rooms, they were twenty-one;
He placed the keys intae her hands,
    Sayin', "Ye're lady owre the Denty Doonby."

"O," says the auld man, "what wull we dae?"
    "O," says the auld wife, "we'll dance tae we dee."
"O," said the auld man, "I think I'll dae that tae
    Since she's made lady owre the Denty Doonby."

39. The Laird o' the Denty Dounby

Under the title, "The Dainty Downby," David Herd noted in his manuscript: "This song is sung to a very fine old Scots tune not hitherto published in any collection of Scots musick" (Hecht 1904: 221; Herd 1776, 2:232). In all recently published variants, the melodic character has a general resemblance to the tune of "Johnnie Cope" in *The Scots Musical Museum* (James Johnson 1790: 242–43), especially in the closing cadence of Lucy Stewart's rendering (Kennedy 1975: 407). Other published versions are in Buchan and Hall 1973: 88 (Lizzie Higgins) and MacColl and Seeger 1977: 110–12 (Maggie McPhee). Burns commented in his MS that the air for "Johnnie Cope" was the tune for the old song, "Will ye go to the coals in the morning?," published by Ritson in his *Scotish Songs* (1794). The air is in Oswald's *Caledonian Pocket Companion*, volume 11 (1759), MacLean's *Scots Tunes* (ca. 1772), and Aird's *A Selection of Scotch, English, Irish and Foreign Airs*, volume 2 (1782); see Cook, in Dick 1962: 102. While one cannot easily posit identity between the two tunes in this case, the tonal and melodic patterns are undeniably close. The plot of the song has drawn some speculation: Child associated with "The Wylie Wife of the Hie Town Hie" (his no. 290; see the note in Child 1882–98, 5:153). Greig (MS 1909–14: 35) got a version from Bell Robertson that he felt was a transformation of "The Parks o' Keltie" (Kinloch had printed songs under both titles in his 1827 collection; cf. also "The Bonnie Parks o' Kilty," in Ord 1930: 113–14). MacColl and Seeger 1977: 110 believe that the plot of Maggie McPhee's variant to be nearer to "The Broom of Cowdenknows" (Child 217). These correspondences do not necessarily imply filiation, either from Child 217 or 290 via "The Parks o' Keltie." They may all be variations on the common theme of the maiden seduced but subsequently honored by one of the minor gentry ("denty" suggests small, compact landholdings). The protagonist's taking the girl by the "lily-white hand" *after* sexual intercourse and the girl's subsequent pregnancy, not before, is notable since it reverses the usual sequence of signals.

Recorded versions: SA 1952/33; 1953/198; 1960/200; SX 1960/2; Prestige International 13006; Lizzie Higgins, Topic 12T185.

Additional references: Gower and Porter 1972; Stephanie Smith 1975.

40. The Laird o' Drum (Child 236)

The Laird o' Drum a-huntin' gaen,
    All in the mornin' early O;
An' it was there that he spied a weel fair maid,
    She was shearin' her faither's barley O.

"O lassie, wid ye fancy me,
    An' let your shearin' be O?
An' will ye gang wi' me tae the Castel o' Drum,
    An' could ye fancy me O?"

"I widnae fancy you, kind sir,
    Nor let my shearin' be O;
And I'm owre low tae be the Lady o' Drum,
    An' your miss I scorn tae be O."

"If ye'll gang tae my faither dear,
    He is shepherd in yonder hill O;
And if he gies ye hees consent,
    I will mairry ye at his wull O."

"My dochter cannae read or write,
    Tae a school she's never been O;
But weel she can tak' a coggie on her knee,
    An' she can milk the cou O."

"She'll bake your breid an' brew your ale,
　　An' gang tae the mill an' kil' O;
And in time o' need she will saddle your steed,
　　An' I can dra' your boots masel' O."

"O ye'll tak' aff that aal' grey goun,
　　Pit on the silks an' scarlets O;
An' if ye'll gang wi' me tae the Castel o' Drum,
　　Ye'll neither be miss or harlot O."

Five an' twenty noblemen
　　Stood at the gates of Drum O;
But nae a man lifted aff his hat,
　　When the Lady o' the Drum walked in O.

Up an' spoke his brither dear,
　　And a angry man wis he O;
"Ye have teen a wife below your degree,
　　Ye're a disgrace tae a' oor kin O."

"The first wife that ere I had,
　　She wis owre high abeen my degree O;
I couldnae enter the room she wis in
　　Withoot my hat abeen my knee O."

"Gin he were dead and I wis dead,
　　An' baith in one grave laid O;
Gin seven lang years were past an' gaen,
　　Wha's tae ken hees dust frae mine O?"

---

40. The Laird o' Drum (Child 236)
Jeannie probably learned this particular variant of the ballad from her husband, for Donald was known to sing it well. He himself may have become attached to it partly because of the sentiments expressed in the last verse. It is all the more surprising that Lizzie, who drew so many songs and tunes from her father's stock, had not assimilated it with confidence in 1970, when she sang three stanzas only (Stephanie Smith 1975: 145). The ballad may not have appealed to her aesthetic sense. Jeannie's air conforms readily to Bronson's class A, especially in the case of those tunes numbered from 8 to 19, with the identifying close of the first strain on the topic, and the high arch of the second strain to the upper mediant and back. Kinloch, Child, and Greig and Keith all discourse on the fortunes of the historical Laird of Drum and his marriage, in 1681 or 1682, to his lowly second wife, Margaret Coutts. According to Lizzie, the then Laird of Drum permitted Jeannie to sit in the Mary Queen of Scots Chair at the Castle

(Stephanie Smith 1975: 147). The suggestion that the ballad is parent to "love among the heather" ditties such as "The Fair o' Balnafannon" is suspect, even though these lyric songs all postdate the earliest ballad text. They share the central encounter but little else of the picturesque dénouement essential to the plot. Without direct evidence of filiation, the argument is difficult to sustain.

Recorded versions: SM 1956/2; Prestige International 13075; Lizzie Higgins, SA 1970/20; Lucy Stewart, Folkways FG 3519; Jane Turriff, Topic 12T180.

Additional references: Bronson 1959–72, 3:395–406; 4:506; Child 1882–98, 4:322–32; Coffin 1977: 135–36; Ford 1899: 4–9; Hall 1969; Henderson 1992: 38–39; Morton 1969: 6; Shuldham-Shaw and Lyle 1990: 249–66, 552–53.

41. I Will Lay You Doun

For I will lay you doun, love, I'll treat you dacent,
    I will lay you doun, love, I'll fill your can;
I will lay you doun, love, I'll treat you dacent,
    For Bolerl he is a solid man.

For as I strollt out on a summer's evening,
    Down by the waters of the pleasant Bann;
And as I was walking sure I could hear them talking,
    And saying, "Bolerl, he's a solid man."

I will lay you doun, love, I'll treat you dacent,
    I will lay you doun, love, I'll fill your can;
I will lay you doun, love, I'll treat you dacent,
    For Bolerl he is a solid man.

41. I Will Lay You Doun

Maria Stewart apparently had a number of verses for this Irish-American music-hall song with the title, "Muldoon, the Solid Man." Two of the stanzas she sang are in Dean 1922: 102–3, with this refrain:

    So come with me and I'll use you dacent,
        I'll get you drunk and I'll fill your can;
    As I walk the street each friend I meet
        Says, "There goes Muldoon, he's a solid man."

The tune is the versatile "The Galway Shawl," which Jeannie also used for "Carrbridge Castle," "Susan Pyatt," and "I Was Drunk Last Night." Several recorded versions have shown influence from her singing of the lyric (which has transformed it into a frankly erotic song). Buchan and Hall 1973: 67 print Jeannie's first two stanzas with two added by Enoch Kent. Jean Redpath also contributes an extra verse in her recording.

Recorded versions: SA 1959/15/104; HMV 7EG 8534; Enoch Kent, Gordeanna MacCulloch, Topic 12T164; Jean Redpath, Folk-Legacy FSS-49; Norman Kennedy, Folk-Legacy FSS-34.

Additional reference: Wright 1975: 497.

42. Carrbridge Castle (The Lady of Carlisle, Laws O25)

At Carrbridge Castle there lived a lady,
 She had ten thousand pounds a year;
But she could dress as gay as any,
 And few with her there could compare.

But she was courted by two lovers,
 And both of them were brothers bold;
They were both alike in rank and station,
 They were both alike and she loved the two;
They were both alike in rank and station,
 But what could she, a poor lady, do?

She ordered her carriage to get ready,
    All early by the break of day;
And a horse and saddle she did prepare,
    As quickly as she rode away.

When she came to the den of lions,
    She dropped her fan in the lions' den;
"For any man who wants to gain a lady,
    They will bring me back my fan again."

"Tis up spoke the bold sea captain,
    He was bound to the *Tiger* of the many wars;
"For it's I have ventured my life in danger
    On the many warships;
But I will not venture my life in danger,
    For to gain a lady fair."

But it's up spoke the poor lieutenant,
    And a bravely-spoken young man was he,
"For it's I will enter the den of lions,
    And I'll bring you back your fan again."

42. Carrbridge Castle (The Lady of Carlisle, Laws O25)
Jeannie's air for this song is usually known as "The Galway Shawl," and she used it for other items in her repertoire (e.g., "Susan Pyatt," "I Was Drunk Last Night"). A tune in the Greig MS 1909–14, 3:165, is a cognate, and there are three other versions of the song in the Greig MS. One meets with substantial variation in the setting of the opening line, from "In London City" (Teresa Maguire; Kennedy 1975: 309) to "In sweet Argyll . . . " (Eddie Butcher). Cecil Sharp believed the plot to derive from an actual incident in sixteenth-century France. Literary versions by Schiller, Browning, and Leigh Hunt are extant. Lucy Broadwood pointed out that traditional texts end with a happy marriage, while in the literary workings, the hero throws his glove in the lady's face (e.g., the finale of Leigh Hunt's poem). The reference to a lion's den is possible because lions were kept at the Tower of London till 1834 (cf. Kennedy 1975: 329). Laws 1957: 237–38 discusses the list of variants, and others are in Kennedy 1975.

Recorded versions: SA 1952/33; SX 1958/2; Teresa Maguire, Caedmon TC1164/Topic 12T196; BBC LP 24842; Eddie Butcher, Free Reed FRR003 (1976), Leader LED 2070.

Additional references: Brunnings 1981; Gower and Porter 1972: 155; Greig 1963: 67; Huntington and Herrmann 1990: 488–89; Karpeles 1974, 1:313–15; Shields 1981: 77–78; *Spin* 3/8.

43. O Haud Your Tongue, Dear Sally

O haud your tongue, dear Sally,
   Or I ging tae the toun;
I'll buy tae you a jauntin'-car
   An' a braw white muslin goun.
I'll buy tae you a jauntin'-car
   An' a braw white muslin goun,
An' besides a little wee lap dog
   Tae folly your jauntin'-car.

May the deil go wi' your lap dog,
   An' your jauntin'-car an' a';
For I wad raither hae a young man
   Tae roll me fae the wa'.

I wad raither hae a young man
    Withoot a penny ava,
Before I'd hae a auld man
    To roll me fae the wa'.

For your chanter's never in order,
    Your pipes is never in tune;
I wisht the deevil had you
    And a young one in your room.
I wisht the deevil had you
    And a young one in your room,
As I wad raither hae a young man
    To roll me fae the wa'.

But now my auld man's deid and gone,
    But left tae me a gey fee;
He left to me ten thousand pounds,
    Besides my lands quite free.
He left to me ten thousand pounds,
    Besides my lands quite free,
And besides a little wee lap dog,
    To follow my jauntin'-car.

But now I've got a young man
    Withoot a penny ava,[5]
Now I've got a young man
    Tae roll me fae the wa'.[6]
He broke my china cups and saucers,
    He lay an' broke them a',
And he's killt my little wee lap dog
    That folliet my jauntin'-car.

43. O Haud Your Tongue, Dear Sally
Jeannie recalled, "I heard my mother singin' it about thirty-six years ago" (SA 1952/
43). Although some Irish elements appear in this text (the name Sally, the term
jaunting-car) and Jeannie regarded it as an Irish song (SA 1960/113), a decidedly Scots
version is extant in Charles Kirkpatrick Sharpe's *Ballad Book* (1824), entitled "The
Lady's Misfortune" (176–77). This version bears the comment: "The old man is said to
be one of the Earls of Home, who was married to the heiress of Pittenweem." Stanzas 3
and 4 are:

But haud your tongue, dear Jeany,
Till I gang to the fair,
An' I'll buy you a lap-dog
To lay your chanting care:
A pox on you and your lap-dog,
Your chanting cares an' a';
Gin I had but a kind young man
To row me to the wa'.

O haud your tongue, dear Jeany,
Till I gang to the town,
An' I'll buy you a scarlet cloak,
But an' a damass gown.
A pox on your scarlet cloaks
An' damass gowns sae braw;
Gin I had but a kind young man
To row me to the wa'.

The text is marked "from Skene MS." This must refer to the collection of James Skene of Rubislaw, the correspondent of Scott and middleman for the "Old Lady's Collection" (see Buchan 1972: 63, 225). It may be that the text has been filtered through the sensibility of Irish migrant workers or travellers, or it may have been taken to Ireland by Scots travellers and there recast through cultural contact. The forthright Scottish diction suggests the latter possibility, although the sexual symbolism of broken crockery in Jeannie's final verse is a widespread image. The air is more usually found in Irish variants, often under the name "It Was in Dublin City," which is used for "Bold Jack Donohue" (see Jolliffe 1970: 40) or for "The Titanic" (see David Hammond 1978: 30); cf. also the tune for "Johnny Hate" (O Lochlainn 1939: 174).

Recorded versions: SA 1952/43; 1954/72/105; Selection JES 4001.

Additional reference: Gower and Porter 1972.

44. A Pretty Fair Maid (Laws N42)

Version 1 (Original Version)

A pretty fair maid, her garden walking,
  When a brisk young sailor came walking past;
He steppit up to her on purpose to view her,
  He said: "Young fair maid, could you fancy I?"

"It's seven long years since I courted a sailor,
  It's seven long years since he went away;
It's seven long years since I courted a sailor,
  But he'll come back, and he'll marry me."

"For maybe he's married, or perhaps he's drownded,
  Or maybe he sails on the ocean blue."
"But if he's married I wish him pleasure,
  And if he's drownded I hope him rest;
And if he sails on the wide blue ocean,
  For he'll come back and he'll marry me."

"It's do you see yon high, high castel,
  All decorated with lilies white?
I'll give you gold, I will give you silver,
  If you say you will be mine this night."

"For what care I for your high, high castel,
  Or what care I for your lilies white?
Or what care I for your gold an' silver,
  If my dear Willie was here this night?"

He put his hand into his pocket,
    His fingers bein' long and small;
He pulled out a ring which had once broke between them,
    And as she saw it she droppit down.

He picked her up into his arms,
    And he gave to her a sweet loving kiss;
"For I'm your true love, and I'm your Billie,
    And I've come back for to marry you."

Version 2 (Ritchie Version)

A pretty fair maid, a-workin' in the garden,
    When a bright young soldier came a-ridin' by;
He said, "Kin' miss, don't you want to marry,
    Or could you fancy such a one as I?
    Or could you fancy such a one as I?

"I have a true love in the army,
    He's been in the army for seven long years;
And if he's gone for seven years longer,
    Not a man on earth will marry me;
    Not a man on earth will marry me."

"For maybe your true love has been drownded,
    Or maybe he's lying on some battlefield slain;
Or maybe he took some poor girl married,
    And you may never see him again;
    And you may never see him again."

"For if my true love has been drownded,
  Or maybe he's lying on some battlefield slain;
Or if he took some poor girl married,
  I will love the girl that married him;
  I will love the girl that married him."

He took his hand from out of his pocket,
  His fingers bein' both neat and small;
An' seven gold rings upon hees fingers,
  Down at her feet he let them fall;
  Down at her feet he let them fall.

She gathered them up along her pretty fingers,
  And the kisses she gave him one, two, three;
"I am your own, your single soldier,
  Returning home for to marry you;
  Returning home for to marry you."

44. A Pretty Fair Maid (Laws N42)

Jeannie sometimes knew and sang two different versions of a song (e.g., "The Over-gate," "Trooper and Maid," "Little Musgrave"). Her first recording of this widely-diffused piece stands in contrast to the later version she learned from Jean Ritchie on the latter's visit to Britain and Ireland in 1961–62. Jeannie's singing of the Ritchie traditional variant omits one stanza (the second), as Ritchie sings it on the *Field Trip* album, and there are minor variations in the words; repetition of the last stanza is maintained. The tune and text have a number of parallels in Sharp's Appalachian collection (1932, 2:70–73). A variant of Jeannie's own text and tune, sung by Maggie McPhee, is printed by MacColl and Seeger 1977: 129–30. Poetically, Jeannie's original contains the image of the high castle decorated with lilies as a symbol of riches and temptation, part of the returned lover's test. (Note the close correspondence of the final four stanzas in "Green Grows the Laurels," song 64 below.) Ritchie's verses lack this and are generally straightforward in comparison. Laws lists broadsides by Catnach and Such 1957: 224–25. Local versions of the text are in Christie 1876: 264–65; 1881: 200–201, Greig 1963: 23, and Ord 1930: 326.

Recorded versions: (original) SA 1953/195; 1960/202; (Ritchie version) SA 1962/25; Jean Ritchie, Collector CLE 1201; Sarah Makem, Topic 12T182.

Additional references: Brunnings 1981; Cazden, Haufrecht, and Studer 1982; Henry 1923–29, 2:12, 2:320; Huntington and Herrmann 1990: 317–18; Laws 1957: 224–25.

45. Cruel Fate

> Though cruel fate should us part
>   As far as the pole an' line;
> Her dear idea around my heart
>   Should tenderly entwine.
>
> Though mountains groan and deserts howl
>   And oceans roar between,
> Yet dearer to my deathless soul
>   I still wad love my Jean.

45. Cruel Fate

Jeannie recited this for Hamish Henderson, having first found the words in what she called "a Burn auld, auld song book—a big auld song book, lang, lang ago, when I was jeest a lassikie. But there was no air attached til it. So therefore I put a hauntin' kind o' air til it mysel'." She then sang "Cruel Fate" with the tune she had composed for it. The words, with slight variation, are those of Burns as published in *The Scots Musical Museum* (James Johnson 1788: 122) to the tune "The Northern Lass." A manuscript of the words older than that in the British Museum marks them to be sung to "She rose and let me in." Johnson could not use this tune because it had already been printed in the first volume of *The Scots Musical Museum* (cf. Dick 1962: 373).

Recorded versions: SA 1952/43; 1959/8; 1962/26.

Additional reference: Gower 1968.

46. The Laird o' Windy Wa's

For I'm the Laird o' Windy Wa's,
　An' I cam' here withoot a cause;
But I've got mair than thirty fa's,
　Comin' oot owre the plain.

Refrain:
O let me in this ae nicht,
　This ae, ae, ae nicht;
Let me in this ae nicht,
　An' I'll never seek back again.

O ile the door or it be's weet,
　An' it'll neither chirrup or cheep;
An' it'll neither chirrup or cheep,
　An' I'll get slippin' in.

When he got in he wis sae gled,
　He throwed his bonnet from of his head;
He kissed her on the cheek sae red,
　An' the aul' wife heard the din.

Refrain:
O but weel she likit that ae nicht.
    That ae, ae, ae nicht;
O weel she likit that ae nicht,
    She let the laddie in.

When he got in he wis sae gled,
    He knockit the bottom boards oot o' the bed;
He stole the lassie's maidenhead,
    An' the aul' wife heard the din.

46. The Laird o' Windy Wa's

Several versions of this old bawdy song, more often than not sung by women and all to the same air, have been current among Northeast travellers (cf. that of Maggie McPhee in MacColl and Seeger 1977: 160–62). The tune generally used is not that published in *The Scots Musical Museum* (James Johnson 1792: 320–21) or in Thomson's *A Select Collection of Original Scotish Airs* (1805: 156) under the name "Will you lend me your loom, lass?" (see Oswald's *Caledonian Pocket Companion*, 1752, 4:21). Jeannie's text, like the others in traveller tradition, is an analog of that in Herd's MS (Hecht 1904: 149–52), with its insistent chorus, "Let me in this ae nicht," which often has given the song its title. Her first stanza corresponds to Herd's fourth, though the promiscuity is toned down; Herd has "And I hae gotten mony fa's/Upon a naked wame o!". In a satirical piece of this kind, traveller singers might not wish to paint too flattering a picture of one too often their social adversary. Jeannie's second verse resembles Herd's fifth, and her last his ninth. Some additions, omissions, and recasting have taken place over the years. Burns produced a polite version for the *Museum;* plainly dissatisfied, he made two more attempts to rewrite the old words. The next version he discarded, and the last was published in Thomson's 1805 collection, the first stanza and chorus being from the original song.

Recorded versions: SA 1954/90; 1959/106/108; 1960/201; HMV 7 EG 8534; Prestige International 13006.

Additional reference: Shuldham-Shaw and Lyle 1990: 120–23, 539.

47. The Bonnie Lassie's Pleydie's Awa'

Refrain

There wis a bonnie lassie, an' she wis ga'n tae Crieff,
    She met in wi' a butcher laddie an' he wis sellin' beef;
First he took her in his airms, an' doun the twa did fa',
    An' the wind blew the bonnie lassie's pleydie awa'.

O ma pleydie's awa', an' awa' wi' the win',
    Ma pleydie's awa' an' it cannae be fund;
What will the aal' folk, the aa' folk say ava?
    O I cannae say the win' blew ma pleydie awa'.

47. The Bonnie Lassie's Pleydie's Awa'
This was learned from Maria, with the usual "White Cockade" tune. This tune bears a
close resemblance, in its first phrase, to the Gaelic tune "Cuir a nall duinn am botal,"
noted by Lucy Broadwood in Arisaig in 1907 (Broadwood 1911: 154). Ford 1899: 74–

75 relates that his friend, D. Kippen of Crieff, believed the words to have been written by an Irishman living there in the early nineteenth century and familiarly known as "Blind Rob." Ford's and Ord's texts of ten stanzas and refrain are partially reproduced in the variant recorded by Jimmy MacBeath (q.v.), though the sentimental ending of "Now Rab and his lassie are hand in hand/They live as contented as ony in the land" has been removed. The refrain has elements in common with texts of "The Elfin Knight" (Child 2). "Selling beef" is, no doubt, a euphemism for male lust. A children's parodic variant is included by Montgomerie 1948: 81.

Recorded versions: SA 1954/104; 1955/176; Caedmon TC 1143/Topic 12T158; Topic 10T52 (12T96); Jimmy MacBeath, Topic 12T173.

Additional references: Bronson 1959–72, 1:9–15, 4:439–40.

48. The Braes o' Killiecrankie

For on a thistle I sat doun,
   I nearly jumpit tae the moon;
I nearly jumpit tae the moon,
   For the lass that stole my hankie.

Refrain:
O too-ral-oo-ral-oo-ral-ay,
   O fal-da-doodle-aye-do-ay;
O fal-da-doodle-aye-do-ay,
   On the Braes o' Killiecrankie.

For Jean MacNeil she's fair an' fat,
   An' she wears her hair below her hat;
She wears her hair below her hat
   On the Braes o' Killiecrankie.

For her feet is big an' her face is flat,
   An' her curly locks hang doun her back;
Her curly locks hang doun her back
   On the Braes o' Killiecrankie.

For Jean she began tae curse,
   Her bloomers fell doun an' her stays did burst,
She gied her aul' erse a twust
   An' she caa'd it through a windae.

48. The Braes o' Killiecrankie

A parody of Hogg's "Killiecrankie," this comic squib was part of Maria's legacy. A version of Hogg's original is in Buchan and Hall 1973: 150. The overall tone is one of caricaturing sexual mishap (simulated orgasm suggested in verse 1). For the School of Scottish Studies Archive, Jeannie substituted "fit" (foot) for "erse" in the final stanza (SA 1959/78). Because she had sung an unexpurgated version of the song both on disc and in public, one must assume that the nature of the audience (Linkum Ceilidh) led her to replace the original word. The title of this song is not to be confused with the parody of Burns' "Banks o' Aberfeldy" in Lyle 1975: 153. Some affinity exists between Jeannie's tune and the class of melodies associated with "Tree in the Wood (Valley)." See the first air used by John Reilly, the Irish traveller singer, for his rare version of "The Maid and the Palmer" (Child 21; cf. Bronson 1959–72, 4:457, reprinted from *Ceol*).

Recorded versions: SA 1954/88; 1959/15/74/78/82; HMV 7 EG 8534.

Additional reference: Hogg 1819–21; Legman 1975: 814–21.

49. The Thorn Bush (The Cuckoo's Nest)

For there is a thorn bush in oor kailyaird,
There is a thorn bush in oor kailyaird;
At the back o' thon bush there stands a lad an' lass,
An' they're busy busy herryin' at the cuckoo's nest.

Refrain:
O, it's hey the cuckoo 'n' ho the cuckoo 'n' hey the cuckoo's nest,
It is hey the cuckoo 'n' ho the cuckoo 'n' hey the cuckoo's nest;
I'll gie ony body a shullin' an' a bottle o' the best
If they'll rumple up the feathers o' the cuckoo's nest.

It was thorned, it was sprinkled, it was 'compassed all around,
It was thorned, it was sprinkled, and it wasn't easy found;
For she said, "Young man, you're plunderin'," I said it wisnae true,
But I left her with the makin's of a young cuckoo.

49. *The Thorn Bush (The Cuckoo's Nest)*

Jeannie sang this item frequently, and it has been a universal favorite throughout Britain and Ireland. Buchan and Hall 1973: 69 have published a version of her singing. Kennedy 1975 includes an Irish version sung by Annie Jane Kelly or Keady, Armagh, called "The Magpie's Nest" (410–11). The hornpipe nature of the tune, especially the refrain, has contributed to its widespread popularity. It appeared in such eighteenth-century publications as Rutherford's *Compleat Collection of 200 of the Most Celebrated Country Dances* (1750–76) and Straight and Skellern's *204 Favourite Country Dances* (1771). Hogg's *The Jacobite Relics of Scotland* (1819–21, 1: iii) has a song, "The Cuckoo," set to a version of this air. As to the textual tradition, Burns, Lady Nairne, and others tried their hand at reworking the old song (see James Johnson 1796: 508; a combination of Burns and Nairne is in R. A. Smith's *The Scotish Minstrel* [1821, 1:22]). Ford 1899: 178–79 adds another text written "a number of years ago by an Edinburgh man whose name I have heard and forgotten." All these *refacimentos*, even that of Burns, eliminate the erotic symbolism.

Recorded versions: SA 1952/33; 1954/105; 1956/169; 1957/98; 1959/74/80/83/84; 1960/109; 1962/75; Folktracks FSA 067; SX 1953/2; 1960/5; Selection JES 8; Prestige International 13075; Caedmon TC 1143/Topic 12T158; Annie Jane Kelly, BBC 18475, Caedmon TC 1142/Topic 12T157; Jimmy MacBeath, Collector CLE 1201; Ewan MacColl, Argo (Z) DA 85.

Additional reference: David Buchan 1984: 110.

50. A Dottered Auld Carle

vv. 2, 4, and 6.

A dottered auld carle cam' owre the lea,
 Aha, but I widnae hae him;
He cam' owre the lea an' a' tae coort me,
 Wi' his grey baird newly shaven.

My mither tellt me tae open the door,
 Aha, but I widnae hae him;
I opened the door an' he totter'd in owre,
 Wi' his grey baird newly shaven.

My mither tellt me tae gie him a chair,
 Aha, but I widnae hae him;
I gied him a chair an' he sit on the flair,
 Wi' his grey baird newly shaven.

My mither tellt me tae gie him some meat,
    Aha, but I widnae hae him;
I gied him some meat but he'd nae teeth tae eat,
    Wi' his grey baird newly shaven.

My mither tellt me tae gie him a drink,
    Aha, but I widnae hae him;
I gied him a drink an' he began tae wink,
    Wi' his grey baird newly shaven.

My mither tellt me tae gie him a kiss,
    Aha, but I widnae hae him;
If ye like him sae weel ye can kiss him yersel',
    Wi' his grey baird newly shaven.

Wi' his grey baird newly shaven,
    Wi' his grey baird newly shaven;
If ye like him sae weel ye can kiss him yersel',
    Wi' his auld grey baird newly shaven.

50. A Dottered Auld Carle

With its satirical partner, "A Auld Man Cam' Coortin' Me," this song was frequently performed by Jeannie at *ceilidhs* and concerts. The short, cumulative text, Jeannie's dramatic ability to draw broad, comic strokes, and her skillful adaptation of the pipe tune "Leaving Port Askaig" must account for the song's popularity. The song was much printed during the eighteenth century, appearing in most of the well-known collections after *The Tea-Table Miscellany* and *Orpheus Caledonius*. Ford 1899: 142–43 reports that it was widely sung in country districts of Scotland; Jeannie's text is fairly close to the second of the two that Ford prints. The song has also been distributed over Britain and Ireland; see Dean-Smith 1954: 95 and Kennedy 1975: 333. A transcription of Jeannie's version is in Kennedy 1975: 316.

Recorded versions: SA 1958/25; 1959/15/106; 1962/12; SM 1956/2; Caedmon TC 1142/Topic 12T157; Prestige International 13075.

Additional references: Greig 1963: 149; Herd 1769–1776, 1:33–34; Shuldham-Shaw and Lyle 1990: 207–9, 546–47.

51. The Overgate

For as I gaed doun the Overgate,
   I met a bonnie wee lass;
For she winked to me wi' the tail of her e'e
   As I went walkin' past.

Refrain:
Rickey-doo-dum-die, doo-dum-die,
   Rickey-dickey-doo-dum-day.

I asked her what her name might be,
   She said, "Jemima Rose;
And I live in Blaeberry Lane
   At the fit o' the Beefcan Close."

I asked her what was her landlady's name,
   She said it was Mrs. Bruce;
And wi' that she invited me
   To come awa' tae the hoose.

As we went up the windin' stairs,
   And it bein' lang and dark;
For I slipped my money through my inside pooch,
   And I tied it to the tail o' my sark.

I scarcely had got in the hoose,
   When she took me tae her room;
It was there we pulled a bottle oot,
   And then we baith sat doun.

For a' nicht lang I dreamt I was lyin'
In the airms o' Jemima Rose;
But when I waukened I was lyin' on my back
At the fit o' the Beefcan Close.

Come a' ye jolly plooman lads,
That gang oot for a lark;
Just slip your money tae your inside pooch,
And tie it to the tail o' your sark.

51. The Overgate

Learned "amongst our people," this item was sung by Jeannie in two different melodic and textual variants, one associated with the city of Aberdeen, the other with Dundee. In recent published recordings and texts, it is the latter that has received greater attention (cf. Kennedy 1975: 418; MacColl and Seeger 1977: 175–77), though it is the former variant that Jeannie sings here (and that Lizzie also knew; Stephanie Smith 1975: 238). The refrain of Jeannie's tune is related to the version of "I'm Seventeen Come Sunday" published by Sharp 1921: 104. According to Ford 1899: 102–5, the type with the "rolling eye" refrain was well known in Perthshire and Fife through the singing of Alexander Smith ("Singing Sandy" or "Rolling Eye"), an itinerant musician of the nineteenth century. Burns recovered a song for *The Scots Musical Museum* (James Johnson 1790: 298, "A Waukrife Minnie") from a country girl in Nithsdale, though whether it can be regarded as an antecedent of the present song is debatable, since the dénouement is different and the implicit moral absent; the same is true in comparisons of "Trooper and Maid" and "As I Roved Out." It may be that "The Overgate" came into existence in more or less its present forms as nineteenth-century reworkings of a common situation (encounter of the sexes, invitation by the girl to her house, drinking and love making, interruption and/or departure by the man) by "Singing Sandy" or others, but now localized, in tune with the experience of bothy farmworkers visiting the big city, and with a Victorian moral lurking in the background. Metaphorically, "Jemima Rose" suggests virginal charms, "beefcan close" sexual intercourse. The refrain marks the difference between the two versions known to Jeannie, and additional textual variations are apparent (cf. Gower and Porter 1977: 82–86). There are four texts in the Duncan MS, none to Jeannie's tunes. John MacDonald, who sang a version of the Dundee "Overgate" for MacColl and Seeger (1977: 175–77), uses the tune Jeannie had for another encounter ditty, "She Was a Rum One."

Recorded versions: (Aberdeen): SA 1954/104; 1955/176; 1958/25; 1959/81/84/106; 1960/109/201/203; SX 1959/1/5; BBC 27810; Riverside RLP 12-633; Prestige International 13075; (Dundee) SA 1954/104; 1960/201; Jazz selection JES 4; Prestige International 13006; Belle Stewart, Topic 12TS307; Davie Stewart, Topic 12T293; Jimmy MacBeath, BBC 21089; Norman Kennedy, Topic 12T178.

Additional references: *A Collection of Scots Songs*, 1972: 26–28.

53. Cuttie's Weddin'

Busk an' go, busk an' go,
 Busk an' go tae Cuttie's weddin';
Fa's the lassie and the lad
 That widnae gang an they were bidden?

Cuttie he's a lang man,
 O he'll tak' hissel' a wifie;
Gin he tak's on tae the toun lawn,
 Gin she tak's on her fykie fykie.

Cuttie he cam' here yestreen,
 Cuttie he fell owre the midden;
He wat his hose an' tint his sheen,
 Courtin' at the canker'd maiden.

53. Cuttie's Weddin'
"The little story that I heard about the song, which is the history of the song, was that Cuttie wis a man, he wis a fisherman, at St. Fergus, that's down the Buchan. And it was Prince Charles Stuart's own fiddler that composed the song, which is really a pipe tune too" (BBC Schools Program, November 28, 1960). Variant words of the song appear in Charles Kirkpatrick Sharpe's MS (NLS 210), from 1824:

Busk and go, dearie go,
Busk and go to Cutty's wedding;
Busk &c.
Cutty is a bonny lad,
And he has a little wifie,

He's gae to the town his lane,
When she taks ony fiekie fikie.

Busk and go, dearie, go
Busk and go to Cutty's wedding,
Busk, &c.
Dadie says he winna gae,
Mammy says she wisnae bidden,
I'll put on my ruffled cuffs
And slide awa to Cutty's wedding.

A three-stanza version of the words, which Jeannie's text resembles more closely, is in Chambers 1829: 400–401, with the additional stanza:

He sat him doun upon the green,
    The lass cam til him wi' ae biddin';
He says, 'Gin ye were mine, my dame,
    Monie ane's be at our weddin.'
        Busk and go, etc.

A tune is included in Alexander McGlashan's *A Collection of Strathspey Reels* (ca. 1780). Songs about ill-matched or grotesque couples, or about Rabelaisian weddings, are common in traditional Scots song.

Recorded versions: SA 1957/98; 1958/25; 1959/78/81/84/106; 1961/44; 1962/12/75; SM 1956/2; SX 1959/5; Jazz Selection JES 1; Prestige International 13075.

54. Roy's Wife o' Aldivalloch

Refrain:
Roy's wife o' Aldivalloch,
   Roy's wife o' Aldivalloch,
But quot ye foo she diddled me
   As I came owre the Braes o' Balloch?

She vow'd, she swore she would be mine,
   And said she lo'ed me best o' ony;
But O the fickle faithless quean,
   She's taen the carle an' left her Johnnie.

O she was a cantie quean,
   An' she could dance the Hielan' walloch;
O if only she'd be mine,
   Or if I'd been Roy o' Aldivalloch.

Her hair so fair, her een so clear,
   Her wee bit moothie sweet an' bonnie;
To me she ever will be dear,
   Tho' she's for ever left her Johnnie.

---

54. Roy's Wife o' Aldivalloch
Jeannie learned this song when she was ten (SA 1953/247), and it has probably found favor among travellers as a result of its national popularity (ca. 1792–1820). The words have remained fairly constant in oral tradition, at least, since Mrs. Grant of Carron (ca. 1745–ca. 1814) wrote them. They appeared first in *The Bee*, June 19, 1791, and James

Johnson added them to *The Scots Musical Museum* (Johnson 1792: 352) shortly afterwards. "Ruffian's Rant," the old air first printed by Bremner in his *A Collection of Scots Reels or Country Dances* (1759), was used for setting the words. The same tune serves Burns' "In Comin' by the Brig o' Dye" (*The Caledonian Museum,* 1770, no. 156), and three songs in *The Merry Muses* are directed to be sung to it (Legman 1965: 37–38; 46–47; 95–97). Another name for the tune was "Cog na scalan" (a basket for oatcakes, a baking-board, or dough trough; see Graham 1908: 139). It is found under that name in the Mcfarlan MS (1740) and in Cumming's *Collection of Strathspeys or Old Highland Reels* (1780). Glen located it as "Lady Wemys' Reel" in Walsh's *24 Country Dances for the Year 1742.* The tune gained in popularity as the association with the words became welded. Other printings are in Gillespie's *A Collection of the Best and Most Favourite Tunes for the Violin* (1768, as "Ruffian's Rant"), *An Evening Amusement* (1789), Urbani's *A Selection of Scots Songs* (1792-1804), Napier 1792 ("Harmony by Haydn"), and *The Caledonian Museum* (1770) (marked "largo"). Maidment 1859: 159–60 supplies the background for the plot. John Roy of Aldivalloch married Isabel Stewart on February 21, 1727. Much younger than her husband, she ran off with one David Gordon of Kirktown but was pursued and brought back after a chase over the Braes of Balloch. The last descendant of the Roys of Aldivalloch, Margaret Roy (who died in 1860), asserted that the song was created by a local shoemaker (cf. Glen 1900; MacColl 1965: 68). This claim apparently has never been substantiated. Graham (1861, 2:79) records how the celebrated soprano Catalani, in one of her first appearances in Edinburgh (ca. 1821; see Farmer 1947), sang "Roy's Wife" to great applause.

Recorded versions: SA 1953/247; SX 1958/2; Prestige International 13075; Topic 10T52 (12T96).

Additional references: Rogers 1855, 1:50–51; Shuldham-Shaw and Lyle 1990: 72, 534; Stenhouse 1853: 320–21, 368–69.

O Maggie a-milkin' one fine summer's day,
    When by came wee Jockie, to her he did say:
"O Maggie, O Maggie, your milk's runnin' free,
    For if I sit doun beside thee, it's will you milk me?"

Refrain:
Rick-a-too-ral-i-a-die, rick-a-too-ral-i-ay,
Rick-a-too-ral-i-a-die, right fal-al-the day.

For Maggie lay doun and she pulled up her clothes,
    And Jockie he gave her ye may's weel suppose.
For she milkit wee Jockie and she milkit him dry,
    And she sent him tae the Highlands amongst the dry kye.

55. Maggie A-Milkin'
Maria Robertson, who sang this ribald piece, apparently had additional verses she
would not permit Jeannie and the other children to hear. Jeannie's received text looks
like a parody of the pastoral ditty, "Lovely Molly," printed in Ford 1899: 225–26 as a
song commonly performed at country social meetings in Perthshire in the mid-nine-
teenth century (see also Greig 1963: 50). A version entitled "As Molly Was Milking"

appeared in the *Journal of the Irish Folk-Song Society* 20 (1923): 59. The tune, usually associated with the song "Logie o' Buchan" (written about 1736–37 by George Halket, schoolmaster at Rathan), is undoubtedly older. Halket's song with the tune appeared in the *Aberdeen Magazine* for 1788; but the earliest printing of the air, with the title "Logie o' Buchan," is in *The Caledonian Museum* (ca. 1770). As an independent tune, it first emerges in the Atkinson MS (1694), with the name "Tak tent to the ripells, Gudeman," and it appears later in the Macfarlan MS (1740). As "The Taylor fell through the bed," it was associated with the Incorporation of Taylors; and with this designation, it is attached to the song "I rede you beware o the ripples" in *The Merry Muses*. R. A. Smith (1824) published an expurgated version of the words. It is probable that the bawdy associations of the tune have persisted in Jeannie's oral tradition, bypassing the sentimental "Logie o' Buchan" development, even though the text here has transferred the action to a pastoral context.

Recorded version: SA 1954/104.

Additional references: Gower and Porter 1977: 76–78; Legman 1965: 5–6, 138–39; MacColl 1965: 74.

56. Ainst Upon a Time

O ainst upon a time,
    Fin I was young and bonnie;
Ainst I had a bonnie wee lad,
    But nou I hinnae onie.

Fin I was cook aboot the hoose,
    Fin he wis bit a laddie,
I gied him a' my breid an' milk
    Tae tickle up ma baggie.

O dinna thin, my bonnie lad,
    That I'm mad aboot ye;
For I caud dae wi' a man,
    But I can dae withoot ye.

56. Ainst Upon a Time

The words as they stand in Jeannie's version may approximate a traditional song text circulating at the time Hector MacNeill (1746–1818) wrote his popular verses beginning, "Dinna think, bonnie lassie, I'm gaun to leave you." These appeared toward the end of *The Scots Musical Museum* (James Johnson 1803: 574–75), though without his name as author. G. F. Graham 1861 (2:42; 3:165) points to a version by Susanna Blamire (1747–94), a lady from Cumberland who spent much of her life in Scotland because of a sister's marriage in 1767 to Colonel Graham of Duchray. Her first stanza begins: "O dinna think, my bonny lass, that I'm gaum to leave thee/I nobbet gae to yonder town, and I'll come and see thee/Gin the nicht be ne'er sae dark, and I be ne'er sae weary, O!" Blamire's poem predates MacNeill's, and it is possible that he modeled his poem partly on her lines. But the evidence suggests a traditional song in existence prior to both literary versions. The tune can be traced in print as far back as the third part of Playford's *Apollo's Banquet* (1687), where it is called "Long cold nights." The Thomson MS 1702 includes it under a similar name, and further on as "The banks of Yaro." Thereupon the melody begins to be associated with the song "Mary Scott," under which title the tune, and song, were widely popular during the eighteenth century in Scotland. Meanwhile, a close variant of the air, "O minie" or "O dear mother what shall I do?," had come into being (Sinkler MS, 1710; Macfarlan MS, 1740; Oswald's *Caledonian Pocket Companion*). It found great favor as an instrumental tune, from Walsh's *Country Dances* of 1740, where it is entitled "Carrick's Reel," to Angus Cumming's *Collection* (1780). It appears in *An Evening Amusement* (1789) with the comment, "Clurie's Reel—from Mary Scott." Gow modified it for the reel "The Braes of Auchtertyre" in the *Repository*, but as a fiddle tune it is best known in modern times as "The Smith's a Gallant Fireman." It is found in Northumberland as "Sir John Fenwick's the Flower among Them" or "Fenwick's Lament" (cf. Bruce and Stokoe 1965 [1882]: 158–59). A composite version of Jeannie's song, with five verses added by Ray Fisher, appears in Buchan and Hall 1973: 63. A wider study of the song "Mary Scott" and the tune complex is in Porter 1983.

Recorded versions: SA 1955/154; HMV 7EG 8534; Folktracks FSA 067.

Additional reference: Gower and Porter 1977.

57. Brush Ye Back My Curly Locks

> O, brush ye back my curly locks
>   An' lace my middle sma',
> An' nane'll ken by my rosy cheeks
>   That my maidenheid's awa'.
>
> For I'll gang back to Dundee
>   Lookin' bonnie, young, and fair;
> An' I'll pit on my buskit stays
>   And kaim back my bonnie brown hair.
>
> For I'll pit on my buskit stays
>   Tae mak' my middle sma',
> And wha will ken by my rosy cheeks
>   That my maidenheid's awa'?

57. Brush Ye Back My Curly Locks
Challenging rather than sardonic in tone, this song became commercially available in a recording by Enoch Kent and The Reivers (Topic 12T128). Her virginity gone, the protagonist looks forward to amorous encounters as she celebrates her sexuality. Virginity and its social implications in Scotland since the Middle Ages are dealt with by Marshall 1983. See also Mitchison and Leneman 1989.

Recorded versions: SA 1954/104; SX 1958/2.

58. Hap An' Rowe

O hap an' rowe, hap an' rowe,
Hap an' rowe the feeties o't;
I didnae ken I had a wee thing
Till I heard the greeties o't.

58. Hap an' Rowe

This quatrain forms the burden to "The Reel o' Stumpie" (in *The Scots Musical Museum:* James Johnson 1839 [1787–1803]: 457), one verse of which was also printed in James Johnson 1792: 470. According to Legman 1965: 156–57, two more stanzas were omitted by MacNaught 1911 and Ferguson 1985 in their editions of Burns, *The Merry Muses*, these stanzas possibly being the addition of Burns himself. Stenhouse 1853: 403 notes that the "lively old reel tune" lacked words, and that Burns supplied the single stanza and refrain in the *The Scots Musical Museum*. Chambers 1829: 536–37 attributes variant words to the pen of William Creech, sometime bookseller and Lord Provost of Edinburgh, author of *Edinburgh Fugitive Pieces* (1791), but these lack the eroticism of Burns' verses. The tune, explicitly called "Hap and row the feetie o't" in Chambers, has other names: "Stumpie" in Aird's *Selection of Scotch, English, Irish and Foreign Airs* (1782), "Lady Betty Wemyss' Reel" in Bremner's *Collection of Scots Reels or Country Dances* (1757). Stenhouse believed it formerly to have been called "Jocky has gotten a wife," which Coffey selected for one of his songs ("And now I am once more set free") in the opera *The Female Parson, or Beau in the Suds Caledonian Country Dances* (ca. 1734) under the name "Butter'd pease." This tune lacks the initial identifying feature of tones 3-5-1, making it only a first cousin rather than an immediate relative. It is printed as a pipe tune by Polwarth and Polwarth 1969: 39 with the original halves reversed. A transcription of the singing of Isabella Strachan, Banchory, is in *Tocher* 14 (1974): 211.

Recorded versions: SA 1954/100.

Additional references: MacColl 1965: 66; Mackay 1854: 307; Montgomerie and Montgomerie 1948: 96; 1964: 118; Barke and Smith 1959: 80–81.

59. The Lassies in the Cougate

The lassies in the Cougate
   Kaim doun their yella hair,
The lassies in the Cougate,
   They sing for evermair.
But woe be to the rovin' boys
   That sings the rantin-roo,
And woe be to the sailor lads
   That fills the lassies fou.

59. The Lassies in the Cougate
"I heard my mother singin' it. But it was long—I don't remember it" (SA 1954/105). A
version of the text is printed in Charles Kirkpatrick Sharpe's *Ballad Book* (1824) with
the note, "From Mrs. Campbell of Monzie, the present General Campbell's mother,
and by grandaunt." See Henderson 1964: 227–28 for a discussion of the song's origin.
The image of sexuality in the combing of hair is one of many dealt with by Andersen
1985, who suggests that the act implies a readiness to be courted or approached.

Recorded versions: SA 1954/105; 1955/154; 1957/107; 1959/107; SX 1958/2.

Additional reference: Gower and Porter 1977: 73.

60. The Banks o' Red Roses

When I was a wee thing I heard my mother say,
  Before I would wark I would raither sport and play;
Before I would wark I would raither sport and play
  Wi' my Johnnie doun among the red roses.

For he took her to his house and advited her to tea:
  "Rise my bonnie Mary and come alang wi' me;
Rise my bonnie Mary and come alang wi' me,
  Tae the bonnie, bonnie banks beneath the roses."

He pulled out his tune box to play his love a tune,
  And in the middle of the tune she stood up an' cried:
"O Johnnie dear, O Johnnie dear, it's dinnae leave me
  At the bonnie, bonnie banks beneath the roses."

60. The Banks o' Red Roses
While Jeannie learned this song in her youth from hearing older travellers sing it, Lizzie maintains that she herself picked it up from her father (Stephanie Smith 1975: 244). It is likely that both Jeannie and Donald were exposed to the same, or very similar, performed variants. The song has had considerable currency throughout Britain and Ireland (see *Journal of the Folk-Song Society* 2 (1906): 4, 254). Burns remarked that the song, "The Beds of Sweet Roses," was very popular in Ayrshire when he was a boy (Dick 1962, appendix 3; James Johnson 1787: 7). W. Macnie of Stirling printed a chap text with a first stanza similar to that quoted by Burns. Joyce 1909: 65 offers "The Banks of the Daisies," a version different from that in Stanford-Petrie. O Lochlainn (1960: 158, 226) mentions how his mother learned the song

from her father, John Carr of Limerick (1819–90), adding that he gave it to Donal O'Sullivan for inclusion in *Journal of the Irish Folk-Song Society* 18 (1921): 30–31. Frank Kidson, Ethel Kidson, and Moffat also published a version in *English Peasant Songs* (1929), and there are thematic connections with English songs such as "The Nightingales Sing" (see Kennedy 1975: 414–15, 434). Smith notes the twin themes of love and death in many texts. One type of plot is simply the seduction of a girl by a soldier, who is usually married; the other is a murder story in which the maiden is killed for refusing his advances. The "banks o' red roses" image suggests sexual satiety or fulfillment but might also hint at both blood and the profusion of flowers in funeral wreaths—i.e., death. "Tune box" can, as in other scenarios where music and lovemaking are closely related, be taken as a sexual metaphor (cf. "fiddle" in many versions). Lizzie's text has the murder motif that Jeannie's and Macnie's chap versions lack, as have the two most recently published variant texts (Buchan and Hall 1973: 52, sung by Ruby Kelbie; and MacColl and Seeger 1977: 235–37, sung by John MacDonald). All the various tunes are related.

Recorded versions: SA 1953/247; Sheila Douglas SA 1971/243; Lizzie Higgins, Topic 12T185; Sarah Makem, Topic 12T182; Ella Ward, Collector CLE 1201.

Additional references: Gower and Porter 1977; Joyce 1909; Munro 1984: 280–92.

61. Three 'Stralion Dragoons
(Trooper and Maid, Child 299)

Three 'Stralion dragoons, coming home from the war,
    The night was dark and dreary;
"For I wid know my own soldier boy,
    Because I love him dearly."

She took his horse by the bridle-head,
    An' laid it in the stable;
Hay an' corn for a pretty soldier's horse,
    For to eat while it was able.

She took the lad by the lily-white hand,
    An' led him tae her chamber;
Cakes an' wine for a pretty soldier boy,
    For to eat while he was able.

She went up the stair for to make her bed,
    Then soft and easy;
For she stript off her lily-white goun,
    Beside his hat an' sabre;
For he stript off his boots and his spurs,
    And they both lay down together.

They weren't very long into bed,
    When the bugle't did sounded;
For the bugle it did play an' the trumpet it did say:
    "Bonnie lassie, I maun leave you."

"O when will you come back, my bonnie soldier boy,
  To be the wee thing's daddie?"
"When cockleshells grow in silver bells,
  Bonnie lass, we'll get mairried."

61. Three 'Stralion Dragoons (Trooper and Maid, Child 299)

A song that circulated widely among Aberdeenshire travellers, this ballad was added by Jeannie to her repertoire about the time that Hamish Henderson recorded it from her aunt, Maggie Stewart, who sang it for him in 1954 during a lengthy session in Jeannie's Causewayend house. Henderson also heard a fragment, with the same text and tune, in the Castle Gate of Aberdeen in 1969 (Henderson to JP, March 1969). Jeannie seems to have known the more familiar version of the ballad with its "Bonnie lassie, I'll lie near ye" refrain, since she taught it to Lizzie (Stephanie Smith 1975: 167–68). On SA 1959/106, this version is wrongly attributed to Jeannie's singing; the singer is Hamish Henderson (see also Bronson's variant 19, *Traditional Tunes*, 4:432–33). In terms of narrative metaphor, the lady's stabling of the horse is suggestive for what follows, and use of "lily-white" for both the *soldier's* hand and the lady's gown is unusual. The bugle, and cockleshells and silver bells add to the complex of sexual imagery. The similarity of Jeannie's air to that for her "Lord Lovat" (77) suggests a melodic model peculiar to her, yet one that is also found elsewhere (see the first phrase of Greig and Keith's tune for "The Mermaid," 1925: 242–43). Bronson sees a further connection, in regard to "Lord Lovel," with the English tunes for "Lord Thomas and Fair Eleanor" (Child 73) and "Lady Isabel and the Elf Knight" (Child 4), no doubt because of the 6/8 meter and the corresponding cadence points.

Recorded versions: SA 1963/84; Lizzie Higgins, SA 1970/22.

Additional references: Child 1882–98, 5:172–74; Coffin 1977: 161–62; Gower and Porter 1970: 57–58.

62. Lovely Molly

I onc't was a ploughboy, but a soldier I'm now,
  I courted wee lovely Molly, as I followed the plough;
I courted wee lovely Molly, at the age of sixteen,
  But now I must leave her, for to serve James, my king.

Refrain:
O Molly, lovely Molly, I delight in your charms,
  And there's many's the night I have lay in your arms;
But if ever I return again, it will be in the spring,
  When the mavis and the turtle dove and the nightingale sing.

You can go to the market, you can go to the fair,
  You can go to the church on Sunday, and meet your love there;
But if anyone loved you as much as I do,
  Then I won't stop your marriage, so farewell, adieu.

62. Lovely Molly
Hamish Henderson learned this song from Jock MacShannon while engaged in field-work in Kintyre (Stephanie Smith 1975: 241). He then taught it to Jeannie, who substituted "James" for MacShannon's "George" in the first stanza, presumably because of the number of Stuart kings of Scotland with that name. She subsequently taught it to Lizzie, who has recorded the song on disc. Smith has suggested that the change of names was to make the text more Scottish, or more local, and the presence of words like "mavis" (thrush) hints at a nineteenth-century reworking and localization of a text such as that recorded by Sam Henry (1923–29, 2:282) from a County Antrim infor-

mant. The last line of verse 2 has "When the lark and the linnet and the nightingale sing." Henry's first stanza runs:

> I once was a ploughboy but a soldier I'm now;
> > I courted lovely Molly, a milkmaid I vow;
> I courted lovely Molly, I delight in her charms,
> > For many's the long night I rolled in her arms.

No king is mentioned in Henry's five stanzas, the last of which introduced the "rue and thyme" motif familiar from variant texts of "Green Grows the Laurels." It is probable that Jock MacShannon came by the song from Kintyre-Ulster contact.

Recorded versions: Prestige International 13075; Lizzie Higgins, Topic 12T185.

Additional references: Huntington and Herrmann 1990: 346.

63. Bonnie Barbara O (The Bonnie Lass o' Fyvie)

> There aince come a troop o' Irish dragoons,
> > Come marchin' doun through Derby O;
> For the captain fell in love wi' a bonnie servant maid,
> > And I think they ca'd her bonnie Barbara O.

> "Come doun the stair, bonnie Barbara O,
> > Come doun the stair, bonnie Barbara O;
> Come doun the stair, an' kaim back your yalla hair,
> > An' tak' the last farewell o' your mammy, O."

"What wey can I come doun, bonnie Sandie O?
  What wey can I come doun, bonnie Sandie O?
What wey can I come doun, when I'm lockit in a room,
  An' a deep dra'-well below ma windie O?"

"For I will buy you ribbons, an' I will buy you rings,
  And I will buy you beads o' the ember O;
I'll buy you silken gouns for to rill you up an' down,
  If I follae you intae your chamber O."

"I dinnae want your ribbons, an' I dinnae want your ring,
  I dinnae want your beads o' the ember O;
As for your silken gouns I widnae pit them on,
  An' ye'll no' follae me tae ma chamber O."

"What wid your mammy think, bonnie Barbara O,
  What wid your mammy think, bonnie Barbara O?
What wid your mammy think if she heard the guineas clink,
  An' her dochter follyin' a sodger O."

63. Bonnie Barbara O (The Bonnie Lass o' Fyvie)

It is likely that Jeannie only added this song to her active repertoire late in her public career, probably because it was performed often during the Revival. Her text is almost identical to the first six stanzas in Ford 1899: 133–35, less so to the "Fyvie" verses in Ord 1930: 304–5. Cecil Sharp 1932, 2:59–61, recovered four texts and tunes in the Appalachians, three from Kentucky with airs not unrelated to the usual Scottish one, and another from North Carolina. A version of this latter type, with a heroine named Peggy rather than Barbara (and with the "Fyvie" localization) is in Buchan 1962 (reprinted in Buchan and Hall 1973: 90–91). Greig 1963: 15 has discussed the ballad, and the tune most closely associated with it is adapted to other ballads (cf. Greig and Keith 1925: 11, 181, as one of the airs for "Binorie," Child 10, and "The Earl o' Aboyne," Child 235). Standard texts with the tune are in MacColl 1965: 18 and Dallas 1972: 62–63. A version called "Handsome Polly O," recorded from Thomas Moran of Mohill, County Leitrim, by Seumas Ennis, is on *Folk Songs of Britain*, volume 8.

Recorded version: SA 1963/83.

64. Green Grows the Laurels

Green grows the laurels an' sweet falls the dew,
  Sorry was I when I parted from you;
But I hope the next meeting, I hope you'll prove true,
  And we'll change the green laurels to the violets so blue.

He passes my window both early an' late,
  And the looks that he gives me it makes my heart break;
And the looks that he gives me it makes my heart break,
  And we'll change the green laurels to the violets so blue.

He wrote me a letter, a sweet rosy line,
  But I wrote him another all twisted an' twined;
Saying, "Keep your letters and I will keep mine,
  You can write to your sweetheart and I'll write to mine."

"It's do you see yon high, high castel,
  All decorated with lilies white?
I'll give you gold, I will give you silver,
  If you say you will be mine this night."

"For what care I for your high, high castel,
  Or what care I for your liles white?
Or what care I for your gold an' silver,
  If my dear Willie was here this night?"

He put his hand into his pocket,
  His fingers they bein' long an' small;

He pulled out a ring which had once broke between them,
    And as she saw it she droppit down.

He picked her up into his arms,
    And he gave to her a sweet loving kiss;
"For I'm your true love, and I'm your Billie,
    And I've come back for to marry you."

64. Green Grows the Laurels

This song was popular not only among Scots travellers but also with Gypsy families in the south of England (see Kennedy 1975: 379). A version akin to Jeannie's was sung by Charlotte Higgins of Blairgowrie (in MacColl and Seeger 1977: 212–14). Kennedy 1975: 358 prints another recently recovered variant from Robert Cinnamond of Belfast, again with a related tune. Ewan MacColl has recorded the song as learned from his mother in 1947: "Two girls skip back to back, and reverse their positions at the beginning of every couplet" is the description he gives for it as a game song (*Streets of Song*). The origin and diffusion of the texts, the symbolism of the plant refrain, and the sex of the singer are discussed by Coffin 1952. He perceives two basic groups of texts, according to refrain content: Group A (British, with "we'll renew," "orange and blue," as sung by a man); Group B (American, with "I hope," "Red, white, and blue," as sung by a girl). Gilchrist 1914 sees political significance in the colors of the refrain words in some versions; Coffin does not quote her opinion. Jeannie's text, falling as it does into the second group, follows the pattern of Greig's and Ord's verses, though it is obvious that the words are sung by a girl rather than a man.

Recorded versions: SA 1962/74; Caedmon TC 1142/Topic 12T157; Charlotte Higgins, Prestige International 25016; Robert Cinnamond, BBC 18784; Jack Fuller, BBC 18717; Lal Smith, BBC 18302; Ewan MacColl, Topic 12T41.

Additional references: Brunnings 1981; Dean-Smith 1954: 97; Greig 1963: 2, 70, 84, 87; Henry 1924: 165, 479, 624; Hughes 1936, 4:91–93; Huntington and Herrmann 1990: 260; Karpeles 1974, 1:637; Meek 1978: 34–35; Ord 1930: 182; Sharp 1932, 2:211; Shields and Shields 1975: no. 175.

65. The Moon Shined on My Bed Last Night

For the moon shined on my bed last night,
   No rest I could not find;
For thinkin' on the bonnie boy
   The boy I left behind.
If he were here, that I love dear,
   I'd go to my bed an' sleep;
But instead of sleep all night I weep,
   And there's many's a tear I shed.

Young men so full of jealousy,
   Young girls so frank an' free;
If it was my will I wid be still
   In my love's company.
If he were here, that I love dear,

I'd go to my bed an' sleep;
But instead of sleep all night I weep,
  And there's many's a tear I shed.

For a old man came a-coortin' me,
  And he asked me for his bride;
My parents they advised me
  To give up my own true love.
He had a little money,
  It was all they did endure;
But I will live in poverty,
  And wed the lad I adore.

For it's some they speak of my true love,
  Yet many more speaks of me;
But I let them a' say what they will,
  But I'll keep his company.
I'll let them a' say what they will,
  And I'll do the best I can;
For I'm bound to leave this counterie,
  An' folly my nice young man.

65. The Moon Shined on my Bed Last Night

"The song," observed Jeannie, "actually is about a girl that had a young man, ye see. And of course, people had talked about her an' him. So her people didn't want her to take him, they wanted her to throw her lover over and take this old man with the money, ye see. An' she widnae huv that, so she said she would rather live in poverty, an' wed the lad she adored, ye see" (*What a Voice*). Jeannie's own experience in eloping with Donald may be reflected in this account of the song, though the idea of marrying for romantic love is deeply embedded in the traveller ethos. Jeannie's mother sang this as "one of her old songs." It was the last song that Jeannie taught her nephew Stanley Robertson before she died (Robertson to HG, July 17, 1979). The theme seems to bridge the satire of "An Auld Man Cam' Coortin' Me" and "A Dottered Auld Carle" (50), and songs that show resolve, usually to follow the girl's true love, such as "Far Over the Forth" (71) and "O Haud Your Tongue Dear Sally" (43). Sam Henry recovered a song, "The Banks of Cloughwater," in County Antrim that has echoes of Jeannie's text in verse 2:

On my bed last night, the moon was bright, when I no rest could find,
  Still thinking of the company that I had left behind,
They are modest, tall and neat young men, fair maidens just and free;
  If I had my will, wouldn't I be still in my love's company?

Recorded versions: SA 1952/33; 1953/198; Folktracks FSA 067; Prestige International 13075; Transatlantic XTRA 5041.

66. When I Was Nou But Sweet Sixteen

When I was nou but sweet sixteen,
　In beauty jist in bloomin' O;
O little, little did I think
　At nineteen I'd be greetin' O.

Refrain:
O the plooman lads, they're gey weel lads,
　They're false and deceivin' O;
They sail awa' and they gang awa'
　And they leave their lassies greetin' O.

O hishie ba, O I'm your ma,
　But the Lord kens fa's your daddie O;
For I wouldnae be sittin' at your fireside
　Cryin' hishie ba, my bairnie O.

For if I hadda kent whit I dae ken,
　An' taen my mither's biddin' O,
I wouldnae be sittin' at your fireside
　Cryin' hishie ba, my bairnie O.

66. When I Was Nou But Sweet Sixteen

Hamish Henderson 1957: 246–48 discusses a version of this song, "Peggy on the Banks of Spey," recorded from Mrs. Elsie Morrison of Spey Bay in 1956. Transcriptions of her variant and Jeannie's appear in *A Collection of Scotts Songs* (1972: 17–18). Jean

Redpath adds to Jeannie's text another stanza that she learned from Lucy Stewart via Arthur Argo: "It's keepit me frae loupin' dykes/Frae balls and frae waddins O/It's gi'en me balance tae my stays/And that's the latest fashion O." The text, and one of two tunes based on Jeannie's singing but collated with other printed versions, are in *The Seeds of Love* (Sedley 1967: 106–7). Buchan and Hall 1973 also print a transcription of Jeannie's rendering (81). The tune is related to that entitled "Jockey's gray Breeches" in Oswald's *Caledonian Pocket Companion* (ca. 1745, 2:32). One text of the song, without tune, is in the Greig MS and Duncan MS.

Recorded versions: SA 1952/33; 1960/203/205; SX 1953/2; 1958/4; Topic 10T52 (12T96); Riverside RLP 12-633; Jean Redpath, Folk-Legacy FSS-49.

67. Young Emslie (Edwin in the Lowlands Low, Laws M34)

Young Emslie loved a sailor boy,
   Young Emslie loved a sailor boy,
Because he ploughed in the lowlands low.

"For if you go to a public house,
   A public down by the shore,
An' if you chance to enter in,
   Don't let my parents know."

As young Edward sat a-drinking,
    As young Edward sat a-drinking,
Little, little was he thinking
    That sorrow crowned his haid.

As young Emslie lay a-slumbering,
    As young Emslie lay a-slumbering,
She dreamed a fearful dream.

She dreamed the' murderit her own true love,
    That robbit him an' stabbit him,
An' the' sank his body low.

"O mother dear, O mother dear,
    Come tell tae me no lie;
What did ye do with the stranger
    You had here last night?"

"O daughter dear, O daughter dear,
    To you we'll tell no lie;
We robbit him an' we stabbit him,
    An' we sank his body low."

"O you cruel, cruel parents,
    O you cruel, cruel parents;
All for the murder of my own true love,
    You shall die on a public shore."

---

67. Young Emslie (Edwin in the Lowlands Low, Laws M34)

Jeannie heard this song from her mother who, according to Lizzie, sang it every day. Jeannie believed the story to be based on fact: "When the young sailors came off the boats with their money, they'd tae get them into these drinkin' places where they gave them a bed and drink, and of course they robbit them and they usually did them in, and then they throwed the bodies in the watter again" (SA 1954/103). Laws 1957: 197–98 indicates four nineteenth-century broadside texts of the song, and it has been suggested that the present one came by way of the expanding fish trade at that time (Hall 1969). Greig 1963: 123 has a version entitled "Young Emma," and numerous textual variants have been noted in North America (cf. Stephanie Smith 1975: 306). Like Jeannie, Lizzie sings three-line stanzas in verses 4 and 5; the ABBC form of the melody lines then becomes ABC for these stanzas and for verse 1 also. Lizzie, however, makes her first stanza a four-line one with the additional "An' why she loved that sailor boy." One must assume that Jeannie's memory is responsible for the truncated verse, though to propose this reason for verses 4 and 5 would be conjectural. It may be, as

Stephanie Smith 1975: 191–92 believes, a result of the oral process that the three-line stanzas have become a fluid part of the song. Another transcription of Jeannie's singing is in *Tocher* 9 (1973): 16–17.

Recorded versions: SA 1954/103; SX 1958/4; Lizzie Higgins, Topic 12T185; Peter Bellamy, Topic 12TS400; George Hanna, Topic 12TS 372; Louis Killen, Topic 12T126; Betty Smith, Folk Legacy FSA 53; Doug Wallin, Folkways FA 2418.

Additional references: Dean-Smith 1954: 119; Henry 1923–29, 1:102; Huntington and Herrmann 1990: 434, 449; Morton 1969: 53–54; Karpeles 1974, 1:290–91.

68. The Butcher Boy (Laws P24)

My parents gave me good learning,
    Good learning they gave unto me;
They sent me to a butcher's shop,
    For a butcher boy to be.

It was there I met with a fair young maid,
    With dark and rolling eyes;
And I promised for to marry her,
    On the month of sweet July.

I went up to her mother's house,
    Between the hour of eight and nine;

And I asked her for to walk with me,
 Down by the foamin' brine.

"Down by the foamin' brine we'll go,
 Down by the foamin' brine;
For that won' be a pleasant walk,
 Down by the foamin' brine."

But they walked east and they walked west,
 And they walked it all alone;
Till he pulled a knife from out of his breast,
 And stabbed her to the ground.

She fell upon her bended knee,
 Help and mercy she did cry;
Roarin', "Billy dear, don't murder me,
 For I'm not prepared to die."

But he took her by the lily-white hand,
 And he dragged her to the brim;
And with a mighty downward push,
 He pushed her body in.

But he went home til his own mother's house,
 Between the hour of twelve and one;
But little did his mother think
 What her only son had done.

He asked her for a hankychief,
 To tie around his head;
And he asked her for a candlelight
 To show him up to bed.

But no sleep, no rest could this young man get,
 No rest he could not find;
For he thought he saw the flames of hell
 Approachin' his bedside.

But the murder it was soon found out,
 And the gallows was his doom;
For the murder of sweet Mary Ann,
 That lies where the roses bloom.

68. *The Butcher Boy (Laws P24)*

This was, according to Lizzie, one of Jeannie's favorite songs (Stephanie Smith 1975: 201). She learned it from "an old woman about twenty-five or twenty-six years ago" (SA 1953/247). Her text and air are quite similar to two texts (E, F) and the three tunes contained in the Greig MS (Shuldham-Shaw and Lyle 1983: 45–48). Greig 1963: 137 prints a text close to Jeannie's, the first of that particular subtype to be recorded (cf. his 179). In its final phrase, Jeannie's tune resembles the close of some recent melodies from "The Cherry Tree Carol" (cf. Bronson's Aa group, *Traditional Tunes*, 2:4–7). The second line, with its cadence on the fourth degree, brings it into the orbit of tunes like that for "The False Bride" (72). Laws 1957: 104–22 has probed the ramifications of the ballad plot and its textual complexity, deriving all variants from an eighteenth-century broadside entitled "The Berkshire Tragedy; or the Wittam Miller" (Wytham is in Berkshire, not far from Oxford). The present plot seems to be a recasting of "The Cruel Miller," a version found on a later broadside (Laws 1957: 104). MacColl and Seeger 1977: 237–39 print a variant sung by "Queen" Caroline Hughes, a Dorset Gypsy, in which elements of "Died for Love" are grafted onto the main story. Phoebe Smith, another Gypsy from Suffolk, recorded a version of "The Oxford Girl" for Peter Kennedy in 1956, in which her ninth stanza recalls Jeannie's ninth verse: "I asked him for a candle/To light me up to bed/I asked him for a handkerchief/To bind my aching head" (Kennedy 1975: 713).

Recorded versions: SA 1953/247; SX 1958/4; Riverside RLP 12-633; Caedmon TC 1163; Topic 12T195; Lizzie Higgins, SA 1970/22; Enoch Kent, Topic TOP 81.

Additional references: Gower and Porter 1972; Lloyd 1967: 235.

69. Bonnie Udny

O Udny, bonnie Udny, you shine whaur you stand,
  And the mair I gaze upon you, the mair my hairt yearns;
The mair I gaze upon you the mair my hairt yearns,
  For a' your lands in Scotland, bonnie Udny for me.

For it's you'll pull the red rose and it's I'll pull the thyme,
  For it's you drink tae your love, and I'll drink tae mine;
We'll drink tae we're merry, we will drink tae we're fou,
  For there's lang walks of Udny, they are a' tae go through.

We will drink an' be merry, we will drink an' gang hame,
  For if we bide here onie langer, we'll get a bad name;
And tae get a bad name, love, for that wad never dee,
  For a' your lands in Scotland, bonnie Udny for me.

For it's you'll pull the red rose and it's I'll pull the thyme,
  For it's you drink tae your love, and I'll drink tae mine;
We will drink tae we're merry, we will drink tae we're fou,
  For it's lang walks of Udny, they are a' tae go through.

They have stolen my sweethairt, and they've put him on the spree,
  They have stolen my sweethairt and they've teen him frae me;
And to keep my eyes from weeping what a fool I wad be,
  For a' your lands in Scotland, bonnie Udny for me.

69. Bonnie Udny

According to Lizzie, this song has been in the family for a considerable time, and it was her own particular favorite (Stephanie Smith 1975: 228). A comparison of Jeannie's six stanzas with Lizzie's four reveals the medley-like nature of the text commented upon by Greig 1963: 32. The textual variants extend back to the eighteenth century. Ritson 1784: 44 prints a song with the title, "The Pleasures of Sunderland," whose final stanza runs:

> Sunderland's a fine place, it shines where it stands,
> And the more I look upon it the more my heart warms,
> And if I was there I would make myself free,
> Every man to his mind, but Sunderland for me.

Peter Buchan published another *refacimento*, perhaps from the original broadside text, in his 1828 collection (as "Portmore"; another broadside text is in Wright 1975: 345). The title and tune of "Bonny Portmore" are in Bunting 1840, who got the latter from an Ulster harper, Daniel Black, in 1796. The Portmore connection refers to the Castle of Portmore, built by Lord Conway on the side of Portmore Lough in 1664. The castle was destroyed after his death, and the Great Oak of Portmore that had been blown down in 1760 was, with the rest of the estate, sold off in 1761. One must presume that this destruction inspired the broadside from which the many variants stem. Croker 1886 imagined (196–99) Tom Moore responsible for the popular variant text, "The Boys of Kilkenny." O Lochlainn 1939: 73 mentions a version that his father, a native of South Kilkenny (b. 1859), learned in childhood. Moffat 1897: 346 suggests Michael Kelly as the author. A variant called "The Chaps of Cockaigny" was recovered by Sharp in Somerset in 1904 (Karpeles 1974, 1:633–34), and there are three in the Hammond MS from Dorset, 1905–6. Textual affinity is evident, again, in the versions of Baring Gould and Sharp 1906: 46 and Joyce 1909: 73; further analogs are in Chappell, Christie, and O'Neill. Sam Henry noted a version called "Bonny Portrush" in 1938 (Huntington and Herrmann 1990: 171). Greig considers the scattered textual offshoots; in his MS, he has three tunes, none of them the present one (which Hall 1969 sees as a variant of that for the Irish recruiting song, "Johnny Gallagher"). Duncan's MS, 67, has the title of "Bonnie Wudny" with the note that this name was used by John Wilson of Premnay, "who furnishes complete words." Ord 1930: 341–42 includes a somewhat literary text without a tune. In his singing of "Glenlogie" (Child 238), John Strachan offers yet another transformation of the lines:

> O Bethelnie, O Bethelnie, it shines where it stands,
> And the heather bells o'er it shine o'er Fyvie's lands.

Buchan and Hall 1973: 103 print a version of Jeannie's text and tune, but with three stanzas only. Another transcription is in *A Collection of Scots Songs* (1972: 13).

Recorded versions: SA 1952/147/154; 1955/82; SX 1958/5; Lizzie Higgins, Topic 12T185.

Additional references: Chappell 1858–59; Christie 1876–81; Gower and Porter 1977: 88–92; Henry 1923–29, 2:277; O Boyle 1976: 50–51; O'Neill 1903.

70. I Made Up My Mind
(The Trail to Mexico, Laws B13)

I made up my mind to change my ways,
    And quit the crowd that was so gay;
And leave the girl that promised me her hand,
    And ride on south to the Rio Grande.

It was in the spring of '53,
    When A. J. Stinson said to me:
"For I say, young fellay, how'd you like to go,
    And ride this herd down to Mexico?"

It was a long and toilsome road,
    As we rode down to Mexico;
With laughter light an' cowboy song,
    To Mexico as we rode along.

But when I reach'd that distant land,
    I wanted my love, an' I could not stand;
So I wrote her a letter, a letter to my dear,
    But never a word from her could I hear.

But when I reached my native land,
    They said she'd married a richer man;
They said she'd married to a richer life,
    "Therefore, wild cowboy, take another wife."

O curse your gold, and your silver too,
    Confound the girl that can't prove true;
But I'll go out west where the bullets fly,
    And ride this trail till the day I die.

70. I Made Up My Mind (The Trail to Mexico, Laws B13)
Jeannie learned this from the singing of Pete Seeger (recorded on Folkways FP 48-5;
also on FP 5003, FH 5003), to the commonly sung tune. Her small changes to Seeger's
words, however, give some idea of the evolution through which such texts can pass.
Laws 1964: 139 describes the hiring of the narrator as taking place in 1883, and not, as
in Jeannie's and Seeger's texts, "'53." Cox 1925: 358 links the song to the British piece,
"Early in the Spring," printing four texts of this song from North American tradition.

Recorded versions: SA 1960/114; 1962/25.

71. Far Over the Forth

Far over the Forth, I look to the North,
    But what is the North and its Highlands to me?
The South nor the East gae ease to my breast,
    It's the far foreign lands or the wild roarin' sea.

I look to the West as I ging tae my rest,
That happy my dreams and my slumbers may be;
For far in the West lives he I lo'e best,
The laddie that's dear to my bairnie an' me.

But his father he frowned on the love of his boyhood,
And O his proud mother looked cauld upon me;
But he follied me aye tae my hame in the shielin',
And the house of Breadalbane rung wild wi' our glee.

A' the lang summer day mid the heather an' braicken,
O the joy an' the light o' his bonnie blue e'e!
But little I thought that the wild westren ocean
Wid be rollin' this day 'tween ma laddie an' me.

But we plighted our faith on the cairn o' the mountain,
The deer and the roe stood bride-maidens to me;
And the bride's tryin' glass was the clear crystal fountain:
What then was the world to my laddie an' me?

But I look to the West as I gae to my rest,
That happy my dreams an' my slumbers may be;
For far in the West lives the lad I lo'e best,
Tha laddie that's dear to my bairnie an' me.

71. Far Over the Forth

This song was learned from Lizzie, who, according to Jeannie, heard an older traveller woman sing it (SA 1952/43). Lizzie, however, told Stephanie Smith (1975: 221) that she learned it from her father as a child. There are some differences in the two renderings: Jeannie has inserted Lizzie's final verse after her first one, so that her first two stanzas follow *The Scots Musical Museum* text closely (James Johnson 1790: 434). Lizzie's third and fourth stanzas are transposed by Jeannie here. The two-stanza text in the *Museum* is set to part of Niel Gow's "Charles Graham's welcome hame," but Burns did not care for the cadence in its second part and suggested that Stephen Clarke might conceive a better one (see Gow's *Second Collection*, 1788: 20). The air used by Jeannie is essentially that which Ewan MacColl also sings to "Lord Randal" (cf. Bronson 1959–72, 4:449; *A Collection of Scots Songs*: 39).

Recorded versions: SA 1952/43; 1962/25; Lizzie Higgins, Topic 12T185; Ray Fisher, Topic 12T128.

Additional reference: Glen 1900: 193.

72. She's Only My Auld Shoes
(The False Bride)

For I saw my own bonnie lass to the church go,
    Gold rings on her fingers, white gloves on her hands;
Gold rings on her fingers, white gloves on her hands,
    She was away to get wed to another.

I said, "My own bonnie lass, wait a wee while,
    For you are false beguiled;
For you are false beguiled,
    But you're only my auld shoes when he's got you."

It was servin' the glasses of brandy and wine,
    Here is health to the bonnie lass that should have been mine;
Here is health to the bonnie lass that should have been mine,
    But she's only my auld shoes when you've got her.

But the ladies and gents they inquired off of me:
    "How many blackberries grows roun' a salt sea?"
But I gare them one back with a tear in my e'e:
    "How many ships sail in a forest?"

She has broken my hert and forever left me,
    She has broken my hert and forever left me;
But it's not onc't or twice that she's lain now with me,
    For she's there and she cannae deny it.

But I'll lay doun my heid and I'll tak' a lang sleep,
Youse can cover me over by lilies so sweet;
Youse can cover me over by lilies so sweet,
For that's the only way I'll ever forget her.

72. She's Only My Auld Shoes (The False Bride)

Jeannie's text of six stanzas makes for instructive comparison with the ten stanzas Henderson and Kennedy recorded from Lucy Stewart in 1955 (Kennedy 1975: 352). Jeannie's first, third, fourth, and fifth verses correspond to Lucy's second, sixth, tenth, and ninth. While Lucy's version has a more linear narrative, Jeannie's provides a lyrical ending that welcomes death. The song text shows a few recorded variants in Northeast tradition (cf. Christie 1876–81, 2:134–35; Greig 1909–14: 24; Ord 1930: 175), probably finding its way north during the nineteenth century. A broadside by John White of Newcastle, and another in the *Euing Collection*, indicate a seventeenth-century date for the first printed appearance of the text (cf. Kennedy 1975: 375; Stephanie Smith 1975: 197). Most versions of the song recovered in recent times have been English or North American and bear as title "The False Bride" or "The Week Before Easter." Greig, in proposing a southern origin for the song, remarks how English texts often end with a verse in which the protagonist asks for a grave to be dug, while in the Scottish ones he is resigned to finding another love. The riddling stanza in Jeannie's and Lizzie's variants is not present in the otherwise fuller texts in the Greig and Duncan MSS. Jeannie's tune, which is a cognate of Lucy's, is found in the Rymour Club's *Miscellanea*, and there are other close parallels from Somerset and Gloucestershire in Karpeles 1974: 268–73.

Recorded versions: SA 1954/105; 1957/98; 1959/16/107; 1960/109/201; 1962/13.

Additional references: Gower and Porter 1972: 149; O Lochlainn 1939: 170–71; Seeger and MacColl 1960: 31; Shields 1981: 41.

73. I Wish, I Wish
(Love Has Brought Me to Despair, Laws P25)

What a voice, what a voice, what a voice I hear,
    It is like the voice of my Willie dear;
But if I had wings like that swallow flyin',
    For I would clasp in the arms of my Billy Boy.

When my apron it hung low,
    My true love followed through frost and snow;
But now my apron it's tae my shins,
    And he passes me by and he'll ne'er speir in.

It was up onto the white house brae,
    That he called a strange girlie to his knee,
And he tellt her a tale which he once told me.

O I wish, I wish, O I wish in vain,
    I wish I was a maid again;
But a maid again I will never be
    Till a aipple it grows on a orange tree.

O I wish, I wish that my babe was born,
    And smilin' on some nurse's knee;
And for mysel' to be dead and gone,
    And the long green grass growin' over me.

For there's a blackbird sits on yon tree;
   Some says it's blind and it cannae see;
  Some says it's blind and it cannae see,
    And so is my true love to me.

73. I Wish, I Wish (Love Has Brought Me to Despair, Laws P25)

Other titles for this song, which Jeannie learned from Maria, are common; it belongs to the "Died of/for Love—The Bold/Brisk Young Sailor/Farmer" story complex. A note by Lucy Broadwood (in *Journal of the Folk-Song Society* 19 [1915]: 186–87) indicates a probable ancestor of the text in Laing's *Broadside Ballads* (ca. 1700) with the title "Arthur's Seat shall be my bed, or Love in despair." The essence of the theme has been compared to stanzas of "Waly, Waly" in *Orpheus Caledonius* (1725) and the later version in the *The Scots Musical Museum* (James Johnson 1788: 166; see also Ritson 1794, 1:235–36). The further textual connection with "Jamie Douglas" (Child 204) is well known. Bronson 1959–72, 3:258 firmly believes that the makers of the ballad used a popular lament to fill out its verses, singing it to the same tune. Christie 1876: 248 includes a version of the song in his first volume. It appears in the Duncan MS as "The Student Boy," and the first of five tunes in the Greig MS is entitled "Arthur's Seat." The most recent Scottish variants are in: Buchan 1962: 61, with the title, "Will Ye Gang, Love?"; Buchan and Hall 1973: 93, a version by Lizzie Mary Hutchison; and MacColl and Seeger 1977: 194–98, sung by Charlotte Higgins. The air used by both Lizzie Mary Hutchison and Charlotte Higgins is closely related to Jeannie's, and she herself uses it for "The Famous Flower of Serving Men" (Child 106). It appears again in MacColl and Seeger 1977 as that for "The Convict Song," sung by John MacDonald (291). The earliest English printed variants are in Kidson 1891: 44–46, Baring Gould and Sheppard 1892: 184–85, and the Hammond MS (1905). Dean-Smith 1954: 63 gives a list of published versions. See also Gilchrist 1938: 192–93 and 1946: 16–17, Lloyd 1953: 103, and Palmer 1973: 278. See also Reeves 1958: 43–45, 90–92; and Reeves 1960: 96–98. There is an analog (in *Journal of the Folk-Song Society* 27 (1930): 110–12) called "The Shannon Water, or Mabel Kelly," and another immediately following, "Happy the Worm Lies Under the Stone." The Stanford-Petrie collection has it as no. 811, "I wish, I wish, but I wish in vain," and there are two fragments in Bunting 1796. Henry recovered it from Mrs. H. Dinsmore of Coleraine as "The Apron of Flowers" (Huntington and Herrmann 1990: 393). Several versions of the text have been recovered in North America, where it has been linked to "Careless Love" (cf. Lomax 1960: 585). Laws 1957: 61 names it "Love Has Brought Me to Despair" (P25) and notes versions from Indiana and Illinois. Additional texts are in Combs 1925: 205, Cox 1925: 353–57, Korson 1949: 48–49, Owens 1950: 134–35, and Randolph (1950: 268–69); see also the "Lullaby" in Grover n.d.: 24. "Floating" stanzas, lines, and images link the verses to similar stories of unhappy love, such as "The Butcher Boy" (68 above; Laws P24) or "The Sailor Boy" (Laws K12). The imagery of the apron (pregnancy), white house ("alehouse"), strange girl, apple on the orange tree, burial beneath long green grass, and the blind girl are retained in most English and Scottish versions of the text.

Recorded versions: SA 1952/33; 1953/195; SX 1958/2; 1956/2; Topic 10T52; Collector CLE 1201 (Jean Ritchie's recording of Jeannie singing stanzas 2, 3, 4, 6); Folktracks FSA 067; Lizzie Higgins, Lismor LIFL 7004; Isla Cameron, Columbia KL 206; Amy Birch, Topic 12TS349; Campbell Family, Topic 12T120; Martin Carthy, Topic 12TS344; Audrey Coppard, Folkways FP 917; Frank Hinchcliffe, Topic 12TS308; Roscoe Holcomb, Folkways FA 2374; Norman Kennedy, Topic 12T178, Folk-Legacy FSS-34; Geoff Ling, Topic 12T236; Walter Pardon, Topic 12TS392; Frank Profitt, Folk-Legacy FSA 1; Jasper Smith, Topic 12TS304; Joseph Taylor, Leader LEA 4050; Tom Willett, Topic 12T84.

Additional references: Child 1882–98, 4:90–105; Gower and Porter 1977: 67–70; Henry 1923–29, 2:194; Joyce 1909: 134; Kennedy 1975: 349, 372; Loesberg 1980, 2:60–61; Lyle 1975: 108; Moulden 1979: 13.

74. Mary Hamilton (Child 173)

Yestreen there were four Maries,
    This night they're only three;[7]
There was Mary Seton an' Mary Beaton
    An' Mary Carmichael an' me.

A knock cam' to the kitchen door,
    It sounded through a' the room;
That Mary Hamiton had a wean
    To the highest man in the toun.

"Where is that wean you had last night,
    Where is that wean, I say?"
"I hadnae a wean to you last nicht,
    Nor yet a wean today."

But he searched high and he searched low,
    And he searched below the baid;
And it was there he found his ain dear wee wean,
    It was lyin' in a pool o' blood.

Yestreen there was four Maries,
    This night they're only three;[8]
There was Mary Seaton and Mary Beaton
    An' Mary Carmichael an' me.

O little did my mither ken,
    The day she cradlit me;
The land I was to travel in
    Or the death I was to dee.[9]

For oftimes I hae dressed my queen,
    An' put gowd in her hair;

But little I got for my reward,
    Was the gallows to be my share.

O happy, happy is the maid
    That's born o' beauty free;
For it was my dimplin' rosy cheeks
    That was the ruin o' me.

Yestreen there was four Maries,
    This night they're only three;
There was Mary Seton an' Mary Beaton
    And Mary Carmichael an' me.

74. Mary Hamilton (Child 173)

Old people recited this ballad, Jeannie remarks, "like a poetry" when she first heard it as a child in Blairgowrie. The reference is to stanzas 2, 3, and 4, in particular, though Jeannie herself usually sang rather than spoke them. Lizzie's version, as included by Stephanie Smith 1975: 170, suggests plasticity in the order of verses: Lizzie's second stanza is Jeannie's seventh, Lizzie's third Jeannie's eighth, and so on. To say that this flexibility is evidence for the "lyric" nature of many variant texts is perhaps warranted, though to assume that the lyrical bent undermines the singers' conception of this song as a narrative one is to take a devolutionary view of the traditional ballad (cf. Coffin 1957). The organic process of folk tradition involves more than simple linear progression through time (cf. the note on "The Gypsy Laddie," 14 above). Jeannie's tune belongs to Bronson's class D, which he characterizes as late in the record.

Recorded versions: SA 1953/196; 1960/201; Caedmon TC 1146/Topic 12T161; Riverside RLP 12-633; Folktracks FSA 067; Lizzie Higgins, SA 1970/21; Isabel Sutherland, Topic 12T151.

Additional references: Bronson 1959–72, 3:150–55 and 4:494; Child 1882–98, 3:379–99; Coffin 1977: 114–15; Gower and Porter 1970: 17–18; Shuldham-Shaw and Lyle 1983: 36–38.

75. Willie's Fate (Willie's Fatal Visit, Child 255)

For Willie's gaen owre yon high, high hill,
    An' doun yon dowie den;
For it was there he met a grievous ghost,
    That would fear ten thousand men.

For he's gaen owre yon high, high hill,
    An' doun by Mary Stile;[10]
Wan an' weary was the ghost,
    On him that grimly smiled.

"Aft hae ye travellt this road, Willie,
    Aft hae ye travellt in sin;[11]
An' nae a thought of your poor soul,[12]
    When your sinful life is done."

"Aft hae ye travellt this road, Willie,
    Your bonnie new love tae see;
Aft hae ye travellt this road, Willie,
    And ne'er a thought on me."[13]

"Aft hae ye travellt this road, Willie,
  Your bonnie new love tae see;
But you'll never travel this road again,
  For this night avenged I'll be."

Then she has ta'en her perjurt love,
  Reived him frae gair tae gair;
And on likae side o' Mary Stile,
  Of him she hung a share.

His father an' mither baith made moan,
  His new love muckle mair;
His father an' mither baith made moan,
  And his new love reived her hair.

75. Willie's Fate (Willie's Fatal Visit, Child 255)

Having learned this ballad from Maria, Jeannie in turn began to teach it to Lizzie in 1973 (Stephanie Smith 1975: 124). After Peter Kennedy's recordings and also those for *The Travelling Stewarts,* some fragmentation in Jeannie's text is perceptible. Infrequent performance of the song and, later, poor health may account for this, although the variant published by Bronson (2) is the most confident of the three extant. Jeannie's melody may be related to that printed by Christie 1876–81, 1: 218, for the second half of her tune, as Bronson asserts, resembles the first half of Christie's, with its distinctive octave leap (cf. "The Gypsy Laddie" subgroup with this trait). The fragment of "Clyde's Water" (Child 216) sometimes sung by Jeannie was set to this air. A transcription of Lizzie's tune is in Stephanie Smith 1975: 271. Lizzie's words show some differences that may have arisen as Jeannie's memory failed after several strokes, or as spontaneous or deliberate changes. The text is fundamentally from Peter Buchan, beginning at stanza 13. Child believed that the first part of the ballad (not sung by Jeannie or Lizzie) was a medley of "Sweet William's Ghost," "Clerk Saunders," and "The Grey Cock." The suggestion that the ghost is Willie's former lover, however, is not present in Buchan's text.

Recorded versions: SA 1962/74; Caedmon TC 1146/Topic 12T161; Topic 12T179; Lizzie Higgins, SA 1973/174; BBC REC 293.

Additional references: Bronson 1959–72, 4: 64–65; Child 1882–98, 4: 415–16; Munro 1984: 186–88.

76. The Twa Brithers (Child 49)

There were twa brithers at the schill,
  An' when they got awa';
It's "Will ye play at the stane-chuckin',
  Or will ye play the ba'?
Or will ye gae up tae yon bonnie green hill,
  An' dare we'll wrestle a fa'?"

"I winnae play at the stane-chuckin',
  Or will I play at the ba';
But I'll gae up tae yon bonnie green hill,
  An' there we'll wrestle a fa'."

They wraslit up, they wraslit doun,
  Till John fell to the ground;
But a dirk fell out of William's pooch,
  Gave John a deadly wownd.

"O lift me, lift me on your back,
  Tak' me tae yon well sae fair;
An' wash the blood frae aff my wownd,
  That it may bleed nae mair."

He's liftit him upon hees back,
  Ta'en him tae yon well sae fair;
He's washed the blood frae aff hees wownd,
  But aye it bled the mair.

"O ye'll tak' aff my holland sark,
　　Reeve it frae gair tae gair;
He's stapped it in the bloody wownd,
　　But it bled mair an' mair.

"O lift me, lift me on your back,
　　Tak' me tae Kirklan' fair;
An' dig a grave baith wide an' deep,
　　An' lay my body there."

"Ye'll lay my arrows at my head,
　　My bent bow at my feet;
My sword an' buckler by my side,
　　As I wis wont tae sleep."

76. The Twa Brithers (Child 49)

It is possible that Jeannie and Lizzie both learned this ballad from Donald, since Lizzie affirmed that she first got it from her father; she and Jeannie sing virtually corresponding texts and tunes (cf. Stephanie Smith 1975: 120). The song may have been in a number of travelling families for generations. Hamish Henderson relates how Nellie MacGregor, then living in Aberdeen, alerted him first to the continuing existence of a ballad that Greig and Duncan had not encountered among the farming folk; after 1954, "versions came pouring in from all over Central and North East Scotland" (Henderson 1975: 8). Other traditional variants, in addition to those of Jeannie and Lizzie (who often sang it in folksong clubs), performed by Lucy Stewart, Belle Stewart, and Sheila MacGregor, are on commercial recordings. All the melodic forms in the published recordings are related in their plagal hexatonic structure (see Bronson 1959–72, 4:462–64). The verses that Lucy Stewart sang for Kenneth Goldstein in 1959 are closer in many respects to those of the Perthshire Stewarts than those of Jeannie's family, although both Lucy and Jeannie lived in Aberdeenshire (cf. Child's C and E texts). In the Stewart versions, the rest of the family is to be informed of the brother's death, and there is still the implication of plotting by the stepmother. Still, the knife-wound is explicitly accidental in the Higgins and Blairgowrie Stewart texts, while in Lucy's it points to murder. Whether this suggestion of murder has any connection with the "plot" of "Edward" (Child 13) is an open question, though Maggie Stewart, Jeannie's aunt, sang a line in that ballad, "And a good scholar I'll come home," which recalls Sheila MacGregor's seventh stanza. The solution of such differing texts must be that travelling families retain their own versions even when they come into contact with families from other parts of the country, or with other families from the same county who have particular versions of a song. For Belle Stewart, for instance, the ballad had special significance for two reasons: first, it was one of her father's favorite songs; and second, she had learned it from her brother Donald MacGregor, one of two brothers left in a family of nine (four older brothers and two sisters had died before Belle was born) (Porter 1985). Common, at least, to all the recorded texts here is the folkloric notion of blood from a wound, maliciously inflicted or not, being unstaunchable (cf. some texts of Child 20, "The Cruel Mother," and Shakespeare's *Macbeth*). The ballad may well have remained in favor with the travelling folk for internecine reasons that have little to do with the supposed historical origin of the ballad story.

Recorded versions: SA 1957/44/51; 1958/25; 1959/8/77/86; SX 1960/3/5; Jazz Selection JES 4; Lizzie Higgins, SA 1970/21; Topic 12TS260; Lucy Stewart, Folkways FG 3519; Caedmon TC 1145/Topic 12T160; Belle Stewart, Topic 12TS307; Sheila MacGregor, Tangent TGNM 119/D; Isabel Sutherland, Topic 12T151.

Additional references: Child 1882–98, 1:434–44; Coffin 1977: 55–57; Gower and Porter 1970.

77. Lord Lovat (Lord Lovel, Child 75)

Lord Lovat he stands at his stable-door,
   He was brushing his milk steed down;
When who passed by but Lady Nancy Bell,
   She was wishing her lover good speed,
   She was wishing her lover good speed.

"Where are you going, Lord Lovat?" she said,
   "Come promise, tell me true."

"Over the sea, strange countries to see;
    Lady Nancy Bell, I'll come and see you,
Lady Nancy Bell, I'll come an' see."

He was away a year or two,
    But he scarcely had been three,
When a mightiful dream cam' into his head:
    "Lady Nancy Bell, I'll come and see you,
Lady Nancy Bell, I'll come an' see."

He passed down by the village church,
    An' down to Mary's Hall;
An' all the ladies were weeping forth,
    An' all the ladies were weeping forth.

"Who is dead?" Lord Lovat he said,
    "Come promise, tell me true."
"Lady Nancy Bell died for her true-lover's sake,
    And Lord Lovat that was his name."

He ordered the coffin to be opened up,
    And the white sheet rolled down;
He kissed her on the cold-clay lips,
    An' the tears came trickin' down,
An' the tears came tricklin' down.

77. Lord Lovat (Lord Lovel, Child 75)

Well, he went away overseas, an' he promised tae come back before long, but he went away an' he was about three years away. And suddenly he remembered, that he promised Nancy Bell that he would come back til her. But he'd overstayed the time, and of course, when it came into hees head, he suddenly made up his mind that he would come back. And when he came back to the place where he'd left her, he went down through the village, and when he came down upon a place they called St. Mary's Hall, he saw all the ladies weepin', so he went in about an' he askit them what they were all weeping for. And they said that they were weeping for Lady Nancy Bell who had died for her true lover's sake. And of course, he went in, for to see her, when she was lying before she was buried. (*What a Voice*)

Jeannie learned the song when she was about nine, from "a very old woman in Aberdeenshire. . . . but I think she came from Perthshire. It was Cameron or something they called her" (SA 1953/247). Lizzie recounted how Jeannie would sing the ballad to her instead of the lullabies that Lizzie disliked, and how, through Jeannie's singing, she came to love the song and presumably to assimilate it (Stephanie Smith 1975: 22). A suggestive distinction in the learning process is that Lizzie would pick up songs from her mother without deliberately seeking them out, whereas Jeannie was often helped by Maria in her learning of traditional songs. Lizzie, rather, explored her father's repertoire (SA 1972/22; Stephanie Smith 1975: 49–50). In many ways it is the readily identifiable air that has kept this ballad alive (cf. Bronson 1959–72, 2:189 and 4:471–72; in the latter, Jeannie's variant text and the tune of the first stanza are transcribed). A closely related text and tune are sung by Charlotte Higgins (MacColl and Seeger 1977: 70–72). The earliest printed version of the tune is in Davidson 1847: 148, and Child includes an 1860 variant of it from Aberdeen in his "Musical Appendix" (in Child 1882–98, 5:416). Parodies of the ballad may well have been aided by the dominant tune, which has an opening strain akin to Burns' "Last May a Braw Wooer." Sam Cowell, the English comedian, is reported to have sung a parody, about 1850–55 in Aberdeen (Greig and Keith 1925: 57); Lomax 1960: 401 asserts that it was probably the most widely sung Child ballad in North America during the nineteenth century. Many North American versions of the ballad are from the Civil War period or earlier (cf. Coffin 1977: 73). Kinloch printed it, and Bell 1877: 134 relates how J. H. Dixon told him of seeing a black-letter broadside copy from the time of Charles II, in which the hero, Bell continues, may have been a member of the Loveles or Delavelles family of Northumberland that is celebrated in "Chevy Chase" (Child 162).

Recorded versions: SA 1953/247; 1959/80; SX 1957/3; 1958/8; 1960/3; Topic 10T52; Riverside RLP 12-633; Folktracks FSA 067; Lizzie Higgins, SA 1970/20; Topic 12TS260; Ethel Findlater, Topic 12T160.

Additional references: Child 1882–98, 2:204–13; Gower and Porter 1970; Munro 1970; Lyle 1975: 54–55.

78. Mill o' Tifty's Annie
(Andrew Lammie, Child 233)

At Mill o' Tifty there lived a man,
    In the neighbourhood o' Fyvie;
He had a lovely daughter fair,
    Whose name was bonnie Annie.

Her cheeks were like the bloomin' rose,
    That hails the rosy mornin',
With innocent heart and graceful mien
    Her beauteous face adornin'.

Lord Fyvie had a trumpeter,
    Whose name was Andra Lammie;
For he had the art to gain the heart
    Of Mill o' Tifty's Annie.

Lord Fyvie he rose by the door,
    His trumpeter before him;
His trumpeter rode him before,
    Even this same Andra Lammie.

Her mother called her to the door:
    "Come here to me, my Annie;
Did you ever see a prettier man
    Than the trumpeter o' Fyvie?

She sighed sore, but said no more,
 Alas for bonnie Annie!
For she durst not own that her heart was won
 By the trumpeter o' Fyvie.

At night when all went to their bed,
 All slept full soun' but Annie;
Love so oppressed her tender breast,
 And love will waste her body.

"For the first time me an' my true love met,
 Was in the woods o' Fyvie."
For his lovely form and speech so soft
 Soon gained the heart o' Annie.

"He called me mistress, but I said no,
 That I was Tifty's bonnie Annie;
With apples sweet he did me treat,
 And kisses soft and many."

But now alas! her father heard
 That the trumpeter o' Fyvie
Has had the art to gain the heart
 Of Mill o' Tifty's Annie.

Her father soon a letter wrote,
 And sent it on to Fyvie;
For to tell his daughter was bewitched
 By his servant Andra Lammie.

It was up the stair to his trumpeter,
 He called him soon and shortly:
"Pray tell me soon, what is this you've done
 To Tifty's bonnie Annie?"

It's woe be to the Mill o' Tifty's pride,
 For it has ruint many;
And they have said that she should not wed
 With the trumpeter o' Fyvie.

"But where shall I find a boy so kind,
 That'll carry a letter canny?
And who'll rin on to Tifty's glen,
 Give that to my love Annie?"

"For Tifty he has daughters three,
    And they all are wondrous bonnie;
But you will ken her owre the rest,
    Give that to my love Annie."

"For you will come to the Bridge of Sate,
    Whaur I will come an' meet you;
For it's there we will renew our love,
    Before I gang an' leave you."

"I'll buy tae you a braw new goun,
    My love I'll buy it bonnie;
"But ere you come back I will be laid
    In the green churchyard o' Fyvie."

Her father struck her wowndless sore,
    And woe be to her brothers;
They broke her back owre the haal door,
    For the lovin' o' Andra Lammie.

"For if you strike me I will cry,
    And gentlemen will hear me;
Lord Fyvie he'll be ridin' by,
    And he'll come in an' see me."

"O Annie dear, O Annie dear,
    I can hear your couie lowin';
For I widnae gie that couie lowe
    For a' your kye in Fyvie."

"For Fyvie's lands they are broad an' lang,
    As they are wondrous bonnie;
But I widnae gie my ain true love,
    For a' your lands in Fyvie."

78. *Mill o' Tifty's Annie (Andrew Lammie, Child 233)*
The historical truth of this ballad is stressed by Northeastern singers such as Jane Turriff
(*The Muckle Sangs*, where the rich recording of the ballad by the School of Scottish
Studies is documented). Jeannie related the story:

The story of Tifty's Annie it's over three hundred years ago. She wes the miller o'
Fyvie's daughter, what hees name was Tifty. An' she wes called Annie Tifty, ye
see. Because he wes the miller o' Fyvie an' that wes hees name. An' he had three

lovely daughters but she wes the fairest of them all. And of course Lord Fyvie wantit her hand in marriage, he wes in love with her. But he had a trumpeter, he got a trumpeter to the Castle o' Fyvie. And hees name was Andrew Lammie. But of course he wes younger and far far handsomer than the Lord o' Fyvie. And the both o' them fell in love with each other, ye see. So of course her father found out that she wes takin' up with the trumpeter o' Fyvie, an' he told her to give him up, and marry Lord Fyvie. Of course it wes the money that he wes lookin' for. But hees daughter wes not lookin' for that, she wes lookin' for love. An' of course she wouldn't give up Andrew Lammie to please him. So when Lord Fyvie saw that the trumpeter wes takin' up with her, he wesn't pleased either, ye see. So of course—he wouldn't have injured her in any way—but he told her father, an' of course there wes a terrible row got up, an' Annie got hurtit oot owre it, an' of course they were very cruel to her, over the lovin' o' Andrew Lammie. Finally, at the long run they broke her back for it, ye see. That's true history. She's buriet, at the old graveyard at Fyvie. For it's there for anybody tae go an' see. An' there's a stone which they call the Weepin' Stone. It sheds very moisty watter. . . . every now an' again. An' they call it the Weepin' Stone. Her grave's there to be seen by anybody. But Andrew Lammie went amiss an' nobody ever knew what became o' Andra Lammie. He come home from Edinburgh town—when they killed her he left to go to Edinburgh—an' when he came back she wes killed, an' she wes gettin' buried. So of course, he went amiss—but not so very long ago, maybe a hundred years ago or that, I don't know, at Fyvie there was a skeleton gotten which, they couldnae give no account for. An' the way he was dressed an' things, they hid their own ideas. Well Andra Lammie gied amissin', so it's left tae draw your own conclusions. (*What a Voice*)

There are clearly some reminiscences of "Lord Lovat" in this account. Annie's gravestone, bearing the date 1673, is crowned by a nineteenth-century stone on which the leaves of two intertwining trees are carved, while the trumpeter appears as a gargoyle on the roof of Fyvie Castle. Peter Buchan took down a copy of the ballad text "from a very old woman" and published thirty thousand copies of it. According to Peter Buchan 1825: 197, the girl's name was Annie (or Agnes) Smith; his note adds the episode of Lammie's hearing the song of Annie while in Edinburgh and the bursting of his waistcoat buttons when he faints. Willie Mathieson's fifty-stanza version probably derives from that of Mrs. Gillespie in *Last Leaves* (175), as learned by her in the area of Buchan in the 1850s, or from a similar source (see the two texts in Bronson 1959–72, 3:387–89 and 4:503–5). Jeannie's text of twenty-one stanzas corresponds with Mathieson's stanzas 1, 2, 3, 5, 6, 7, 8, 10, 13, 14, 15, 16, 18, 19, 24, 25–27, 37–38, 32, 30, 36. Notable points are: the "literary" cast of lines such as those in Jeannie's verse 3, the use of apples as erotic symbol (verse 9), the substitution of "woundless" for "wondrous" (verse 18), and the image of contempt for human pain in verse 20 ("couie lowin'"). Two variants of Jeannie's tune are printed by Bronson, both from the year 1953 (5, 5.1). This tune falls into the plagal, minor hexatonic Group Aa, a tune family broadly known in the Northeast and elsewhere, and associated with "Barbara Allan" (Child 84) and more particularly with "The Braes o' Yarrow" (Child 214).

Recorded versions: SA 1953/197; BBC SA 20183–4; Folktracks FSA 067; Lucy Stewart, Folkways FG 3519; Jane Turriff, Tangent TGNM 119D; Sheila MacGregor, Tangent TGNM 11/D.

Additional references: Child 1882–98, 4:300–308; Coffin 1977: 135; Greig 1963: 16, 34; Greig and Keith 1925: 174–79.

79. Lord Donald (Lord Randal, Child 12)

"Whaur hae ye been all the day,
　　Lord Donal', my son?
Whaur hae ye been all the day,
　　My jolly young man?"

"Awa' coortin', mither,
　　Mak' my bed soon;
For I am seik at the hert,
　　An' I fain wid lie doun."

"What will ye hae for your supper,
　　Lord Donal', my son?
What will ye hae for your supper,
　　My jolly young man?"

"I hae had my supper,
    Mither, mak' my bed soon;
For I am seik at the hert,
    An' I fain wid lie doun."

"What had ye for supper,
    Lord Donal', my son?
What had ye for supper,
    My jolly young man?"

"I had little sma' fishes,
    Mither, mak' my bed soon;
For I am seik at the hert,
    An' I fain wid lie doun."

"What like were the fishes,
    Lord Donal', my son?
What like were the fishes,
    My gallant young man?"

"Black-backed an' speckled bellies,
    Mither, mak' my bed soon;
For I am seik at the hert,
    An' I fain wid lie doun."

"O I doubt you are poishened,
    Lord Donal', my son;
O I doubt you are poishened,
    My jolly young man."

"What will ye leave tae your father,
    Lord Donal', my son?
What will ye leave tae your father,
    My jolly young man?"

"My houses an' lands, mither,
    Mak' my bed soon;
For I am seik at the hert,
    An' I fain wid lie doun."

"What will ye leave tae your true love,
    Lord Donal', my son?

What will ye leave tae your true love,
My jolly young man?"

"The tow and the helter,
Tae hang on yon tree;
And there for to hang
For the poishening o' me."

79. Lord Donald (Lord Randal, Child 12)

"You know how lang it took me to learn 'Lord Donald'?" Jeannie asked. "It's the longest sang I've got. I learned it from a young chap in one night's time. But it wisnae only because o' the air wi' it. It appealed to me as a good story" (Gower 1968: 121).

As is evident from Jeannie's few recordings of the ballad, it was not one that she felt drawn to compare with, for instance, "Son Davit." While there must be psychological reasons for this, it is true that Greig and Duncan gathered no more than a half-dozen verses of the song in the Northeast (cf. Bronson 1959–72, 1:191–225, nos. 29, 34, 40, 43, 44, 85). In these variants, the title is usually "Lord Ronald," the name that Lizzie employs (Munro 1970: 163; Stephanie Smith 1975: 148). Jeannie may have adopted the name "Donald" because of her husband. The shape of her tune, with its characteristic rise to the higher mediant in the second phrase, is kin to that of Jimmy Stewart of Forfar, listed by Bronson in *The Traditional Tunes of the Child Ballads* (1959–72, 4:449–50) just before Jeannie's text and tune. Both airs are built on a repeated double structure, Jeannie's falling more naturally, perhaps, into a pattern of short quatrains in fifteen stanzas. Is this a hint of the "archaic" formal feature noted by scholars in relation to "Edward" (Child 13; cf. Wilgus 1966: 77–92)? Bronson places Jeannie's and Jimmy Stewart's tunes within his Ab class ("typically of the familiar 'Vilikens and his Dinah' pattern"), which also includes Ewan MacColl's and his mother's distinctive melody (35.2). These two sets are so different in identity, however, that it is probably better to regard this entire class as showing only broad trends in tune construction rather than having any direct correspondence with the "Vilikens" type. Jeannie's text is related to that in Kinloch 1827: 110–13, though it omits the brother and sister in the "testament" sequence, perhaps as a result of memory lapse.

Recorded versions: SA 1957/44; 1960/203; Topic 12T160; Lizzie Higgins, SA 1970/20; Minnie Haman, SA 1974/35; Ewan MacColl, SA 1951/1; Topic 12T103; Argo (Z) DA 66; Folkways FG 3509; Riverside RLP 12 62; MacColl and Betsy Miller, Folk Lyric FL 116 (see fuller list in Huntington and Herrmann 1990: 424–25).

Additional references: Brunnings 1981; Child 1882–98, 1:151–66; Coffin 1977: 36–39; *A Collection of Scots Songs* (1972): 39–40; Dean-Smith 1954; Greig 1963: 112; Greig and Keith 1925: 13–15; Henry 1923–29, 2:316; Huntington and Herrmann 1990: 415; MacColl and Seeger 1977: 54–57; *Tocher* 14 (1974): 222–23 (Minnie Haman).

80. Son Davit (Edward, Child 13)

O what's the blood that's on your sword,
   My son Davit, O son Davit?
What's the blood it's on your sword?
   Come promise, tell me true.

O that's the blood of my grey mair,
   Hey lady mother, ho lady mother;
That's the blood of my grey meir,
   Because it widnae rule by me.

O that blood it is owre clear,
   My son Davit, O son Davit;
That blood it is owre clear,
   Come promise, tell me true.

O that's the blood of my grey hound,
   Hey lady mother, ho lady mother;
That's the blood of my grey hound,
   Because it widnae rule by me.

O that blood it is owre clear,
   My son Davit, O son Davit;
That blood it is owre clear,
   Come promise, tell me true.

O that's the blood of my huntin' haak,
   Hey lady mother, ho lady mother;

That's the blood of my huntin' haak,
 Because it widnae rule by me.

O that blood it is owre clear,
 My son Davit, O son Davit;
That blood it is owre clear,
 Come promise, tell me true.

O that's the blood of my brother John,
 Hey lady mother, ho lady mother;
That's the blood of my brother John,
 Because he drew his sword tae me.

I'm gaun awa' in a bottomless boat,
 In a bottomless boat, in a bottomless boat,
But I'm gaun awa' in a bottomless boat,
 And I'll never return again.

O whan will you come back again,
 My son Davit, O son Davit?
Whan will you come back again?
 Come promise, tell me true.

When the sun and the moon meets in yon glen,
 Hey lady mother, ho lady mother;
When the sun and the moon meets in yon glen,
 For I'll return again.

80. Son Davit (Edward, Child 13)

"I heard my mother sing it when I was about seven or eight years of age, but she had a lot more verses and I can't remember them" (SA 1952/43). "The wey that I mind upon the song, I used to hear the auld people an' ma mother too singin' a two-three verses o' it, but that's all I can remember, "What's the blood 'at's on your sword?" (*What a Voice*; but recorded 1953). These early comments on "Son Davit" suggest that Jeannie subsequently tried to recall or recover as many traditional verses as she could, in an attempt at "completeness." Hamish Henderson notes, as does Peter Kennedy, that she added something fresh at each of the early recording sessions. The changes in her singing of the ballad (text, air, and general style) are dealt with in detail elsewhere (Porter 1976, 1988). Lizzie has recorded a variant that follows the "mare," "huntin' hawk," and "brother John" sequence (SA 1970/21), one rarely if ever used by Jeannie, who, after a TV appearance in which a producer encouraged her to shorten the song, reduced the fourfold pattern to that of "mare," "hound," and "brother John." Lizzie's tempo takes after Jeannie's later, deliberate style rather than her earlier impersonal one (cf. Munro 1970: 171; Stephanie Smith 1975: 175–78). Jeannie's aunt, Maggie Stewart, sang a version of the ballad (Bronson 1959–72, 4:451–52), as did Jeannie's niece, Maria Robertson (MacColl and Seeger 1977: 58–60). In these two versions, the reason for the quarrel is more explicit: it was over " a silly one" (Stewart) and "a silly wand" (Robertson). The air common to all the Robertson family variants is a slow metamorphosis of "O Gin I Were Where Gadie Rins," a song and tune localized in Aberdeenshire (Porter 1978). A version with this tune, "The Back o' Bennachie," is in Buchan and Hall 1973: 80–81. MacColl and Seeger 1977 also publish (174–75) a variant sung by Maggie McPhee.

Recorded variants: SA 1952/43; 1954/105; 1955/62/154; 1958/25; 1959/9/76/82; 1960/111/200/203/205; 1961/44; SX 1953/2; 1955/1; 1956/4; 1957/6; 1958/2; 1960/3/5; Caedmon TC 1145/Topic 12T160; Prestige International 13006; Tradition TLP 1047; Lizzie Higgins, SA 1970/21; Margaret Stewart, SA 1954/102; Paddy Tunney, Caedmon TC 1145/Topic 12T160; Angela Brasil, Caedmon TC 1145/Topic 12T160; Norman Kennedy, Topic 12T133.

Additional references: Bronson 1969: 1–17; Coffin 1949; Taylor 1931; Wilgus 1966.

Commentary

Jeannie Robertson's life is best and most completely perceived through her songs. The "narrative" element in her repertoire is, in a fundamental sense, the narrative of her own experience. The songs do not simply recount emotional high points in this experience, but crystallize and transform the lived reality into formal, coherent expressive structures. In turn, these transformed structures act upon, and sometimes interact with, her audience in diverse contexts: familial, Revival, or disembodied mass-media situations. We are left with a number of important questions. How did she acquire her repertoire and her communicative art? How did individuals, travellers and nontravellers, involved in the Revival, evaluate her singing? What, in material, contextual, and subjective terms, does the process of transformation involve? The first of these questions involves the acquisition of knowledge and particular skills.

Learning and Cognitive Development

Cognition, broadly speaking, involves knowing and learning. It is also bound up with the development of particular talents within the individual. Cognitive psychologists, inspired chiefly by the work of Piaget, lately have identified a series of stages by which a person becomes skilled. One scholar recognizes this process as "movement through a domain," which occurs when someone becomes interested in a field and traverses the levels of mastery.[1] The acquisition of skill can be grouped into seven stages: (1) novice (beginner); (2) apprentice (serious study with a master); (3) journeyman; (4) craftsman; (5) expert; (6) master; and (7) preeminent contributor. This sequence, in which stages 3 and 4, and also 5 and 6 could be merged, corresponds to a similar five-stage developmental model: (1) novice; (2) advanced beginner; (3) competence; (4) proficiency; and (5) expertise.[2]

A developmental pattern of this sort, while inconsistent in shifting from "novice" to skill, contrasts with the five skill domains postulated by Howard Gardner (linguistic, musical, logical-mathematical, spatial, bodilykinaesthetic). The sequences above might apply in each of these domains. Mastery in singing, for example, would represent the highest level in such a skill domain.[3] While the auditory sense is crucial to all musical participation, music and bodily or gestural language are closely linked. Taking the idea of multiple intelligences further, Gardner and Wolf have argued that human development involves both separate streams of specific skill acquisition and common "waves of symbolization," in which a new achievement in one stream spills over into apparently unrelated streams.[4]

Students of women's educational development have emphasized how women, unlike men, come to know in stages, moving from silence and lack of a voice, to recognizing authority, to finding inner voices of subjectivity and reason, and then to integrating earlier stages.[5] Such a model is suggestive for the way in which Jeannie, in her performances of ballads like "Son Davit," transformed the song in accord with merging contexts and her sense of the song's internal coherence. The projection of her repertoire into spacious halls developed from these contexts, while she also was pushed by scholars and apprentice singers to consider the aesthetic form and the significance of particular songs.[6]

These conceptions of cognitive development are illustrated by Jeannie's evolution into a skilled singer, and in her recognition as such by many within her immediate social group. Her early interest in traditional songs, as she absorbed them in the egalitarian context of traveller camps, formed a first stage. Listening intently at seven or eight, she began to develop preferences for certain songs or ways of singing; she was attracted by the dramatic plots of songs like "The Murder of Miss Mary Brown" and began to learn as a "novice" from age nine. She herself described how her mother sang "Son Davit" at night during World War I, when anxiety over the fate of her husband and two sons kept her awake.[7] Jeannie's contention that learning the tune was the key to learning the words of a song suggests an already powerful, developing melodic instinct that later, as her skill in singing grew, was brought into balance with her concept of the song text. In children this developmental stage is marked in music by an increasing ability to classify music explicitly as conforming to rule or style, and by an increasing advantage in memory and perceptual tasks for those sequences that conform to rule.[8] Meanwhile, Jeannie practiced the songs, with some guidance from her mother Maria ("master") and progressed to the second stage: that of apprentice, or advanced beginner.

In her teenage years, in a third stage of development involving "competence," Jeannie worked at acquiring a repertoire of songs, mainly from her mother but occasionally from other sources. This body of songs numbered about 180, over 90 percent of which were "traditional."

With increasing mastery, Jeannie began to be recognized within her circle of traveller kin and acquaintances as a singer of unusual proficiency. At gatherings in her little house in Aberdeen, according to her daughter Lizzie, Jeannie was often asked to sing by her relatives and friends.[9] This can be identified as the fourth stage, one difficult to distinguish from the fifth and last stage of expertise, since her mastery was already accepted within her group by the time she reached middle age, the point at which she became exposed to the wider environment of the Folksong Revival.

In Jeannie's acquisition of traditional songs, Maria provided the readiest model, because of her own strong personality as much as by her husband's absence. Jeannie assimilated phrasing, balance, and vocal articulation from her mother, just as Lizzie, to a lesser extent, would from Jeannie.[10] Jeannie regarded her mother's voice as lower in volume than her own, a "mellow" (soft) voice while hers was a "high" (loud) voice. She admired Donald's mother, a cousin of Maria, as a "loud, sweet singer" who preferred not to sing in public. Sitting in the middle of the camp with a child on her knee when no one was about, she would sing to Jeannie and a few other children.

Throughout this negotiation of stages, Jeannie, was engaging in a dialectical process of reality construction and culture maintenance that, in Berger's formulation, involves three stages: externalization, objectivization, and internalization.[11] The first of these stages consists in the outpouring of the individual's physical and mental being into the world: world-building activity is rooted in the biological need to eternalize. With the second, objectivization, the world attains the character of an external and "objective" reality experienced not just by the self but as one experienced in common with others. The third moment in this dialectic, internalization, reabsorbs the objectivized world into consciousness, so that the structures of the world come to determine the subjective structures of consciousness itself. Internalization allows the individual to participate in the outer social world, but it also enables her or him to cultivate a rich inner life. By internalizing the voices of others, we are able to speak to ourselves, since it is through others that we discover ourselves and, more particularly, it is through significant others that we develop a significant relationship to ourselves.[12] Jeannie's immediate family, and above all Maria, because of her presence and personality, played such a role during Jeannie's early cognitive development.

Describing this broad process only creates the outer framework for the specific events that shaped Jeannie's emotional world. These events were not confined to family matters, separation, and the like. One must postulate that the singing events of her childhood were, in all likelihood, experiences of the kind referred to by phenomenological psychologists.[13] In such situations, gifted individuals receive a sense of self and of experience that has been called Cognition of Being, or B-cognition.[14] In turn, this is related to a series of values: wholeness, perfection, completion, justice or "oughtness," aliveness, richness, simplicity, beauty, goodness, uniqueness, effortlessness, playfulness, truth (honesty, reality), and self-sufficiency.[15] Each aspect will come to the foreground of cognition, depending on the operation—such as singing or nurturing a child—that has revealed it. It is the ability to perceive the whole and rise above the parts, however, that characterizes cognition in peak experiences. The person, too, becomes more integrated, individual, spontaneous, expressive, effortless, courageous, and powerful. Thus, affective singing events, such as those in which the young Jeannie participated as an active contributor, constituted peak experiences for her and were central in the gradual integration of her personality.

Song Epistemics

Because the concept of "musical cognition" is a broad one, we might propose the term *epistemics* to denote the specific set of beliefs and attitudes that a singer or musician holds concerning a song or instrumental piece.[16] The term, of course, has the same root as *epistemology* (the study of the method and grounds of knowledge) and has been used both in recent philosophical discourse and in the vocabulary of artificial intelligence. Students of philosophy use the term to denote the extent to which perception involves beliefs. Although some theorists have argued that belief-acquisition is a regular concomitant of perception, it is not a necessary one (i.e., it is "non-epistemic"). It has also been proposed that perceiving is always a matter of belief-acquisition.[17]

In the present context, *epistemics* refers to the subjective beliefs held in relation to a cultural product (a song, for instance), in contrast to any phenomenal properties of the same item. For instance, epistemics can apply to a person's views or notions about a song or about its origin, character, style, structure, aesthetics, nonmusical associations, or interpretation. These beliefs may be subjective rather than phenomenal, but this does not necessarily mean that "native ideas" are being contrasted with so-called scientific reasoning. Rather, we are proposing that these beliefs about a cultural product lead to an important area of inquiry, namely the specific conceptions of the practiced, reflective performer concerning cultural material, not all of which he or she may have in an active repertoire.

Singers may have subjective knowledge and a set of beliefs about songs, whether they sing them or not. These modes of knowing and understanding are to some extent complementary, yet not every skilled singer holds a coherent set of beliefs about each song. To some extent, these two modes contribute to our notion of style in any culture, since both performance features and particular beliefs (about the past, history, or identity) make up the individual character of a "style." Instead of generalizing about musical change from observation of a group as if it were homogeneous, a more orderly methodology would set out to "discover" the beliefs and knowledge held by individuals, working outward in concentric circles to compare performers' beliefs with those of nonperformers. Such investigation can help answer more difficult questions: What does it mean to "know" a song or piece of music? Of what utility or value is epistemic knowledge? Since cognitive perspectives on musical behavior are now of central importance in seeking out musical and cultural meaning, inquiry into individual epistemics is an essential task.

The relationship of epistemic beliefs to knowledge or cognition, then, is a complex one. The relation of knowledge to belief is particularly intricate in traditional societies, where the two often are fused or exist in close proximity. We have adopted here a view of traditional knowledge, or cognition, that relates it closely to belief, since, in the performance of songs, conviction of "truth" is a key factor. Whereas knowledge is often defined in relation to facts, or the phenomenal world, this cannot easily be done in traditional societies. Practical knowledge ("knowing how to") and epistemic belief ("knowing about" or "believing") cannot be rigidly demarcated and, in performative terms, they ought to be analyzed contextually. The important point is that native epistemics provide the perceptual basis for the conceptual act of singing—the act of will, in other words, that transforms belief into action.

Jeannie's epistemics can be deduced from her random remarks and occasional commentaries on songs such as "Harlaw" (number 27 in the section of this book entitled "Songs and Notes about the Songs"), "For the Moon Shined on My Bed Last Night" (65), "Young Emslie" (67), "Lord Lovat" (77), "Tifty's Annie" (78), "Lord Donald" (79), and "Son Davit" (80). The most pointed example of such understanding relates to "Son Davit," which, like most of her repertoire, she learned from her mother under difficult circumstances during World War I, though she came to "relearn" it later. The tune caught her attention first, before the words; she believed the ending of the plot ("I'm gan' awa' in a bottomless boat") referred to David's intention of suicide; David was "the oldest brother, heir to everything," and "the other brother was a very selfish, jealous brother"; while the younger sibling had everything he could want materially, he wanted "to be master . . . o' the castle" and kill his elder brother; the mother liked David better than the younger brother; it was "a natural thing for David to fight to defend his sul'" (David fought him "in a fair fight and killed him"); finally, Jeannie commented, "we hadnae enough o' the ballad, actually, to tell the whole story."[18]

Jeannie's explanation challenges all previous explanations of the oblique plot by scholars, who had assumed from comparative analysis of ballad texts that the motive for the duel was a quarrel over a young girl or, alternatively, some unspecified incestuous relationship. But in Jeannie's view, it is over inheritance rights. David has acquired a moral character in Jeannie's understanding of the story, a justification for his actions unknown in interpretations of other recorded variants. Closely related versions of the song recorded from travellers appear to bear out Jeannie's assertion that the skeletal nature of the ballad text known to them did not make clear the motive for the killing.

Stanley Robertson has supplied a contrasting explanation from his mother, Elizabeth McDonald. A noblewoman bears twin boys, David being the elder. The husband dies when they are young. A dominant figure, the mother raises them; they are trained in weaponry; David, as the son who will inherit the estate, is favored by her; and John, feeling hurt, is rebellious. When fully grown, the brothers fight during a hunt, perhaps after a heated argument over birthright. After killing his brother, David is remorseful and tries to deceive his mother. She can read the signs, however, and is concerned now for David's life. Stanley added, "My mother compared the story with 'The Twa Brothers' and said it was the same story virtually. She also said it could be compared with the biblical story of 'Esau and Jacob,' inasmuch as the mother favored one son more than the other and it was also a story of great deception."[19]

"Son Davit": From Performative to Transformative Modalities

The centrality of "Son Davit" in Jeannie's repertoire has already been emphasized.[20] She was asked to sing the song repeatedly, more than any other song, because it was perceived by the general public (prompted by scholars) as a rare ballad, one that had been scarce in Lowland culture of the twentieth century, even though it has analogies in Europe and North America. Jeannie's recognition of the value placed on "Son Davit" by nontravellers affected her view of the song. It became prized in her repertoire, the pièce-de-résistance of her concert programs. The traveller concept of the song as but one of the "old songs" valued for their use by previous generations (it had vanished from nontraveller oral tradition) was displaced by her identification of it as a "big ballad," as she moved away from traditional aesthetic concepts.

Second, her structural alteration of the song by removing one stanza (the "hunting hawk" verse) at the prompting of a television producer occurred at the same time that she was expanding the number and duration of the song's phrases. By the late 1950s, she had reduced the fourfold repetition of mare, hound, hawk, and brother John to a three-part repetition—perhaps to reduce the overall duration and arrive at the Law of Three proposed by Olrik as one of the "laws" of folk poetry.[21] This expansion, at the cost of reduction on another plane, may be a function of what has been termed the folk artist's spatial mode of apprehension, which works together with a simpler linear mode. Jeannie's changing sense of structure, following external criteria of song evaluation, began to recognize a new set of aesthetic priorities; the song was no longer "presented" to a traveller audience in domestic surroundings. It was "performed": enlarged, projected, and stylized to suit new, anonymous audiences in larger halls, as well as media technicians in empty, soundproof studios.

The last aspect of the song's structural and symbolic transformation can be inferred from remarks Jeannie made in interviews. This concerns the premature loss of her young son, James, who died at the age of eight from meningitis and from whose death Jeannie never fully recovered. As the song "Son Davit" began to achieve a paramount position in her concert programs, Jeannie's whole vision of her life, and especially the trauma of Jeemsie's death, became embodied in the song. It took on the status of a lament. The protagonist, David, whose mother urges him to tell the truth about killing his brother, is in fact Jeannie's own son James, who has right on his side in the quarrel. But he is also, paradoxically, John, now "dead." Jeannie is the "mother," pleading for an explanation of a son's death—one she finds impossible to understand. From the song's characters, she has selected symbolic features that fit her conception and experience of life.

The gradual shift in performance mode seems to reflect a changing emphasis in the three interrelated systems of literary grammar: semantics, concerned with content; syntax, concerned with structural organization; and rhetoric, concerned with diction and style.[22] At first, Jeannie's performance concentrated on the plot of the narrative song (the syntactical aspect). But by 1957–58, she began to be preoccupied with the other two systems (semantics and rhetoric). Her experience in the television studio (1957) and the excision of a stanza and refrain suggest less concern with plot accuracy and more with delivery and timing. By the time of her 1958 performance, she had shifted into a new performance mode, stressing what a theory of poetics would call "diction" or "style." Her final recorded performances of "Son Davit" after 1960 reveal a lyric outpouring. Plot no longer had narrative significance, and style was a vehicle for pure emotion. Distilling the life experience of a masterfully "musical" singer, her delivery had an unforgettable effect on her listeners. Leaning toward the semantic and rhetorical, Jeannie transformed the song from a communally employed "auld sang" into a personal elegy—moving, as it were, from quotidian marker to sonic icon.

Remarkably, the musical proportions of "Son Davit" remained stable in relation to one another throughout this transformation of content, plot, and style. Jeannie was an acknowledged master of phrasing, employing skillful techniques of balance and symmetry despite protracted phrase segments that caused her to break continuity in the musical line. Her demeanor in performance conveyed immersion in the affective world of the song. But that world had left behind the medieval plot of fratricide, confession, and projected suicide, along with its yeoman background, and veered toward personal lament for a deceased child, with the related notion of a life colored by this loss. Jeannie had altered the focus of the original plot, going beyond even a simple identification of herself with David's anxious questioner; she had become an emblem, in fact, of the universal mother.

To some extent, this identification can be detected in her "Lord Donald" ("Lord Randal" [79] and "The Twa Brithers" [76]). Particular concern with the tragic death of young males marks her later performances; the ballads begin to take on the character of dirges, or coronachs, as Sir Walter Scott might have put it. The implications of this shift from performative to transformative modes in relation to specific songs should be clarified. Performance emphasizes process rather than structure; it involves gestures, physical feeling, the pregnant moment. The aesthetic is unsuited to the syntactic criteria of classical music. Performative (ceremonial) "utterances" were identified in linguistic philosophy[23] and, later, in musical aesthetics[24] and performative genres in anthropological studies of southeastern European communities.[25] These performatives, such as dancing, singing, and other enactments, evoke ideas about society and its construction through concrete acts. Yet the notion of performative, while usefully tied to that of gesture and meaning within a social act,[26] needs to be opened up to the possibility of transformation: performance that does not simply celebrate the metaphors of communal experience but actively "remakes" them in a new and reconceived way, so that they are "transformative" and hence bring into being a new perception of the world. Jeannie's performance of "Son Davit" evolved a special treatment in the late 1950s, but by 1960 was something utterly transformed in style, tone, and structure. The "meaning" of the song had changed, for both Jeannie and her audience.

Transformativity and Its Agents

Transformativity, the capacity to stimulate change, is best understood as an artistic process. In sure hands, it is a powerful tool for influencing perception of the world. As a musical and cultural process, it has two principal features. First, it is a means by which a singer enacts change on material, contextual-performative, and subjective levels. Second, it is a device mediating between dichotomies of the folklore process, bridging communal and individual, oral and literate, traditional and innovative. These two features are connected because the second process brings about the first and helps to frame a more detailed discussion of song style. The general concept of transformativity involves the transformation of songs, situations, self. Unlike mechanisms of adaptivity, suggesting a passive reaction to an external stimulus, or of variability, referring to a more general process of change, transformativity connotes the active, transitive capacity of a skilled performer (a singer, say) to bring about qualitative change. Transformativity, then, involves causality and the will of its human agents.

In a semiotic analysis of style, some necessary description of structures must occur. Such descriptions, however, must always to be related to the gesture, to the act of singing or music making and its reception.[27] That is, the description of modes or rhythms must be conjoined to particular examples of performance, in specific contexts and situations. A semiotics of making song and music should consider not only the transformation of material but also the transformation of context and singer. Jeannie's life world and her performance style, that style and the external world, create the twofold basis, not just for a musical semiotics, but also for a critical hermeneutics of musical performance.

Transformativity, too, needs to be seen in terms of human agents, the most important of whom are the singers. Bound to traditional patterns of expression (though not mindlessly so), their singing can be seen as enacting metaphors of experience. It is not just the text's content itself, though that is important, but the existential act that envelops singer and audience and makes the imagined world "present" as if it were real, palpable. In this sense, the "story" of the song exists on multiple levels: the internal narrative; the story of the song's creation and transmission; the story of the singer, specific performance, situation, and audience; the story of the community. Each of these is a transformation of the others and needs to be understood as part of a multiplex, phenomenal set of relations. Considered alone, the verbal text, for example, is but one part of this interdependent, intersubjective reality, in which the singer seeks to transform experience through traditional patterns and sounds into an existential act of communication. It is best, then, to consider the contextual and subjective aspects of transformativity together.

A second agency of transformativity is the mediators, often middle-class intellectuals who, for ideological reasons, have wanted to promulgate knowledge of traditional expressive forms to the local community and the world at large. In this they have failed, if one takes the view that their primary motive was to appropriate the songs for a bourgeois audience.[28] Their reasons, certainly, encompass both a personal ideology of value and a social ideology that has been nationalistic, socialist, or, more recently, ecological, a reaction to such environmental forces as tourism.[29] The contextual levels of folksong transformation which deal with politics or the cultural manipulation of singing have been less studied, though at least one scholar has accused English collectors at the turn of the century, for example, for using material transaction as a device to "acquire" songs from singers and thus effect the transformation of the "Revival."[30]

Other agents of transformation include media specialists, recordists, and producers who often, by electronic techniques, transform a thin voice into an incisive one or persuade the singer to adopt some novel performance style. They also determine, at times, the sequence and number of songs on a commercial disc. Jeannie was exposed to such manipulation in her recordings with guitarist Josh White and later, in her television appearance, when an important stanza of "Son Davit" and its refrain verse were dropped. Her unaccompanied voice, however, and its gradual change, deepening and slowing after a decade, were sufficiently arresting that few producers tampered with it. But the empty, dry studio ambiance often made her final recordings seem disembodied, cut off from the essential interactive presence of others. Technicians, influenced by the practices of "classical music" producers, in the 1960s tended to replicate that dry acoustic and produce "perfect" studio recordings of traditional singers. Only later did they realize that traditional music seeks a live, engaged audience on whose feedback the musicians depend, and this audience feedback is an essential ingredient in the transformative process. Live albums, however, can present more problems than studio records because of their ambiguity about the focus of uniqueness. The listener can be alienated by being excluded from this very quality. The emphasis on the individual, the Other, can be seen as part of a romantic ideology that supports capitalism by casting cultural products as something other than commodities.[31]

Material Transformation

Transformativity of form and content in songs is bound up with their arrangement by the singer. Such form and content are verbal and musical. Analyses of music, it has been argued, are essentially descriptions of sequences involved in different kinds of creative acts;[32] as such, these analyses encompass more than simply a concern for structural organization. Structural analysis of music may answer such questions as these: how does a particular style or piece work? how is it structurally successful? It cannot, however, answer questions concerning the individual or social evaluation of music making.[33] Ethnomusicology, as a holistic discipline, aims at explaining the constraints on musical behavior and on responses to it. Analysis of traditional repertoires, for instance, as one strategy in scrutinizing whole bodies of music or song, can uncover the concepts, preferences, and ordering systems that musicians or singers bring to their overall style, as well as changes they make under certain circumstances.[34]

Analysis of the performance process, similarly, should identify contextual input into the music. An analytical model of traditional performance may include such aspects as community structure and family. But at the center is the performer, whose individual personality and perception of audience response affect her or his choices, both communicative and aesthetic, from the repertoire of available options.[35] Two preliminary steps in building such a model are analysis of the musical idiom into units and rules of combination, and analysis of the performance occasion. Determining the range of variation in idiom and performance context allows the analyst to demonstrate how a specific situation affects the music and its performance.[36] This leads to the question of whether it is possible to identify with certainty the "process of sharing" that is as crucial to musical analysis as the sonic product.[37] Such sharing involves listeners who do not actively perform but who nevertheless provide input; they contribute a notion of how successful the performer is, and the scholar also can use techniques such as videotaping to discover a variety of evaluations.[38] The study of variance in the performance situation is a clear case of how performance can be assessed. Styles then can be understood as resources and techniques that acquire specific meanings when they are used and adjusted or transformed, with reference to one another.[39]

The evaluation of Jeannie's performance style by community and family has been outlined above. These evaluations admittedly were made by practitioners with experiential knowledge rather than by passive listeners. Yet the general acclaim her singing received in public performances, and her emergence as a "public" singer recognized by Revival and mass-media audiences, imply widespread acceptance of her stylistic norms even though these changed dramatically over the years. At the heart of her style, analytically speaking, is a "musical gesture" that had iconic power even after she ceased to sing in public. This "singing gesture," in semiotic terms, may refer to a complete piece such as a song; but it can also be taken to mean the musical phrase, the architectural basis of her style. Jeannie's use of structure is built upon phrases of asymmetrical and varying lengths (see fig. 21). Consequently, the analysis that follows addresses, first, the content and structure of her repertoire; and, second, melodic, rhythmic, and phrasal organization.

Collector: Hamish Henderson

SA 1955/154/B9

Fig. 21. "Ainst Upon a Time" (56 in "The Songs, Annotated").

Thematic Content of Repertoire

A singer often can characterize her or his own repertoire. Thus Granny Riddle distinguished "classic" songs (usually the oldest kind) from, say, children's songs, feeling free to alter the former but not the latter.[40] After contact with scholars and collectors, Jeannie began to refer to certain songs as "big ballads," though the term for these in her circle always had been "auld sangs." She would identify generic subtypes: "battle," "war," "cowboy," or "work" (i.e., occupational) songs. Her daughter Lizzie has remarked that "we jist called them aal'

[old] songs, but now we know it's folksong."[41] Jeannie herself began to be aware of the distinctions that outsiders made among her narrative songs. The close attention given to these by influential scholars led her to emphasize them in her programs, thereby assimilating to some extent values and concepts alien to her community. To her, a "big ballad," as a concept picked up from intellectuals, became one that had to be sung in grand or deliberate style.[42] Such songs, for her, carried emotional weight rather than length or narrative complexity.

Terminology among travellers was not strict, however, even for ballads that fell into the category of "old songs." Lizzie could refer to "The Gallowa' Hills" (33) as a "ballad" in the same category as the narrative "Lord Lovat" (77)— namely, as a lullaby.[43] Travellers did not maintain rigid categories of song types, but changed and modified their conceptions according to situation or usage. Changes in terminology nevertheless reveal significant transformations in the mental sets of singers such as Jeannie and point to shifts in conceptualization that themselves are triggered by social contact. The excitement of scholars at finding rare ballads in her repertoire substantially altered her own conception of such songs. Even though she was not the first traveller singer to be "discovered" with such songs, the power and depth of her singing marked her as one of the most remarkable.

Content analysis of a repertoire can be misleading, since studying "texts" alone neglects the existential communication of the sung entity. In performance, the words can be influenced by the sung shapes so that their plain "prose" meaning is transformed. Words and music, and their relative sense in combination, move both toward and away from each other, at one time the words dominating, at another the melody, although, in the Western stanzaic tradition, a coalescent relationship, a fusion, is the performative ideal. Performance style is another factor that projects particular meanings. Jeannie was adept at satire, for instance, as in songs mocking old men who court young women. But she avoided parody, which amounts to a more radical transformation of style and style renewal. Some caution, then, needs to be exercised in understanding the way music and words interact. In terms of structure, Bronson, for example, has shown how the music shapes the prosody in balladry, affecting both line length and refrains.[44]

Jeannie's repertoire, as noted above, highlights certain well-defined themes that appealed to her and to her audiences at every stage of her development. The big ballads that she found suited to her personality and self-image gained in her estimation with outside praise. The seriousness of this category had to be matched by dignity of expression even when lit by humor, as in "The Laird o' Drum" (40). Some songs had become inactive in her repertoire for various reasons (e.g., "Susan Pyatt," "My Father Built Me a Dandy Bower"). Others were sung intermittently ("Little Matty Groves," Clyde's Water," "The Golden Victory" [30], "Glenlogie," "Trooper and Maid" [61], "Carrbridge Castle" [42], "The Loch o' Shallin"). Ballads that she did not conceive of falling into this category were of a lighter kind ("The Laird o' the Denty Doonby" [39], "The Bonnie Wee Lassie Who Never Said No" [52]), though a hard and fast line is difficult to draw.

Songs like "An Auld Man Cam' Coortin' Me" or "She's Only My Auld Shoes" (72) barely fall into the ballad genre, since the narrative element is slight, while other songs of a lyric character occasionally retain traces of a narrative core ("Up a Wide and Lonely Glen," "The Banks o' Red Roses" [60]). Semantic completeness, a criterion insisted upon by singers such as Almeda Riddle, is lacking in some of Jeannie's songs—e.g., in the plot continuation of "Carrbridge Castle" (42), in the transposition of stanzas in "The Beggar Man" (21), or in the "illogic" of stanza 4 in "The Laird o' the Denty Doonby" (39). Features of her songs that might puzzle the listener or reader stem from common problems in material transmitted orally: the abrupt narrative breaks of "Harlaw" (27) or "Mary Hamilton" (74). Some of these problems have been identified for the British traditional ballad in general, though it is clear that Jeannie attempted to clarify her texts as much as possible.[45] She seldom felt the need to shore up the semantics of a song by interpolating a prose version of the plot, as has been noted with other singers.[46] Such explanations, when they are present, derive either from the stories of songs told to traveller children by their parents or from Jeannie's personal interpretation of a song.

The themes of her songs—that is, the ideas or feelings worked out in a plot or lyrical account—range from childhood, freedom, and social conflict to love in its various modalities and the tragedy that results from obsessive or too intense relationships. These thematic concepts often transcend the common distinction made by scholars between narrative and lyric. "MacPherson's Farewell" (15), for example, has more in common thematically with "Brennan on the Moor" (18) or "Johnny the Brime" (16) than with other songs of a conventional lyric type. Basic affinities in theme, then, permit the grouping of songs which, at the more specific level of plot structure or emotional tone, could be brought together only with difficulty.[47]

Structure of Repertoire

Jeannie's repertoire can be categorized in several content types: lyric songs, 36 percent; narrative songs, 28 percent; children's songs, 20 percent; Harry Lauder music-hall songs, American (blackface and hillbilly) songs, and "drawing room" folksongs, 10 percent; and bawdy songs, 6 percent. These percentages refer to the sample of 128 songs used in this study and do not include the total number of songs Jeannie knew (more than 140). Some songs that she taught to Lizzie, for example, she did not record or sang only rarely. Among them are "I Am a Forester in This Wood" (Child 110), sung to the tune of "Harlaw" and probably for that reason dropped from her repertoire; "Three Times 'Round Went the Gallant Ship" (Child 289), recorded by Jeannie on Prestige International 13006 but in a form close to the standard version taught in Scottish schools; "The Corncraiks Among the Whinny Knowes"; "The Lassie Gathering Nuts"; "Wha's at the Windae?"; and "Macaphee." Jeannie sang very few Northeast bothy songs. While many of these are for or about men and male life in the farm bothies, traveller women have been known to sing them. On the other hand, at least a dozen of the songs she performed regularly were of Irish influence or provenance. A singer's preferences in repertoire are shaped by basic factors: learning, taste, and the learned ability to read different audiences in differing situations, a feedback process that Jeannie mastered as she crystallized her repertoire for effective communication.

Her active repertoire amounted to some seventy songs, about half the total number she knew. These can be arranged in a number of ways, the most illuminating of which is based on frequency of recording. Although mediators, from both the academy and the commercial media, helped to shape her "public" repertoire by influencing the number and kinds of songs Jeannie recorded, live concert tapes reveal Jeannie's structuring for public performance on quite different occasions.

Those songs most often recorded (five or more times), either on commercial disc or by the School of Scottish Studies, number twenty-two. They are:

An Auld Man Cam Coortin' Me
Bonnie Lass Come Owre (36)
The Bonnie Wee Lassie Who (52)
The Braes o' Killiecrankie (48)
Brennan on the Moor (18)
The Cuckoo's Nest (49)
Cuttie's Weddin' (53)
A Dottered Auld Carle (50)
The Gallowa' Hills (33)
The Gypsy Laddie (14)
The Handsome Cabin Boy (26)

The Laird o' Windy Wa's (46)
MacCrimmon's Lament (32)
Mary Hamilton (74)
The Overgate (Aberdeen version) (51)
Rolling in the Dew (38)
She's Only My Auld Shoes (72)
Son Davit (80)
Tullochgorum (23)
The Twa Brithers (76)
When I Was Nou But Sweet Sixteen (66)
Yowie wi' the Crookit Horn (19)

Songs recorded with moderate frequency (not more than four times) are these thirty titles:

The Beggar Laddie (21)

Bonnie Glenshee (34)

The Bonnie Lassie's Pleydie (47)

Bonnie Udny (69)

The Butcher Boy (68)

Cruel Fate

The Deadly Wars (31)

I Ken Where I'm Going (3)

I Will Lay You Doon (41)

I Wish, I Wish (73)

Jock Stewart (17)

Johnnie the Brime (16)

The Laird o' the Denty Doonby (39)

The Lassies in the Coogate (59)

Lord Lovat (77)

Lord Randal (79)

MacPherson's Farewell (15)

The Moon Shined on My Bed (65)

O Are Ye Sleepin' Maggie?

O Haud Your Tongue Dear Sally (43)

O Jeannie My Dear (1)

The Overgate (Dundee version)

A Pretty Fair Maid (44)

Roy's Wife o' Aldivalloch (54)

Rub a Dub Dub (6)

Tak' the Buckles Frae Your Sheen (37)

Ten O'Clock Is Ringing (4)

We Are Three Wee Glesca Molls

What Did He Feck Ye?

Willie's Fate (75)

A third group of songs, recorded only once or twice, comprises the rest of her repertoire and includes traditional Scottish lyrics and ballads, Harry Lauder, Irish songs, and American songs.

We drew the 80 songs in this book largely from the first and second groups just listed, which amount, respectively, to 18 percent and 23 percent of the total sample of 128 songs recorded from Jeannie. The selection process was a difficult one that involved, first, conveying the range of material in her song repertoire; and, second, considering the frequency of performance of specific songs. We decided that the latter criterion was at least a rough guide to her own taste as well as to her audience's taste.

By 1955 Jeannie's repertoire had assumed a pattern that was to characterize it until the late 1960s, when she began to restrict her public singing because of poor health. This pattern was not an invariable or inflexible one, for she could adapt to the character of any audience. But certain kinds of songs were chosen by her more often and were offset by others for the sake of variety and contrast. At the May 1958 meeting of the Edinburgh University Folk Song Society, when she was at the peak of her fame, the sequence of songs in her program segments was: "The Overgate" (51), "Son Davit" (80); then, later, "Harlaw" (27) and "Cuttie's Weddin'" (53); finally, "A Dottered Auld Carle" (50), "The Twa Brithers" (76), and "The Fair o' Balnafannon" (35). She placed longer, more taxing ballads after or between shorter lyric or comic pieces, clearly aiming for balance and contrast. For the "Bothy Ballads and Blues" ceilidh sponsored by Aberdeen Left Club in June 1960, Jeannie's program included: "The Cuckoo's Nest" (49), "The Overgate" (51), "She's Only My Auld Shoes"

(72); then "Twa Recruitin' Sergeants" (25), "An Auld Man Cam' Coortin' Me"; and last, "Bonnie Black E'e," "Ten O'Clock Is Ringing" (4), "We Are Three Wee Glesca Molls," "Soo Sewin' Silk" (10), "I Ken Whaur I'm Going" (3), and "Son Davit" (80).

These sequences grow out of factors both enculturated and "learned." First among such factors was association. Jeannie's observation of older singers in traveller gatherings provided a model for the structure of repertoire that may be seen in her grouping of children's songs at the "Bothy Ballads and Blues" concert. Second, her instinct for contrast meant building program segments by means of variety, by the effective juxtaposing of song types. Third, this variety was enclosed within a move from lighter pieces to weightier ballads. Andy Hunter has confirmed how Jeannie increasingly was inclined to build her programs to a climax. She refused a request to open with "Little Matty Groves" because she preferred to leave it to the end, when the audience would be more receptive. This progression from lyric or children's song to the grandeur of her ballad singing was offset, then, by a striving for contrast in theme, structure, and mood.

Occasionally her choice of songs was dictated by the audience. On one occasion, she was encouraged to perform for a London Irish crowd in the Bedford Tavern. Pressed to sing before people she considered hard to please, she began with "The Gallowa' Hills" (33), sung a little faster than usual. When this won approval, she followed it with a song she believed to be Irish ("O Haud Your Tongue Dear Sally" [43]) because "there was a jauntin' car an' ivrything in it." At another time, she had to trim the length of a song. A television producer asked her to shorten "Son Davit" (80) in the interest of air time, which she did, with permanent results for the version she subsequently sang.[48] These examples indicate a flexibility with respect to audiences and the kinds of songs Jeannie felt to be acceptable and appropriate, even though she might make such changes against her better artistic judgment. Her ability to adjust in this way has been compared to the behavior of Romanies in similar situations. Since Jeannie's audience normally was a native Scottish one familiar with the songs and themes of her active repertoire, she rarely needed to modify a prepared group of songs, either in order or in length.

A final aspect of repertoire is that of song ownership. Because of the wider rivalries between and among traveller families and clans, the notion of song ownership normally is relevant only in the context of the nuclear family. In traveller families, exchange has been much more the norm than exclusive "ownership" of songs, but often family members have well-defined individual repertoires based upon preference and aptitude.[49] In the Higgins family, Jeannie did not know some of Donald's songs. "Proud Lady Margaret" (Child

47), for instance, was taught to Lizzie by her father, whose favorite ballad it was.[50] Lizzie's comment was, "My father would never give it til her. . . . He learned me . . . Jeannie wouldnae poach upon us."[51] In later years, Lizzie, as she took over the role of traditional singer from Jeannie, began to learn more songs from her than she formerly had done. The concept of ownership, of having exclusive rights to a song, then, has only limited relevance in the context of Jeannie's family.

Poetics, Commonplaces

Whereas Jeannie's song texts show thematic variety, a range of affective modes, and structural complexity, the structure of the songs displays a tension between musical phrase and verse line, and in the varieties of stanza, line, and metrical foot. The conventional ballad stanza (ABCB) and iambic tetrameter plus trimeter are the preferred forms in over 40 percent of her songs. Dactylic types of verse rhythm occur in about half that number; the rhyme schemes AAB and ABAB appear in about 30 percent of her songs. She achieves subtlety of stress and accent by mixing dactyls and spondees in such songs as "Twa Recruitin' Sergeants" (25), and a direct, somber effect emerges from the abrupt monosyllables of "Ainst Upon a Time" (56). But it is the musical concept of phrase which, by means of the melodic design and rhythmic pulse, shapes the versification.[52] The commonest phrase scheme for the melodies is, as Bronson found for almost half his 3,450 ballad tunes, the non-recurrent ABCD.

The ballad commonplaces or formulas, with their parallelisms and plangent imagery, recur in Jeannie's song texts: hands, breasts, and gowns are "lily-white"; steeds are "milk-white" (Lord Lovat's mount, by ellipsis, becomes a "milk steed"); a woman's middle is "sma'" and a corn-barn "cauld." Less tightly conventional are the "mightful" dream and "cold-clay" lips in "Lord Lovat" (77). Embedded in "She's Only My Auld Shoes" (72) is a riddle: How many blackberries grow round a salt sea? This device pulls the song into the orbit of other riddle ballads in which an important event lies outside the song, preceding or following the verbal narration.[53] Jeannie commonly employs repetition, both incremental repetition and a simple parallelism, as a device in ballads: "Lord Donald" (79), "Son Davit" (80), and "The Twa Brithers" (76). These mechanisms also are present in lyrics such as "Bonnie Udny" (69) and "I Wish, I Wish" (73). The overall effect of the rhetoric in Jeannie's songs is, as Gerould noted for balladry as a genre, one of intense stylization.[54] Studies of ballad language and individual ballad repertoires have shown the structural and thematic significance of those rhetorical devices, to which the ballad scholar William Motherwell drew early attention.[55] Yet their effectiveness is fundamentally affected by the transformation they undergo in the singing act, and their effect is subject to the musical skill of the singer as communicative agent.

The imagery and metaphors that occur in the song texts are largely those of love, sex, and death, sometimes as a reflection or reinforcement of a theme or plot. That many of the metaphors in folksong are sexual has been pointed out by Reeves and later by Renwick.[56] Andersen has investigated in some detail the significance of commonplaces in English and Scottish ballads, and has demonstrated that these are far from being random or bound by convention, as earlier scholars supposed.[57] The general pattern of images and metaphors in Jeannie's songs follows a widely shared vocabulary; birds, flowers, colors figure prominently. Birds usually are signifiers of love, as are the mavis (thrush), turtle dove, and nightingale in "Lovely Molly" (62); though the hawk of "Son Davit" (80) may suggest a connection to the Otherworld rather than simply being part of the yeoman's accouterments. The blooms in "Banks of Red Roses" (60) hint at sexual satisfaction (rose is often a metaphor for the vagina, or for youthful female sexuality; cf. "Jemima Rose" in "The Overgate," 51) but also at blood and death, while the laurels of "Green Grows the Laurels" (62) are juxtaposed with "violets so blue," indicating that sorrow is to be replaced by true love and fidelity (see also note on the "red, white, and blue" variants). (See also the note to song 62 on the "red, white, and blue" variants.)

White, and more particularly "lily-white," is a common color for the breast (13) and above all the hand, but "lily-white," oddly, is found in "Trooper and Maid" (61) as an attribute of the object (normally passive female, here trooper). In "The Laird o' the Denty Doonby" (39), too, "lily-white hand" occurs after the seduction rather than before, when it normally paves the way for the central act (cf. "The Butcher Boy," 68). Both "lily-white" and "snow-white" are applied to material: pillows in "I'm a Rover" (13), a gown in "Trooper and Maid" (61). Green, as elsewhere in folklore, betokens danger ("green wids" in "Johnnie the Brime," 16) or transformed circumstances (as in the clothes of the beggar man who turns out to be a nobleman in disguise, 21). Yellow is a sign of youthful sexuality, especially in women's hair ("The Lassies in the Cougate," 59; "Bonnie Barbara O," 63). Black is a sign of physical power (as in the horse of "The Gypsy Laddie," 14) and sometimes sexual power (curly black hair, dark eyes). Blue eyes, on the other hand, like blue in general, suggest fidelity rather than treachery, seduction, or murder. Gold is the color of rings or, happily, of a transformed "cold and" in "golden frosty morning" (7).

Jeannie's vocabulary ranges from contemporary Scots and traveller cant at one end of a spectrum to modern English at the other. The Scottish and English broadside songs are readily distinguishable in terms of language, but Jeannie also used alternative forms of a word in the same song: ging/go, nicht/ night, bilin'/boilin'. Her repertoire of traveller songs inject cant as a vital element, in "Jimmy Drummond" (24), "What Did He Feck Ye?," and "Cant Song." In her Scots, conventional archaisms ("holland sark," "cowks at her kail") exist beside rare neologisms ("advited her to tea"). The mixture of linguistic and lexical forms in Jeannie's songs has, as its basis, lowland Scots tempered by cant and modern English. Compared with the poetics of the historical ballad singer Anna Brown (and later, Bell Robertson), on the one hand, and of Jeannie's daughter Lizzie, on the other, differences in usage arise as much from education and social class as from historical erosion. The most palpable changes in Lizzie's everyday language reflect a move away from rural Scots to an urbanized Scots-English, though this development often has left untouched the conservative world of ballad language, which among travellers and other traditional singers retains its archaic power.[58]

The overwhelming majority of Jeannie's songs are cast in four-line stanzas (67 percent), the other types being eight-line (17 percent), six-line (8 percent), five-line (4 percent), and more than eight lines (4 percent). The four-line stanza normally is in conventional form by rhyme scheme (ABCB). There are no couplet types in her repertoire, though a few three-line forms occur.

Refrains that are intercalary, independent, or the final line of the stanza are found in over a quarter of Jeannie's songs (about 27 percent). The intercalary type is seen in "I'll Sing to Ye a Story" (11), the distinct refrain in "Mary Hamilton" (74), and the final line type in "The Gaberlunzie Man" (22). The majority of refrains are the second or distinct type. Some are composed wholly or partly of nonlexical syllables, as in "The Overgate" (51) or "The Cuckoo's Nest" (49). The character of such refrains is suggestive, their structural and artistic function often determined by the song's racy or erotic subject matter. Few of her ballads have a refrain, for in these parallelism tends to make a refrain superfluous. Exceptions to this general rule are "The Jolly Beggar" (22), "Mary Hamilton" (74), "Brennan on the Moor" (18), and "I'm a Rover But Seldom Sober" (13).

Tonal Concepts and Use

Traditional singers normally do not articulate a concept of mode, scale, or tonality but rather are aware of the right and wrong ways of singing a tune and the musical intervals that constitute it. A mode or scale is, after all, an abstract structure even when played on an instrument such as a pipe or fiddle.

Yet a notion of melodic style is more pronounced in some singers than in others.[59] Jeannie's sense of pitch and tonality is keyed to relatively fixed intervals, whatever the mode or complex of tones she uses at any one time. She does not subject individual degrees of a tune to deliberate or involuntary fluctuation, a fact that tends to reinforce the impression of a sure sense of pitch. Within each song, pitch and the relation of tonal degrees to one another remain consistent. Her stable grasp of pitch shows an evident awareness of the range and technical difficulty of individual songs and the effect that these difficulties could have on the pitch level of a song. The real pitch of Jeannie's voice tended to fall in later life as her style grew idiosyncratic and more ponderous.

Jeannie's tonal concepts are oriented towards the six-tone (hexatonic) and five-tone, halftone-less (anhemi-pentatonic) forms of scale disposition considered as abstractions. A total of 82 tunes (64 percent) from the sample of 128 are of the two types, of these 51 being hexatonic (62 percent) and 31 pentatonic (38 percent). The remaining 46 tunes (36 percent of the total 128) are seven-tone (heptatonic) tunes, except for two examples of pentachordal or five-note tunes—the children's songs, "One, Two, Three a Leerie" and "Goodbye Mama, Goodbye Dada" (2)—and one tetratonic tune ("Cant Song"). The first of the two pentachords has placement of fifth through supertonic above, the second of tonic through fifth to the upper octave. "Cant Song" is laid out in the plagal range from lower fourth through tonic, supertonic and major third to the upper fifth. Spontaneity within a generic context (childhood, warning of danger) appears to have shaped the limited but direct tonal character of these three songs.[60]

The hepta- airs in the sample rarely deviate from a norm of seven relatively stable degrees. In a few cases, an interval within a tune will appear in two intentionally discrete forms: the seventh in "Tullochgorum" (23) and "Yowie wi' the Crookit Horn" (19). This seventh corresponds approximately to the major and minor intervals of tempered tuning. On the other hand, the variable third in the second measure of "The Laird o' the Denty Doonby" (39) is less clear-cut, but in the recorded versions settles down, in the course of the song, to a regular minor third. Variability of this kind is comparatively rare in Jeannie's singing. Notes that she altered, deliberately or not, from the concept of a quasi-tempered scale and mode disposition are the exception rather than the rule. This is perhaps surprising, since we might expect the influence of the nontempered tuning of the bagpipe scale on traveller singing to be more percepitble. Collinson, paradoxically, believes the origin of the bagpipe scale to be vocal, arising from the tendency he noted among traditional singers in Scotland (more, one might imagine, in the Highlands than the Lowlands, and in rural than in urban areas) to divide the gap of a minor third in the pentatonic scale by an approximation towards a midway point.[61]

In his analysis of Scottish, English, and Appalachian tunes, Bronson notes that the order of preference in modal configuration for Scottish tunes is as follows:

1. Hexatonic Dorian-Aeolian (six-note scale with a minor third and flat seventh).
2. Ionian (regular major scale).
3. Hexatonic Ionian-Mixolydian (six-note major scale without a seventh).[62]

Of the heptatonic forms in Jeannie's tunes, the great majority (33, or 75 percent) are in the *do* (or Ionian) mode. The *sol* (Mixolydian) and *re* (Dorian) modes account for five songs (23 percent) each; and the *la* (Aeolian) mode only one song (2 percent).

In the hexa- types, the wide interval (formerly referred to as a "gap") is distributed thus:

Degrees	1–2	2–3	3–4	5–6	6–7
Number (Total = 51)	1	3	14	11	22
Percentage of Total	2	6	27	21	43

Overall, the hexa- types incline to a prevailing tonal form of a minor third (86 percent) and the wide interval between degrees 6 and 7 (43 percent). Of the seven songs with a minor third (14 percent), six have the wide interval between 5 and 6, and one ("The Flower of County Down") between 1 and 2.

Jeannie's penta- tunes favor the wide intervals between 3 and 4, and 6 and 7 (i.e., Bronson's penta- 1), 90 percent of these falling into that model form and the remaining three tunes being distributed equally among three other penta-forms (penta- 2, 3, 4). Without doubt, Jeannie's avoidance of the seventh, and to a lesser extent of the 3–4 degree, in two-thirds of her repertoire contributed to the "modal" feel of her song airs and their distance from the world of popular commercial song. It also contributed to the impression of elemental power in her performance of the songs.

Recordings fix the pitch range of Jeannie's voice from about the F below middle C (f) to the C an octave above (c''). Her later, deliberate style tended to confine the voice to its lower octave. The overall tonal range of her songs, on the other hand, extends from a simple tetrachord to examples spanning a twelfth: "Lord Donald" (79) or "The Bonnie Lassie's Pleydie's Awa'" (47). The great majority of tunes fall within the span of an octave or ninth, the latter accounting for a third of the total, slightly more than those with an octave range (31 percent). The prominence of bagpipe airs may be one reason for this pattern. Following these ranges come tunes of a tenth (19 percent), an eleventh (9 percent), and a sixth (5 percent).

The proportions of authentic (*do-dó*), plagal (*sol-sól*), and mixed tunes, in Bronson's terminology, are as follows: 47, 38, and 15 percent, respectively. Comparison within their own modal forms gives:

	Authentic (Percentage)	Plagal (Percentage)	Mixed (Percentage)
Hepta-	59	23	18
Hexa-	47	37	16
Penta-	30	63	7

The high count of plagal penta- tunes suggests that this modal framework constitutes a basic model in Jeannie's tonal thinking and awareness, and consequently in her performance style.

The dominant type in the hepta- forms is that in the authentic *do* mode (52 percent), followed by its plagal (27 percent) and mixed (21 percent) versions. *Sol* mode tunes are mostly in the authentic range (60 percent), the remainder being divided equally between plagal and mixed forms. The *re* tunes are all in the authentic range. A profile of the hepta- tunes in Jeannie's repertoire, then, shows *do* mode types predominating (39 percent), followed by its plagal and mixed forms (20 and 16 percent, respectively). Authentic *re* mode tunes are next in frequency (11 percent), then authentic *sol* mode types (7 percent). Authentic forms of the *la* mode, with plagal and mixed forms of the *sol* mode, make up the remaining 7 percent.

Jeannie's hexa- tunes show that authentic types dominate (47 percent) in range, followed by plagal (37 percent) and mixed forms (16 percent). The majority of the authentic hexa- types combine this characteristic with a preference for the wide interval between 5 and 6 (33 percent), followed by 3 and 4 (29 percent), 6 and 7 (25 percent), 2 and 3 (8 percent), and 1 and 2 (5 percent). Her plagal types incline strongly to place the wide interval between 6 and 7 (63 percent). Next she favors the wide interval between 3 and 4 (21 percent), and 5 and 6 (16 percent). In the mixed forms, she prefers the wide interval between 6 and 7 (50 percent), followed by one between 3 and 4 (37 percent), and 2 and 3 (13 percent).

The prevailing hexa- tune type, then, is in the plagal range with the wide interval between 6 and 7:

Degrees	1–2	2–3	3–4	5–6	6–7
Authentic	2%	4%	13%	16%	12%
Plagal			8%	6%	23%
Mixed		2%	6%		8%

A significant majority of Jeannie's penta- tunes consists of plagal tunes with the wide interval between 3 and 4, and 5 and 6 (penta- 1 = 58 percent). The same type in its authentic and mixed ranges (22 and 10 percent, respectively, of all her penta- tunes) together outnumber the few single instances of other penta- types. The dominant kind of penta- tunes, then, is plagal with the wide interval between 3 and 4 or 5 and 6, followed by the same type in its authentic and mixed ranges (23 and 19 percent, respectively).

Jeannie's preferences in mode and range accord generally with Bronson's statistics for Lowland Scots tunes as a whole.[63] Two-thirds (66 percent) of his sample were of the hexa- or penta- type, and of Jeannie's repertoire 64 percent were. But in modal type her songs differ. Bronson's sample yields a preference for the minor hexatonic with the wide interval between 5 and 6 (his D/AE), followed by the hepta- *do* mode (Ionian) and then the major hexatonic (wide interval 6–7) and also penta- 1. Jeannie's modal inclinations, in contrast, are toward the authentic major hexa- type (wide interval 5–6 = 6 percent), the major hexa- (wide interval 3–4 = 6 percent), and the authentic penta- 1 (11 percent). This pattern strongly suggests an element of broadside sources in her tune repertoire as a counterbalance to songs learned orally from Maria and others in the family circle.

Finals, Anacruses

While the tonic note normally functions as the "final" in Jeannie's tunes, 13 percent end on another note. Of the seventeen tunes that display a final of this kind, ten end on degrees two or three (59 percent), four end on the upper or lower five (23 percent), and three end on six (18 percent). Tunes of this kind have often been dubbed "circular" by scholars (i.e., the last note implies the beginning of another cycle). In those cases where Jeannie's melodies are designated as being in the *sol* mode, the seventh is low because of an idiomatic tonal sequence in Scottish traditional music known as the "double tonic" or the "subtonic juncture."[64] This occurs when a figuration on the tonic triad is followed by one on the triad a tone lower (or higher). The sequence is probably instrumental in origin, stemming from the fingering technique of the nine-note Highland bagpipe.[65] Jeannie provides two clear examples in the songs "Tullochgorum" (23) and "The Gallowa' Hills" (33).

Jeannie begins fully 77 percent of her songs on an upbeat or anacrusis. Of this amount, over half move from tonic to upper third (1–3; 29 percent), or from dominant to tonic (V–1; 25 percent). These are followed by a move 3–5 (8 percent), 5–1 (7 percent), and 5–3 (7 percent), and VII–1 (4 percent). To some extent, her preferences here correspond to the significant proportion of plagal penta- and hexa- tunes, and authentic *do* mode airs in her songs. The proportion of tunes beginning on a strong beat (23 percent) is also comparable in terms of mode and range. Jeannie's favored degree at midcadence is 5 (or V; 32 percent), followed closely by 2 (24 percent), 6 (11 percent), 1 (10 percent), 3 (8 percent), and 4 (7 percent). These figures appear to corroborate the differences Bronson found in his more extensive sampling of British-American tunes.[66]

Rhythmic and Metrical Concepts

The majority of Jeannie's song airs (about 65 percent) are in common time. Triple time accounts for about 16 percent, and about 8 percent are 6/8 tunes. A significant batch of airs has an ambiguous metrical structure, in which the second beat of a measure can be interpreted in two ways (i.e., as a 4/4 measure in which the second beat is a half-note or, alternatively, as a 3/4 bar in which the second beat is a fermata). Tunes of this kind number about eleven (9 percent of the sample); see "Tifty's Annie" (78) and "Carrbridge Castle" (42).

In broad terms, Jeannie's phrasal sense is evident in her breaking up of regular mensural units, as in "Twa Recruitin' Sergeants" (25), a song in which, according to Andy Hunter, "she left the foot-tappers behind." No tune in her performances was ever wholly symmetrical in measure, nor metronomic in rhythm and tempo. At one end of her repertoire spectrum lie dancelike numbers based on strathspey and reel forms, and in these she showed a virtuosic grasp of rhythmic variation ("Tullochgorum" [23]). At the other end were the rhythmically freer types, usually but not inevitably her big ballads, including such songs as "Far Over the Forth" (71) or "I Wish, I Wish" (73).

Though a large group of Jeannie's songs is in common time (4/4), the rhythmic freedom among them is striking. Some are couched in a jaunty march time ("My Auld Man and Your Auld Wife," to the air of "Lovat Scouts") or in a strathspey tempo ("Tammy Doddle" [9], "Yowie wi' the Crookit Horn" [19]). One or two tunes in duple time oscillate between 2/4 and 6/8 ("Harlaw" [27], "The Laird o' the Denty Doonby" [39]). In "Harlaw," notably, Jeannie's performance often would begin in marchlike 2/4 with dotted rhythm, but she would switch at the refrain to a 6/8 time which then was maintained for the remainder of the song. The foregoing percentages refer to the abstracts of sung melody as they appear in transcription. Such abstracts, of course, are but a shadow of the rhythmic subtlety apparent in more descriptive transcriptions.[67]

Melorhythmic Phrase Models

From the above analysis, it is clear that Jeannie forged some dominant models in terms of melody, rhythm, and phrase structure. The musical gesture, in her singing style, is founded on the phrase and its structural components—melodic, rhythmic, textural. One could argue that these melorhythmic models represent the musical gesture in her singing style. They form a significant nucleus of her concert repertoire as it evolved over twenty years. As such, though, these models are neither reductions of her repertoire as a whole nor generative of subsidiary tune types. Rather, as cornerstones of repertoire, they represent favored structures that reflect certain melodic, rhythmic, and phrasal preferences within her performance style. Three model types stand out, based on phrase structure, mode, and range, as well as frequency of performance.

Model 1 is a four-line ABAB′ (ABBA, ABCD) stanza, penta-1 mode in the plagal range, with a midcadence on the fifth (second, sixth) degree. Songs that illustrate the model are "Soo Sewin' Silk" (10), "Davie Faa" (19), "The Jolly Beggar" (21), "Harlaw" (27), "The Bonnie Hoose o' Airlie" (28), "Bonnie Lass Come Owre the Burn" (36), "I Will Lay You Doun" (41), "Carrbridge Castle" (42), "Susan Pyatt," "Cruel Fate" (45), "The Overgate" (51), "When I Was Nou But Sweet Sixteen" (66) and "Son Davit" (80). The melodies for three of these (41, 42, and "Susan Pyatt") are actually identical, though the emphases and timing differ. The solid pentatonic scaffolding allows Jeannie maximum flexibility in nuancing structural discrepancies; she repeats the first two melodic lines to make up the six-line stanza in verses 2 and 5 of "Carrbridge Castle." The strong arch of the melody, the deliberate tempo, and the pliant rhythmic treatment match closely the style and cast of Jeannie's voice. Several other hexatonic songs follow this strong plagal pattern. The model type represents Jeannie's orally learned repertoire.

Model 2 has the melodic line structure ABBA, ABBA′ (or ABCD), while the modal type is hexatonic in the authentic or mixed range (wide interval 3–4 or, if plagal, 6–7). Again, like Model 1, there is sometimes mensural or rhythmic ambiguity in the second or third measure of the phrase. Songs that exemplify this are "Come Up and See My Garritie" (8), "I'll Sing to Ye a Story" (11), "The Gypsy Laddie" (14), "I Hae Ae Bit Son" (29), "Bonnie Glenshee" (34), "A Dottered Auld Carle" (50), ""Bonnie Udny" (69), "I Wish, I Wish" (73), and "My Father Built Me a Dandy Bower." Like Model 1, the song type here is drawn mainly from oral sources.

Model 3 is a much less common type: an eight-lined tune (ABCDCDAB), hexatonic like Model 2 though in the authentic range (wide interval 3–4). But it shows a mensural and rhythmic character quite different from those of Models 1 and 2, using the technique of repeating lines 3–4 for 5–6 with a midcadence on the fifth degree, and then returning in circular fashion to lines 1–2. Songs generated from this model, mostly from broadside, chapbook, or possibly Irish oral sources, are "O Haud Your Tongue Dear Sally" (43) and "The Moon Shined On My Bed Last Night" (65). Model 3 is more representative of songs whose texts stem directly from the tradition of street literature.

The conceptions of range and tonality in these song types are animated, in performance, by rhythms that play in a flexible, free manner with the more spacious melodies or, on the other hand, emphasize strict tempo march or dance time. They suggest a tension between songs in a more contemplative style and those that depend on rhythmic vitality—i.e., those that are essentially internalizations of experience and those that externalize the song's character. This contrast suggests the differentiation of melodic, rhythmic, and stylistic types to which Bartók gave the names *parlando rubato* (free rhythm) and *tempo giusto* (strict tempo). But the variety of Jeannie's rhythmic types covers a wider range of technical possibilities. Sure-footed in the slower intricacies of Child ballad rhythmic and melodic interpretation, she was equally adept at the bagpipe and fiddle snap in tunes such as "Tullochgorum" (23), "Yowie wi the Crookit Horn" (19), "The Braes o Killiecrankie" (48), and "The Cuckoo's Nest" (49). Such songs were not meant to be danced to in her performances of them. Rather, they were portraits of dance songs, geared to Jeannie's own rhythmic impetus.

Contextual Transformativity

The contexts of transformativity emerge from changes in style and performance. We might also speak of a transformativity of contexts, since several contexts are transformed in and through the singing gesture: the performance context, the broader cultural context, the poetic and generic contexts of the song itself, and the historical context.[68] These can be arranged in a hierarchy subordinate to the performance context, which is the locus of the singing gesture, of meaning, and thus constitutes the central fact of transformativity. That is not to suggest that the performance context eclipses other contexts; but it is the only one in which communication and feedback are vital, observable elements. The contexts that are intertwined with the performance context are therefore to be seen not as being in opposition to it, but as multilayered dimensions of an existential act. This act constitutes the grounding of cultural communication, and, in Jeannie's case, was cast in two directions: inward, to her own experience; and outward, progressively, to public audiences rather than, as earlier, to the restricted network of her traveller kin.

The travellers' world of performance has shifted, but it would be a mistake to see this as negative. While rapid change has invaded the intimacy and reciprocity characteristic of traveller clans, it has also offered adaptive strategies: many who were recognized singers and musicians in their own circle adjusted their practical skills to widening spheres and the challenge of new audiences. On the other hand, the experience of some who began to concertize during the 1950s and 1960s has suggested that the further the performer moves from the locus of creativity (kin, restricted network of acquaintances, domestic and local concerns, standards and values), the more stringently are sanctions on communication and meaning enforced, while at the same time the demand for relevance on a more "universal" plane increases.

In such cases, the flexibility of tradition in local contexts—where performer and audience know fairly well how constraints may be extended or where communicative and interpretive codes may be switched—is exchanged for an ostensibly broader structure of repertoire and a wider frame of reference. Actually, these latter are more constricted because the social base of tradition has been altered. Max Gluckman coined the term "multiplexity" for the development of separate roles in a bounded community where formerly such roles were cumulative in individuals.[69] We can believe that the gradual assimilation that the travellers are currently undergoing involves the learning of separate kinds of role behavior that were neither necessary nor useful in their communities a generation ago. The expressive system of the traditional community has been modified by a new set of norms governing performance in particular—namely, the norms of mass entertainment.[70]

This has happened to some travellers and nontravellers alike as their "little tradition" modernizes.[71] A singer like Jeannie Robertson, recognized by her own circle of kin, who moves out of the traditional community into a populous, mobile, and highly commercial world, often has been misunderstood or typecast as naive, primitive, or quaint. Not surprisingly in such contexts, traveller singers have tended to drift into "art" on the one hand (idiosyncratic treatment of repertoire, inspired by an external emphasis on individualism) or "folksiness" on the other (self-parody induced by the exchange of traditional for nontraditional performance contexts). Without local referents and local interpreters, the internal coherence and contextual meaning of a song in performance is liable to disintegrate or gain meanings that are relevant only to the personal.

Traditional singers sometimes have found it difficult to adjust to the anonymity and pace of urban life and to mass-media pressures. Frequently it has been those who somehow were at odds with their community who have adjusted to the wider contexts of club circuit and concert stage. Performers of this kind have mastered several types of context in the performance of traditional songs: first, the domestic, small-scale, and familial kind that corresponds to the norms of the community; second, the milieu of informal ceilidhs and folk festivals, where the audience is composed mainly though not exclusively of local persons; and, third, the full-blown concert tour, which involves audiences of strangers at staged performances in unfamiliar locations. The empty recording studio is yet another context, though the lack of an interactive audience affects the singer adversely, and product-oriented manipulation thwarts the communicative act.[72] These contexts have moved, then, or continue to move, from the communal to the contractual, from the sponsored to the commercial and individualistic.[73]

Lately scholars have argued for studies of musical performance that are context-sensitive, the idea being that the conditions under which music is made, and the possible meanings these may impose on the music or invoke in the listener, are factors integral to the assessment of musical value. They argue that music is a social fact shaped by enculturation and therefore must be studied and evaluated in social (that is, "group") situations. While this argument is valid enough, in more complex societies the composition and performance of music and song often can occur in solitary contexts: individuals practice for reasons ranging from insecurity and sensitivity to perfectionism and delight in their craft, and it is often such reflective individuals who are innovators in form and style.[74] The processes involved in composition, improvisation, or preparation for performance now are receiving some attention.[75]

In relation to traditional singing style, however, "innovation" is a misleading concept. It suggests novelty, perhaps individualistic or radical change, as does the notion of "composition," and Lomax has warned that an apparent change in style may be a temporary experiment.[76] In any case, the term *style* refers to the acts of composing and performing and to the evolution of a performance technique that incorporates not just human physical change (aging and the like) but also conceptual change, when external, contextual forces come to bear upon the music maker. *How* the singer conceives of her or his material lies at the foundation of any notion of musical change and is just as significant as the *what* (subject matter). The *what*, moreover, cannot be studied, at least in communities with a vibrant aural tradition, except through the *how*, and it is mistaken to try to separate the two or, indeed, to separate *musical change* from *social change*, since styles are embodied in individuals who mature, age, and decline.

While it is true that change in a musical style results from individual specialists' bringing their artistic influence to bear on the direction of music making, Jeannie's achievement was both conservative and profound. Her stylistic development, which is best seen in terms of a sequence of events (ceilidhs, concerts, recording sessions) of extraordinary communicative power, transformed her audiences and herself, as well as her songs and their performance. This communicative power lies at the heart of her style, for it was not its novelty but its layered depth that made it persuasive. Her repertoire, too, crystallized as favored songs became stable and standardized in performance. Jeannie, then, was not so much a conscious innovator, in the sense of inventing materials, as she was a singer deeply involved in the cognitive and affective "truth" of her traditional songs.

Jeannie's ability to "read" an audience beforehand, to tailor her repertoire to the demands of the particular situation, was legendary. To be sure, some changes she made in adapting to an audience, such as the excision of stanzas or the expansion of her singing style, were not always acceptable to purists.[77] Jeannie's self-transformation also was bound up with the change of context; her singing gesture evolved as her world both expanded spatially and narrowed as repertoire, themes, and style crystallized. The final summation of this development was her protracted treatment of some big ballads, brought about partly by her isolation on large stages and in empty recording studios and partly by her focusing on a few songs that reverberated with her personal experience of motherhood, family, bereavement.

Subjective Transformativity

The singing of ballads, as the phenomenal recreation of experience through feeling, is the essence of transformativity, not only because singing intensifies emotional depth but because, at a single stroke, it incorporates history and social structure into the ritual process. Ballad singing is not merely a "cultural performance" through which we change in some ways while remaining the same in others,[78] but a way of distilling the life world and its fullnesses in a ritualizing gesture that fuses cognition, feeling, and volition.[79] The components and mechanisms of cultural communication are themselves transformed, no longer in the hierarchical arrangement of speech or even balladry. The cause of their transformation lies in the compulsion—found at its most dramatic among travellers and similar groups living on the margins of materialistic societies and driven by social rejection, fragile living standards, and an identification with natural forces—to test the limits of experience and consciousness, of nature, culture, and gender, by joining present with past and future, the living with the dead, and the here-and-now with the world beyond. Transformativity is, in essence, teleological; it aims to test knowledge and experience and, in testing, to change the world.

As the stranger in society, keenly conscious of its weaknesses and moral pretensions because he or she is constantly marginalized, the traveller singer threatens to turn the world upside down, to invert norms and point to a world-that-could-be.[80] Singing is a potent device, then, for synchronizing diachrony, for converting structure into process and thus turning the lead of everyday life and its struggles into the gold of an idealized existence. The nature-oriented, antimaterialistic, communal, yet individualistic quality of traveller life has maintained this ability to transform experience through singing. By seeing transformativity as a necessary condition of, and reason for, the nature of the sung products, we can construct a more informed epistemology of songs and ballads, of myth and ritual, of oral tradition and culture change.

Oral societies, as Jan Vansina has noted, operate with a notion of change that opposes the present to a single past and not to a variety of pasts. Complex chain reactions through time are not perceived. History is seen as a series of static states in which new items appear but are unconnected to one another; and individuals are responsible for any changes that occur.[81] Levi-Strauss, Edmund Leach, and others have suggested that oral traditions affect a society's present cultural values rather than expressing idle curiosity about that past. There indeed may be complex historical reasons for thematic preferences among travellers and Lowland Scots at times (magic spells, supernatural metamorphoses, internecine feuds); some scholars have sought to explain them by reference to animism, totemism, the witch cult, and older Celtic social customs. We cannot, however, dismiss a continuing, immediate, and organic identification with the natural and preternatural worlds as the basis of these preferences.[82]

The uses of singing among travellers have included lightening mundane tasks, bringing back memories of ancestors, arguing or competing in song, and teaching songs to others. One traveller, Betsy Whyte, whose autobiography was published in 1978, says of the relationship between singing and farm laboring, "You are free to let yourself go, to feel yourself. Being close to the land brings you out of yourself. You are a different person, you feel different all together from being inside. You feel that good you want to sing."[83] This effect of the laboring context on the body, that in turn generates song, can be noted as a form of, or condition of, external transformation. As the body works through repetitive physical tasks, the need for both sublimation of and continuity of expression leads to song rather than speech, especially within a culture keyed to singing's affective power. The bodily contact sometimes described in traveller singing (holding hands, embracing during performance) is a way of transmitting the sensations felt and lived by the singer. The performance has metamusical aspects, and thus song performance transforms human relationships in a palpable and tactile way.[84]

Such singers might also vary their strategies depending on the audience—telling the story of the song first in prose, for example, before singing it, to make sure the audience was interested. Mingled speech and song, chantefable or partially sung stories seem to have been an authentic form of traveller narration. On the generic level, it has been shown that travellers shift from song to prose narrative at indeterminate points of performance for various reasons: to effect a smoother transition from one part of the song to another, sometimes as a result of forgetting the text, or, more remarkably, to explain what the song text leaves poetically opaque.[85] Spoken narrativity thus becomes an important dialectical foil for the singing, ritualizing gesture: the fusion of cognition, feeling, and willing (volition) that singing embodies shifts towards a hierarchical concept in which cognition and volition dominate the affective dimension.

The singer's ability to perform effectively sometimes is aided by alcohol, since this helps soften feelings of grief. The singer finds it difficult to refrain from identifying with the person in the story. Duncan Williamson could not sing his father's "Shanghai Ballad" (a song about his imprisonment) without drinking first, as his father would also.[86] The generic shift from narrativity to lament, as in Jeannie's "Son Davit" or Duncan's "Shanghai Ballad," stems from powerful identification with a relative. But, unlike the lament singers of Finland, who borrow from Kalevala meter songs, Scottish traveller singers reverse the process and project the idea of lament into ballads. While there is an improvisatory element in formal lament traditions, the traveller singer often will shift the emotional gravity of the ballad toward a semi-improvised structure.

In traveller tradition, ballads at times are sung as a way of transforming and renewing interrupted relationships, often with dead relatives; women singers more often than not have been the main figures in this tradition. By practicing the lament as a ritualized structure, or even by pushing other genres like ballads in the direction of the lament, the (usually postmenopausal) female singer in many societies manifests a power unavailable to her during childbearing years.[87] In her study of the lament in Greek tradition, Margaret Alexiou observes how the lament of the Virgin Mary, in telling a story that contains lamentation, has become a balladlike genre in modern times; forms of it are found in all parts of the Greek-speaking world.[88] In a subsequent study, one scholar notes that older Greek women in Epirus transform songs into laments to express certain personal feelings in a non-lament context. Through this third genre, women extend the range of sorrowful expression beyond death rites into the solitary moments of daily life.[89] Discussing similar laments, another study mentions that it is the oppressed woman of the "patriarchal" Greek village who is the manipulator of the magical language of the lament, which can draw bridges across disparate realms, transforming lamentation into equipment for living.[90] Singing a narrative while directing it at departed relatives is more than just a device for coping with grief. The medium transforms the act from an objectivizing gesture replete with descriptive detail into ritual communication, with an implied inversion of the present social order.

Traveller singers (not only women) find an old song meaningful because it is bound up with the person who sang it. Because some ballads embody for travellers the limits of knowledge or experience, the generic boundaries between ballad, legend, and historical tale become blurred. Jane Turriff observed that "there's a story in every song."[91] And about "Tam Lin," Duncan Williamson remarked, "It's really something you can't explain. . . . could be fictional or reality, too far back for us to understand."[92] The meaning of ballads, then, is perceived and discussed not in an abstract way but as bound up with identified relatives, with performance and situation. Moreover, the story, the bare narrative, by itself could not move the listener. Only in singing was the full affective potential of the song realized. "I try to bring the listener's mind to the place and time when the thing really happened, to show the listener, convey to him what took place at that time," comments Duncan Williamson.[93]

Jeannie's self-transformation began in her teens, as she mastered her singing style and repertoire. Her personhood absorbed and transformed the experience of marriage to Donald and the pain of Jeemsie's and Lizzie's arrival. The next stage began with Jeemsie's passing and Jeannie's philosophical acceptance of her fate. By middle age, when Hamish Henderson knocked on her door, her mastery of style in the old songs that she had learned from Maria and others was fairly complete, although it was to shift and crystallize under outside pressure, casting out the popular and religious and elevating the traditional. The timbre of her voice grew darker, richer, fuller. Her phrasing became grander, more spacious, and the pitch of her voice dropped slightly. This stage took perhaps seven or eight years, from 1953 until 1960, when Jeannie ceased singing due to health problems.

Conclusion: Songs as Transformative Experience

Any theory of traditional music making must deal with processes of meaning formation and community values in music, as well as with song structure and style.[94] One noted scholar emphasized that ethnomusicology should embody "the hermeneutic science of human musical behavior."[95] Implicit in this statement is a rejection of both statistical measurement for its own sake and the assumption that traditional music can be treated like urban concert music and its character determined from analysis of its structure alone. Understanding also means rejecting study restricted to the (verbal) text.[96] From such a shift toward a more "humanizing ethnomusicology" we can develop the notion of a critical hermeneutics of the making of music and song.

Critical hermeneutics is to be regarded as positive rather than simply as negative. A positive hermeneutics must acknowledge the utopian aspect of ideology, along with the latter's ability to express collective impulses and desires, while at the same time articulating the privileges of some groups over others. That is, hermeneutics should remain critical of its own ideological basis, while analyzing both positive and negative aspects of power relations in society.[97] The cultural and musical heritages of the modern world are plural, not "universal." They are constructed, not preserved and transmitted in the form of a self-same tradition or core of inevitable meanings. These constructions, in fact, are the locus of conflicting interpretations. This is as true of Jeannie's songs and singing as of the "tradition" of Western classical music. The task of a critical but positive hermeneutics, in terms of song performance and its cultural profile, is to assess the dialogue of contemporary culture as it is forced, through pressure from indigenous and immigrant minorities, to reevaluate its claim to universality.

In a convergence of folk music study and ethnomusicology, the strengths of phenomenology can be linked to an analysis critical of society. Folklore is, after all, a "culture of contestation" in which the communal, informal culture exists in counterpoint to elite culture.[98] The music and song that emerge from such traditional communities into mass society are devalued through commoditization, the traditional concern of sociologists of music who, after Adorno, have argued for an ethical stance against the dehumanizing effects of mass-media culture under advanced capitalism.[99] But this linkage need not be a utopian endeavor, since "folksong" and "folk music" to a large extent have remained outside commercial exploitation, even in the kind of regional, urbanized environment where folk clubs flourish and a range of musical choices exists.[100] The notions of exchange, of reciprocity, and of a community of singers and musicians who practice "traditional music" are very different from the "icon-like relationship between rock star and fan."[101]

More cogently, the question of musical as opposed to textual meaning—one that goes back to the Gestaltists' theories of meaning in particular[102]—engages those concerned with the future of music education and musical taste. Phenomenology is harnessed here to social ends, to a scrutiny of the "inherent" and "delineated" meanings of music, logical moments that interact to produce musical experience. It is in the mediation between music as an objective structure and the consciousness of the producing or listening subject that "inherent" meaning arises. But music also possesses "delineated" meaning, the complex of values, verbalizations, and associations attached to it in specific contexts.[103] The weakness of such analysis, however, is the relative lack of interest in the performer's or composer's conception and realization of the musical gesture. A singer such as Jeannie arranges repertoire in significant ways for performance, channeling meanings toward audiences that are differently prepared.

Interpretively, the arrangement of repertoire and performance of Jeannie's songs in certain sequences might be seen as her device for synchronizing past and present through contrasting ideas. In semiotic theory, Mukařovský emphasized that the semantic gesture integrates structure in a work of art, and essentially links it to its social function.[104] Likewise, the gestural theory of communication developed by G. H. Mead sees meaning emerging from the social act and its phases of gesture and response.[105] Music and song have gestural meaning. just as songs call forth dispositions and responses, we can speak of the gestural meaning of music.[106] The singing gesture involves not only bodily movement and articulation, but the communication of structures, images, textures, correspondences, and associations. Roman Jakobson isolated six discrete functions of communication (referential, aesthetic, emotive, conative, phatic, metalingual), the nature of meaning varying according to which of these functions predominate.[107] Yet, over and above these linguistic and musical significations are metalinguistic and metamusical ones attached to the actions of body movement, voice directioning, or audience proxemics. Such dimensions aid in analyzing a performative process.

It is the performative function of Jeannie's singing that moves this study beyond being a detached semiotic exercise. Buried within this performative, ceremonial communication, however, is a deeper, transformative one. She evolved this transformative gesture as a result of (a) her response to stimulation from outside her community, and (b) her internalization of her life-world experience. The first part of the transformation came about through exposure to scholars and folksong collectors, students and Revivalists, in the 1950s. The second resulted from a crystallizing of her repertoire and of specific songs in it that held meaning for her: the "big ballads," her mother's lyrics, children's songs that evoked her Aberdeen childhood. As she advanced through middle age, secure in her identity and artistic *persona*, these meanings became her "message" to those who came to hear her and learn from her. The meanings were not just abstractions of experience; they *were* experience, they embodied it. The dialectical plight of the mother and son in "Son Davit" or "Lord Donald" was real to her, both as a lived event and as a metaphysical question directed at eternity.

Thus the primary and elemental character of these texts had to be matched by hard-edged melodies, so that the gesture was unified in artistic effect. Even "Lord Lovel," which Bronson referred to as an "insipid" ballad, with Jeannie's realization became "the most famous contemporary version, sung with superb natural artistry."[108] Like this ballad, the very "incompleteness" of her texts gave them the character of frescoes suspended in half-visible space and dimly perceived by her audience. The transformative power of her singing, of her musical gesture, lent scale and proportion to the internal drama of the song, no matter how clipped or oblique the montage. Implicit in these songs and her singing of them, however, was a desire to communicate experience and to inculcate wisdom. Because her model for singing and communicating experience was her mother, she aligned herself with the aesthetic norm dominant for ballad singing. She wanted to build worlds of experience up, to construct an edifice as an example to others. Apart from her songs of childhood, in which a sense of the grotesque is evident, she was not drawn to parody like her brother Davie, who was skilled at representing a culturally acceptable inversion of these norms, at "turning the world upside down." Such differences derived in turn from enculturated models of behavior, Jeannie's primarily from Maria, Davie's from his male relatives, though to some extent Jeannie's models later were reinforced by external, "affirmative" notions of traveller song culture.[109]

As she transformed herself from a "traveller singer" to a "folksinger," she avoided sermonizing and rarely commented on political realities. The world external to hers initially at least was foreign, hostile, inimical to her personal values, despite friendships established with individual nontravellers. Rather than being unconscious of political reality, she and her family remained outside it, liminal but aware, cautious of ancient scorn and calumny. Jeannie sang for left-wing concerts but took no part in the antinuclear rallies or radical causes. Although her family clearly was egalitarian, they were no "fellow travellers." Her own experience had been of other worlds—of birdsong and running brown trout streams, of birth and nurturing, of second sight and the Otherworld. Jeannie's dream of the child's white coffin, for instance, was a precognitive experience filled with dread for her.

The notion of time as multidimensional is central to such extrasensory perception. The problem of conceiving of a future is that language is structured around past, present, future. We superimpose these concepts on time. Most predictions are fulfilled shortly after they are made. Comparing Jeannie's premonitions and Mrs. Martin's "second sight" vision of little Jeemsie raises the issue of "paranormal" phenomena and the human ability to perceive them. Did both women's abilities stem from the same cause? Are second sight and similar phenomena present as potential powers in the human body, or are they from an outside agent? Jeannie had a vision of the child's coffin just before he died, and while Mrs. Martin did not actively "predict" Jeemsie's death, her behavior toward him revealed her "precognition" of his fate.

One hypothesis, comparing what is common to both precognition and short-term memory (which records what is happening now, the brain selectively processing the immediate past), holds that the brain can receive information from the future as well as the past. Information flows through the brain in the form of electrical impulses from neuron to neuron by charges fired between nerve endings, resulting in thoughts and images that can be recalled later. Stimuli from the future then allow the visionary to "remember" the future— i.e., precognition could be thought of as memory in reverse. Similar theories have been advanced for clairvoyance in terms of spatial phenomena. The most likely conclusion, from similar arguments, is that part of the human being exists independent of time and space, and we can hypothesize a kind of telepathy by which psychically gifted persons receive information from the future.[110]

In chapter 3, Jeannie relates her vision of "the Lord" while she was near death with enclampsia. In her dream or vision, the light at the top of the hill fell behind the figure of "the Lord" and created a contrast to the "dark and dreary" place where Jeannie was standing. His white dress added to the contrast. This light, and whiteness, normally represents healing energy, but here, because of the contrast with the normal world and Donald's weeping, no doubt stands for the world beyond, where there is no sorrow or pain. The temptation, then, for Jeannie was to relinquish her fleshly, everyday existence as a mother enduring the aftermath of childbirth. In her semiconscious state, she somehow realized that she had to return to Donald, to her quotidian world. She recorded this struggle to resist "temptation" in the language of religious experience.[111]

The framing world, however, for Jeannie's singing was one in which she revealed the secret of using symbolic information to satisfy existential needs. Singing of the kind she learned is an activity that provides symbolic rather than material feedback. As opposed to traditional rewards like money and status, which are limited and costly, symbolic rewards in principle are inexhaustible and free. The modern world needs to release the potential of symbolic energy by separating existential needs from concrete, material feedback, and artistry of Jeannie's sort is a source of constructive knowledge that is low on energy yet limitless in the amount of information it can provide. Smaller societies recognize this: the practitioners of symbolic skills (dancer, poet, shaman) are held in great esteem. Jeannie and other traveller singers have shown how we may create a world in which recognition of symbolic power will become central and meet the existential needs of a new generation.[112]

Jeannie's worlds, then, convey a sense of elemental perception, elemental feeling, elemental experience. The sonority of her voice was especially suited to conjuring up these dimensions and conveying them through the images and metaphors of ballad phonotactics. Her own accounts in this study suggest that we can learn from her songs, her singing, her worlds, no matter how distant they seem from materialism and bourgeois comforts. Her life is an implicit criticism of intolerance, elitism, and complacency, and it would be surprising if these admonitions were not found in her songs, too. The songs, and the gestures of her singing, have a moral basis. They teach that reciprocity, personhood, and integrity still count, and that we must continually reinvent the world by seeing past its aggressions, angst, and injustice to its poetic potential, to its hidden, balladic Otherworlds that offer the disadvantaged and the powerless equally transformative voices.

Notes: Part II
The Songs, Annotated

About the Songs

1. See Henderson 1992: 142–44.
2. Kennedy 1975: 798.
3. Johnson 1972: 91–92.
4. Dugaw 1989.

The Songs

1. SA 1960/110: stood.
2. SA 1952/154: coortin'. This transcription of the text and tune is from Prestige International 13006.
3. SA 1962/73: chuggies.
4. Prestige International 13006: catch'd.
5. JES 4001: Tae roll me fae the wa'.
6. JES 4001: Withoot a penny ava.
7. SA 1060/201: nicht we'll hae but three.
8. SA 1060/201: nicht we'll hae but three.
9. SA 1960/201: this and the following stanza are transposed.
10. Caedmon TC 1146/Topic 12T161: by Mary Kirk.
11. Caedmon TC 1146/Topic 12T161: and sang.
12. Caedmon TC 1146/Topic 12T161: Nor thought what would come.
13. Caedmon TC 1146/Topic 12T161: Nor thought on pooren me.

Commentary

1. Feldman 1978.
2. Dreyfus and Dreyfus 1986.
3. See Howard Gardner 1984.
4. Gardner and Wolf 1983.
5. See Cook 1989: 97.

6. Gower 1968.

7. Porter 1976.

8. Sloboda 1985: 215.

9. Cf. Stephanie Smith 1975: 23.

10. Ibid.: 54.

11. See Berger 1967.

12. Mead 1934.

13. E.g., Allport 1960.

14. Cf. Maslow 1962.

15. See Hartmann 1959, Maslow 1962: 78.

16. Porter 1986.

17. Foley 1987, Heil 1983, Goldman 1978, Goldman 1986.

18. Porter 1976.

19. Stanley Robertson to JP, Nov. 1987, JP personal files, Los Angeles, Calif.

20. Porter 1976 and 1988.

21. Cf. Olrik 1909.

22. Todorov 1969.

23. Austin 1962, Morris 1946, Pierce 1955.

24. See Coker 1972.

25. Cowan 1990, Herzfeld 1981.

26. Mead 1934.

27. Coker 1972.

28. Harker 1985.

29. Cf. Baumann 1976.

30. Boyes 1990.

31. Stratton 1983: 151–52.

32. Blacking 1971: 95.

33. Cf. Blum 1992.

34. Cf. Kenneth S. Goldstein 1971, Kumer 1981, Nettl and Blum 1968, Nielsen 1974, Riddle 1970, Stephanie Smith 1975, Stekert 1965, Top 1981.

35. Fine 1984, Joyner 1975.

36. See Qureshi 1987.

37. Blacking 1979: 12.

38. Cf. Ruth M. Stone and Verlon L. Stone 1981.

39. Blacking 1967: 195.

40. Cf. Abrahams 1970: 8.

41. Stephanie Smith 1975: 24.

42. Cf. Lloyd 1967: 135.

43. Stephanie Smith 1975: 22.

44. Bronson 1976: xxviif.

45. Cf. Coffin 1977: 8.

46. See Henderson 1975, Tannen 1988, Linda Williamson 1985.

47. Cf. Wilgus 1970.

48. Porter 1976.

49. See MacColl and Seeger 1986, Porter 1978.

50. Stephanie Smith 1975: 183.
51. Ibid.: 74.
52. Cf. Bronson 1976.
53. David Buchan 1985, Coffin 1983, and Shields 1991: 43.
54. Gerould 1932: 116.
55. Andersen 1985, David Buchan 1972, McCarthy 1991, Motherwell 1827.
56. Reeves 1958, Reeves 1960, Renwick 1980.
57. See Andersen 1985.
58. Aitken 1981, Clement 1981, Henderson 1983.
59. MacColl and Seeger 1977: 59.
60. Gower and Porter 1977: 59.
61. Collinson 1966: 166.
62. Bronson 1969a: 156.
63. Ibid.: 155.
64. Cazden 1972: 65.
65. Cf. Johnson 1972: 157–60.
66. Bronson 1969: 155–56.
67. Gower and Porter 1977: 59.
68. Cf. Toelken 1986.
69. Gluckman 1962.
70. MacColl and Seeger 1986: 33.
71. Cf. Singer 1972.
72. Porter 1976, 1985.
73. Cf. Kaemmer 1980.
74. See Barnett 1953.
75. Sloboda 1985: 102f, Koskoff 1987.
76. Lomax 1968.
77. Cf. MacColl 1964.
78. McAloon 1984.
79. Ricoeur 1966.
80. Simmel 1971, Shields 1986.
81. Vansina 1985.
82. Cf. Wells 1950, Wimberley 1928, Wittig 1958.
83. Whyte 1979.
84. Blacking 1977: 22–23.
85. See Gerould 1932: 89.
86. Linda Williamson 1985: 82–85.
87. Koskoff 1987.
88. Alexiou 1974.
89. Auerbach 1987.
90. Caraveli-Chaves 1980.
91. Porter 1978.
92. Linda Williamson 1985: 67.
93. Ibid.: 64.
94. See Gourlay 1978, Keil 1979.

95. Merriam 1977.

96. Ong 1990.

97. Cf. Brenkman 1987, Cowan 1990: 133, Jameson 1981: 289, Marsh 1988.

98. Lombardi-Satriani 1974.

99. Shepherd et al. 1977.

100. Finnegan 1989.

101. Armstrong and Pearson 1979: 100, Ives 1971.

102. See, e.g., Meyer 1956.

103. Green 1988.

104. Tarasti 1979.

105. Mead 1934.

106. Coker 1972: 15.

107. Jakobson 1960.

108. Bronson 1976: 193.

109. Cf. Marcuse 1937.

110. Sutherland 1985.

111. Diane E. Goldstein 1983, Hufford 1977.

112. Csikszentmihalyi 1978: 124–25.

Appendix A

Robertson and Stewart Families

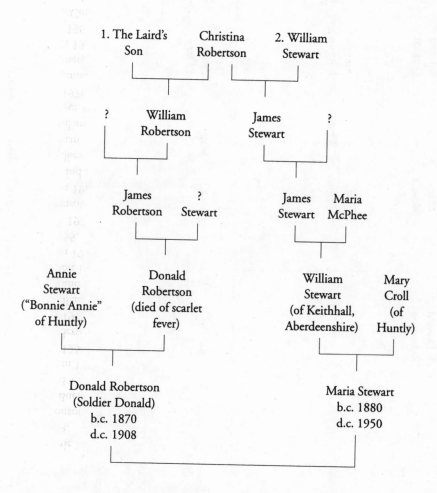

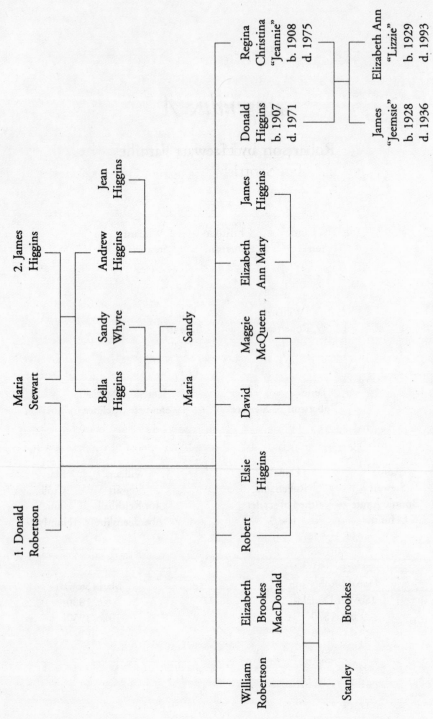

Genealogical Charts by Stanley Robertson, Aberdeen.

Appendix B

Progress Report by Hamish Henderson,
School of Scottish Studies, 1956

South-West Scotland and North-East Ireland may be said (from the point of view of folksong, at any rate), to form a single culture area. Investigation of Lowland folksong can hardly, therefore, be undertaken without reference to similar research-work across the water. An opportunity to start the necessary liaison was given to me in January, when the Northern Irish BBC invited me to contribute to its "Folksong Forum." I made contact with the distinguished Irish collector Sean O'Boyle, and spent a week with him in Armagh listening to his vast collection of Ulster folksong, and comparing notes with him on songs of mutual interest. He showed me his catalogue of the contents of the Sam Henry collection in Belfast, which stands comparison, both as regards quantity and quality, with the Gavin Greig collection housed in King's College Library, Aberdeen. Interesting Scottish material, which has not so far turned up here, has survived in Ireland.

Mr. O'Boyle very kindly lent me records of some of his material, and we now possess copies of these in our archives.

Later the same month I made contact in Dublin with Ciaran MacMathuna, of the folk-music section of Radio Eireann, and had similar discussions with him. He readily made available to me the texts of songs collected by him in Galway. Mrs. Kathleen Behan, in particular, sang a beautiful version of "Lord Randal," which she calls "My Bonny Brown Boy," and which I had ear-marked for recording several years ago. Like many other versions of Child ballads collected in Ireland, it is probably of Scottish origin.

The Behan family has a considerable number of folksongs from Co. Louth and Co. Meath, as well as the Dublin area, and I recorded some twenty of these. I exchanged notes on songs and singers with Sean MacReamoinn as well as Ciaran MacMathuna, and in addition had a long discussion on the various points raised by my Irish tour with Professor Seamus Delargy.

Both Mrs. Behan in Dublin and Mr. O'Boyle in Armagh put me up in their own houses, and treated me with the most open-handed hospitality. In Mr. O'Boyle's case, the invitation extended by the School of Scottish Studies enabled me to repay some of his kindness, both to myself and to Mr. Herschel Gower, who had also at my recommendation visited him in Ireland. He came with me to the Blairgowrie berryfields, gave information about the Irish tinkers to Mr. Farnham Rehfisch, and witnessed something of the richness and exuberance of the Scots Gaelic song tradition in Barra and South Uist.

Mr. Rehfisch's appointment in tinker communities in Perthshire and Aberdeen has carried the "tinker project" a stage further. A detailed anthropological study is now being initiated of a tinker group whose culture has already been extensively recorded, and which continues to yield much fascinating material, in the way of both songs and tales. This year I again spent a fortnight of July camped in the Standing Stones berryfield, and during the picking season Mr. Rehfisch leaguered in the same field. The folktale repertoire of these tinkers can already be seen to outstrip all previous Scots-English collections, both in extent and in artistic excellence; it is possible to collect good versions from people of all ages—from adolescents, and even children. The oral folk-culture is their culture, they have little else; but from what they have it should be possible to reconstruct a whole forgotten chapter of Scottish popular culture, now almost completely obliterated in other sections of the community.

By good fortune, a family of Stewarts from Lewis was also camped at the Standing Stones, and this enabled me to make extensive recordings of the Hebridean tinker folk-culture without stirring from the berryfields. Among Gaelic material recovered was what seems to be a previously unrecorded Jacobite song. While this recording was going on, the sanitary officials of Perth endeavoured to expel our informants from the berryfields on the ground that they had insufficient privy accommodation and unsatisfactory hygiene arrangements. Fortunately Rehfisch and I were able to act on this issue as the tinkers' privy counsellors, and organized the winning of the court-case which was one result of these ongoings. Our prestige, for that reason, continues high, both among the nomads and the settled tinks.

In December, acting on information obtained in the berryfields, I tracked down a tinker family in Glasgow, and obtained, among other things, a version of a rare Border ballad, "Tom Lane." When in Kintyre, I took the opportunity of contacting the local tinkler-gypsies, mainly Townsleys—a poor crew compared to their North-country cousins. Further tinker intelligence has also been provided by Mr. Maurice Fleming, who throughout the year had continued his researches among these folk in various parts of Perthshire; during the berry-picking season he again joined forces with me, and gave me much valuable assistance.

Earlier in the year I temporarily shelved the tinker project to take part in the Glenlivet scheme. Planned by the research staff to illustrate the advantages of co-operative teamwork, the scheme got under way in the Spring. After a preliminary recce [*sic*] tour, I spent two longer spells in the area with Dr. Whitaker, investigating the local folksongs and traditions. The advantages of a combined approach were quickly obvious. Glenlivet's folk-culture offers many features of interest: it is a peripheral Highland area in which the North-East dialect of Scots has supplanted Gaelic, but in which the Lowland culture pattern has been modified somewhat by contact with the older culture. A dozen good folk-singers were discovered, and one first-rater: Mrs. Elsie Morrison, a native of Ballindalloch, who now lives in Spey Bay. Mrs. Morrison recorded some 40 songs for me, including several classical ballads.

In December I took advantage of a brief lecture tour in Argyll to investigate the folksong situation in Kintyre. In Campbeltown I located a butcher, Willie Mitchell, who had already recorded dialect material for the Linguistic Survey; on the song side he turned out to be a discovery of the first importance. For over ten years he has himself been collecting songs and ballads from older singers and writing them down in a book, together with facts regarding their provenance, and comments—often very illuminating. At least thirty of the songs in his book are previously unrecorded folksongs, or interesting new versions of known ones. Willie helped me to find a retired shepherd James MacShannon, from whom I collected song-texts in 1940, and he laid on a ceilidh for several older singers in his own house—thus enabling me to put on tape at one blow the best of the songs in his collection. When I left Kintyre he entrusted the MS book to my care, and I have brought it to Edinburgh so that it can be photo-stated. *Campbell McLean?*

From a Sutherland-born minister in Campbeltown I recorded not only versions of Gaelic folksongs but also a fragment of the ballad "Young Beichan" (Child 53), which he had learned in childhood from his grandfather near Scourie—a striking example of the inter-penetration of cultures so evident among the gaberlunzie clans of the Central and Northern Highlands.

Last month the School of Scottish Studies' broadcast "For the Record" stimulated an Ayrshire lady to write in offering to record a folksong taught her by her mother. I recorded this song in December—it is a weaver's song from the Beith area—and the same informant recorded as well as number of Ayrshire children's rhymes.

Progress Report by Hamish Henderson, 1956 · 315

When in Campbeltown I gave a lecture to the local school which enabled me to collect Kintyre variants of these bairnsangs.

Fresh information about that esoteric ploughman's cult, the Horseman's Word, has come to light recently in the Kirriemuir area. From Mr. James Neave, "high heid horseman in Angus," I have received (confidentially) lengthy versions of the initiation catechism, rhymes, toasts and shibboleths. Although the cult is moribund in Aberdeenshire, it shows obstinate signs of life around Kirriemuir; the latest initiation of young horsemen into the cult took place at Martinmas 1956. I also began to muster evidence during my Irish tour in January of a link between the Horseman's Word and the agrarian secret societies of 18th-century Ireland.

Transcriptions of Scots song-texts has been accelerated thanks to the voluntary labours of Dr. Robert Botsford. In addition, Mr. Tom Scott has transcribed texts of Edinburgh children's rhymes collected to date. Child ballads in our collection, and songs deriving from or related to them, have been brought together on four tapes. Mr. Collinson is in process of transcribing the tunes of these.

Twice this year I visited Allan Glen's School in Glasgow, where the poet Maurice Blythman has succeeded in transforming the current folksong "revival" from a bobby-soxer vogue into a flourishing and many-sided artistic movement—the schoolboys of Allan Glen's are creating their own songs, and singing the old ones, both Gaelic and Lowland, with a creative spontaneity and verve which augurs well for the future of Scottish folksong. Recordings of them have also been added to the archives.

December, 1956

Appendix C

Letter from Hamish Henderson to Herschel Gower, 1956

17 December, 1956
27 George Square
Edinburgh

Dear Herschel,

Here, at long last, is the letter I've been meaning to sit down to for weeks and weeks—in fact, ever since I got your fine letter about Professor [Donald] Davidson's reactions to Jeannie's singing (a letter since then much quoted by me in various quarters). It arrived just before "Pleasure of Scotland" opened in the Assembly Hall, and I read it to Jeannie on the first night. Needless to say, she was delighted with it, and when at the end of the show she was guest of honour at a party in Compton Mackenzie's house, she proudly quoted it.

"Pleasure of Scotland" was pretty good, all things considered. I had arrived back from Barra only a day before (this was the joint trip with Sean O'Boyle— see Progress Report enclosed) and consequently hadn't been in on any of the rehearsals; I didn't even know which songs of Jeannie's George Scott Moncrieff had selected for the show. I had a free seat in the front of the Assembly Hall— prize, as you can imagine, for my "advisory" services—and this turned out to be a lucky chance. For when the great moment came for Jeannie's appearance, there was a moment of anxiety—no Jeannie, and then there she was on stage, visibly "puffed" after being hurried from her dressing room. (The idiot who was supposed to call her had forgotten, and she had to be summoned in a hurry.) Well, there she was, dressed in the North-East Fisher-wife get-up the Festival had provided for her, and she launched into the heroic ballad of "The Battle of Harlaw." But when she came to the chorus, she was too out of breath to sing it—there was another split second of anxious silence—and I sang the chorus myself. And so it went on, right to the end of the ballad—verse from Jeannie and chorus from myself. (I learned afterwards that 99% of the folk present believed it was all part of the show.) Then, when "Harlaw" was finished, she sang "Son David"—to great applause. After the show, I found Scott Moncrieff and told him that it was ridiculous to expect Jeannie to sing 2 of the biggest ballads in her repertoire one after the other. So, on all subsequent nights she sang first "Son David," and then "An Auld Man Cam A-Courtin' Me" . . . Your bouquet she was overjoyed with, of course, and carried it back with her finally to Aberdeen.

Jimmy Macbeth also did famously in "Pleasure of Scotland"—he was dressed more or less like a broken-down ostler in a Hogarth print, and he was the least "stage-conscious" of any singer present. His "He Widna Wint His Gruel" was probably the most successful single song of the Festival.

Sean's trip to Scotland went off very well indeed—first of all, he came to Blairgowrie, met Jeannie (who was down for the picking season), and had one or two great ceilidhs in Bella Higgins's house. Needless to say, he was a "succes fou" with the tinkers—and "fou," now I come to think of it, is the "mot juste." Alec and Belle, especially, who were at that time a bit worried about the "privy case" (see below), completely forgot their legal problems when Sean was present and sang up like linties.

After Perthshire, we made tracks for the Western Isles, and there Sean was in his glory—especially on Barra, which completely captured his allegiance. It was great fun being with him; in fact, there was never a dull moment, his sympathy and wit are so lively, keen and kindly. Everything in the islands, from the priests to the pagans, came in for an appreciative lick of his tongue.

Earlier on, when I was camped at the Standing Stone berryfield, an episode took place which was a bit like "Clochemerle" in reverse. No sooner had I finished putting up my tent on the same site Frank Vallee and I were camping on the year before than the local polis arrived and told me I was contravening a by-law. "What by-law?" I asked. He didn't bother to give me a reply, assuming—very understandably—that I was a tinker. And then it began to get really funny—the sanitary officials in Perth began an offensive to clear the tinker-owned berryfields of tinkers, and they actually issued a lot of summonses—but they were so confident of victory that they wrote any old thing on these summonses and left themselves wide open to counter-attack from anyone who cared to read the by-laws. I went to Edinburgh, and enlisted the services of Lionel Daiches—who had acted for the lads charged in the conspiracy trial—the surest-footed mouthpiece I could lay my hands on. Lionel took one look at the by-laws, and declared with emphasis that they were riddled through and through with absurdities. Well, to cut a long story short, he came up to Perth and spoke up for the poor folk—completely confounding the evil machinations of Perthshire sanitation squads.

The joke was that there were—for the first time—a few rough and ready privies erected at the Standing Stones berryfield. I used one myself—once. The experience was instructive. After that I emulated the other tinkers and used the woods—a much more convenient and aesthetically satisfying course of action.

This summer I added a number of Child ballads to our collection—among these "The Elfin Knight" (2) and a fragment of "The Demon Lover." But in many ways the most interesting new finds were folktales, which you can even collect in Perthshire from the tinker children. Two kids, one of 14, the other of 15, had fascinating wonder-tales which have not yet, as far as I know, been given numbers in the Aarne–Stith Thompson type index. Calum Maclean is making a list of the various stories in our collection, and affixing numbers to them—but for the wonder-tales, it seems, he is having to allot new numbers, provisionally. The style of the tinker story-tellers, according to him, is equal to the best of the Hebrideans.

Farnham Rehfisch, the Californian anthropologist who was appointed to study the Blairgowrie tinkers, has produced a report which is very interesting indeed. He is now in Aberdeen, adding a study of the urbanised tinkers to what he has got already. The Gallowgate market is his happy hunting ground—that and the "Hairy Bar," where the more hirsute of the fraternity come to slacken their eternal drought. (It was in that bar that Jeannie's brother Dave, "The Iron Man," had one of the classic fights of the century.)

A fortnight ago I went to Argyll, having been invited by the Workers' Educational Association to lecture on our folksong collection in Campbeltown and Inverary. Campbeltown, where I prospected for songs as long ago as 1940, yielded a great deal—including a song "The Boys of Callieburn" which descends from Jock Cameron's "King Fareweel"—the Jacobite song on the Marshak tape. In Kintyre "King Fareweel" has turned into an emigrants' song—and, Herschel, emigrants to your own country whose descendants, I gather, still live in a bunch together at Willow Creek, Ohio. Mackinley and Ralston are two of the most frequently heard names there, I believe—and they are the characteristic names of the Campbeltown emigrants of the 1830's and 1840's—especially the "hungry 40's," when the West Highlands had a famine almost as severe as Ireland's.

The old boys who sing the "Boys of Callieburn" render it with great feeling, especially the chorus, when they lift their pints and raise the roof on the final "Fareweel." Here are two verses of the song—(you'll get a copy of it on your tape, needless to say)—

> Jack Blair and I hae taen the notion
> To cross the wide Atlantic ocean.
> Rob MacKinlay's gone before us

And he'll keep us all in order.

    Hame fareweel

    Friends fareweel

And ye boys of Callieburn

    Fare ye weel.

Macrihanish bright and bonny—

On thy head the waves are rolling,

Macrihanish I adore thee—

Never more shall I behold thee.

The words, as you can see, are a bit stilted and imperfectly assimilated into folksong—but the tune is superb, possibly the best version of the tune now recorded.

One very interesting thing about the song is the use of assonance instead of rhyme throughout—an indication that previous Gaelic literary models had been carried over into Scots.

Good wishes to you, incidentally, from a whole battery of folk in Edinburgh and other parts of Scotland. Jeannie is never finished telling me to send you her love and warm greetings, and all the folk in the office who knew you have been asking to be remembered to you. And among other folk who have asked me to include their good wishes is Andrew Tannahill, the secretary of the Glasgow branch of the Saltire Society—he tells me that you came over to hear David Daiches lecture some months ago.

Sandy and I have been preparing a tape for you which I think you'll judge a worthy successor of the HG tapes of this summer. It includes "Young Beichan" (a version of "Lord Bateman," the nearest thing to Child's Scottish versions of this which I've yet recorded). Also "Tam Lin," which I tracked down after following a trail which led through Barlinnie Prison—the nephew of the woman who sings it was doing eighteen months for stealing a Buick in Oban! Last, but not least, I've added Thurso Berwick's "Scotland Hasnae Got a King":

    O Scotland hasnae got a King

    —And it hasnae got a Queen!

    Ye cannae hae the second Liz

    When the first yin's never been.

    O her husband's the Duke o Edinburry—

    He's one of the Kilty Greeks.

    O dinna blow my kilts awa

    For Lizzie wears the breeks.

At the moment the tape is only two-thirds finished, so rather than hurry the completion of it I've kept it here to do a proper job on it next week. You should have it fairly early in the New Year.

Two nights ago I was lecturing in Glasgow myself, to the Saltire Soc., and I included swatches of Joyce's and Sandy's rendering of "Johnny Gibb o' Gushetneuk." As an interlude between the songs it took a rare trick. Those two rich Buchan voices carried onto the Glasgow evening air like a pipe tune heard in the Libyan desert.

What Professor Davidson says about Jeannie's "high ballad style" is absolutely true, I think. In this particular tinker strain it has been preserved probably better than anywhere. The North-country tinkers have kept what the farm servants have to some degree lost—a dignified, almost aristocratic "grand manner" when singing the tragic ballads. Maggie and Nellie hit it here and there, but in both there's also noticeable a less attractive tinker strain—that petulant wail which in certain songs can be effective and even attractive, but which lifts the lid from what wells, ye gods, of savaged human kindness and shiftless self-pity.

Well, Herschel, when I say that we all miss you I'm only telling you a well-verified fact in and around No. 27. "The lang, lang balladologist" made more friends in a comparatively short time than anyone else we've had around. And we're all hoping that the time [that] elapses before you appear again in our midst is as short as possible. Please write soon, and let me know how your own ballad-study is progressing.

All the very best, then, for a great Hogmanay, and a wad of good songs in the New year! Slainte mhor!

Yours ever
Hamish
PS: Transcriptions of texts on HG III and HG IV will be on their way in a couple of months.

Recording No.	Text	Context	Performance
7. SA 1960/205	Crystallized	Clifton Rooms Ceilidh ?Oct. 1960 Audience, spacious arena	Duration: 6'34" Manner: prolonged
8. SA 1961/44	Crystallized	Huntly recordings ?Aberdeen July 1961 Audience, spacious arena, microphone distant	Duration: 5'44" Manner: slow
9. Prestige International 13006	Crystallized	Studio ?	Duration: 5'49" Manner: slow

Glossary

aa	all	*cowk*	choke
aafie	awfully, very	*cried, cry*	called, call
abeen, abune	above	*croft*	small farm
ae	one	*croosie*	cheerful
ain	own	*cryin's*	banns
ainst (eenst)	once	*dee*	do
aneth	beneath	*diddle*	deceive, cheat
ava	at all	*dottered*	feeble-minded
aye	always, ever	*dram, drammie*	small drink
bade, bide	lived, live	*duddies*	clothes
bairns	children	*durst*	dare
bate	beaten	*dyke*	dry stone wall
beckit	beckoned	*een, eenst*	one, once
ben	interior of house	*erse*	buttocks
blaan	blown	*fae, frae*	from
bothy	a cottage housing	*far, fat*	where, what
	servants	*farden*	farthing coin
bowdy	bow-legged	*fauld*	fold
brae	hill	*feart*	afraid
braicken	bracken	*firbyes*	forbye, also
busk	get ready	*flatties*	nontravellers
buskit	fastened	*fleen*	flying
byre	cattle shed	*follie*	follow
caa	knock, push	*forrit*	forward
cannie	careful	*fykie*	fidgety
cantie	cheerful, merry	*gaberlunzie*	the man who carries
carle	fellow		the wallet
ceilidh	a gathering, party	*gadgie*	fellow
chiel	fellow	*gair*	strip of cloth, gusset
chorin'	stealing	*gaun*	going
chuck	cast, throw	*geet*	bastard
chuggies	police	*gey*	very
coggie	pail, measure	*gied*	went
cottar	tenant farmer	*gin*	if, than

ging	go	quean	young woman
greetin'	weeping	richt	right
guttery-sharny	manure-covered	rowe	roll
haill	whole	sark	shirt
hap	enfold	scaldies	nontravellers
heid	head	scroggs	stunted bushes, low trees
herryin'	harrying, raiding		
helter	halter	sheen	shoes
hibber	stammer (speech)	sodger	soldier
hornies	police	soorins	sour dish
hummel cou	lacking horns	sowens	flummery
hussle	gurgle	spreckled	flecked, mottled
ilka	each	sprogs	shoots
inby	through	styte	abode, place
kaim	comb	teen	taken
kent	knew	thackit	thatched
kye	cattle	thon	yon, yonder
laird	landowner	thraw	pull
leal-licht	loyal	til	to
lippen	listen to	tint	lost
loon	lad	tow	rope
loup	leap	unco	very
mind	remember	undaantin'	undaunted
muckle	great	walloch	dance
nicht	night	wean	child, infant
nickin'	cheat, trick	wecht	weight
oxter	cradle of the arm	weel-faured	well-favored, handsome
owre	over, too		
owsen	oxen	widden	wooden
plaidie	cloak	windae	window
pleydie	an outer loose bit of tartan worn by Highlanders	wir	our
		wyde	wade
		wyme	womb, stomach
pooch	pocket	yarbon	rough-cut
puckle	small quantity	yowie	ewe
putten on	dressed, garbed		

Bibliography

1. Manuscripts

Atkinson MS. 1694. Society of Antiquaries Library, Newcastle-upon-Tyne, England.

Drummond Castle MS. 1734.

Duncan MS. 1905–11. Aberdeen University Library, Aberdeen, Scotland.

Gairdyn MS. Ca. 1729–35. National Library of Scotland, Edinburgh.

Gardiner MS. 1905–9. Cecil Sharp House, London.

Greig MS. 1909–14. Aberdeen University Library, Aberdeen, Scotland.

Guthrie MS. Ca. 1675–80. Edinburgh University Library, Edinburgh.

Hammond MS. 1905–9. Cecil Sharp House, London.

Mcfarlan MS. 1740. National Library of Scotland, Edinburgh.

Macmath MS. Ca. 1880–85. Hornel Library, Broughton House, Kirkcudbright, Scotland.

Mansfield MS. Ca. 1776. Hornel Library, Broughton House, Kirkcudbright, Scotland.

Rowallan MS. 1612–28. National Library of Scotland, Edinburgh.

Sinkler MS. 1710. National Library of Scotland, Edinburgh.

Skene MS. Ca. 1620. National Library of Scotland, Edinburgh.

Thomson MS. 1702. National Library of Scotland, Edinburgh.

2. Journals

Ceol: A Journal of Irish Music. 1963–88. Dublin.

Chapbook. N.d. 5 vols. Aberdeen, Scotland.

Folklore: Journal of the Folklore Society. 1890– . London.

Folk Music Journal: Journal of the English Folk Dance and Song Society. 1965– . London.

Journal of American Folklore: Journal of the American Folklore Society. 1888– . Austin, Tex.

Journal of the English Folk-Dance and Song Society. 1932–64. London.

Journal of the Folk-Song Society. 1899–1931. London.

Journal of the Irish Folk-Song Society. 1904–23. Dublin.

Scottish Studies: Journal of the School of Scottish Studies. 1955– . Edinburgh.

Spin: The Folksong Magazine. 1963– . Wallasey, Cheshire, England.

Tocher. 1971– . School of Scottish Studies, Edinburgh.

3. Reference Works

Abrahams, Roger. 1969. *Jump-Rope Rhymes: A Dictionary*. Austin: U. of Texas Press.

Bronson, Bertrand H. 1959–72. *The Traditional Tunes of the Child Ballads*. 4 vols. Princeton, N.J.: Princeton U. Press.

——. 1976. *The Singing Tradition of Child's Popular Ballads*. Princeton, N.J.: Princeton U. Press.

Brunnings, Florence E. 1981. *Folk Song Index: A Comprehensive Guide to the Florence E. Brunnings Collection*. New York: Garland.

Child, Francis J. 1882–98. *The English and Scottish Popular Ballads*. 5 vols. Boston: Houghton Mifflin.

Coffin, Tristram P. 1977. *The British Traditional Ballad in North America*. 3d ed. Revised, with a supplement, by Roger deV. Renwick. Austin: U. of Texas Press.

Dean-Smith, Margaret. 1954. *A Guide to English Folk-Song Collections, 1822–1952*. Liverpool: U. of Liverpool Press.

Laws, G. Malcolm, Jr. 1957. *American Balladry from British Broadsides*. Philadelphia: American Folklore Society.

——. 1964. *Native American Balladry*. Philadelphia: American Folklore Society.

Montgomerie, William. 1966–67. A Bibliography of Scottish Ballad Manuscripts, 1730–1825. *Studies in Scottish Literature* 4:3–28, 4:79–88, 4:194–227, 5:107–32.

Wehse, Rainer. 1979. *Schwanklied und Flugblatt in Großbritannien*. Artes Populares: Studia Ethnographica et Folkloristica 3. Frankfurt-am-Main: Peter Lang.

4. Published Collections and Commentaries

Aird, James. 1782–1803. *A Selection of Scotch, English, Irish and Foreign Airs*. 6 vols. Glasgow.

Allingham, William. 1877. *Songs, Ballads, and Stories*. London: G. Bell.

Baring Gould, Rev. Sabine; and Cecil J. Sharp. 1906. *English Folk Songs for Schools*. London: Curwen.

Baring Gould, Rev. Sabine; and H. Fleetwood Sheppard. 1889–92. *Songs and Ballads of the West*. 4 parts. London: Patey and Willis.

Barke, James, and Sydney Goodsir Smith, eds. 1959. *The Merry Muses of Caledonia*. New York: Putnam.

Barsanti, Francis. 1742. *A Collection of Old Scots Tunes*. Edinburgh: A. Baillie, and Hamilton and Kincaid.

Bell, Robert. 1877. *Early Ballads Illustrative of History, Traditions, and Customs*. London: G. Bell.

Brown, Colin. 1884. *The Thistle: A Miscellany of Scottish Song*. London and Glasgow.

Bruce, Rev. J. Collingwood, and John Stokoe. 1965 [1882]. *Northumbrian Minstrelsy*. Newcastle-upon-Tyne, England: Society of Antiquaries.

Buchan, David. 1984. *Scottish Tradition: A Collection of Scottish Folk Literature*. London: Routledge and Kegan Paul.

Buchan, Peter. 1825. *Gleanings of Scotch, English, and Irish Scarce Old Ballads*. Peterhead: P. Buchan.

————. 1828. *Ancient Ballads and Songs of the North of Scotland.* 2 vols. Edinburgh: Laing and Stevenson.

Buchan, Norman, ed. 1962. *101 Scottish Songs.* Glasgow: Collins.

Buchan, Norman, and Peter Hall, eds. 1973. *The Scottish Folksinger.* London: Collins.

Bunting, Edward. 1796. *A General Collection of the Ancient Irish Music.* Dublin W. Powers.

Bremner, Robert. 1757–61. *A Collection of Scots Reels or Country Dances.* 14 parts. Edinburgh.

————. 1765. *A Collection of Scots Reels or Country Dances.* London: R. Bremner.

Broadwood, Lucy, and J. A. Fuller Maitland. 1893. *English County Songs.* London: Cramer.

Buchan, David, ed. 1984. *Scottish Tradition: A Collection of Folk Literature.* London: Routledge and Kegan Paul.

Bunting, Edward. 1840. *The Ancient Music of Ireland.* Dublin: Hodges and Smith.

Burns, Robert. 1965 [1800]. *The Merry Muses of Caledonia.* Edited by G. Legman. New Hyde Park, N.Y.: University Books.

The Busy Bee or Vocal Repository. 1790. London: J. S. Barr.

The Caledonian Muse. 1795. London.

The Caledonian Museum, or the Beauties of Scottish Harmony. 1770. Edinburgh.

The Caledonian Musical Repository. 1809. Edinburgh.

Campbell, Alexander. 1816–18. *Albyn's Anthology of a Select Collection of the Melodies and Vocal Poetry Peculiar to Scotland and the Isles.* 2 vols. Edinburgh: Oliver and Boyd.

Campbell, Donald. 1862. *A Treatise on the Language, Poetry, and Music of the Highland Clans.* Edinburgh: D. R. Collie.

Campbell, Joshua. 1786. *A Collection of Reels.* Edinburgh: Neil Stewart.

Cazden, Norman; Herbert Haufrecht; and Norman Studer, eds. 1982. *Folk Songs of the Catskills.* Albany: State U. of New York Press.

Chambers, Robert. 1829. *The Scottish Songs.* Edinburgh: William Tait.

Chappell, William. 1858–59. *Popular Music of the Olden Time.* 2 vols. London: Cramer, Beale and Chappell.

The Charmer: A Choice Collection of Songs, English and Scots. 1749. Edinburgh: J. Yair.

Chilton, Charles. 1965. *Victorian Folk Songs.* London: Essex Music, Ltd.

Christie, William. 1876–81. *Traditional Ballad Airs.* Edinburgh: Edmonston and Douglas.

Collinson, Francis M. 1946. Songs Collected by Francis M. Collinson. *Journal of the English Folk Dance and Song Society* 5: 13–22.

Combs, Josiah H. 1925. *Folk-Songs du Midi des Etats Unis.* Paris: Université de Paris.

Cooke, B. 1793. *Selection of Twenty-One Favourite Original Irish Airs.* Dublin.

Cox, John Harrington. 1925. *Folk-Songs of the South.* Cambridge, Mass.: Harvard U. Press.

————. 1964. *Traditional Ballads and Folk-Songs Mainly from West Virginia.* Ed. George W. Boswell. N.p.: American Folklore Society.

Craig, Adam. 1730. *A Collection of the Choicest Scots Tunes.* Edinburgh.

Croker, T. Crofton. 1886. *Popular Songs of Ireland*. London: G. Routledge.

Cromek, R. H. 1808. *Reliques of Robert Burns*. London: T. Cadell and W. Davies.

Cumming, Angus. 1780. *A Collection of Strathspeys or Old Highland Reels*. Edinburgh.

Dallas, Karl. 1972. *The Cruel Wars*. London: Wolfe.

Dauney, William. 1838. *Ancient Scotish Melodies*. Edinburgh: Edinburgh Printing and Publishing Co.

Davidson, George Henry. 1847–49. *Davidson's Universal Melodist*. London: G. H. Davidson.

Davie, James. 1829. *Caledonian Repository*. London.

Dean, M. C. 1922. *Flying Cloud and One Hundred and Fifty Other Old Time Songs and Ballads*. Virginia, Minn.: Quickprint.

Dewar, James. 1826. *Popular National Melodies*. Edinburgh.

Dixon, James Henry. 1846. *Ancient Poems, Ballads and Songs of the Peasantry of England*. London: Percy Society.

[Drummond, William, of Hawthornden]. 1684. *Polemo-Medinia inter Vitarvam et Nebernam*. Edinburgh.

D'Urfey, Thomas. 1959 [1719–20]. *Wit and Mirth, or Pills to Purge Melancholy*. Introduction by Cyrus L. Day. 6 vols. New York: Folklore Library.

An Evening Amusement. 1789. Edinburgh.

Ford, Robert. 1899–1901. *Vagabond Songs of Scotland*. 2 vols. Paisley: Alexander Gardner.

Gainer, Patrick W. 1975. *Folk Songs from the West Virgina Hills*. Grantsville, W. Va.: Seneca Books.

Gerish, W. B. 1895. Norfolk Nursery Rhyme. *Folk-lore* 6: 202.

Gillespie, James. 1768. *A Collection of the Best and Most Favourite Tunes for the Violin*. Perth.

Gillington, Alice. 1911. *Songs of the Open Road*. London: Williams.

Glen, John. 1900. *Early Scottish Melodies*. Edinburgh: J. and R. Glen.

Gomme, Alice Bertha. 1894–98. *The Traditional Games of England, Scotland, and Ireland*. 2 vols. London: D. Nutt.

Gow, Niel. 1788. *A Second Collection of Strathspey Reels*. Edinburgh.

———. 1799–1817. *A Complete Repository of Original Scots Slow Strathspeys and Dances*. Edinburgh: Gow and Shepherd.

Graham, George Farquhar. 1861. *The Songs of Scotland*. Edinburgh: Wood.

———. 1908. *The Popular Songs of Scotland*. Revised by J. Muir Wood. Glasgow: Bayley and Ferguson.

Greig, Gavin, and Alexander Keith. 1925. *Last Leaves of Traditional Ballads and Ballad Airs*. Aberdeen: Buchan Club.

Grover, Carrie. N.d. *A Heritage of Songs*. Edited by Ann L. Griggs. Bethel, Me.

Halliwell, J. O. 1843. *The Nursery Rhymes of England, Obtained Principally from Oral Tradition*. 2d ed. London: J. R. Smith.

———. 1849. *Popular Rhymes and Nursery Tales*. London: J. R. Smith.

———. 1860. *The Nursery Rhymes of England*. 6th ed. London: J. R. Smith

Hammond, David, ed. 1978. *Songs of Belfast*. Dublin: Gilbert Dalton.

Hammond, H. E. D. 1908. *Folk Songs from Dorset*. London: Novello.

Hardiman, James. 1831. *Irish Minstrelsy, or Bardic Remains of Ireland.* 2 vols. London: James Hardiman.

Healy, James, ed. 1965. *Ballads from the Pubs of Ireland.* Cork: Mercier Press.

Hecht, Hans, ed. 1904. *Songs from David Herd's Manuscripts.* Edinburgh: William J. Hay.

Henry, Sam, ed. 1923–29. *Songs of the People.* Coleraine, Ireland: Northern Constitution.

Herd, David. 1769–76. *The Ancient and Modern Scots Songs, Heroic Ballads.* 2 vols. Edinburgh: Dickson and Elliot.

Hogg, James. 1819–21. *The Jacobite Relics of Scotland.* 2 vols. Edinburgh: W. Blackwood.

———. 1834. *The Domestic Manners and Private Life of Sir. Walter Scott.* Glasgow: J. Reid.

———. N.d. *The Border Garland.* N.p.

Holloway, John ed. 1971. *The Euing Collection of English Broadside Ballads.* Glasgow.

Hughes, Herbert. 1909–36. *Irish Country Songs.* 4 vols. London: Boosey.

Humble, B. H., ed. 1934. *The Songs of Skye.* Stirling, Scotland: E. Mackay.

Johnson, James. 1839 [1787–1803]. *The Scotish Musical Museum.* 6 vols. Edinburgh: W. Blackwood and Sons; and London: Thomas Cadell. Orig. issued as *The Scots Musical Museum*; Edinburgh.

Jolliffe, Maureen, ed. 1970. *The Third Book of Irish Ballads.* Cork: Mercier Press.

Joyce, Patrick W. 1909. *Old Irish Folk Music and Songs.* Dublin: University Press.

Karpeles, Maud, ed. 1974. *Cecil Sharp's Collection of English Folksongs.* 2 vols. London: Oxford U. Press.

Kennedy, Peter. 1951–54. *The Fiddler's Tune-Book.* Oxford, England: Oxford U. Press.

———. 1975. *Folksongs of Britain and Ireland.* New York: Schirmer.

Kidson, Frank. 1891. *Traditional Tunes.* Oxford: C. Taphouse.

Kidson, Frank; Ethel Kidson; and Alfred Moffat. 1929. *English Peasant Songs.* London: Ascherberg, Hopwood and Crew.

Kinloch, George R. 1827. *Ancient Scottish Ballads.* London and Edinburgh.

———. 1828. *A Ballad Book.* Edinburgh.

Korson, George. 1949. *Pennsylvania Songs and Legends.* Philadelphia: U. of Pennsylvania Press.

Loesberg, John. 1980. *Folksongs and Ballads Popular in Ireland.* 2 vols. Cork: Ossian Publications.

Lomax, Alan. 1960. *The Folk Songs of North America.* New York: Doubleday.

Lyle, Emily B., ed. 1975. *Andrew Craufurd's Collection of Ballads and Songs.* Vol. 1. Edinburgh: Scottish Texts Society.

MacColl, Ewan. 1953. *Scotland Sings: A Collection of Folk Songs and Ballads.* London: Scottish Branch of the Workers' Music Association.

———. 1965. *Folk Songs and Ballads of Scotland.* New York: Oak Publications.

MacColl, Ewan, and Peggy Seeger. 1977. *Travellers' Songs from England and Scotland.* Knoxville: U. of Tennessee Press.

MacDonald, Alexander. 1922. *Transactions of the Gaelic Society of Inverness, 1914–19.* Vol. 29. Inverness.

McGibbon, William. 1762. *A Collection of Scots Tunes*. 4 books. London: R. Bremner.

McGlashan, Alexander. 1780. *A Collection of Strathspey Reels*. Edinburgh: N. Stewart.

MacKay, Angus. 1838. *A Collection of Ancient Piobaireachd or Highland Pipe Music*. Edinburgh: MacLachlan.

Mackay, Charles. 1854. *The Illustrated Book of Scottish Songs*. London: Illustrated Library.

MacLean, Charles. 1772. *A Collection of Favourite Scots Tunes*. Edinburgh: N. Stewart.

Maidment, James. 1859. *Scottish Ballads and Songs*. Edinburgh: T. G. Stevenson.

Meek, Bill, ed. 1978. *Songs of the Irish in America*. Dublin: Gilbert Dalton.

Mercurius Democritus. 1652–61. London.

Moffat, Alfred. 1895. *The Minstrelsy of Scotland*. London: Augener.

———. 1897. *The Minstrelsy of Ireland*. 4th enlarged ed. London: Augener.

Montgomerie, William, and Norah Montgomerie, eds. 1948. *Sandy Candy and Other Scottish Nursery Rhymes*. London: Hogarth.

———. 1964. *The Hogarth Book of Scottish Nursery Rhymes*. London: Hogarth.

Morton, Robin, ed. 1970. *Folksongs Sung in Ulster*. Cork: Mercier.

Motherwell, William. 1819. *The Harp of Renfrewshire*. Paisley: J. Lawrence, and Glasgow: W. Turnbull.

———. 1827. *Minstrelsy: Ancient and Modern*. Glasgow: John Wylie.

Moulden, John, ed. 1979. *Songs of the People: Selections from the Sam Henry Collection, Part One*. Belfast: Blackstaff Press.

Napier, William. 1792. *A Selection of Original Scots Tunes*. London.

Nicholson, William. 1878. *The Poetical Works of William Nicholson*. Castle-Douglas: S. Gordon, and Kirkudbright: J. Nicholson.

Northall, G. S. 1892. *English Folk-Rhymes*. London: K. Paul, Trench, Trübner.

O'Boyle, Sean. 1976. *The Irish Song Tradition*. Dublin: Gilbert Dalton.

O'Canainn, Thomas, ed. 1978. *Songs of Cork*. Dublin: Gilbert Dalton.

O'Keefe, Daniel. 1955. *The First Book of Irish Ballads*. Cork: Mercier.

O Lochlainn, Colm. 1960. *Irish Street Ballads*. Dublin: Three Candles.

———. 1965. *More Irish Street Ballads*. Dublin: Three Candles.

O'Neill, Francis. 1903. *O'Neill's Music of Ireland*. Chicago: Lyon and Healy.

———. 1907. *The Dance Music of Ireland*. Chicago: Lyon and Healy.

Opie, Iona, and Opie, Peter. 1951. *The Oxford Dictionary of Nursery Rhymes*. London: Oxford U. Press.

———. 1959. *The Lore and Language of Schoolchildren*. Oxford, England: Clarendon Press.

Ord, John. 1930. *The Bothy Songs and Ballads of Aberdeen, Banff and Moray, Angus and the Mearns*. Paisley: Alexander Gardner.

Oswald, James. 1743–59. *The Caledonian Pocket Companion*. London: Straight and Skillern.

O'Sullivan, Donal. 1960. *Songs of the Irish*. Dublin: Browne and Nolan.

Owens, William A. 1950. *Texas Folk Songs*. Austin: Texas Folklore Society.

Palmer, Roy. 1973. George Dunn: Twenty-One Songs and Fragments. *Folk Music Journal* 2 (4): 275–96.

Playford, John. 1650–51. *The English Dancing Master*. London.

————. 1666. *Musick's Delight on the Cithren.* London.

————. 1687. *Apollo's Banquet.* 5th ed. London.

Polwarth, Gwen and Mary Polwarth. 1969. *North Country Songs.* Newcastle-upon-Tyne, England: Frank Graham.

Purslow, Frank. 1965. *Marrowbones: English Folk Songs from the Hammond and Gardiner MSS.* London: EFDSS Publications.

————. 1972. *The Constant Lovers.* London: EFDSS Publications.

Ramsay, Allan. 1724. *The Tea-Table Miscellany.* Edinburgh.

Randolph, Vance. 1946–50. *Ozark Folksongs.* 4 vols. Columbia, Mo.: State Historical Society.

Ravenscroft, Thomas. 1609. *Pammelia.* London.

Reid, H. G. 1859. *Songs and Poems by J. Skinner.* Peterhead.

Rimbault, E. F. 1851. *A Little Book of Songs and Ballads.* London: J. R. Smith.

Ritchie, James. 1964. *The Singing Street.* Edinburgh: Oliver and Boyd.

Ritson, Joseph. 1784. *The Bishopric Garland or Durham Minstrel.* Stockton.

————. 1794. *Scotish Songs.* 2 vols. London.

————. 1802. *The North-Country Chorister.* Durham.

————. 1810. *Gammer Gurton's Garland, or The Nursery Parnassus.* Enlarged edition. London: Harding and Wright for R. Triphook.

Rogers, Charles. 1855–57. *The Modern Scottish Minstrel.* 6 vols. Edinburgh: Adam and Charles Black.

Rutherford, David. 1750–76. *Compleat Collection of 200 of the Most Celebrated Country Dances.* London.

Rymour Club. 1906–28. *Miscellanea of the Rymour Club.* Edinburgh.

School of Scottish Studies. 1972. *A Collection of Scots Songs.* Edinburgh.

Sedley, Stephen. 1967. *The Seeds of Love.* London.

Seeger, Peggy, and Ewan MacColl, eds. 1960. *The Singing Island.* London: Mills Music.

Sharp, Cecil J. 1921–23. *English Folk Songs: Selected Edition.* London: Novello.

————. 1932. *English Folk Songs from the Southern Appalachians.* Edited by Maud Karpeles. 2 vols. London: Oxford U. Press.

Shuldham-Shaw, Patrick, and Emily B. Lyle, *et al.* 1981–95. *The Greig-Duncan Folk Song Collection.* Vols. 1–6. Aberdeen: Aberdeen U. Press.

Slocombe, M. 1953. Seven Songs Recorded by the BBC from Mrs. Costello of Birmingham. *Journal of the English Folk Dance and Song Society* 7: 96–105.

Smith, R. A. 1820–24. *The Scotish Minstrel.* 6 vols. Edinburgh.

Stanford, Charles V., ed. 1902–5. *The Complete Petrie Collection.* 3 parts. London: Boosey.

Straight and Skillern. 1771. *204 Favourite Country Dances.* London.

Struthers, John. 1819. *The Harp of Caledonia.* 3 vols. Glasgow: Sommerville.

Sutton-Smith, Brian. 1972. *The Folkgames of Children.* Austin: U. of Texas Press.

Tannahill, Robert. 1815. *Poems and Songs, Chiefly in the Scottish Dialect.* London: Gale, Curtis and Fenner.

Thomson, George. 1793–1805. *A Select Collection of Original Scottish Airs.* 4 vols. Edinburgh.

Thomson, William. 1725–33. *Orpheus Caledonius.* London.

Thorp, N. Howard ("Jack"). 1966. *Songs of the Cowboys*. Edited by Austin E. Fife and Alta Fife. New York: Bramhall House.

Urbani, Peter. 1792–1804. *A Selection of Scots Songs*. 4 vols. Edinburgh.

Vaughan Williams, Ralph, and A. L. Lloyd, eds. 1959. *The Penguin Book of English Folk Songs*. Harmondsworth, England: Penguin.

Walsh, John. 1733–62. *Caledonian Country Dances*. 9 books. London: John Walsh.

———. 1739. *Twenty-Four Country Dances for the Year 1740*. London.

———. 1741. *Twenty-Four Country Dances for the Year 1742*. London.

Walton's 132 Best Irish Songs and Ballads. N.d. Dublin.

White, Newman Ivey, ed. 1952. *The Frank C. Brown Collection of North Carolina Folklore*. Durham, N.C.: Duke U. Press.

Winstock, Lewis. 1970. *Songs and Music of the Redcoats*. London: Leo Cooper.

Wright, Robert L., ed. 1975. *Irish Emigrant Ballads and Songs*. Bowling Green, Ohio: Bowling Green U. Popular Press.

5. Studies

Abrahams, Roger D. 1970. Creativity, Individuality, and the Traditional Singer. *Studies in the Literary Imagination* 1: 5–34.

Aitken, Adam J. 1981. The Good Old Scots Tongue: Does Scots Have an Identity? In *Minority Languages Today*. Edited by E. Haugen, J. D. McClure, and D. Thompson, 72–90. Edinburgh: Edinburgh U. Press.

Alexiou, Margaret. 1974. *The Ritual Lament in Greek Tradition*. Cambridge: Cambridge U. Press.

Allport, G. 1960. *Personality and Social Encounter*. New York: Beacon.

Andersen, Flemming G. 1982. The Living Oral Tradition: Jeannie Robertson's "Little Mattie Groves" (Cf. Child no. 81). In *The Ballad as Narrative: Studies in the Ballad Traditions of England, Scotland, Germany and Denmark*. Edited by Flemming G. Andersen, Otto Holzapfel, and Thomas Pettitt, 85–100. Odense: Odense U. Press.

———. 1985. *Commonplace and Creativity*. Odense: Odense Univ. Press.

Andersen, Flemming G., and Thomas Pettitt. 1979. Mrs. Brown of Falkland: A Singer of Tales? *Journal of American Folklore* 92: 1–24.

Andersen, Flemming G.; Otto Holzapfel; and Thomas Pettitt, eds. 1982. *The Ballad as Narrative: Studies in the Ballad Traditions of England, Scotland, Germany and Denmark*. Odense: Odense U. Press.

Armstrong, Frankie, and Brian Pearson. 1979. Some Reflections on the English Folk Revival. *History Workshop Journal* 7: 95–100.

Auerbach, Susan. 1987. From Singing to Lamenting: Women's Musical Role in a Greek Village. In *Women and Music in Cross-Cultural Perspective*. Edited by Ellen Koskoff, 25–43. Westport, Conn.: Greenwood Press.

Austin, J. L. 1962. *How to Do Things with Words*. Oxford, England: Clarendon Press.

Barnes, Bettina. 1975. Irish Travelling People. In *Gypsies, Tinkers and Other Travellers*. Edited by Farnham Rehfisch, 231–56. London: Academic Press.

Barnett, H. G. 1953. *Innovation: The Basis of Cultural Change*. New York: McGraw-Hill.

Barry, Phillips. 1961. The Part of the Folk Singer in the Making of Folk Balladry. In *The Critics and the Ballad*. Edited by MacEdward Leach and Tristram P. Coffin, 59–76. Carbondale: Southern Illinois U. Press.

Barth, Fredrik. 1955. The Social Organization of a Pariah Group in Norway. *Norveg* 5: 126–43.

Bascom, William R. 1955. Verbal Art. *Journal of American Folklore* 68: 245–52.

Baskerville, Charles Read. 1921. English Songs of the Night Visit. *Publications of the Modern Language Association* 36: 565–614.

Bauman, Richard. 1984 [1977]. *Verbal Art as Performance*. Prospect Heights, Ill.: Waveland Press. Originally published Rowley, Mass.: Newbury House.

Bauman, Zygmunt. 1973. *Culture as Praxis*. Boston: Routledge and Kegan Paul.

Baumann, Max-Peter. 1976. *Musikfolklore und Musikfolklorismus*. Winterthur: Amadeus.

Bausinger, Hermann. 1986a. A Critique of Tradition: Observations on the Situation of Volkskunde. In *German Volkskunde: A Decade of Theoretical Confrontation, Debate, and Reorientation (1967–1977)*. Edited by James R. Dow and Hannjost Lixfeld, 26–40. Bloomington: Indiana U. Press.

———. 1986b. Towards a Critique of Folklorism Criticism. In *German Volkskunde: A Decade of Theoretical Confrontation, Debate, and Reorientation (1967–1977)*. Edited by James R. Dow and Hannjost Lixfeld, 113–23. Bloomington: Indiana U. Press.

Bayard, Samuel. 1950. Prolegomena to a Study of the Principal Melodic Families of British-American Folk Song. *Journal of American Folklore* 63: 1–44.

———. 1954. Two Representative Tune Families of British Tradition. *Midwest Folklore* 4: 18–33.

Belenky, M. F.; B. M. Clinchy; N. R. Goldberger; and J. M. Tarule. 1986. *Women's Ways of Knowing: The Development of Self, Voice and Mind*. New York: Basic Books.

Ben-Amos, Dan. 1984. Seven Strands of Tradition: Varieties in Its Meaning in American Folklore Studies. *Journal of Folklore Research* 21: 97–131.

Ben-Amos, Dan, and Kenneth S. Goldstein, eds. 1975. *Folklore: Performance and Communication*. The Hague: Mouton.

Benjamin, Walter. 1968. Theses on the Philosophy of History. In *Illuminations*. Trans. Hannah Arendt, 255–66. New York: Harcourt, Brace and World.

Berger, Peter. 1967. *The Sacred Canopy*. Garden City: Doubleday.

Berne, Eric. 1959. The Mythology of Dark and Fair: Psychiatric Use of Folklore. *Journal of American Folklore* 72: 1–13.

Blackie, John Stuart. 1876. *The Language and Literature of the Scottish Highlands*. Edinburgh: Edmonston and Douglas.

———. 1889. *Scottish Song: Its Wealth, Wisdom, and Social Significance*. Edinburgh and London: Blackwood.

Blacking, John. 1967. *Venda Children's Songs: A Study in Ethnomusicological Analysis*. Johannesburg: Witwatersrand U. Press.

———. 1971. The Value of Music in Human Experience. *Yearbook of the International Folk Music Council* 1: 33–71.

———. 1977. Towards an Anthropology of the Body. In *The Anthropology of the Body*. Edited by J. Blacking, 1–28. SAS Monograph No. 20. London: Academic Press.

———. 1979. Some Problems of Theory in the Study of Musical Change. *Yearbook of the International Folk Music Council* 9: 1–26.

———. 1981. The Problem of "Ethnic" Perceptions in the Semiotics of Music. In *The Sign in Music and Literature*. Edited by Wendy Steiner, 184–94. Austin: Univ. of Texas Press.

———. 1983. The Structure of Musical Discourse: The Problem of the Song Text. *Yearbook for Traditional Music* 14: 15–23.

———. 1992. The Biology of Music-Making. In *Ethnomusicology: An Introduction*. Edited by Helen Myers, 301–14. New York: Norton.

Blankenhorn, Virginia. 1977. Traditional and Bogus Elements in "MacCrimmon's Lament." *Scottish Studies* 22: 45–67.

Blum, Stephen. 1992. Analysis of Musical Style. In *Ethnomusicology: An Introduction*. Edited by Helen Myers, 165–218. New York: Norton.

Bourdieu, Pierre. 1979. *La distinction: critique sociale du jugement*. Paris: Editions de Munuit. English version is *Distinction: A Social Critique of the Judgement of Taste*. Translated by Richard Nice. London: Routledge and Kegan Paul, 1984.

Bowers, Jane. 1989–90. Feminist Scholarship and the Field of Musicology. Part 1, *College Music Symposium* 29: 81–92. Part 2, *College Music Symposium* 30: 1–13.

Bowers, Jane, and Urban Bareis. 1991. Bibliography on Music and Gender—Women in Music. *The World of Music* 33: 65–103.

Boyes, Georgina. 1990. The English Folksong Revival: Collecting as Transaction and Transformation. In *Recent Ballad Research*. Edited by Tom Cheesman, 2:75–90. London: Folklore Society Library Publications.

Brenkman, John. 1987. *Culture and Domination*. Ithaca, N.Y.: Cornell Univ. Press.

Broadwood, Lucy. 1911. Additional Notes on the Gaelic Scale System. *Journal of the Folk-Song Society* 4: 154.

Bronson, Bertrand H. 1969a. *The Ballad as Song*. Berkeley: U. of California Press.

———. 1969b. Mrs. Brown and the Ballad. In Bronson, *The Ballad as Song*, 64–78. Berkeley: U. of California Press.

Brown, Mary Ellen.1984. *Burns and Tradition*. Urbana: U. of Illinois Press.

———. 1985. The Street Laureate of Aberdeen: Charles Leslie, alias Musle Mou'd Charlie, 1677–1782. In *Narrative Folksong: New Directions. Essays in Appreciation of W. Edson Richmond*. Edited by Carol L. Edwards and Kathleen B. Manley, 364–78. Boulder, Colo.: Westview Press.

Brown, Mary Ellen, and Paul S. Smith. 1982. *Ballad and Folksong*. Sheffield: Centre for English Cultural Tradition and Language.

Buchan, David. 1968. History and Harlaw. *Journal of the Folklore Institute* 5: 59–67.

———. 1972. *The Ballad and the Folk*. Boston: Routledge and Kegan Paul.

———. 1985. The Wit-Combat Ballads. In *Narrative Folksong: New Directions. Essays in Appreciation of W. Edson Richmond*. Edited by Carol L. Edwards and Kathleen B. Manley, 382–400. Boulder, Colo.: Westview Press.

Burton, Thomas G. 1978. *Some Ballad Folks*. Johnson City: East Tennessee State U. Press.

Cafagna, Albert Carl. 1960. A Formal Analysis of Definitions of "Culture." In *Essays in the Science of Culture.* Edited by Gertrude E. Dole and Robert L. Carneiro. New York: Crowell.

Caraveli-Chaves, Anna. 1980. Bridge Between Worlds: The Greek Women's Lament as Communicative Event. *Journal of American Folklore* 93:129–57.

Cazden, Norman. 1972. A Simplified Mode Classification for Traditional Anglo-American Song Tunes. *Yearbook of the International Folk Music Council* 3: 45–78.

Clement, David. 1981. The Secret Languages of the Scottish Travelling People. *Grazer Linguistische Studien* (Sprachliche Sonderformen) 15: 17–25.

Clements, William M. 1980. Personal Narrative, the Interview Context, and the Question of Tradition. *Western Folklore* 39: 106–12.

Clifford, James. 1988. *The Predicament of Culture: Twentieth-Century Ethnography, Literature, and Art.* Cambridge, Mass.: Harvard U. Press.

Coffin, Tristram P. 1949. The Murder Motive in "Edward." *Western Folklore* 8: 314–19.

———. 1952. A Tentative Study of a Folk Lyric: "Green Grows the Laurel." *Journal of American Folklore* 65: 341–51.

———. 1957. Mary Hamilton and the Anglo-American Ballad as an Art Form. *Journal of American Folklore* 70: 208–14.

———. 1983. Four Black Sheep Among the 305. In *The Ballad Image: Essays Presented to Bertrand Harris Bronson.* Edited by James Porter, 30–38. Los Angeles: Center for the Study of Comparative Folklore and Mythology.

Coker, Wilson. 1972. *Music and Meaning: A Theoretical Introduction to Musical Aesthetics.* New York: Free Press.

Collinson, Francis. 1966. *The Traditional and National Music of Scotland.* London: Routledge and Kegan Paul.

Cook, Susan C. 1989. Women, Women's Studies, Music and Musicology: Issues of Pedagogy and Scholarship. *College Music Symposium* 29: 93–100.

Coser, Lewis A. 1988. *A Handful of Thistles.* New Brunswick, N.J.: Transaction Books.

Court, Artelia. 1985. *Puck of the Droms.* Berkeley: U. of California Press.

Cowan, Jane K. 1990. *Dance and the Body Politic in Northern Greece.* Princeton, N.J.: Princeton U. Press.

Cowdery, James. 1990. *The Melodic Tradition of Ireland.* Kent, Ohio: Kent State U. Press.

Crawford, Thomas. 1963. Jean Armour's "Double and Adieu." *Scottish Studies* 7: 37–46.

Cray, Ed, ed. 1992 [1969]. *The Erotic Music.* New York: Oak Publications. 2d ed. Urbana: U. of Illinois Press

Csikszentmihalyi, Mihaly. 1978. Phylogenetic and Ontogenetic Functions of Artistic Cognition. In *The Arts, Cognition, and Basic Skills.* Edited by Stanley S. Madeja, 114–27. St. Louis, Mo.: Cemrel.

Dallas, Karl. 1975. The Singer Not the Song. *Melody Maker,* 29 March, p. 75.

d'Andrade, Roy. 1984. Cultural Meaning Systems. In *Culture Theory: Essays on Mind, Self, and Emotion.* Edited by Richard A. Shweder and Robert A. LeVine, 88–119. Cambridge, England: Cambridge U. Press.

Degh, Linda. 1969. *Folktales and Society: Storytelling in a Hungarian Peasant Community*. Bloomington: Indiana U. Press.

Dick, James C. 1962. *The Songs of Robert Burns*. Hatboro, Penn.: Folklore Associates.

Dolby-Stahl, Sandra. 1977. The Personal Narrative as Folklore. *Journal of the Folklore Institute* 15: 9–30.

———. 1985. A Literary Folkloristic Methodology for the Study of Meaning in Personal Narrative. *Journal of Folklore Research* 22: 45–69.

Dorson, Richard. 1956. Paul Bunyan in the News, 1939–1941. *Western Folklore* 15: 26–39.

Douglas, Sheila. 1982. *Sing a Song of Scotland*. Surrey, England: Thomas Nelson.

———. 1992. *The Sang's the Thing: Scottish Folk, Scottish History*. Edinburgh: Polygon.

Dreyfus, Hubert L., and Stuart E. Dreyfus. 1986. Why Skills Cannot Be Represented by Rules. In *Advances in Cognitive Science*. No. 1. Edited by N. E. Sharkey, 315–35. New York: Halsted.

Dugaw, Dianne. 1989. *Warrior Women and Popular Balladry, 1650– 1850*. Cambridge, England: Cambridge U. Press.

Dundes, Alan. 1964. Text, Texture, Context. *Southern Folklore Quarterly* 28: 215–65.

———. 1984. Defining Identity through Folklore. *Journal of Folklore Research* 21: 149–63.

Dunn, Ginette. 1980. *The Fellowship of Song: Popular Singing Traditions in East Suffolk*. London: Croom Helm.

Eisenstadt, S. N. 1969. Some Observations on the Dynamics of Traditions. *Comparative Studies in Society and History* 11: 451–75.

Fabian, Johannes. 1983. *Time and the Other: How Anthropology Makes Its Object*. New York: Columbia U. Press.

Farmer, George Henry. 1947. *A History of Music in Scotland*. London: Hinrichsen.

Feld, Steven. 1986. Orality and Consciousness. In ed., *The Oral and the Literate in Music*. Edited by Yosihiko Tokumaru, 18–28. Tokyo: Academia Music.

Feldman, David. 1978. A Response to Csikszentmihalyi: Discussion of Phylogenetic and Ontogenetic Functions of Artistic Cognition. In *The Arts, Cognition, and Basic Skills*. Edited by Stanley S. Madeja. St. Louis, Mo.: Cemrel.

Ferguson, J. De Lancey. 1985. *The Letters of Robert Burns*. 2d ed. Edited by G. Ross Roy. Oxford, England: Clarendon Press.

Fine, Elizabeth C. 1984. *The Folklore Text: From Performance to Print*. Bloomington: Indiana U. Press.

Finnegan, Ruth. 1977. *Oral Poetry: Its Nature, Significance and Social Context*. New York: Cambridge U. Press.

———. 1989. *The Hidden Musicians: Music-Making in an English Town*. New York: Cambridge U. Press.

Foley, Richard. 1987. *The Theory of Epistemic Rationality*. Cambridge, England: Harvard U. Press.

Fox, William S. 1980. Folklore and Fakelore: Some Sociological Considerations. *Journal of the Folklore Institute* 17: 244–61.

Friedman, Albert B. 1983. The Oral-Formulaic Theory of Balladry: A Re-rebuttal. In *The Ballad Image: Essays Presented to Bertrand Harris Bronson*. Edited by James

Porter, 215–40. Los Angeles: Center for the Study of Comparative Folklore and Mythology.

Gadamer, Hans-Georg. 1972. *Wahrheit und Methode: Grundzüge einer philosophischen Hermeneutik*. 3d ed. Tübingen, Germany: Mohr.

Gailey, Alan. 1982. Folk Culture, Context and Culture Change. In *Folklorismus*. Edited by Edith Horandner and Hans Lunzer, 73–103. Neusiedl-See.

———. 1989. The Nature of Tradition. *Folklore* 100: 143–61.

Gardner, Howard. 1984. The Development of Competence in Culturally Defined Domains: A Preliminary Framework. In *Culture Theory: Essays on Mind, Self, and Emotion*. Edited by Richard A. Shweder and Robert A. LeVine, 257–75. Cambridge, England: Cambridge U. Press.

———. 1985. *Frames of Mind: The Theory of Multiple Intelligences*. New York: Basic Books.

Gardner, H., and D. Wolf. 1983. The Waves and Streams of Symbolization: Notes on the Development of Symbolic Capacities in Young Children. In *Acquisition of Symbolic Skills*. Edited by D. Rogers and J. A. Sloboda, 19–42. New York: Plenum Press.

Gardner-Medwin, Alisoun. 1976. Miss Reburn's Ballads: A Nineteenth-Century Repertoire from Ireland. In *Ballad Studies*. Edited by E. B. Lyle, 93–116. Totowa, N.J.: Rowman and Littlefield.

Gentleman, Hugh, and Susan Swift. 1971. *Scotland's Travelling People: Problems and Solutions*. Edinburgh: HM Government Stationery Office.

Gerould, Gordon Hall. 1932. *The Ballad of Tradition*. New York: Oxford U. Press.

Gilchrist, Anne G. 1914. The Orange and the Blue. *Journal of the Folk- Song Society* 5: 70–71.

———. 1915. Died of/for Love. *Journal of the Folk-Song Society* 6: 186–87.

———. 1938. I Wish in Vain. *Journal of the English Folk Dance and Song Society* 3: 192–93.

———. 1946. I Wish, I Wish. *Journal of the English Folk Dance and Song Society* 5: 16–17.

Glasser, Howard. 1974. Ray Fisher: A Tremendous Sort of Feeling. *Sing Out* 22 (6): 2–8.

Glassie, Henry. 1970. "Take That Night Train to Selma": An Excursion to the Outskirts of Scholarship. In H. Glassie, E. D. Ives, and John F. Szwed, *Folksongs and Their Makers*, 3–68. Bowling Green, Ohio: Bowling Green Popular Press.

Gluckman, Max. 1975 [1962]. Les rites de passage. In *Essays on the Ritual of Social Relations*. Edited by Max Gluckman, 1–52. Manchester: Manchester U. Press.

Gmelch, George. 1977. *The Irish Tinkers: The Urbanization of an Itinerant People*. Menlo Park, Calif.: Cummings Publishing Co.

Gmelch, Sharon. 1986. *Nan: The Life of an Irish Travelling Woman*. New York: Norton.

Goldman, Alvin I. 1978. Epistemics: The Regulative Theory of Cognition. *Journal of Philosophy* 75 (10): 509–23.

———. 1986. *Epistemology and Cognition*. Cambridge, Mass.: Harvard U. Press.

Goldstein, Kenneth S. 1971. On the Application of the Concepts of Active and Inactive Traditions to the Study of Repertoire. *Journal of American Folklore* 84: 62–67.

———. 1966. Robert "Fiddler" Beers and His Songs: A Study of the Revival of a Family Tradition. In *Two Penny Ballads and Four DollarWhiskey: A Pennsylvania Folklore Miscellany*. Edited by Kenneth S. Goldstein and Robert H. Byington, 33–50. Hatboro, Penn.: Folklore Associates.

———. 1968. Liner notes to *Sara Cleveland, "Ballads and Songs of the Upper Hudson Valley."* Folk-Legacy FSA 33.

———. 1991. Notes Toward a European-American Folk Aesthetic. *Journal of American Folklore* 104: 164–78.

Goldstein, Diane E. 1983. The Language of Religious Experience and Its Implications for Fieldwork. *Western Folklore* 42: 105–13.

Gower, Herschel. 1968a. Jeannie Robertson: Portrait of a Traditional Singer. *Scottish Studies* 12: 113–26.

———. 1968b. Burns in Limbo. *Studies in Scottish Literature* 5: 229–37.

———. 1983. Analyzing the Revival: The Influence of Jeannie Robertson. In *The Ballad Image: Essays Presented to Bertrand Harris Bronson*. Edited by James Porter, 131–47. Los Angeles: Center for the Study of Comparative Folklore and Mythology.

Gower, Herschel, and James Porter. 1970. Jeannie Robertson: the Child Ballads. *Scottish Studies* 14: 35–58.

———. 1972. Jeannie Robertson: The "Other" Ballads. *Scottish Studies* 16: 139–59.

———. 1977. Jeannie Robertson: The Lyric Songs. *Scottish Studies* 21: 55–103.

Gourlay, Kenneth. 1978. Toward a Reassessment of the Ethnomusicologist's Role. *Ethnomusicology* 22: 1–36.

Grainger, Percy. 1908. The Impress of Personality in Traditional Singing. *Journal of the Folk-Song Society* 3: 163–66.

Green, Lucy. 1988. *Music on Deaf Ears: Musical Meaning, Ideology, Education.* New York: Manchester U. Press.

Greig, Gavin. 1963. *Folk-Song in Buchan and Folk-Song of the North East.* Transactions of the Buchan Field Club 9, 1906–7. Hatboro, Pa.: Folklore Associates.

Grierson, H. J. C. 1935. *The Letters of Sir Walter Scott, 1823–1825.* Vol. 8. London: Constable.

Hall, Peter. 1969. Liner notes to LP disc, *Princess of the Thistle.* Topic 12T185.

———. 1975. Scottish Tinker Songs. *Folk Music Journal* 3: 41–62.

Halpert, Herbert. 1964. Truth in Folk-Songs—Some Observations on the Folk-Singer's Attitude. In John Harrington Cox, *Traditional Ballads and Folk-Songs Mainly from West Virginia.* Edited by George W. Boswell, 13–20. N.p.: American Folklore Society.

Harker, Dave. 1985. *Fakesong: The Manufacture of British "Folksong": 1700 to the Present Day.* Philadelphia: Open U. Press.

Hartman, R. 1959. The Science of Value. In *New Knowledge in Human Values.* Edited by A. H. Maslow. New York: Harper.

Hawkes, Terence. 1977. *Structuralism and Semiotics.* Berkeley: U. of California Press.

Headlee, Linda. 1976. Bessie Whyte. *Tocher* 23: 249–76.

Hecht, Hans, ed. 1904. *Songs from David Herd's Manuscripts.* Edinburgh: William J. Hay.

Heil, John. 1983. *Perception and Cognition.* Berkeley: Univ. of California Press.

Heimann, Walter. 1977. Zur Theorie des musikalischen Folklorismus: Idee, Funktion, und Dialektik. *Zeitschrift für Volkskunde* 73: 181–209.

Henderson, Hamish. 1957. "Peggie on the Banks o' Spey." *Scottish Studies* 2: 246–48.

———. 1964. "The Lassies in the Cougate." *Scottish Studies* 8: 227–28.

———. 1965. Liner notes to LP disc, *The Stewarts of Blair*. Topic 12T138.

———. 1972. Jeannie Robertson as a Storyteller. *Tocher* 6: 169–78.

———. 1974. Davie Stewart. *Tocher* 15: 262–80.

———. 1975. Liner notes to LP disc *The Muckle Sangs*. Tangent TGNM 119/D.

———. 1978. Scots Folk-Song Discography, part 3. *Tocher* 28: 262–64.

———. 1979a. Jeannie Robertson Talking. *Tocher* 32: 113–21, *Tocher* 33: 196–201.

———. 1979b. Scots Folk-Song Discography, part 4. *Tocher* 30: 404–6.

———. 1979c. Scots Folk-Song Discography, part 5. *Tocher* 32: 132–33.

———. 1980. The Ballad, the Folk and the Oral Tradition. In *The People's Past: Scottish Folk, Scottish History*. Edited by Edward J. Cowan, 69–107. Edinburgh: Edinburgh U. Student Publications Board.

———. 1983. "At the Foot o' Yon Excellin' Brae." The Language of Scots Folksong. In *Scotland and the Lowland Tongue*. Edited by J. Derrick McClure, 100–128. Aberdeen: Aberdeen U. Press.

———. 1992. *Alias MacAlias: Writings on Songs, Folk and Literature*. Edinburgh: Polygon.

Henderson, Hamish, and Francis Collinson. 1965. New Child Ballads from Oral Tradition. *Scottish Studies* 9: 1–33.

Herndon, Marcia, and Suzanne Ziegler, eds. 1990. *Music, Gender, and Culture*. Wilhelmshaven, Germany: Florian Noetzel.

———. 1991. Women in Music and Music Research. *World of Music* 33 (2).

Herzfeld, Michael. 1981. Performative Categories and Symbols of Passage in Rural Greece. *Journal of American Folklore* 94: 41– 57.

Heymowski, Adam. 1969. *Swedish Travellers and Their Ancestry: A Social Isolate or an Ethnic Minority*. Uppsala: Almquist and Wiksells Boktryckeri.

Hobsbawm, Eric, and Terence B. Ranger, eds. 1983. *The Invention of Tradition*. Cambridge, England: Cambridge U. Press.

Holbek, Bengt. 1987. *Interpretation of Fairy Tales: Danish Folklore in a European Perspective*. Folklore Fellows Commmunications 239. Helsinki: Academia Scientiarum Fennica.

Hufford, David. 1977. *The Terror That Comes in the Night: An Experience-Centered Study of Supernatural Assault Traditions*. Philadelphia: U. of Pennsylvania Press.

Huntington, Gale, ed. 1990. *Sam Henry's Songs of the People*. Revised by Lani Herrmann. Athens: U. of Georgia Press.

Hymes, Dell. 1975. Breakthrough into Performance. In *Folklore: Performance and Communication*. Edited by Dan Ben-Amos and Kenneth S. Goldstein, 11–74. The Hague: Mouton.

Ives, Edward D. 1964. *Larry Gorman: The Man Who Made the Songs*. Bloomington: Indiana U. Press.

———. 1971. *Lawrence Doyle: The Farmer-Poet of Prince Edward Island*. Orono, Me.: University Press.

————. 1978. *Joe Scott: The Woodsman-Songmaker.* Urbana: U. of Illinois Press.

Jakobson, Roman. 1960. *Grundlagen der Sprache.* Berlin: Akademie- Verlag.

James, William. 1948. *Psychology.* New York: World.

Jameson, Fredric. 1981. *The Political Unconscious: Narrative as a Socially Symbolic Art.* London: Methuen.

Jansen, William Hugh. 1957. Classifying Performance in the Study of Verbal Folklore. In *Studies in Folklore in Honor of Distinguished Service Professor Stith Thompson,* 110–18. Bloomington: Indiana U. Press.

Johnson, David. 1972. *Music and Society in Lowland Scotland in the Eighteenth Century.* London: Oxford U. Press.

Jones, James H. 1961. Commonplace and Memorization in the Oral Tradition of the English and Scottish Ballads. *Journal of American Folklore* 74: 97–112.

Joyner, Charles. 1975. A Model for the Analysis of Folklore Performance in Historical Context. *Journal of American Folklore* 88: 254–65.

Kaemmer, John E. 1980. Between the Event and the Tradition: A New Look at Music in Socio-cultural Systems. *Ethnomusicology* 24: 61–74.

Keil, Charles. 1978. Who Needs "the Folk"? *Journal of the Folklore Institute* 15: 263–65.

————. 1979. *Tiv Song.* Chicago: U. of Chicago Press.

Keith, Alexander. 1922. *Burns and Folk-Song.* Aberdeen: D. Wyllie and Sons.

Kennedy, Peter, and Alan Lomax. 1961. Liner notes to *The Child Ballads,* vol. 2 (*The Folk Songs of Britain,* vol. 5). Caedmon TC 1146/Topic 12T161.

Klusen, Ernst. 1986. The Group Song as Object. In *German Volkskunde: A Decade of Theoretical Confrontation, Debate, and Reorientation (1967–1977).* Edited by James R. Dow and Hannjost Lixfeld, 184–202. Bloomington: Indiana U. Press.

Korson, George. 1949. *Pennsylvania Songs and Legends.* Philadelphia: U. of Pennsylvania Press.

Koskoff, Ellen, ed. 1987. *Women and Music in Cross-Cultural Perspective.* Westport, Conn.: Greenwood Press.

Kumer, Zmaga. 1981. Singers' Repertories as a Consequence of Their Biographies. *Lore and Language* 3 (4–5): 49–54.

Langer, Suzanne. 1967. *Mind: An Essay on Human Feeling.* Baltimore, Md.: Johns Hopkins U. Press.

Langness, L. L. 1965. *The Life History in Anthropological Science.* New York: Holt, Rinehart and Winston.

Langness, L. L., and Gelya Frank. 1981. *An Anthropological Approach to Biography.* Novato, Calif.: Chandler and Sharp.

Legman, G. 1964. *The Horn Book: Studies in Erotic Folklore and Bibliography.* New York: University Books.

————. 1968. *No Laughing Matter: An Analysis of Sexual Humor.* Vol. 1. Bloomington: Indiana U. Press.

————. 1975. *No Laughing Matter: An Analysis of Sexual Humor.* Vol. 2. Bloomington: Indiana U. Press.

————. 1990. Unprintable Folklore: The Vance Randolph Collection. *Journal of American Folklore* 103: 259–300.

Lloyd, A. L. 1953. I Wish, I Wish. *Journal of the English Folk Dance and Song Society* 7: 103.

———. 1967. *Folk Song in England*. London: Lawrence and Wishart.

Lomax, Alan. 1967. The Good and the Beautiful in Folk Song. *Journal of American Folklore* 80: 213–35.

———, ed. 1968. *Folk Song Style and Culture*. Washington, D.C.: American Association for the Advancement of Science.

Lombardi-Satriani, Luigi. 1974. Folklore as Culture of Contestation. *Journal of the Folklore Institute* 11: 99–121.

Lord, Albert B. 1956. Avdo Mededovic, Guslar. In *Slavic Folklore: A Symposium*. Philadelphia: American Folklore Society.

———. 1960. *The Singer of Tales*. Cambridge, Mass.: Harvard Univ. Press.

Lyle, Emily. 1976. *Ballad Studies*, Folklore Society: Mistletoe Series. Totowa, N.J.

MacAloon, John J. 1984. Introduction: Cultural Performance, Culture Theory. In *Rite, Drama, Festival, Specatcle: Rehearsals toward a Theory of Cultural Performance*. Edited by John J. MacAloon, p. 1. Philadelphia: U. of Pennsylvania Press.

McCarthy, Willam B. 1990. *The Ballad Matrix: Personality, Milieu, and the Oral Tradition*. Bloomington: Indiana U. Press.

MacColl, Ewan. 1953. *Scotland Sings: A Collection of Folk Songs and Ballads*. London: Scottish Branch of the Workers' Music Association.

———. 1958. Liner notes to the disc, *The Singing Streets*. Folkways.

———. 1964. The Singer and the Audience: Some Thoughts on the Folk Revival in Britain. *Sing Out!* 14 (4): 16–20.

———. 1965. *Folk Songs and Ballads of Scotland*. New York: Oak Publications.

MacColl, Ewan, and Peggy Seeger. 1977. *Travellers' Songs from England and Scotland*. Knoxville: U. of Tennessee Press.

———. 1986. *Till Doomsday in the Afternoon: The Folklore of Scots Travellers, the Stewarts of Blairgowrie*. Dover, N.H.: Manchester Univ. Press.

Mackay, William. 1921. The Battle of Harlaw: Its True Place in History. In *Transactions of the Gaelic Society of Inverness. 267–85*.

Mackinnon, Niall. 1993. *The British Folk Scene: Musical Performance and Social Identity*. Philadelphia: Open U. Press.

MacLean, Magnus. 1925. *The Literature of the Highlands*. Glasgow: Blackie.

MacNaughton, Adam. 1985. Hamish Henderson—Folk Hero. *Chapman* 42: 22–29.

———. 1991. Hamish Henderson. *Tocher* 43: 2–5.

McPherson, J. M. 1929. *Primitive Beliefs in North-east Scotland*. London.

Marcuse, Herbert. 1968 [1937]. The Affirmative Character of Culture. In *Negations*. Translated by Jeremy J. Shapiro. Boston: Beacon.

Marsh, James L. 1988. *Post-Cartesian Meditations: An Essay in Dialectical Phenomenology*. New York: Fordham U. Press.

Marshall, Rosalind Kay. 1983. *Virgins and Viragos: A History of Women in Scotland from 1080 to 1980*. London: Collins.

Maslow, Abraham H. 1962. *Toward a Psychology of Being*. New York: D. Van Nostrand.

Mason, Redfern. 1911. *The Song Lore of Ireland*. New York: Bake and Taylor.

Mead, George Herbert. 1934. *Mind, Self, and Society: From the Standpoint of a Social Behaviorist.* Ed. Charles W. Morris. Chicago: U. of Chicago Press.

Means, Andrew, and Sara Gray Means. 1975. Jeannie Robertson: More Than a Myth. *Sing Out!* 24 (3): 22–23, 27.

Merleau-Ponty, Maurice. 1948. *Sens et Non-Sens.* Paris: Nagel.

Merriam, Alan P. 1977. Definitions of "Comparative Musicology" and "Ethnomusicology": An Historical-Theoretical Perspective. *Ethnomusicology* 21: 189–204.

Meyer, Leonard B. 1956. *Emotion and Meaning in Music.* Chicago: U. of Chicago Press.

Meyer, Leonard B., and G. Cooper. *The Rhythmic Structure of Music.* Chicago.

Mitchison, Rosalind, and Leah Leneman. 1989. *Sexuality and Social Control: Scotland, 1660–1780.* Oxford, England: Blackwell.

Morris, Charles. 1946. *Signs, Language, and Behavior.* New York: Prentice-Hall.

Morton, Robin, ed. 1973. *Come Day, Go Day, God Send Sunday.* London: Routledge and Kegan Paul.

Moser, Hans. 1962. Vom Folklorismus in unserer Zeit. *Zeitschrift für Volkskunde* 58: 177–209.

Muir, Willa. 1965. *Living with Ballads.* London: Hogarth.

Munro, Ailie. 1970. Lizzie Higgins and the Oral Transmission of Ten Child Ballads. *Scottish Studies* 14: 115–88.

———. 1984. *The Folk Music Revival in Scotland.* London: Kahn and Averill.

———. 1991. The Role of the School of Scottish Studies in the Folk Music Revival. *Folk Music Journal* 6 (2): 132–68.

Neat, Timothy. 1978. The Summer Walkers: Aspects of the Life and Culture of the Travelling People in the Highlands of Scotland. In *Seer*, 40–49. Dundee: Duncan of Jordanstone College of Art.

Nettl, Bruno. 1983. *The Study of Ethnomusicology: Twenty-Nine Issues and Concepts.* Urbana: U. of Illinois Press.

Nettl, Bruno, and Stephen Blum. 1968. Toward the Comparative Study of the Structure of Traditional Repertoires. *Journal of the International Folk Music Council* 20: 47–50.

Newall, Venetia. 1987. The Adaptation of Folklore and Tradition. *Folklore* 98: 131–51.

Nielsen, Svend. 1974. *Den Gode Vise—Den Sande Vise.* Copenhagen: Dansk Folkemindesamling.

———. 1988. Songs with a Sting: Songs of Satire and Protest: A Social Weapon for the Powerless. *ARV: Scandinavian Yearbook of Folklore 1987* 43: 109–45.

Nygard, H. O. 1978. Mrs. Brown's Recollected Ballads. In *Ballads and Ballad Research.* Edited by Patricia Conroy, 68–87. Seattle: U. of Washington Press.

O'Boyle, Sean. 1976. *The Irish Song Tradition.* Dublin: Gilbert Dalton.

Olrik, Axel. 1909. The Epic Laws of Folk Narrative. In *The Study of Folklore.* Edited by Alan Dundes, 131–41. Englewood Cliffs, N.J.: Prentice Hall.

O'Neill, Francis. 1910. *Irish Folk Music: A Fascinating Hobby.* Chicago: Lyon and Healy.

Ong, Walter J. 1982. *Orality and Literacy: The Technologizing of the Word.* New York: Methuen.

———. 1990. Foreword. In P. Zumthor, *Oral Poetry: An Introduction.* Translated by K. Murphy-Judy, ix–xii. Minneapolis: U. of Minnesota Press.

Orlov, Henry. 1981. Toward a Semiotics of Music. In *The Sign in Music and Literature*. Edited by Wendy Steiner, 131–37. Austin: U. of Texas Press.

Partridge, Eric. 1984. *A Dictionary of Slang and Unconventional English*. 8th ed. New York: Macmillan.

Petrie, Elaine C. 1983. Odd Characters: Traditional Informants in James Hogg's Family. *Scottish Literary Journal* 10 (1): 30–41.

Pinto, Vivian deSola, and Allan Edwin Rodway, eds. 1957. *The Common Muse: An Anthology of Popular British Ballad Poetry, XVth–XXth Century*. New York: Philosophical Library.

Porter, James. 1976. Jeannie Robertson's "My Son David": A Conceptual Performance Model. *Journal of American Folklore* 89: 7–26.

———. 1978. The Turriff Family of Fetterangus: Society, Learning, Creation and Recreation of Traditional Song. *Folk Life* 16: 5–26.

———. 1979. "O Gin I Were Where Gadie Rins": A Note on Tune Relationships and Local Song-Making. *Folk Music Journal* 3: 479–87.

———. 1983. The Mary Scott Complex: Outline of a Diachronic Model. In *The Ballad Image*. Edited by James Porter, 59–94.

———. 1985. Parody and Satire as Mediators of Change in the Traditional Songs of Belle Stewart. In *Narrative Folksong: Essays in Appreciation of W. Edson Richmond*. Edited by Kathleen R. Manley and Carol L. Edwards, 303–38. Boulder, Colo.: Westview Press.

———. 1986. Ballad Explanations, Ballad Reality, and the Singer's Epistemics. *Western Folklore* 45: 110–25.

———. 1988. Context, Epistemics and Value: A Conceptual Performance Model Reconsidered. *Selected Reports in Ethnomusicology* 7 (Issues in the Conceptualization of Music): 69–97.

———. 1993. (Ballad-)Singing and Transformativity. *ARV: Scandinavian Yearbook of Folklore 1992* 48: 165–80.

Qureshi, Regula B. 1987. Musical Sound and Contextual Input: A Performance Model for Musical Analysis. *Ethnomusicology* 31: 56–86.

Reeves, James. 1958. *The Idiom of the People*. New York: Macmillan.

———. 1960. *The Everlasting Circle*. New York: Macmillan.

Reagan, Charles E., and David Stewart, eds. 1978. *The Philosophy of Paul Ricoeur: An Anthology of His Work*. Boston: Beacon Press.

Recanati, Francois. 1987. *Meaning and Force: The Pragmatics of Performative Utterances*. Cambridge, England: Cambridge U. Press.

Rehfisch, Farnham. 1975. *Gypsies, Tinkers and Other Travellers*. London: Academic Press.

———. 1961. Marriage and the Elementary Family among the Scottish Tinkers. *Scottish Studies* 5: 121–48.

Renwick, Roger deV. 1980. *English Folk Poetry: Structure and Meaning*. Philadelphia: U. of Pennsylvania Press.

Rickman, H. P. 1961. *Wilhelm Dilthey: Pattern and Meaning in History*. New York: Harper.

Ricoeur, Paul. 1966. *Freedom and Nature: The Voluntary and the Involuntary.* Translated by Erazim V. Kohák. Evanston, Ill.: Northwestern U. Press.

Riddle, Almeda. 1970. *A Singer and Her Songs.* Ed. Roger D. Abrahams. Baton Rouge: Louisiana State U. Press.

Robertson, Carol E. 1987. Power and Gender in the Musical Experiences of Women. In *Women and Music in Cross-Cultural Perspective.* Edited by Ellen Koskoff, 225–44. Westport, Conn.: Greenwood Press.

Robertson, Stanley. 1988. *Exodus to Alford.* Nairn, Scotland: Balnain Books.

Sarkissian, Margaret. 1992. Gender and Music. In *Ethnomusicology: An Introduction.* Edited by Helen Myers, 337–48. New York: Norton.

Schuetz, Alfred. 1967. Phenomenology and the Social Sciences. In *The Phenomenology of Edmund Husserl and Its Interpretation.* Edited by J. J. Kockelmans, 450–72. New York: Doubleday.

———. 1967a. The Stranger. In Schuetz, *Collected Papers,* vol. 2: *Studies in Social Theory,* 95–96. The Hague: Nijhoff.

Scotland's Travelling People. 1982. Third Report of the Secretary of State's Advisory Committee on Scotland's Travelling People. Edinburgh: HM Stationery Office.

Seeger, Charles. 1958. Prescriptive and Descriptive Music Writing. *Music Quarterly* 44: 184–95.

Sharp, Cecil J. 1965. *English Folk Song: Some Conclusions.* 4th ed. Revised by Maud Karpeles. Belmont, Calif.: Wadsworth.

Shepherd, John. 1987. Music and Male Hegemony. In *Music and Society: The Politics of Composition, Performance and Reception.* Edited by Richard Leppert and Susan McClary, 151–72. Cambridge, England: Cambridge U. Press.

———, et al. 1977. *Whose Music? A Sociology of Musical Languages.* London: Latimer.

Shields, Hugh. 1972a. The Dead Lover's Return in Modern English Ballad Tradition. *Jahrbuch für Volksliedforschung* 17: 98–114.

———. 1972b. Old British Ballads in Ireland. *Folk Life* 10: 68–103.

———. 1981. *Shamrock, Rose and Thistle: Folksinging in North Derry.* Belfast: Blackstaff Press.

———. 1982. Literacy and the Ballad Genre in Ireland. In *12de Internationale Volksballadentagung, Alden Biesen 22–26 Juli 1981.* Edited by S. Top and E. Tielemans, 151–65. Brussels: Centrum voor vlaamse volkscultuur.

———, ed. 1986. *Ballad Research, Dublin 1985.* Dublin: Folk Music Society of Ireland.

———. 1991. Popular Modes of Narration and the Ballad. In *The Ballad and Oral Literature* (Harvard English Studies 17). Edited by Joseph Harris, 40–59. Cambridge, Mass.: Harvard U. Press.

———. 1993. *Narrative Singing in Ireland: Lays, Ballads, Come-All-Yes and Other Songs.* Dublin: Irish Academic Press.

Shields, Hugh, and Lisa Shields. 1975. Irish Folk-Song Recordings, 1966–72: An Index of Tapes in the Ulster Folk and Transport Museum. *Ulster Folklife* 21: 25–54.

Simmel, Georg. 1971 [1908]. Der Fremde. In Simmel, *On Individuality and Social Forms: Selected Writings.* Translated by D. N. Levine, 143–49. Chicago: U. of Chicago Press.

Singer, Milton. 1972. *When a Great Tradition Modernizes: An Anthropological Approach to Indian Civilization.* New York: Praeger.

Sloboda, John A. 1985. *The Musical Mind: The Cognitive Psychology of Music.* Oxford, England: Clarendon Press.

Smith, Stephanie. 1975. A Study of Lizzie Higgins as a Transitional Figure in the Oral Tradition of Northeast Scotland. M. Litt. thesis, U. of Edinburgh.

———. 1988. A Contextual Study of Singing in the Fisher Family. Ph.D. thesis, U. of Edinburgh.

Solie, Ruth ed. 1993. *Musicology and Difference: Gender and Sexuality in Music Scholarship.* Berkeley: U. of California Press.

Stekert, Ellen J. 1965. Two Voices of Tradition: The Influence of Personality and Collecting Environment upon the Songs of Two Traditional Folksingers. Ph.D. diss., U. of Pennsylvania.

Stenhouse, William. 1853. *Illustrations of the Lyric Poetry and Music of Scotland.* Edinburgh: W. Blackwood and Sons.

Stewart, Susan. 1978. *Nonsense: Aspects of Intertextuality in Folklore and Literature.* Baltimore, Md.: Johns Hopkins U. Press.

Stone, Ruth M., and Verlon L. Stone. 1981. Event, Feedback and Analysis: Research Media in the Study of Music Events. *Ethnomusicology* 25: 215–25.

Stratton, J. 1983. Capitalism and Romantic Ideology in the Record Business. *Popular Music* 3: 143–56.

Stubbs, Ken. 1963. The Life and Songs of George Maynard. *Journal of the English Folk Dance and Song Society* 9: 180–96.

Sutherland, Elizabeth. 1985. *Ravens and Black Rain.* London: Constable.

Sutton-Smith, Brian. 1972. *The Folkgames of Children.* Austin: U. of Texas Press.

Szwed, John F. 1970. Paul E. Hall: A Newfoundland Song-Maker and His Community of Song. In *Folksongs and Their Makers.* Edited by H. Glassie, E. D. Ives, and John F. Szwed, 149–69. Bowling Green, Ohio: Bowling Green Popular Press.

Tannen, Holly Joyce. 1988. That's No' a Story, Laddie, That's a Song! Traditional Ballads as Prose Narratives among the Travelling People of Scotland. M.A. thesis, U. of California, Berkeley.

Tarasti, E. 1979. *Myth and Music: A Semiotic Approach to the Aesthetics of Myth in Music.* The Hague: Mouton.

Taylor, Archer. 1931. *Edward and Sven i Rosengård.* Chicago: U. of Chicago Press.

Thompson, Paul. 1978. *The Voice of the Past: Oral History.* Oxford, England: Oxford U. Press.

Titon, Jeff Todd. 1980. The Life Story. *Journal of American Folklore* 93: 276–92.

Todorov, Tzvetan. 1969. *Grammaire du Decameron.* The Hague: Mouton.

Toelken, J. Barre. 1969. A Descriptive Nomenclature for the Study of Folklore. Part 1: The Process of Tradition. *Western Folklore* 28: 91–100.

———. 1967. An Oral Canon for the Child Ballads: Construction and Application. *Journal of the Folklore Institute* 4: 75–101.

———. 1986. Context and Meaning in the Anglo-American Ballad. In *The Ballad and the Scholars: Approaches to Ballad Study,* 31–52. Los Angeles: William Andrews Clark Memorial Library.

————. 1990. Metaphorical Ambiguity and Narrative Meaning in the English-Scottish Popular Ballad. *ARV: Scandinavian Yearbook of Folklore 1989* 45: 125–37.

Top, Stefaan. 1981. Studien zum Repertoire einer 88jährigen flämischen Volksliedsängerin: Zielsetzung, Problematik und erste Ergebnisse. In *11. Arbeitstagung über Probleme der europäischen Volksballade vom 22. bis 24. August 1980 in Jannina, Griechenland.* Edited by R. W. Brednich, 187–98. Jannina: Univ. of Jannina, Department of Folklore.

Udal, J. S. 1889. Dorsetshire Children's Games, Etc. *Folk-lore Journal* 7: 202–64.

Vansina, Jan. 1985. *Oral Tradition as History.* London: James Currey.

Wagner, Roy. 1975. *The Invention of Culture.* Englewood Cliffs, N.J.: Prentice-Hall.

Watson, Lawrence C. 1976. Understanding a Life History as a Subjective Document: Hermeneutical and Phenomenological Perspectives. *Ethos* 4: 95–131.

Weber, Max. 1949. *The Methodology of the Social Sciences.* Edited and translated by Edward A. Shils and Henry A. Finch. Glencoe, Ill: Free Press.

Wehse, Rainer. 1980. The Erotic Metaphor in Humorous Narrative Songs. In *Folklore on Two Continents: Essays in Honor of Linda Degh.* Edited by N. Burlakoff and C. Lindahl, 223–32. Bloomington: Indiana U. Press.

Wells, Evelyn K. 1950. *The Ballad Tree.* New York: Ronald Press.

Whyte, Betsy. 1979. *The Yellow on the Broom: The Early Days of a Traveller Woman.* Edinburgh: Chambers.

Wilgus, D. K. 1965. Fiddler's Farewell: The Legend of the Hanged Fiddler. *Studia Musicologica* 7: 195–209.

————. 1966. The Oldest (?) Text of "Edward." *Western Folklore* 25: 77–92.

————. 1970. A Type-Index of Anglo-American Traditional Narrative Songs. *Journal of the Folklore Institute* 7: 161–76.

————. 1973. "The Text Is the Thing." *Journal of American Folklore* 86: 241–52.

————. 1981. Andrew Jenkins, Folk Composer: An Overview. *Lore and Language* 3: 109–28.

Williamson, Linda J. 1985. *Narrative Singing Among the Scots Travellers: A Study of Strophic Variation in Ballad Performance.* Ph.D. diss., U. of Edinburgh.

Wimberly, Lowry C. 1928. *Folklore in the English and Scottish Ballads.* Chicago: U. of Chicago Press.

Winstock, Lewis S. 1970. *Songs and Music of the Redcoats.* London: Leo Cooper.

Wittig, Kurt. 1958. *The Scottish Tradition in Literature.* Edinburgh: Oliver and Boyd.

Wolf, John Quincy. 1967. Folk Singers and the Re-Creation of Folksong. *Western Folklore* 26: 101–11.

Wolff, Janet. 1983. *Aesthetics and the Sociology of Art.* London: George Allen and Unwin.

Woods, Fred. 1979. *Folk Revival: The Rediscovery of a National Music.* Poole, Dorset, England: Blandford Press.

Wright, Robert L., ed. 1975. *Irish Emigrant Ballads and Songs.* Bowling Green, Ohio: Bowling Green Popular Press.

Discography

Jeannie Robertson

Jeannie Robertson: Songs of a Scots Tinker Lady. 1954. One 12" 33-⅓ rpm disc. Riverside Records (Bill Brauer Productions, New York City) RLP 12-633. Jeannie's first single. Edited by Kenneth S. Goldstein. Has "occasional guitar accompaniments by Josh MacCrae." Contains: The Bonnie Wee Lass Who Never Said No; Brennan on the Moor; The Broken Token; The Butcher Boy; The Four Marys; Go Away from My Window; The Gypsy Laddies; Lord Lovat; MacCrimmon's Lament; The Overgate; What a Voice; When I Was Noo but Sweet Sixteen.

The Gallowa' Hills: Jeannie Robertson Sings Solo. Recorded London, 13 Oct. 1958. One 7" 45 rpm disc. 1958. Jazz Selection JES 1. Contains: The Gallowa' Hills; The Reel of Tullochgorum; O Jeannie My Dear Would You Marry Me; Bonnie Lassie Come Owre the Burn; Cuttie's Waddin'; The Yowie Wi' the Crookit Horn.

Jeannie Robertson: Twa Brothers. Recorded London, 30 Jan. 1959. One 7" 45 rpm disc. 1959. Jazz Selection JES 4. Contains: Twa Brothers; Davy Faa; The Overgate [Rovin' Eye].

Jeannie Robertson: I Ken Where I'm Going. Recorded London, Jan. 1959. One 7" 45 rpm disc. 1959. Jazz Selection JES 8. Contains: I Ken Where I'm Going; The Thorn Bush (Cuckoo's Nest); McPherson's Farewell; Oh Nellie My Darling; The Handsome Cabin Boy.

Jeannie's Merry Muse: Tender and Ribald Songs of Scotland Sung By Jeannie Robertson. One 7" 45 rpm disc. 1959. EMI Records 7EG 8534. Contains: Eenst Upon a Time; The Laird o' Windy Wa's; Bonnie Wee Grainne; Killiecrankie; I'll Lay Ye Doon; Busk, Busk, Bonny Lassie.

Lord Donald: Sung By Jeannie Robertson. Recorded London, 1959. One 10" 33-⅓ rpm disc. 1959. Jazz Selection JES 4001. Contains: Lord Donald; The Twa Recruitin' Sergeants; Rollin' in the Dew; Haud Yer Tongue, Dear Sally; Braes o' Balquidder.

Jeannie Robertson. One 12" 33-⅓ rpm disc. 1959. Topic 10T52. Contains: The Bonny Wee Lassie Who Never Said No; What a Voice; My Plaidie's Awa'; The Gypsy Laddies; When I Was New But Sweet Sixteen; MacCrimmon's Lament; Roy's Wife of Aldivalloch; Lord Lovat.

Jeannie Robertson: The Great Scots Traditional Ballad Singer. One 12" 33-⅓ rpm disc. 1959. Topic 12T96. [A reissue of Topic 19T52]

Jeannie Robertson: The World's Greatest Folksinger. One 12" 33-⅓ rpm disc. [1960]. Prestige International 13006. Contains: An Aul' Man Cam' Coortin' Me; Son David; The Overgate [Rovin' Eye]; The Deadly Wars; Tak the Buckles Fae Your Sheen; The Laird o' the Denty Dounby; Ten O'Clock Is Ringing; Bonny Black Ee; Johnny the Brime; The Laird o' Windy Wa's; Soo Sewin' Silk; Jock Stewart; A Maiden Come From London Town; Street Games and Songs: (a) We Are Three Wee Glasgow Molls, (b) Three Times Round Went Our Gallant Ship, (c) I Ken Whaur I'm Gaun, (d) What's Poor Mary Weepin' For?

Jeannie Robertson: The Cuckoo's Nest. One 12" 33-⅓ rpm disc. [1960]. Prestige International, 13075. Contains: Cuttie's Weddin'; The Moon Shined on My Bed Last Night; Roy's Wife o' Aldivalloch; Bonnie Lass Come Owre the Burn; I Once Was a Ploughboy; Connemara Dan; I Hae Ae Bit Son; The Overgate; A Dottered Auld Carle; The Laird o' Drum; Cuckoo's Nest (The Thorn Bush); O Are Ye Sleepin' Maggie?

Jeannie Robertson: Songs of a Scots Tinker Lady. One 12" 33-⅓ rpm disc. [1961]. Riverside, RLP 12-633. Contains: The Broken Token; When I Was Noo But Sweet Sixteen; The Butcher Boy; Brennan on the Moor; Go Away From My Window; Lord Lovat; The Overgate; The Four Marys; The Bonnie Wee Lassie Who Never Said No; The Gypsy Laddies; MacCrimmon's Lament; What a Voice.

What a Voice: Documentary of a Scottish Folksinger: Jeannie Robertson. One cassette recording. 1975. Folktracks, FSA 067. Recorded by Peter Kennedy in 1953, 1958. Contains: My Son David (talk before and after); The Loch of Shallin (talk before and after); Never Wed a' Auld Man (talk before and after); Go Away from My Window (talk before); Andrew Lammie (story, ballad recited, tune hummed); The Old Witch Woman (story—cumulative); Dandling and Children's Songs, Rhymes, and Fragments: We're A' Blin' Drunk; Bonnie Lassie O; Maggie; Rub-A-Dub-Dub; Flashy Dashy Petticoats; Eenst upon a Time; The Crooked House; Eenty Feenty (counting-out rhyme); My Dadda Wouldna; The Cuckoo's Nest; The Bonny Wee Hielan Man; Lord Bateman/Susan Pyatt (two verses of ballad); talk about Jeannie's family and her early life; The Overgate (talk before); The Braes of Balquidder (talk before); talk about ballad reciting; The Four Maries; Lord Lovat (first verse, story of ballad, last verse); The Moon Shined on my Bed Last Night (talk before and after); What a Voice (talk before).

BBC Archive Recordings. Recorded by Peter Kennedy:

21088-9	Never Wed a' Auld Man	1953
21090	She Was a Rum One (subsequently withdrawn)	1953
21092	The Butcher Boy	1953
21093	Up a Wide and Lonely Glen	1953
27809	Davie Faa	1953
27809	The Laird o' the Denty Dounby	1958
27810	The Overgate [Ricky-doo-dum-dey]	1953
29543	I Saw My Own Bonnie Lass	1964

Other Recordings Issued by Topic Records Featuring
Jeannie Robertson

12T157 (Caedmon, TC 1142). *The Songs of Courtship* (*Folk Songs of Britain,* vol. 1). Contains: Green Grows the Laurels; Old Gray Beard Newly Shaven.

12T158 (Caedmon, TC 1143). *Songs of Seduction* (*Folk Songs of Britain,* vol. 2). Contains: The Bonnie Wee Lassie Who Never Said No; The Cuckoo's Nest; Never Wed a' Auld Man.

12T160 (Caedmon, TC 1145). *The Ballads* (Child Nos. 2-95; *Folk Songs of Britain,* vol. 4). Contains: Lord Randal; Edward (fragment); Young Beichan (fragment).

12T161 (Caedmon, TC 1146). *The Ballads* (Child Nos. 110-299; *Folk Songs of Britain,* vol. 5). Contains: The Four Maries; The Gypsy Laddie (fragment); The Jolly Beggar; Willie's Fate.

12T179. *The Travelling Stewarts.* Contains: Willie's Fate.

12T181. *Festival at Blairgowrie.* Contains: MacCrimmon's Lament.

12T194. *Sailormen and Servingmaids* (*Folk Songs of Britain,* vol. 6). Contains: The Handsome Cabin Boy.

12T195. *Fair Game and Foul* (*Folk Songs of Britain,* vol. 7). Contains: The Butcher Boy.

12T196. *A Soldier's Life For Me* (*Folk Songs of Britain,* vol. 8). Contains: The Deadly Wars.

12T198. *Songs of Animals, Marvels* (*Folk Songs of Britain,* vol. 10). Contains: Rub-A-Dub-Dub.

TPS 189. *A Prospect of Scotland.* Contains: The Bonnie Wee Lassie Who Never Said No.

Index

Crawford, Jean, 88
Crawford, Tom, 88
"Cruel Fate," 44
cultural practice, xxvi, xxxiv

Daiches, David, 320
Daiches, Lionel, 318
Davidson, Donald, 317, 321
"Death of Queen Jane," xxxii
Delargy, Seamus, 314
"Demon Lover," 319
distancing (objectifying), xii
Dublin, 313–14

Edinburgh, xxiv, 318
Epirus (Greece), 300–1
epistemics (of song), 272–74

"Farewell to Lochaber, Farewell to My
    Jean," 90
finals (of songs), 292–93
Finland, 300
Fisher, Archie, 46, 54
Fisher, Ray, xxix–xxx, 45–47, 58, 66, 69,
    71, 79, 89
Fleming, Maurice, xvi, 315
"Flow Gently, Sweet Afton," xvi, xxxii,
    105
"Flower of the County Down," xxxii,
    290
folklore, folklorism, xxvii–xxviii
freedom, xxxi

Gaelic
—folksongs, 315
—literary models, 320
Gallowgate, 8, 12–14, 20, 21, 26, 40, 42,
    58, 59
Gardner, Howard, 269
Garioch, Robert, xvi
gender, music and, xxiv–xxvi
Gerould, Gordon Hall, 286
Glasgow, 314, 320–21
Glenlivet (Perthshire), 315
"Glenlogie," 282

Gluckman, Max, 296
Goldstein, Kenneth, xxxiii
Gower, Dona, 62–65
Greig, Gavin, 40, 54, 72, 313
"Gypsy Laddie," 59

"Harlaw," xxvi, 317–18
Hart, Russell, 59
"He Widna Wint His Gruel," 318
Headlee (Williamson), Linda, xxv, xxxvi
Henderson, Hamish, xi–xii, xxxi, 3, 4,
    40–42, 43, 45, 54, 58, 60, 66, 67, 71,
    79, 90–93, 301
Henry, Sam, 313
hermeneutics, xv, xvii, 302
Higgins, Bella, 312, 318
Higgins, Christina, 17
Higgins, Colin, 40, 41
Higgins, Donald "Donty" (husband),
    xxii, xxv, 4, 17, 18, 21, 64, 85, 86, 88,
    90, 91, 285, 301, 305
Higgins, Isaac (brother-in-law), 20, 31,
    38, 54, 58, 59, 83, 86, 92, 93
Higgins, Isaac "Wee Froggie" (nephew),
    40, 41, 81
Higgins, James "Jeemsie" (son), xxiii, xxv,
    xxix, 20, 22, 24, 26, 27, 30–35, 80,
    88, 275, 305
Higgins, James (stepfather), 4, 10, 18
Higgins, Jim (Donald's father), 17, 18,
    40, 83, 84
Higgins, Lizzie (daughter), 8, 12, 13, 18,
    20, 22, 26, 27, 30, 34–38, 40, 61, 79,
    85, 86, 88, 89, 91–93
Higgins, Maria Stewart Robertson
    (mother), xxxv, 3, 4, 6, 11, 82, 83,
    93, 270–71, 292, 304
"Hobo's Lament," xvi
Homer, xxxv
Horseman's Word, 316
Hunter, Andy, xiv, xxx, 45, 58, 77, 79–
    83, 86, 88–90, 92, 93, 293
Hutchinson, Bella, 69, 71, 92
Hutchinson, Bobby, 41, 69, 71, 81, 84,
    90, 92

"I Am a Forester in This Wood," 283
identity, xxvii
improvisation, xxxvi, 297
intersubjectivity, xviii, xxxvi–xxxvii

Jakobson, Roman, 303
James, William, xvii
"Jeannie My Dear Will You Marry Me?" 46
"John MacFadyen," 82
"Johnny Gibb o' Gushetneuk," 320

Kalevala meter songs, 300
Karpeles, Maud, 43
Kennedy, Norman, 54
Kennedy, Peter, xxxi, 40, 42
"King Fareweel," 319
Kirriemuir (Angus), 316

"Laird o' Drum," 86
"Lassie Gathering Nuts," 283
Lauder, Harry, xxxii, 77, 105
Laurie, John, 50
Leach, Edmund, 299
learning and cognitive development, 269–72
Levi-Strauss, Claude, 299
life history, life story, xv, xviii–xix
"Little Mattie Groves," 75, 77, 282
Lloyd, A. L., 3, 40
"Loch o' Shallin," 282
Lomax, Alan, 3, 40–42, 47, 48
Lord, Albert Bates, xxxv–xxxvii
"Lord Darnley," 75
"Lord Donald," 76
"Lord Lovat," xxxii
"Lovely Molly," xxxii

MacAllister, Marybird, xxxii
"Macaphee," 283
MacBeath (MacBeth), Jimmie, xxxiii, 54, 80, 318
MacColl, Ewan, 40, 45, 50
MacCrae, Josh, 80
MacDonald, Elizabeth, 274

MacGregor, Nellie, 321
MacKenzie, Lady, 49
MacKenzie, Sir Compton, 49, 317
MacLean, Calum, 319
MacMathuna, Ciaran, 313–14
MacReamoinn, Sean, 314
MacShannon, James, 315
Maguire, John, xxxv
marginality, xxi–xxii
Martin, Mrs. (of Tarland), 30–33, 305
"Mary Hamilton," 76
McCarthy, William, 74
Mead, G. H., 303
meaning, xviii
—artistic, xxxiv
—epistemic, xxxiv
—"inherent," "delineated," xxxiv, 302–3
—of "Son Davit," 276
Mededovic, Avdo, xxxii
memorization, xxxvi
Merleau-Ponty, Maurice, xvii
Mermaid Theatre, 52
metrical concepts, 293–94
Mitchell, Willie, 315
models, melorhythmic phrase, 294–95
"Moon Shone on My Bed Last Night," xxvi, xxxii, 88
Morrison, Elsie, 315
Motherwell, William, 73
Mukarovsky, Jan, 303
"Murder of Miss Mary Brown," 270
music and gender, xii, xxiv–xxvi
"My Auld Man and Your Auld Wife," 293
"My Father Built Me a Dandy Bower," 281, 294

narrative, personal, xix
Neave, James, 316

Oban (Argyll), 320
O'Boyle, Sean, 313–14, 317
Olrik, Axel, 275
"One, Two, Three a Leerie," 289
"Oor Jeannie," 63, 64, 66
Opie, Iona and Peter, 70

Appendix D

Recordings of "Son Davit"

Recording No.	Text	Context	Performance
1. SA 1952/43	As crystallized, with v. 7 omitted (break after v. 6); no "bottomless boat"	?Jeannie's house ?Oct. 1952 Confined space	Duration: 3'02" Manner: brisk
2. SA 1954/105	As 1 (8 verses)	4th People's Festival Ceilidh Aug. 1954 Audience, spacious arena	Duration: 3'16" Manner: slowing
3. SA 1955/154	Addition of "huntin' haak" and "bottomless boat" stanzas (11 verses)	Edinburgh Festival Ceilidh Sept. 1955	Duration: 4'16" Manner: spacious
4. SA 1958/25	Crystallized in 9 stanzas	Edinburgh Univ. Folksong Society May 1958 Audience, spacious arena	Duration: 5'03" Manner: dramatic
5. SA 1959/9	Crystallized	Northern Hotel, Aberdeen ?Sept. 1959 Microphone close	Duration: 5'47" Manner: slow, deliberate
6. SA 1960/111	Crystallized	Both Ballads and Blues Ceilidh, Aberdeen June 1960 Audience, spacious arena	Duration: 5'51" Manner: slow, deliberate